The crime novelist Margery Allir
life as skilfully as those to her pl
Jessica Mann *Sunday Telegraph*

She emerges from this thorough and conscientious biography as a woman of courage and charm and ebullience who remained, for most of the time, as her father said of her, curiously sane.
Isabel Colegate *The Spectator*

Julia Thorogood reveals a personality much more complex than the jolly buxom hostess known to her friends... this is an important and enthralling biography .. A notable achievement.
J.E. Morpurgo *Yorkshire Post*

This is a first class biography, well researched, detailed and nicely presented.
F.E. Pardoe *Birmingham Post*

Julia Thorogood has told the story of Margery Allingham's remarkable career with sympathy and admiration.
Violet Powell *Evening Standard*

Margery Allingham is an acquired taste ... (this biography) will make the acquisition easier still. It confirms her status as a major writer and as an exceptional individual.
Robert McLaughlan *Glasgow Herald*

...what a model biography this is! Deftly written, solidly researched and sometimes quite breathtakingly penetrating, it is hard to imagine how it could be bettered.
Lynn Barber *Independent on Sunday*

Julia Jones was formerly known as Julia Thorogood. She lives in rural Essex with her partner, Francis Wheen, and their children. The attic is filled with boxes of Herbert Allingham's papers which were bequeathed to Julia by Margery's sister, Joyce. This unique archive has provided Julia with an obsessive interest for most of the past seven years but it will move to a permanent home at the University of Westminster later in 2009 when her next biography *Fifty Years in the Fiction Factory: the Working Life of Herbert Allingham* is finally complete.

In Suffolk Julia has an alternative obsession as the part-owner (with Francis) of Arthur Ransome's ketch, *Peter Duck.* She dreams of following in Ransome's wake as a writer for children as well as a sailor.

The Adventures of Margery Allingham

Margery Allingham: a biography
was dedicated, with deep affection,
to Joyce, Christina and Gloria
the keepers of the Tolleshunt D'Arcy Studio.

·

The Adventures of Margery Allingham
is dedicated to Francis
and to my children, my daughters-in-law
and grandchildren
with love.

The Adventures of Margery Allingham

JULIA JONES

with a foreword by Nicci Gerrard

First published in Great Britain in 1991 by William Heinemann Ltd
as *Margery Allingham: A Biography* by Julia Thorogood

This edition published in 2009 by
Golden Duck (UK) Ltd
Sokens,
Green Street,
Pleshey, near CHELMSFORD,
Essex
CM3 1HT

www.golden-duck.co.uk

ISBN 978-1-899262-01-4

Cover design by Roger Davies
rogerdaviesdesign@btinternet.com

Foreword

An awful lot happens in Margery Allingham's novels. They are not just dense with multiple murders, locked rooms, cunning plots, sudden reversals, devilish twists, but also with goofy comic turns and sudden anti-climaxes that are reminiscent of PG Wodehouse rather than Agatha Christie, and with unearthly portents, supernatural events, shadows and moonlight and troubling dreams, whose wildness takes us into the world that Wilkie Collins evoked in novels like *The Woman in White* and *The Moonstone.*

Allingham's extraordinary creation, the bespectacled, buck-teethed, garrulous and apparently dim-witted Albert Campion - part-aristocrat, part-detective, part-criminal, part-genius, part fool - leads the reader through this maze, from the very English surface, where characters are decent coves and jolly old fruits and murder a bit of a bother, to the darkness and perversity that lies beneath. And Julia Jones - no fool, but certainly an indefatigable detective - leads us through the same contradictions in Margery Allingham's own life, which on the surface seemed so uneventful but which contained much suffering and turbulence. She shows us her cheerfulness and her very English stoicism, and also the dark days of her depression. There is never a moment when we do not feel in safe hands.

This is a wonderful and evocative biography, sympathetic, fair-minded, intelligent, always interesting both about her subject and the world that she came from, managing to gather up the personal details and place them in a cultural and social context. Some biographies manage to close a life down, but this one opens it up, evoking an age that has vanished and a body of writing that has survived. And it triumphantly passes the acid test of any literary biography: leads you back to the beguiling works themselves.

Nicci Gerrard

Albert Campion by A.J. Gregory (*c.*1939)

Contents

Illustrations

Photographs following page 190

Illustrations

Photographs following page 286

Russell Meiggs on holiday at Skreens Park, Summer 1938

Acknowledgements

Many people helped me to write *Margery Allingham: a Biography*. Eighteen years later the list has a somewhat melancholy, autumnal feel as so many of those who had known Margery as a friend or colleague have since died. Joyce Allingham shared her childhood memories and allowed me as long as I liked with family papers. Herbert Bullard described Dr Salter who was such a God-like figure in Margery's childhood. Mrs Saunders just remembered Margery at the Perse school and Betty Carter encountered her as a teenager and honorary cousin several years before they became sisters-in-law: Mary Brown (Orr) and Josephina Banner (de Vasconcellos) remembered Margery from the Regent Street Polytechnic (University of Westminster): Barbara Muir (Gowing) and Sir Robert Lusty were friends from the 1920s: Dwye Evans, Noel (Bill) Gee, Max Martyn and the Hon Mrs Valentine Richardson (Crittall) knew Margery in the 1930s and the closest of all was Christina Carter who came to work for Margery as a housemaid in 1934 and stayed with her until she died. Pauline Meiggs (Gregg) talked to me about her husband, Russell, and Jack Morpurgo, who met Margery's husband Pip during the Second World War, did his best to ensure that I was not overly partisan in my presentation of their marriage. Margery's god-daughter Sally Everitt (Reid) described her from a child's perspective and Gloria Greci, who came to work as Margery's secretary in the 1950s, also stayed with her until her death and spoke of her as a dear friend as well as an employer. Barbara Noble, Oriel Malet, Graham and Dorothy Watson, Ken McCormick and the Rev Aubrey Moody contributed their memories of the older Margery and Dr Russell Barton, former superintendent of Severall's Hospital Colchester, was determined that I should gain the fullest possible understanding of Margery's illnesses and her 'genes of genius'.

The Ealing local historian John Foster White, the social historian E.S, Turner, staff at the Essex Record Office, Mrs Mee and Mrs Miller at the Perse School, Mrs Chamberlain of the Old Persean Guild, Penny Pope, archivist at the then Polytechnic of Central London,

Richona Zimring of the Bienecke Rare Book and Manuscript Library at Yale University, Jean Rose of the Heinemann archive, Michael Bott who managed the Chatto archive at Reading University, were all knowledgeable and kindly.

Mr & Mrs Beckwith, Hugh Boscawen, Andrew and Georgia Brain, Derek Bright, Lettice Cooper, Tony Doncaster, Margaret Eden, Nicholas Evans, Fletcher le Fleming, Mike Freeth, Trevor Guest, Rev Keith Lovell, Larry Hughes, Sir John Margetson, Richard Martin, Tony Medawar, Mr & Mrs Morris, Charles Pick, Julie Ramos, 'Dodo' Rose, Deirdre, Countess of Roseberry, Laura Runyon, Hugh Saint, Roger Smith, Elizabeth Stevens, Pat Watt, Dame Veronica Wedgewood, Sylvia Williamson and Guy Wilson answered letters and queries and gave their time generously in other ways.

P & M Youngman Carter Ltd and the Estate of Margery Allingham gave me permission to quote from her published books and articles, as did the various publishers concerned. Permissions were also forthcoming from Carcenet Press (*Master of None: an autobiography* by J.E. Morpurgo), The Book Guild (*Toasted Cheese and Cinders* by Sybil Brand), Boydell and Brewer (John Fowles's introduction to *Mehalah*), Faber and Faber (*In the First Watch* by William McFee), The Perse School for Girls and the Polytechnic of Central London (material in magazines and official histories).

Joyce Allingham gave me permission to quote from all her sister's unpublished material and family papers. The Bienecke Rare Book and manuscript library gave permission to quote from William McFee's letters: Sally Everitt gave permission to quote from a letter written by her father, Mr Ronnie Reid; Julia Ramos similarly allowed quotation from her father Sir Henry Rushbury and Larry Hughes gave permission to quote from his own letter. Bantam, Doubleday, Dell allowed quotation from Malcolm Johnson and Mrs Rosalind Hicks gave permission to quote an extract from her mother, Agatha Christie's, appreciation of Margery.

Joyce Allingham, the Master and Fellows of Balliol College Oxford, Josephina Banner, Derek Braddy, Sally Everitt and Barbara Noble kindly allowed me to reproduce photographs in their possession.

Margery Allingham: a Biography was my first book and would never have come into being without Bridget Featherston-Godley, Michael and Diana Mann, Pippa Thistlethwaite, Jenny Uglow, Amanda

Conquy, Gloria Ferris and Arne Soova. It was immeasurably improved by the final thorough reading, comments and suggestions made by my uncle, Rivers Scott. He, together with Gloria Ferris and Joanna Prior, held my hand though all the later stages of production. I was more thankful than I probably told them at the time and I mean no diminution in my gratitude if I say that this time the process seems likely to be rather more fun.

June Turner of Essex Libraries triggered the idea of republication in paperback, Barry Pike of the Margery Allingham Society (**www.margeryallingham.org.uk**) and Tamsen Harward of Chorion Ltd were enthusiastic and a completely unexpected late legacy from Joyce Allingham provided the money. Once again people have been generous and forthcoming with their memories and explanations: Rosalind Barwise, Barry and Sylvia Williamson have talked about Russell Meiggs and provided a new photo: Margie Burn (Reid) and Ciaran Tyler (Madden) remember Margery from their childhood and, as the daughters of two of her doctors, they also contribute their indirect insight into her health problems: Natalie Wheen first told me the story of Pip Youngman Carter and Nancy Spain's relationship: Rose Collis, Nick Laurie, Dick Laurie, Ann Capon and Tom Carter have been utterly brilliant in helping me understand it in its human, emotional, slightly messy aspects. Barry Pike and Gloria Greci reminded me how this unexpected information affected Joyce and Ian Hislop added his editorial glimpse of the political Tom. My warmest thanks naturally go to Tom himself. On reflection I feel sad that he and Joyce never met. I think that they might have liked one another.

What has made this project so much jollier (so far) is the support of friends and family. Who could be downhearted with a foreword from a friend like Nicci Gerrard? My neighbours Jeremy Beale and (especially) Roger Davies have contributed practical expertise in the publishing process and my children are old enough to be dragooned into helping without me feeling like an early Victorian gangmaster. I have tried, with only minimal success, not to exploit the love and literary skill of my partner Francis Wheen but find I cannot cope at all without his talent for punctuation. Which leaves only Dot the dog to blame for all mistakes and inadequacies. Oh, and myself, of course.

Margery at her typewriter *c.*1934
By A.J. Gregory
(sketch on a brown paper bag)

‘

‘A Curiously Sane Girl’

Introduction to the First Edition

When Margery Allingham died in 1966 she left a husband a household and some thirty published volumes. The amount most people knew about her could have fitted neatly onto the back cover of one of them. A ‘Margery Allingham’ had a flavour of its own and a place in popular esteem; the character, Margery Allingham, was more elusive.

It has become accepted form to refer to Margery with Agatha Christie, Dorothy Sayers and Ngaio Marsh as ‘Golden Age’ ‘Queens of Crime’ and then express surprise that they were all ‘very private’ people. A visiting friend once said to Margery, ‘My dear Marge though you write crime novels you do have a dainty drawing room!’ ‘What did she expect?’ wrote Margery, ‘Did she think I would keep a corpse under the sofa?’

In her lifetime Margery had seen her books, such very English books, widely translated and sold throughout the world. She sometimes wondered what readers in Japan or Iron Curtain Czechoslovakia made of her Adventures. She knew they were enjoyed in America, Canada, New Zealand, Italy, Portugal, Scandinavia and Germany. One of the earliest letters she received from a fan was written in 1943 from a prisoner-or-war camp and addressed not to her but to her detective, Albert Campion, at his fictional home, 17A Bottle Street.

Margery had written her first thrillers with their silly ass hero to amuse a smart group of youngsters of her own age. She had no idea that then that either her work or the mystery novel would prove so durable. When, more than thirty years later, she found those same early novels were being read by a whole new generation, she suggested that the genre, the ‘box’ in which she had spent almost all of her professional life, had become part of the century's folk literature. Adventure and detective stories might be compared to the morality plays performed in the market places of the fifteen century. Both, in Margery's view, 'stated an elementary theory of Right or Wrong, Growing or Dying in a cheerful, popular way.'

Appreciations of Margery as a popular novelist, specifically as a practitioner of detective fiction have produced a small but fascinating shelf-load. On the shelf stand contributions from experts and collectors, from historians of popular culture and from scholars who have concentrated on the technical aspects of her work - such as narrative structure of reader response. Margery was proud of her status and would have found the discussions of her work by fellow detective novelists of particular interest. There has already been a biographical study which in tandem with the detail of her life seeks to provide 'a serious critical study' of her writing.

Margery herself made a distinction between books written to entertain or instruct the reader and books written out of the author's need. The best novels in any sphere, she believed, were conceived for the second reason but in their execution succeeded in fulfilling the aims of the first. Margery chose to write a certain kind of fiction but her Campion novels were not written to a formula. Although she was shrewd and knowledgeable about technical matters, she saw herself first and foremost as 'an instinctive writer whose intellect trots along behind, tidying and censuring and saying "Oh My!" She wrote 'as I have to' and because she had to. The mystery novel genre provided a camouflage beneath which she could escape. Not escape in any facile or non-realistic sense but seek escape from perceptions that were pressing on her, experiences which troubled or had hurt her. She could distance these things by putting them into a story thus giving them a new form of their own. 'The whole of life is about escape,' she once said in an interview. 'As long as you face every problem that's presented to you it's not wrong to escape a little. After all you only escape from insanity into sanity and that must be a very good thing.'

I did not come to Margery's life and work through a special knowledge of the detective novel. I had read most of her books quite indiscriminately among a mass of other fiction. Very often I read them again for the sheer pleasure of their style and the indefinable impression of being welcomed into someone else's world. They were also good stories. The book which alerted me to the personality of my hostess, and the matters from which she might be seeking relief, was one which had slipped from popular view, Margery's World War II testament, *The Oaken Heart.* This was a commissioned book written with a propaganda purpose. It was at the same time a book which helped its author put a frightening time into perspective. When I read it I found many things explained, not only about Margery but about some attitudes of a generation that was not my own.

The Oaken Heart is an allusive and somewhat obscure book which leaves as many questions raised as answered. Reading it was like hearing one side only of a conversation. 'In the course of a very happy if strenuous life,' wrote Margery, 'I have had many mental and moral adventures. As *The Oaken Heart* is a book written for those who stayed at home I couldn't quite see what she meant. It sent me back to reread her novels in the order that she had written them and to try to discover more about her life.

Viewed as a single opus compiled over forty years, the Campion novels comment and develop aspects of each other; sometimes taking up matters of theme, sometimes problems of form. Within her detective box Margery did not play safe. She described herself as an experimental writer and, within these bounds, the description is valid. Her relationship with her chief character, Albert Campion, grew increasingly complex and intimate. 'Mr Campion has wandered through them all as, indeed, so have I,' she wrote towards the end of her life. 'As far as I am concerned one is just about as real as the other.' More and more insistently the action of her books demands interpretation on different levels. Her adventures were, as she said, 'mental and moral', and for that her material was all around her.

Margery had been brought up in the tradition of adventure fiction rather than of armchair detection. Robert Louis Stevenson had been a literary influence from her earliest years – but Stevenson had sailed the South Seas as well as tramped the city street. She was sometimes worried by the unadventurousness of her life as she settled into her Essex village and sought warm quiet corners of the house in which to write. 'I envy you, you know,' she wrote to her younger sister Joyce who was serving with the WRNS in Singapore in *The Oaken Heart* days, but she took comfort from the examples of other women writers such as Jane Austen, who lived parochially, or Elizabeth Barrett Browning , confined by her health to a sofa. Both of them, thought Margery, were adept at 'guessing correctly' about life. Perhaps, she added, 'they were not so remarkable in that they knew so few people, as in that they knew a few people very well indeed. It may well be, she concluded, 'that I am best where I am and that *any* people can teach me what I need to know.'

As I read Margery's books more thoroughly, their relationship to her life began to appear extraordinarily close. People simply stepped across. I found Margery's mother-in-law selling flowers outside a bank, her friend (Alan) Joe Gregory as a mid-Atlantic villain, herself as a part American painter, her husband as 'an old cad.' 'I should be dense indeed if I did not recognise some of your originals,' wrote her uncle Ted in 1935 and twenty years later, in 1955, her secretary Gloria noticed, with a lurch of embarrassment, her own work-roughened pair of hands picked up and made use of in the latest Campion.

There was more to this than everyday observation. Although Margery clearly enjoyed playing with real-life material in her fiction and brilliantly juggled her separate worlds, she also possessed a powerful, even turbulent, imagination. There were moments in her life when she was afraid that this might run out of control. Her notions of time and levels of reality were complicated and she sensed danger in a collision or confusion of her inner and outer worlds.

Nor were the limitations of her life entirely voluntary. Her poor health and increasing unwieldy body were a prison – to what extent only she knew. 'I should be more mobile,' she said once, 'but so should grand pianos.' Margery was a big personality with ambitions and emotions to match. In the confined sphere of domestic life there were inevitably occasions when she had to discover means by which to vent her feelings in secret.

She kept a diary. It is usually brief and by no means complete. Sometimes she started new years with diligence but her entries petered out by the spring. In other years it is virtually entire and it is tempting to assume that those were years in which the private record played an important part. That would, however, be extremely rash. In her diaries Margery reveals aspects of herself that passed unnoticed in her lifetime – her depression and insecurity above all. Joyce, Margery's sister, allowed me complete freedom to read and make use of these diaries and to rummage unhindered through the mass of family material in Margery's last writing room. She had been saddened, and to some extent shocked by what she had read and her generosity enabled me to glimpse the extent of the troubles Margery had been seeking to assuage.

If there could be a prize for the perfect literary legatee I would like to propose Joyce Allingham. Margery's theories of inheritance were important to her but I have sometimes wondered whether she realised what burdens, as well as benefits, she was passing to her younger sister. Not least in the delicate matter of dealing with a biographer. Margery had been intensely protective of her reputation in her lifetime. She was convinced that the reading public liked a clear, comprehensible image of its authors – if it wanted an image at all. Usually she preferred her books to speak for her. She was anxious that her publishers and the people she dealt with professionally should not regard her as a difficult personality. This was partly her literary tradesman's upbringing, partly her complicated lack of confidence. She welcomed the mystery story camouflage. 'Nobody blamed the mystery writer for being no better than himself ... no one, not even in the literary columns, wrote to analyse his twisted ego or to sneer at his un-formed philosophy. Nobody cared what the mystery writer *thought* as long as he did his work and told his story.' She destroyed some letters because she was afraid they might be misinterpreted or cause pain domestically. She did not anticipate that anyone would wish to write about her life apart from her work.

Time and again in letters to her publishers or interviews with journalists Margery makes the best of things. This was characteristic of her approach to life and was important to her. It would have been so easy for Joyce to consider that the brave face must be upheld after her death. But she did not take that view. When I asked her to read what I had written she was scrupulous in checking facts but did not ever seek to influence my opinions or my selection of material.

I hope, through this, that the brave face has been reaffirmed. Margery had to content with many problems within her personality and her circumstances. She possessed a power of insight into other people's characters and motivations that was sometimes hard to live with. But she kept on living with and liking them. Her cheerfulness was not false. Laughter was crucial if she was to keep a steady view of life. Depression was one aspect but gaiety was another and both aspects came together in her novels. By writing her bitter comedies she kept tragedy at bay. 'My bet is,' she said, 'that grave and gay people are born not made. One either finds life entertaining or one does not and what happens in one's life has remarkably little effect upon that basic outlook.'

'A curiously sane girl,' her father called her once. And that I think she was.

'Dear Miss Reporter'

Introduction to the Second Edition

'Dear Miss Reporter,' wrote Margery on the verge of breakdown, 'I am sorry that I cannot greet you and give you my life story but there is a story here if you will look for it I think. Be very honest or the consequences will be disastrous.'[i]

Some months after the publication of *Margery Allingham: a Biography* in 1991 I received an unexpected telephone call from Sylvia Williamson, older daughter of Russell Meiggs, the man who had meant so much to Margery in the difficult years immediately before the Second World War. Her father, Herbert, had died, her relationship with Pip, her husband, was coming under strain and, most important of all, she realised that her work was changing. Her Campion novels needed to be written 'from the basic Marge' to achieve high literary quality and this process was exhausting. 'What is the meaning of me?' she wondered.

Russell Meiggs, two years older than Pip and Margery but with the boyish eagerness of the dedicated scholar and the charm of bachelorhood, arrived in her life at party time. Margery felt an immediate and powerful attraction and for the next two years Meiggs was the person who helped her think out answers to these essential questions: 'thereason forbeingalive and whathappenswhenyoudie?'[ii] They met perhaps a half a dozen times in that period – though these were house-party visits that could last overnight or for a long weekend. Mainly theirs was a relationship conducted by correspondence; 'I only want to talk. Regard yourself as my dead letter office,' she told him. Some of the letters were sufficiently important that Margery drafted and re-drafted them, leaving copies in the Tolleshunt D'Arcy archive. Others were later shown by Meiggs to Richard Martin, Margery's first biographer and quoted by him in *Ink in Her Blood.* By the time I came to research this period in Margery's life Russell Meiggs was dead. I met his widow, the scholar Pauline Gregg, who talked to me about her husband but did not offer sight of the complete letter collection.

When Sylvia Williamson rang she regretted that her mother hadn't wanted to say more and offered to donate the letters to the Allingham Society when the time came that her mother no longer minded. Sylvia and her sister Rosalind kept that promise and all the surviving letters written by Margery are now in the Albert Sloman library at Essex University. Joyce Allingham had told me that Margery destroyed the letters she had received from Meiggs and so much reticence began to make me wonder whether there had been something to conceal. I had stated my opinion that Margery and Meiggs had not had a physical affair. Perhaps I had been naïve?

The first letter I opened read like a prohibition from the grave. 'Look here,' Margery wrote. 'An infatuation which springs up at first sight and is nurtured at the three or four yearly or bi-yearly party meetings in an atmosphere of moonlight and alcohol and which dies happily and comfortably (leaving a lot of affection behind it) at the first normal encounter ... is one of those dear little corpses which should be allowed to lie quiet and pretty along with the other delightful and silly little emotional experiences of life.'

Miss Reporter can so easily mis-report ...

I wondered, fleetingly, whether I should do as my subject asked and close the file but she had also said that 'There is a story here if you will look for it.' So, predictably, I disregarded the instruction and carried on. The collection of letters donated by Sylvia and Rosalind confirm that Margery had been intensely physically attracted by Russell Meiggs. She refers to his sex appeal, the 'aphrodisiacal' effect of his personality. But she claims that she has learned to see these characteristics as qualities to be allowed for and disregarded by her;

acknowledged and protected against by him.

Evidently such rationality came later. The 'dear little corpse' which she wished to have left undisturbed is the fact that she had initially responded so strongly – to the brink of infidelity. 'No bloody woman is proof against a great wave of S.A. like a blast furnace,' she writes rather angrily. A sentiment that is echoed by her coolest character, Amanda Fitton, in *Traitor's Purse,* the novel written in 1939 after Margery had completely recovered her poise. Unlike the fictional Lee Aubrey, however, Meiggs was far from being a seducer. His personality was charismatic but he was also a Christian, moral and somewhat unworldly character. In the single letter that has survived from him to Margery he admits, 'I was frankly frightened by the events last year.'[iii]

'Why, in case I leapt up on you?' Margery scribbles back.

Meiggs digs himself in deeper by confessing that he had been only partially 'reassured' on a later visit.

This provokes outrage.

'Think of this, Read it. *Reassured* that I was not going to wreck my life for a man I'd seen three or four times?'

Margery sounds flustered as well as furious. 'The suggestion that you have been terrorised by my unmatronly advances however true (and I think you must be unduly sensative [sic] in this respect) is shocking bad manners and quite extraordinarily ungentlemanly.'

She sent back his letter 'corrected'. She may also have wanted to get it out of her house in case Pip, her husband, picked it up. 'Carter reading this as he easily might have done must have thought that I had fallen in love with you, told you so and been gently rebuked – a circumstance that would have hurt his pride much more than it would mine.'

Reading an exchange such as this is undeniably close to eavesdropping. Margery spells out that 'this infatuation of mine ... was after all my own private affair and kept rigerously [sic] to myself as much as possible.' The other sixteen letters – one of them extending over 43 pages – can be checked against

Margery's diary entries and dated to show when and how the 'infatuation' ran its course. In these letters Margery wrote nakedly about God, the Church, household finance and despair. They're a rich source for understanding 'the basic Marge', from which she was now writing, and even in the angry exchange which marked the end of the intensity, Margery acknowledges with gratitude that her embarrassing sexual response has provided her with 'another precious piece of information about myself and women generally together with a rather lovely discovery and a thing which "grew me up"' a bit more.'

This letter is the only one of the collection which feels intrusive to read – unless we are squeamish about watching someone struggling to make personal sense of religion. Among the reasons Margery later gave for choosing the detective novel as her camouflage was that 'Nobody cared what the mystery writer *thought* as long as he did his work and told his story.' This is not necessarily true but even if we feel we can pass up on Margery's belief in everyday miracles and the stages of despair (and I don't think we should) yet the relationship between her personal experience and novels is surely of interest. This same letter offers an unusual moment of insight into the process whereby the 'mental and moral' adventures of her life were turned into the fiction for which she is remembered.

Margery was writing *Dancers in Mourning* when she fell for Meiggs. By the time she had recovered herself *The Fashion in Shrouds* was complete. The letter that earned Meiggs such a scolding was written shortly after *Shrouds* was published. He mentions that he 'read a lot into the button episode.'

'I'm sorry about the button,' replies Margery, 'but my dear sweet ape! Fiction is my art, my profession. For me it is a highly technical business comparable with dispensing. Personal adventures are always distilled in to the drugs to be used but I would no more dream of putting anything in whole or undigested than I'd think of throwing a whole belladonna root into the family soup.'

Although she is clearly warning against literalism, this exchange does imply that there had been a real button. The fictional object was the yellow hand-painted souvenir that Albert Campion picked up in *Dancers in Mourning*, where he had been so uncomfortably in love with Linda Sutane, a married woman. *Dancers* had included a scene showing how the initial physical attraction caught Campion unawares. 'He ... got up lazily with every intention of kissing her. It was a completely casual, unpremeditated movement, arising naturally out of the unselfconscious exuberance of his mood, and he was halfway across the rug to her when the world returned to him in a rush and he became acutely aware of himself and who and where and what he was. For the second time that day he was seized with a sudden terror that he had gone completely out of his mind.'[iv]

Campion's middle-aged infatuation was inescapably painful and unconsummated – the wrongness of 'pinching' someone's wife is central to *Dancers'* plot. Linda Sutane is scarcely developed as a character at all – it is simply given in the story that she has this disturbing effect on him. Nevertheless Meiggs makes the link between her button and their real-life relationship and Margery does not deny that there was something there for her to use. The fictional button had been appropriated as a souvenir towards the end of *Dancers in Mourning* and was jettisoned early in *The Fashion in Shrouds.* It had been discovered in one of Campion's pockets by Magersfontein Lugg, the character who seems to represent the subconscious elements of Margery's mind. Lugg hands the trophy back to Campion who tosses it out of the window. This must be the incident which helped Meiggs feel 'reassured'.

The button falls into the street from whence it is immediately retrieved by Campion's true love, Amanda Fitton. She has a lot to say about the dangers of infatuation – 'cake-love' as she calls it – and presents herself as being full of 'bread and butter', the real thing. At the end of the letter where

Margery spells out the extent to which she believes Meiggs has mis-read her situation, she uses identical terminology. "Carter and I really love each other ... It's bread and butter stuff..."

Margery Allingham: a Biography left many readers uncertain how to interpret Margery's relationship with her husband. The material that has come to light since publication has not made this any easier. (Readers may skip now to the Afterword but that would be a little like choosing to read the final chapter without allowing the plot to unfold.) This letter, and the link to the idealised fictional marriage of Campion and Amanda, reminds us that Margery continued to regard her marriage to Pip as the central 'bread-and-butter' relationship in her life – despite the financial strain she experienced as she continued to provide him with actual bread and butter and abundance of cake besides.

The Fashion in Shrouds is the first of a number of novels (others are *Coroner's Pidgin* and *Tiger in the Smoke*) to present a conventionally desirable type of marriage as the freely chosen partnership of an active, dominant male and a cherished and protected female (invariably also slim and lovely). Oh, if only ... we might think, as we look from Margery's life to her stories and remember what she wrote about the pleasures of escaping into fiction. However, these conventional characters are often the most wooden of Margery's creations – consider Meg and Geoffrey at the centre of *Tiger in the Smoke,* for instance – and the portrayal of the Dowager Lady Carados in *Coroner's Pidgin* depicts a woman irritatingly and dangerously infantilised by a lifetime of cosseting.

The Beckoning Lady, written after a marital crisis in the 1950s, represents Margery's single attempt to make fiction of an unconventional partnership that has resemblances to her own. The names of the characters (Minnie and Tonker) suggest an unusually direct link between life and story and *Margery Allingham: a Biography* therefore got into trouble with one reviewer for backing away from the scene, reported by a child, where Tonker takes his wife to the bedroom. He shouts at her and smacks her till she cries. Then he kisses her until she laughs and they both come down stairs to pour out drinks for lots of visitors. Does this reveal a sado-masochistic element in Margery's own marriage, I was asked?

'Be very honest, Miss Reporter.'

But I really don't think I can answer. Yes, on one occasion in her diary, twenty years earlier, Margery reported that 'Cocky hit me' but four years before that she wrote 'Had a fight with Pip, *hitting each other* really hard'[v] (my italics). *The Beckoning Lady* incident suggests only that, at that point, twenty seven years into the real-life marriage, physicality may have been an issue – smacking and kissing could be actual happenings, on a par with pouring out drinks for lots of visitors (which Pip and Margery certainly did) or they could be nostalgia or fantasy – or, indeed, pure fiction. The reviewer thought I had been unduly polite in staying outside the bedroom door. I believe it would be not so much discourteous as stupid to chuck the whole belladonna root into the soup by any over-simplistic interpretation. Yes, there is a story within this marriage and *The Beckoning Lady* may provide a clue to its interpretation. But it could well be a clue to a looking-glass world where longings are more potent than everyday experience. When considering Margery's relationship to Pip I frequently find myself remembering some advice she once gave to Gloria Greci. 'If you're going to hold a man up, you might as well hold him up the right way.' Then I remember that she also asserted that 'only the really lovable is beloved for long.'

Returning to the biography after eighteen years is a little like friends reunited. You haven't changed a bit! I exclaim. But is that true?

I see my mistakes, of course (or some of them). Inexcusably I missed Winifred Nerney from the index, cited H.C. Bailey as the author of *Trent's Last Case* when it should have been E.C. Bentley and repeated with unthinking confidence that Herbert Allingham attended Ardingly College and then read theology at Cambridge when my more recent research proves that neither fact is accurate. I'm grateful to Robert Kirkpatrick for pointing out that the unidentified artist of the Fleet Street hack portrait is the well-known illustrator Tom Browne, creator of Weary Willie and Tired Tim, but this makes me less confident that Joyce's tentative identification of the subject as her own 'wild uncle John' is reliable. Nevertheless these are not (I hope) sufficiently serious errors to leave the biography so much non-recyclable waste. Neither has the new material substantially altered my interpretation. Reading the full collection of letters to Meiggs has added depth and colour to 'the basic Marge' and emboldened me to use the adventure title I had originally wanted. Learning the story of Tom Carter has added poignancy and dissonance. The overall portrait remains the same – though possibly with wrinkles.

There was a moment when I wondered whether I'd got Margery's attitude to children completely wrong: Rosalind Barwise (Russell Meiggs's younger daughter) told me how little she and her sister had enjoyed their single visit to D'Arcy House and what a neglectful godmother Margery had been to her older sister Sylvia. This didn't fit with the person I thought I knew. Then, fortunately, I was put in touch with Margie Burn, one of surgeon Ronnie Reid's twin daughters ('Blue Drawers & Yellow Drawers' of *The Beckoning Lady*.) She described the lavishness of a Christmas meal with Margery and Pip at Tolleshunt D'Arcy in the 1950s: the champagne, the old ladies looking grim and Edwardian in their furs and long dresses, the Soho exotics, the free-loaders, the presents 'that were as good as the ones your parents might have given' and the feeling of incipient naughtiness – that at any moment 'uncle Pip' might produce a set of crackers that had naked ladies springing out of them. Above all she remembers Margery hurrying to greet each individual child and clasp her or him to the ample bosom, warmly urging them to have some ginger-beer 'which you wanted to accept even if you didn't normally like ginger beer.' For Margie, Margery's welcome for the children marked her out from the other adults. 'She liked you to be lively, even a bit cheeky.' Her sympathy was direct and sometimes unconventional. Once, when Margie was a teenager and told Margery about a fierce row she'd had with her mother, Margery made some comment that took away the youngster's guilt and then presented her with a ten shilling note, 'which was a lot of money in those days'.[vi]

Another child who attended those exuberant parties was Ciaran Tyler, Dr James Madden's daughter. She too remembered the quality of Margery's welcome for children. 'Come on darling,' Margery would say, enveloping the child in an enormous hug and sweeping her along in her long dress like a mother hen with a chick under the wing. Ciaran chose not to read *Margery Allingham: a Biography* but took issue, correctly, with a reviewer who suggested that Margery's thyroid condition had not been properly diagnosed. She knew that her father, Margery's GP, had cared for Margery to the best of his professional ability and it had been Margery herself who chose to ignore the cancer that finally killed her. Margery was 'a strong-minded person', and for most of her life she could not be made to accept treatment that she didn't want. At the end, when she was compelled, she was very frightened 'and a lot of things came out.'

This hiding of her eyes was a fatal inconsistency in someone who asserted her belief in the necessity of facing 'every problem that is presented to you.' Joyce Allingham had told me that Margery 'didn't agree' with operations unless they were to save life and I was intrigued to notice, from her letters to Meiggs, that she had taken time to understand the Christian Scientist ideas on healing. She did not become an adherent, however. The most likely reason that Margery chose to ignore dormant medical problems was her need to work: a condition such as sinusitis would stop her working so needed dealing with, a lump in the breast wouldn't. Like her father before her Margery felt the responsibility of the family on her shoulders and was convinced that it would be disastrous for everyone if she took time off. Ronnie Reid told Margie that he thought

Margery was finally exhausted by the burden she'd been carrying – specifically the burden of her husband.

Returning to Margery's life includes returning to her fiction. This has been an intrinsically different experience to re-reading the biography. As if the novels have had the opportunity to shift and refresh themselves with the passing of time. Eighteen years older I find myself more ready to criticise and to admire. Criticise where she seems mannered, over-directive and unconvincing (probably because unconvinced). Admire, hugely, the individuality of her language and the sheer beauty of her writing as well as her inventiveness, craftsmanship and – her oddity. Margery is not an easy writer to sum up or categorise. Some new commentaries have appeared in recent years and the Margery Allingham Society is indefatigable in filling its twice yearly *Bottle Street Gazette* with additional information and viewpoints.[vii] As the novels recede through datedness towards historical status there's possibly a tendency to use Margery as a quarry to mine nuggets of information about changing social attitudes. Her professionally-developed powers of observation ('I ... must always be watching and noting and putting experience in communicable form') as well as her personal enthusiasm for 'the surfaces of life' make this a briefly rewarding pastime. It's also a useful way of talking about her writing other than in the context of detective fiction – bracketing her with other twentieth century women novelists in the Second World War, perhaps. It acknowledges her rare forays outside the box (especially *The Oaken Heart*). The temptation then is to look at what is comparable or representative in Margery's writing – what makes her 'middlebrow' – rather than do as her fellow mystery writers have frequently done, which is seek to identify the qualities that make her different or outstanding within their common genre.

One of the most consistent points of agreement among her admirers is that the novels are, to some extent, *sui generis* – both in their cast of characters and descriptive style. Margery's mature style is energetic and highly coloured: it usually involves description though simile and metaphor, describing people, locations or objects in terms of something other. Unexpectedness is a prime quality, though this is only unexpectedness within a prescribed form.

One reviewer of *Margery Allingham: a Biography* (Robert McLaughlan writing in the *Glasgow Herald*) described Margery unhesitatingly as 'a major writer and as an exceptional individual'. Critical thinking has struggled to resolve the question as to whether 'major writers' can be found within category fiction, Margery's detective 'box'. The politically correct answer is yes – twenty-first century professors study the form with perception and respect – but today's mystery novelists or the writers of psychological thrillers still don't make the shortlist for the most prestigious literary awards. Back in 1938 Margery was delighted when Torquemada described *The Fashion in Shrouds* as 'by any standards a distinguished novel' but the full quote opened with a reference to her detective, Albert Campion, and the tone was one of surprise that such a thing could be. I am not convinced that the situation is fundamentally different now.

McLaughlan referred to Margery's work as 'an acquired taste' and was generous enough to say that the biography might facilitate the acquisition of this taste. I was naturally delighted and began to speculate whether it would be a good idea to print dates or series numbers on the spines of Margery's Campion novels in order to help readers make links to the stages of her life and thus appreciate the extraordinary deepening of creativity that is apparent in her best books – specifically the sequence extending from *More Work for the Undertaker* to *Hide My Eyes*.

The idea is obviously fatuous. If Margery is 'a major writer' she doesn't need numbering any more than, say, Dickens does. Her books have the capacity to entertain and impress whether they are read chronologically or not. They are imbued with her literary personality which is something closely connected to but also quite separate from the Margery who hurried to embrace visiting children, wrote with secret passion about her religious belief and, apparently, closed her eyes to sickness and betrayal in order to continue loving and writing. The story disinterred by this Miss Reporter is the story of an exceptional individual who was quite well aware of the potential for sofas to conceal corpses but usually managed to sit upon hers with imagination and élan

i p. 299 (Jean Hind)

ii A fuller discussion of Margery's letters to Russell Meiggs together with my revised cataloguing and dating can be found in the *Bottle Street Gazette: Journal of the MargeryAllingham Society* Issue no 26 (Autumn 2008).

iii This letter and Margery's reply were written in August 1938. I do not correct Margery's spellings as she said she particularly disliked such interference.

iv *Dancers in Mourning* (1937) p.51

v p.161

vi Telephone conversations with Margie Burn and Ciaran Tyler took place in December 2008

vii Margery is included in Susan Rowland's *From Agatha Christie to Ruth Rendell* (Palgrave, 2000), Jenny Hartley's *Millions Like Us: British Women's Fiction of the Second World War* (Virago 1997) and Nicola Humble's *The Feminine Middlebrow Novel 1920s to 1950s: Class, Domesticity and Bohemianism* (Oxford University Press, 2001). Many briefer pieces, including several by practising detective novelists were brought together in *Margery Allingham: 100 Years of a Great Mystery Writer* edited by Marianne Van Hoeven for the Margery Allingham Society (Lucas Books 2004)

I

The Allinghams

1904–1909

Margery Louise Allingham was born in Ealing on May 20th 1904. Whatever impression new-born babies can or can't sense, it is unlikely that she felt a warm maternal welcome. When she was older, her mother, Emily (usually known as Em or Emmie), confirmed that she had not wanted children and having them had not changed her attitude. She deserved considerable credit, she thought, for the sacrifice she had made in agreeing to conceive at all.

Margery was Em's first child – and a sizeable one. Her difficult birth did nothing to foster their mother–daughter bond. Em's labour was painful and protracted, culminating in a forceps- assisted delivery. She saw no reason to suffer in silence. Years later, when Margery had a younger brother, Phil (born in 1906), and a very much younger sister, Joyce (born in 1913), Em was still to be heard regaling acquaintances with the intimate details of this first bruising ordeal. Joyce remembers how Margery, always shy and, as a girl, sometimes gauche in company, shrank inwardly as she endured her mother's loud narrations. Em had a talent for setting others at a disadvantage. She left her elder daughter in little doubt that she held her responsible for every twinge. How her husband, Herbert Allingham, felt is not known. It seems probable that he too had to shoulder his share of the blame.

Feeling as Em did about motherhood it is surprising that she consented to have children at all. She was aggressively independent and despised the sexual relationship – it was 'horrid', 'men were beasts', she told a happily honeymooning friend. Most married women so early in the twentieth century had little choice in matters of conception. Yet, for a few, contraception was discussable and even feasible. Em and Herbert could have been among those few. 'Modern', 'forward-thinking' and 'advanced' were among the adjectives Margery, as an adult, used to describe them. Up-to-date Edwardians, working in Fleet Street, admirers of Shaw and convinced by the Fabians, they could certainly have talked over the possibilities of a marriage without children – and discovered the means by which this could be achieved. Em herself had a special regard for the work of Annie Besant, who, with Charles Bradlaugh, had championed birth control before channelling her energies into theosophy. The celibate marriage, a partnership of equals, was also considered by high-minded contemporaries.

Margery's parents were not quite so avant-garde. Though in the early days of their marriage they had enjoyed long talks with idealistic friends in the Fabian atmosphere of Clifford's Inn, and the ABC café nearby, they did not put into practice any such radical departures from convention. Their rebellions were smaller and more personal: Herbert had rejected the path mapped out for him by his parents; Em was temperamentally in utter contradiction to every one of her own mother's qualities – which included the loving and cherishing of the very young. Both Herbert and Em were idiosyncratically religious. Neither was inclined to take an outright stand against the whole system of Victorian values.

On the subject of potential parenthood, tradition was formidably embodied in the person of Herbert's mother, Louise. She was an erect, dumpy little lady who looked, like so many matriarchs of the period, as if she had modelled herself on The Great Queen. From her Margery inherited her middle name and her beautiful dark brown eyes. She may have owed her some debt for her existence. Louise was 'mater' to eight sons and made it clear to their wives that she expected grandchildren. Margery was her first. Visits between the older and the younger Allingham family were formal occasions. Manners were minded and the regular demand to say or play one's party piece could be daunting. Louise derived pride and pleasure from her eldest granddaughter. 'Guard her well,' she urged Herbert from the solemnity of her deathbed in 1920, 'for she is a good girl and there are many wicked men.'

Apart from her mother-in-law, no-one else was able to push Em into a course of action she disliked. Her children knew her as a loud, domineering personality with no cosiness and a wounding tongue. In the parlance of the time, Em was a 'cough-drop'. She made scant pretence of affection and Margery, Phil and Joyce grew up convinced that whatever they did could somehow be found inadequate. Joyce, the youngest, reckons a major achievement of her own childhood was learning to slip in and out of a room without being noticed. She finds it hard, still, to consider their mother objectively.

Em died in 1960, looked after at the end by her daughters in what seems an exemplary manner. Almost twenty years later Joyce struggled to include her in a brief family biography. 'It is true to say that were I to have written about Emmie in her lifetime, no picture depicted by my pen would have done either of us justice. Margery, although she suffered most, was more generous and quicker to recognise her worth.' She goes no further. In Margery's various attempts at autobiography, her mother is barely mentioned. When she is, it is with a guardedness, a careful giving-of-her-due, that reeks of old hurt.

Emmie Allingham had not had an easy life before she married Herbert. To a late-twentieth-century understanding, the events of her childhood and adolescence seem to have been sufficiently traumatic to explain quite a number of inhibitions about sex, marriage and motherhood. As a young wife, moreover, she lacked the personal status within the family that could have enabled her to ignore the pressure to have children and to defy those social and religious conventions personified by her mother-in-law.

Louise's strength was in her certainty. Joyce writes: 'She kept a strong hold over her children, bringing them up as a close-knit band and instilling in them a belief that they belonged to an important family, a famous family. Everyone connected with her was made to feel that the Allingham boys were special and held a unique place in the universe. When two or more of them were gathered together, their enthusiasm and ability to entertain did much to confirm this myth. Such was her influence that her grandchildren were well in their teens before they got a more realistic outlook on their paternal uncles and on the family as a whole.'

By birth, Em too was a member of this clan. Her mother, Emily Jane, and Herbert's father, William James, were brother and sister – making her her husband's first cousin. Their close ties of blood were never a direct factor in any family-planning discussion as they might have been today. They mattered only insofar as Em – and Emily – may have suffered the subtle stigma, in Louise's eyes, of being one of their 'poorest and most despised relations'. This phrase comes from Margery's 'family' novel, *Dance of the Years* (published in 1943). As an adult she attempted no direct account of her father's family but, in a series of novels beginning with *Police at the Funeral* (published in 1931 and dedicated 'to my seven paternal uncles'), she puzzled fictionally over aspects of her family heritage. *Dance of the Years*, never to date reprinted, was acknowledged by her as the closest record of the facts. In this novel, for various ideological reasons (discussed in Ch. XV), she set herself to explore, as directly as she could, what made the Allingham family the entity into which she had been born.

The bulk of *Dance of the Years* (called *The Galantrys* in America) tells of the birth and growth of James. James is important for his genetic mix – the offspring of a Georgian country gentleman and a gypsy – and for his early-Victorian success. He is the fictional representative of Margery's great-grandfather who was 'born in 1800 and left ten thousand pounds and the injunction that "no gentleman ever works". He devoted his considerable powers to laying out his money judiciously and lived like a rich man.' As Margery never knew her great-grandfather *Dance of the Years'* much briefer portrait of his 'son', William, is of more interest to the biographer. William stands for her paternal grandfather, Louise's husband, whom Margery encountered on many family occasions until he died in 1920, the same year as his wife. Margery brought *Dance of the Years* to a disappointingly hasty end. Only in its last chapters does she reach those generations closest to her own and offer her version of the situation that existed in the period immediately preceding her birth.

Her narrative implies an unworthy involvement of William Galantry, publisher of a nondenominational magazine, *The Converted World*, in the marriage of his sister, Debby, to a drunken and unbalanced widower, Walter Raven. Margery's actual grandfather, William James Allingham, ran an advertising agency, 'J. G. Francis', and was the publisher of a nondenominational magazine, *The Christian Globe*. Was he also unworthily responsible for the marriage of Margery's grandmother, his sister, Emily Jane, to William Walter Hughes, a widower who drank too much? It could have been so. Writing about their mother's parents, Joyce states, 'This marriage was blighted by some unfortunate financial dealings for which the husband blamed the Allinghams and which caused him to take to drink with sad repercussions.'

One of the main features of *The Christian Globe*, William Allingham's paper, was its regular front-page portrait photograph of a popular preacher or visiting missionary. William Walter Hughes, Margery and Joyce's other, unknown, grandfather, was a photographer. Perhaps his profession holds a clue to these 'unfortunate financial dealings'? Margery could only have been guessing or retailing family gossip here. The 'sad repercussions' of the 'unfortunate financial dealings' were however a matter of family fact.

Margery and Joyce's grandmother Emily Jane Hughes (née Allingham) was married to William Walter for at least ten years. They had four children, Em, Maud, Walter and Hilda. Emily Jane also took charge of Phoebe, the daughter of her husband's previous marriage. She is said to have sold her jewels to support him in a lawsuit (though the details of this are not known) and to have covered up for him inventively when he was too inebriated to function professionally. Emily Jane had a profound and straightforward Christian faith – duty, loyalty, self-abnegation and long-suffering were among her most obvious characteristics. Some time in the 1890s she left her husband, taking all five children with her.

It was a drastic step. Joyce believes that only violence against the children could have persuaded 'Granny' to act with such dramatic independence. Em, Joyce and Margery's mother, was the eldest of the Hughes children (apart from her half-sister Phoebe) and may have seen most of the unhappiness at home. Neither she nor her sister Maud (whom Margery and Joyce knew well) later chose to talk of their childhood. As adults they were individual, assertive and alarmingly self-reliant. They paid little more than lip service to the conventional contemporary roles of women. Perhaps this was in their nature, perhaps it was a compensatory reaction to the years of poverty and insecurity that followed their mother's decision – or to the insecurity which may have preceded it. It did not make them easy to live with. Their mother, Emily Jane, remained humble, grateful, deeply religious and naive. Of her Margery wrote, 'She was not clever and she was not amusing but she was the most remarkable source of human peace and security I have ever known.'

Life must have been very hard for 'Granny' after she left her husband. She had been scrupulous in not taking with her anything apart from her own and the children's clothes. Family legend preserves the tale of a memorable scene when Walter Hughes discovered his wife's initial refuge. Emily Jane and the children heard him coming. It sounded as if he had been drinking. She grouped her family around a table on which lay the household's Bible and urged them to busy themselves with some work. When Walter entered, he halted abruptly, apparently sobered by this scene of quiet industry. He saw the Bible and took it. 'Mine, I believe,' he said, and walked out, never to trouble them again.

It is likely that Emily Jane received sufficient financial help from her brother William to keep herself and her children from actual starvation. *Dance of the Years* stigmatises this charity as 'the kind which gave charity its false name'. Help is offered patronisingly and with some contempt, particularly by the character who represents Grandmama Louise. Charity's 'true name', love, is conspicuously absent in the novel. How Margery's grandmothers treated each other in life is not known. Although (or because!) Emily Jane had received a young lady's education, culminating in a period at a finishing school in Germany, she had no marketable talents – except her quality of willingness, some skill with a needle, and an instinct for survival that led her to dress her elder daughters prettily and send them in her stead to the baker's shop when she had no ready money to buy food. They were grindingly poor but Emily Jane did her best to maintain her standards of decency. A characteristic story was passed down through the family that, in the days of their poverty, she used to sweep the floor with her hairbrush as they possessed nothing else. What later impressed Margery was Granny's Victorian 'iron personal discipline' which would never have allowed her to leave a floor unswept, whatever the circumstances.

Whether before or after the family break-up, the youngest daughter, Hilda, died. The others lived through it and were not willing to discuss whatever scars they might have suffered. Phoebe found work as a governess and spent some time in Russia; Em worked as a milliner before her marriage, then learned to write fiction; Maud was initially employed in the Post Office and built herself a career in magazines. Their brother, Wal, emigrated to Canada.

When her daughters had established homes of their own, Emily Jane lived with them and tried to make herself useful. This was fortunate indeed for Em's children. Granny bathed them, prayed with them, taught them to read and loved them. She also told them stories. In later life Margery claimed that her grandmother had 'tucked away in the top drawer of her chest where the curlers and the screw-topped jar of barley sugar were kept . . . an exercise book with the first chapters of a Victorian three-decker novel in it'.

The exercise book that survives today contains nothing quite so ambitious but, tucked between the household hints and copied sentimental poetry, there are brief, homemade stories that seem typical of Granny. They tell tales of Mr and Mrs Blackbird and the helpful sparrow, and of two little girls named Minnie and Margy. It may be significant that many, many years later, when Margery wished to put herself quite directly into a novel, she called that character 'Minnie'. As an adult she took it for granted that children possessed imaginary friends. It may be that Minnie's adventures formed part of a make-believe world which, as a little girl, Margery had shared with her Granny. Joyce, too, remembers long episodic narratives being told to her by Granny at bath-time. For all the upheavals of her personal life, Emily Jane was able to offer her grandchildren a cosy view of the world, where God was in his heaven ready to reward good and punish evil, directly and unequivocally, and where all doubts and disappointments could be smoothed away with the promise of 'a nice long day tomorrow'. No wonder Margery cites 'the prospect of Granny being called away' as one of her abiding childhood anxieties.

Em, Margery's unmaternal mother, had married Herbert in 1902. He was 35 and she was 23. In the fictional world of *Dance of the Years*, Margery interpreted the marriage as a gesture of quixotic chivalry by the character who represents her father. Through marrying his cousin he hopes to atone for the wrongs inflicted by his own father when he forced his sister into the initial disastrous union. Though the validity of this explanation outside the novel cannot be ascertained, it is founded on some truths about Herbert Allingham's personality. 'The one thing I remember most about him,' wrote A. M. Burrage, a fellow-author, who met him in about 1906, 'was that directly I stepped into his presence, I knew that he was kind.' It is clear from his surviving diaries that Herbert also possessed a compelling sense of family duty – a quality he passed on to Margery. He would have wanted to help his impoverished first cousin as she struggled to earn her living in the milliner's shop. Herbert had one staple remedy for financial difficulty – work. He gave Burrage a serial story commission when he was desperate and taught Em their trade.

Herbert had been editor of a family magazine, *The London Journal*, since 1890 and had been writing since he was a boy. Allingham family tradition has it that William and Louise, believing that their second son was too idealistic for success in the advertising agency, intended him to follow a religious career. It would have been a more gentlemanly occupation than manufacturing slogans for products such as Beecham's Pills – 'Worth a Guinea a Box'.

Herbert was educated at Ardingly and went on to Cambridge University to study theology as a non-collegiate student. However, a glance at his diary for 1886 (when his future wife aged seven was surviving life at home with her drunken father) shows how far his inclination had strayed from his studies. His lecture notes on St Paul's epistles have been abandoned and the diarist is engrossed by analysis of the market for boys' fiction and the excitement and anxiety of seeing his own first story published. He is well aware that he should be working to retake failed exams but, 'My thoughts wandered from one thing to another in that easy manner which is so harmful to the discipline of the mind yet so enjoyable to experience.'

The young Herbert Allingham, thoughtful and idealistic, knew that there were elements in the fiction trade which neither his parents, nor those parts of himself that were still influenced by them, could possibly approve. There was, for instance, 'wild Uncle John', and all that he represented.

John Allingham, younger brother of Herbert's father William, was very different from that 'bearded patriarch'. He belonged to a group of writers and publishers for boys in the 1870s and '80s who frequently identified themselves with their own most popular character (Uncle John called himself 'Ralph Rollington') – and who behaved accordingly. They drank too much, played practical jokes on each other, squandered their money and had to have their clothing redeemed from pawn shops. Though Uncle John's doings frequently scandalised the respectable household of the proprietor of *The Christian Globe*, he might have been forgiven more readily if his business projects had been more profitable. 'Yes, that publication did have a chequered career . . . and you can perhaps remember we only saved the editorial carpet from the wreckage,' he wrote cheerfully in his memoirs about one of his magazines.

Slightly priggish misgivings had tempered Herbert's youthful delight when, in 1886, Uncle John offered to print his first school story in the initial number of his latest magazine, *The New Boy's Paper* – and paid him for it, 'the first money I have ever earned'. Once again the paper folded after only a handful of issues ('Uncle is such a fool!') but by then Herbert had tasted the thrill of paid publication and was committed to the world of Ralph Rollington and Co. He took his B.A., gave up theology and came back to work in Fleet Street. He also said goodbye to the charming and educated girl, Lilian Robinson, with whom he had enjoyed a romantic friendship in the genteel households of Cambridge. Forty years later, her son, Pip, married his daughter, Margery.

Herbert's parents may have been disappointed by his decision. In *Dance of the Years*, Margery is certain that they were. The characters of Jeffrey and Belle are the fictional counterparts of Herbert and Em.

'James "remembered" that there had been an almighty row in the family when Jeffrey married Belle, for after suddenly throwing up his preparations for the Church and taking to painting saleable, if uninspired, illustrations to children's religious books, he had avowed himself a Socialist . . . and then, still abruptly and unexpectedly, had married his music-hall cousin . . .'

Herbert's socialism was not a political conviction; it was founded on an interest in the ideals and theories of Fabianism, a recognition of female equality and a profound, if somewhat naive, admiration for 'the Common People'. Even as a youngster, Herbert had secretly disliked newly-rich business friends of his father's who spoke of their servants as if they were scarcely human. As he grew older it became more and more important to him to prove that he was not a snob. Marrying Em could have been part of this compulsion. Idealism apart however, Herbert later wrote to his greatest friend, the novelist and seaman, William McFee, stating his opinion that 'the right and reasonable motive for getting married is that a man wants a particular girl and can't bear to think of anyone else having her.'

Cousin Em, by 1902 when she and Herbert married, had grown up to be a strikingly handsome young woman. She was perhaps not beautiful to modern eyes – as J. B. Priestley wrote (in 1970) of the most-photographed beauties of that day 'a Garbo at her best would make them all look like pink marsh-mallows'. Em's photos show a broad, likely-to-be-stubborn face yet she possessed the soft brown hair, lovely complexion and full figure that were so well complemented by Edwardian fashion. She seemed full of self-confidence and her milliner's training gave her the skills to make the most of her appearance. Margery's choice of 'music-hall' for the fictional character is both acute and privately unkind. They had all loved the music-halls, Herbert in particular, but there was no doubt, certainly by 1942–3 when Margery was writing *Dance of the Years,* that 'music-hall' was 'low'. As a young woman, Em was colourful, witty, lively and completely uneducated. When she swept into a theatre or a restaurant she attracted attention both for her stylish appearance and for what seemed, to her daughters at least, her excruciatingly vulgar conversation. Herbert, following unobtrusively, enjoyed the sensation she caused.

It was an odd marriage. Pip, his future son-in-law, portrayed him as 'that gentle, austere man' who wrote 'with donnish precision' and who 'even in his working dressing-gown looked like a successful actor of the old school or an intelligent bishop off duty.' Photographs show Herbert to have been of medium height, stockily built though not plump, with a lean, likeable, serious face. During Margery's infancy he sported a profuse and fashionable walrus moustache. He enjoyed chess, walks and thoughtful discussion; was responsible, hard-working, frequently anxious and a migraine-sufferer. His daughters say at once that 'tolerance' was his most outstanding quality.

This is only half the story. Herbert hated to be bored. He had after all rejected Lilian, Cambridge and theology, choosing Fleet Street and the boys' adventure fiction of 'wild Uncle John' instead. His friend William McFee was at this time travelling the world in ocean tramps. Although, with age, Herbert's way of life became increasingly circumscribed, when he was in London he scarcely spent an evening at home. He went to the theatre, music-hall, cinema, chess-club, talks, and the homes of relatives, almost always alone or with a single close companion. There was a time when this was Em and a later time when it was more often Margery. When on holiday or in the country his children grew used to his sudden 'sultanic' demand to be entertained – with tricks, charades, recitations or reading. In 1909 and married for seven years, Herbert resigned from his editorial positions, moved to the country and worked meticulously day after day at his fiction. In parallel with his modest life ran melodramas in which, to quote Pip Youngman Carter again, 'children were lost, fathers went blind and failed to recognise their heirs and generations were born and died.'

Herbert seems to have been instinctively attracted to a partner with the potential to disrupt, someone who would stretch his quality of tolerance to its limits. 'All my dull days came to me before I married,' he told McFee. 'Since that time I have often been furiously angry and sometimes driven to the verge of insanity but I have never been dull.' As the children grew older they were appalled by the way their mother alternately ignored and browbeat their father. Yet Herbert rather doggedly carried on loving her. He was no nonentity. There were rare and sudden lashings out of anger either at his children or at the powers that be (frequently the editors or newspaper proprietors upon whom he depended for his living and from whom, as a 'hack', he suffered much). Never towards Em. Occasionally he tried to protect her when she didn't wish to be protected but generally he suppressed his own feelings and stood by, an interested spectator, as she ran her life. Occasionally he noted with gratitude in his diary 'think she is turning to me again.'

What attracted Em to marry Herbert is less easy to define. She was egotistical but not introspective and has left few records of her feelings. William McFee, who enjoyed a lively correspondence with her from the early 1900s until the 1920s when she 'took up' religion, described her then as 'intelligent' and a 'realist'. She may have relished Herbert's admiration, the increased material security he was able to provide and the sensation that through her marriage she was regaining her rightful place in society and the family. Moreover her sober, gentlemanly cousin must have been the most reassuring of potential husbands. He was as unlike Walter Hughes as she was unlike 'Granny'. He took her opinions seriously (and she was quick to complain if he did not!), appreciated her wit, and was restrained by his principles as well as his personality from trying to control or dominate her. And yet

Em was essentially self-sufficient. When she was feeling affectionate, Herbert was her 'dear old boy'; when she found a man who mattered to her deeply, he was quite a different person from her husband.

Em and Herbert's first home and Margery's birthplace – 5, Broughton Road, Ealing – was practical, unpretentious and up-to-date. It, and the first twelve houses of the street, were destroyed by enemy action during World War II and have been replaced by a block of flats. The remainder of Broughton Road is much as it must have been when Margery was an infant, wide enough to catch the sun, lined with trees and leading nowhere in particular. The houses, red-brick, semi-detached, sporting more or less decorative woodwork, were probably not more than ten years old when Herbert and Em started their family. They employed a nursemaid to help care for the children. Ealing possessed plenty of quiet lanes and open spaces through which Margery may have been pushed in a well-sprung pram. 'I loved my pram,' she said wistfully towards the end of her life.

Ealing was also a prosperous, well-managed suburb with advanced urban facilities and frequent transport to central London. For the first five years of Margery's life her father commuted regularly to the *London Journal* offices in New Fetter Lane. William McFee never forgot 'that terrible old building where the Old Boy was editing *Spare Moments*, and *The London Journal* and *The Christian Globe*, wearing a frock-coat and a top hat and working in a room like a dust-bin while the building shook to the presses downstairs.'

The London Journal was owned by its printers, C. W. Bradley, and was conveniently round the corner from the office – at 185, Fleet Street (until quite recently home for Express Newspapers) – of William Allingham's advertising agency, 'J.G. Francis', and *The Christian Globe*. For the children it was a prime spot from which to view the annual Lord Mayor's procession. Margery remembered seeing 'just below me in the narrow way, the hawkers selling the long paper strips which pulled out concertina fashion and showed the whole glory. The air smelled strongly of soot and oranges . . . and the dark sky . . . seemed to come down and swallow up the colours of the uniforms as the cavalcade advanced up Ludgate Hill.'

Two of Herbert's brothers were employed there in the 'J. G. Francis' office and Uncle John was precariously in Salisbury Square. Before his move to Ealing Herbert had lived in Goldhawk Road, Hammersmith. Several other members of the family were nearby in Chiswick. Marriage brought little initial slackening of the close social as well as business ties that bound Herbert to his brothers and, in more tempestuous fashion, Em to her sister Maud.

The Allinghams were not unusual in having several members and different generations of the family working simultaneously around Fleet Street. The cheap popular periodicals with which they were involved could soak up contributions from sons as well as fathers and very often from wives and sisters too. It was a matter of knowing the trade. Links of friendship between families as well as business ties were made. Herbert had taken on the editorship of *The London Journal* from just such a family friend. That friend, Pierce Egan, had been instrumental initially in advising Uncle John Allingham to publish Herbert's first story. His own father, Pierce Egan the Elder, had been well known as a writer of shockingly sensational stories for *The London Journal* in its earlier days. It was a tight little world.

The London Journal had had a long and successful (if not exactly consciousness-raising) history. Founded as a penny weekly in 1845, it had built up a large and loyal mass-market readership almost entirely on the strength of its serial fiction. It was not the lowest of the low, but catered for those readers who found Scott and Dickens over-complicated or insufficiently exciting. Mary Elizabeth Braddon, Mrs Henry Wood, Charles Reade, Eugène Sue and Alexandre Dumas were among favourite *London Journal* authors whose names are remembered today. The heyday of the paper had passed long before Herbert inherited the editorship. Alfred Burrage, who was eighteen when he encountered Herbert, dismissed it as a 'ghastly Victorian weekly . . . publishing old fiction which must have appeared first in the 1860s'. Herbert did what he could to modernise it but Burrage's assessment is brutally fair.

From the 1890s onwards, the penny publishing world was dominated by new men – Newnes, Harmsworth and Pearson. They altered readers' expectations of entertainment – much as *The London Journal* had itself done in its early days – and they significantly raised the financial stakes. *The London Journal* could not compete. Neither Herbert nor the proprietors of the paper had either the flamboyant style or the monetary muscle that was needed to attract readers back from *Answers* or *Titbits*. Between 1900 and 1907 trade was stagnant. From his editorial chair Herbert lamented, 'In these days when there are so many popular periodicals, the old personal relations which used to exist between a reader and his favourite paper do not prevail as they used to. People buy a paper as they buy a packet of cigarettes and they are not always very particular what paper it is as long as it will serve to pass an idle half-hour.'

The goal of both manufacturers of cigarettes (Herbert was a compulsive smoker) and editors of magazines is to achieve 'brand-loyalty'. In the early months of 1906, when Margery was a toddler and her brother Phil a baby, Herbert had expended much of his energy, and a certain amount of the printers', C. W. Bradley's, money, in a re-launch of *The London Journal* that was intended to make it appear competitive and up-to-date without losing any of the diminishing band of Victorian loyalists. Though he changed the layout and the typeface, called it *The New London Journal* and introduced snippety features in the *Titbits* style, he had little prize money to offer and the same old fiction reprinted again. He also took on his Uncle John's many-times sold, re-launched and re-sold *The New Boy's Paper*. Neither venture stood a chance against the vigorous and proliferating periodicals of Alfred Harmsworth, Lord Northcliffe. By 1909 *The New London Journal*'s proprietors were talking of selling their magazine and the competition was lapping at the profits even of backwater papers like *The Christian Globe*.

There was a growing sense of crisis within the Allingham family at this time. Their self-confidence was starting to crumble, individually as well as commercially. Though Herbert was never officially editor of *The Christian Globe* he did write weekly leaders for it and held a consultative position on the fiction side. When his father admitted that this enterprise too was in financial difficulties, Herbert commented gloomily, 'Looks as though Em and I will have to support the whole family in a year's time or so unless we too break down. Then the whole family goes under.'

As it turned out, 1909 heralded the most prosperous period in Herbert's married life and, for Margery, the best years of her childhood – the Edwardian summer of the Allinghams.

'Wild Uncle John?'
by Tom Browne

II

A House, a Garden and a Room of her Own

1909–1911

The Old Rectory, Layer Breton, could have provided any 'Golden Age' detective novelist with the perfect setting for a Murder in the Vicarage. Spacious and decaying, it had become an anachronism. The house was Georgian with a modest sweep of gravelled drive, outbuildings and stabling. It had a separate wing, The Glebe, which would have housed the servants, alibi-ing them from the central action behind the traditional green baize door. There were few neighbours – just enough to provide a manageable list of suspects. With a meadow, a large garden and a view to the estuary, the Old Rectory was, on a good day, redolent of rural ecclesiastical comfort in the early years of the nineteenth century.

When Herbert and Em arrived with their two older children nine years into the twentieth century, the comforts had run threadbare. The Early English church was tiny and disused. In the years which preceded the First World War, it was used for agricultural storage. The Rectory itself had been standing empty since the death of the last octogenarian incumbent and the garden was growing wild. The rector of nearby Birch had added Layer Breton parish to his responsibilities. He too was elderly and left matters of practical administration to his son who acted as his curate. In 1909 the Rev. Edwin Luard decided to spend as little money as he could tidying up Layer Breton Rectory, then offer it for rent. Herbert was its first lessee.

The Allinghams' move to the country had been Em's idea. The house in Broughton Road was probably beginning to feel cramped as Margery and Phil grew larger and more energetic. There was always 'a girl' living in to help with the children and the housework, and often Granny staying too. Herbert had supplemented the income from his editorships by spending two days a week writing fiction at home. There are the occasional jocular references in *The New London Journal* to the difficulty of writing even a simple article in a house with young children. In an issue published in July 1906 the harassed editor is asked to come and watch 'little Margy' in her bath. 'A little impatience on my part was, I think, pardonable, "My dear I have seen baby in her bath. One cannot spend all one's life looking at naked babies." "Don't be cross dear but be quick. Fancy, she has learned to splash all by herself!" ' As the readership of his own magazines declined, so the money he – and Em – could make by writing stories for his more prosperous competitors grew steadily in importance. If it was to become their sole source of revenue, more space and seclusion would be vital.

The proximity of the grown-up brothers and sisters in London was also causing problems. Herbert's diary for January 8th 1909 reads: 'E. and M. have a row – more talk about Phil. House rocking with feminine emotions. Work difficult.' Em's younger sister, Maud, and Herbert's brother Phil ('Big Phil' as he was often called to differentiate him from Young Phil or P.W., Margery's brother), were then involved in a stormy romance. Even at this distance one may feel relief that it eventually came to nothing. They were both determined, hot-tempered characters with the potential for disaster simmering throughout their separate lives. Herbert was regularly drawn into their troubles: 'Had tea with Em, discussed Phil. Had tea with Phil, discussed Maud.' Worried about his father's business difficulties, worried about his brother, worried about his sister-in-law, worried about his own editorial problems – it is not surprising that Herbert's diary frequently carries the brief entry 'Bad head – no work'.

In April 1909 he and Em had spent an unusually pleasant weekend out of London, staying with their mutual cousin Grace at Pope's Hall, Chappel, in Essex. Herbert's friend and fellow-writer, Richard Starr, and his wife had a cottage nearby, and by their return to Ealing, Em had decided that they too should try living in the country. 'She wants me to take Brook Farm, said to be vacant from September,' noted Herbert. 'Will has written for particulars.'

Nothing came of this but cousin Grace was keen to have members of her family close by and continued to look out for suitable houses. She was the only member of Herbert and Em's generation who was invariably a source of comfort rather than anxiety to them. Her father was wild Uncle John, her mother claimed descent from the Red Indian Princess Pocohontas. Their children's upbringing had been unorthodox, a source of scandalised amazement to the more conventional members of the family. 'Ralph Rollington' took home the parrots and monkeys he had acquired in the course of less than successful publicity stunts. If his children displeased him he had been known to toss them into the water butt.

Grace, the eldest daughter, had gone onto the music-hall stage in the 1890s, calling herself Nelly Vaughan. She did not attain stardom. As a 'chorister' in the pantomime Santa Claus at the Theatre Royal, Birmingham, she was paid thirty shillings a week and a third-class fare, outward journey only – 'all fleshings, tights, boots, shoes and wigs to be found by the said artist'. Though Grace loved theatre life she was probably fortunate to attract a kindly and generous 'stage-door johnny'. He was a business man named Richard Cheffins, older than she and well-to-do.

A fashionable way to spend a day out in the 1900s was to join a champagne-drinking excursion to a country house auction. On one such trip, 'Dicky' spent £450 buying Pope's Hall for Grace. It was a delightful small Tudor farmhouse above the Colne valley hidden down a long track and with an orchard, fields, and outbuildings around it. Grace fell in love with it. Dicky and she did not marry but lived there happily for many years. Though she called herself 'Mrs Cheffins' she failed to mix comfortably with her indigenous Essex neighbours. Richard Starr remembered local men with resounding Biblical names – Golden Goody, Moses Percival, Elijah Evans. The children of Chappel felt kindly towards Grace as she allowed them freely into her meadows to pick blackberries or gather wild watercress. After

Dicky Cheffins died, Grace continued to live at Pope's Hall. Dicky had done what he could to provide for her. Gradually the 'chorister' became submerged in the smallholder as she clumped about gamely in wellington boots with cows to milk and apples to pick. She married for companionship several years later.

Throughout her life at Pope's, Grace offered affectionate hospitality to her relatives, either for weekends or holidays – or when they were ill, unwanted or bereaved. It became a focal point for family gatherings of a more relaxed and enjoyable kind than was possible at the older Allinghams'. Grace loved grand gestures. Once she had the floor of the billiard room entirely covered with sand to make somewhere for Margery and Phil to play. Herbert's eldest brother, Will, had already settled nearby at Southey Green. Some years after Herbert and Em had left London, William, Louise and their youngest son 'Tod' moved to Sible Hedingham, a few miles from Chappel. Twenty years later, Margery and her husband Pip rented their first out-of-London home, Viaduct Farm, in the same village. In the summer of 1909, Grace heard of the Old Rectory. Layer Breton is some fifteen miles away from Chappel on the seaward side of Colchester. After slight hesitation, Herbert resigned his editorships and the family moved there in November.

A greater contrast to the cosy convenience of 5, Broughton Road, Ealing could scarcely be imagined. William McFee came to stay at the Old Rectory in the summer of 1911 and offered his own account of its inaccessibility. He had left his ship at Glasgow, then walked down through the midriff of England, thinking of Cobbett and Arthur Young. 'It took the best part of a week before I came, footsore and very tired, to the door of my host in a place called Layer Breton . . . I got lost among the narrow side roads, and the local people were not much help. In fact they were no help, for they could not understand why anyone who wanted to go to Layer Breton would not know where it was. I had heard of suicides being buried at cross-roads and it occurred to me that the suicides were of travellers who had tried to follow the directions of mellow-voiced villagers. They had killed themselves in despair, after tearing their clothes on brambles trying to read illegible signposts, and listening to sing-song yokels giving contradictory counsel.'

There were few modern conveniences at the Old Rectory. Guests huddled round the open fire and were told to 'Get your candles in the hall'. Long afterwards, during the first winter of World War II, Margery was vividly reminded of this period of her childhood and described 'the hard, paraffin-lit winters' when 'we could be comfortably marooned for days . . . If Mr Whybrow, the carrier, could not get into [Colchester] on his weekly visits, we were cut off indeed and the situation approached the calamity stage which I always secretly enjoyed, being at that age and in private rather a one for calamities. However, I learned then that to sit by a fire after battening down the house before a tearing blizzard off the sea and to listen to the frustrated howling of the elements is one of the great pleasures in life.'

The Old Rectory provided Margery with her first glimpse of the slightly spartan, definitely insular way of country life which contributed much to 'classical' English detective fiction. One of her strengths as a novelist proved to be her ability to portray houses and their unique atmospheres. The Old Rectory was the house which first fostered this sensitivity in her. Her time there was the essential period of her childhood. When it ended prematurely in 1916, she determined to return some day – and came close to succeeding. She nowhere mentions her infancy in Ealing; she found her personality at Layer Breton and considered it her essential home.

Margery, a brown-haired five-year-old in befrilled white pinafore and bow, responded eagerly to the new freedom of meadow and garden. There had been a garden at 5, Broughton Road; a long narrow strip behind the house, walled and safe, not unattractive but evoking no special magic. In the garden at Layer Breton there were trees and secret places. She could climb and hide and create new worlds for herself. Her favourite play areas were mapped and privately populated.

> 'Over the edge of the primrose bank
> Where the oak trees stand in a row

Lies the really truly fairy land –
I've been there, so I know.

'And if you go there late at night,
Perhaps they'll give you leave
You'll see them, sure you'll see them
You've only got to believe.'

This poem is typical of Margery's early imaginings. It was addressed to her sister, Joyce, born at the Old Rectory in 1913, when Margery was almost nine. The children left the house in 1916 and it is natural to assume that the poem was written between these dates. That is not necessarily so; fairies, and their companion anthropomorphic birds and small animals, continued to populate Margery's verse and fiction from seven to seventeen. The first play that she persuaded her teenage companions to perform at The Perse School, Cambridge in 1919 was called *Fairy Gold* and contained characters like 'Binkie-Woo' the talking owl. He seems certain to have been one of the more important inhabitants of Margery's fairy garden at the Old Rectory. The literary example of J. M. Barrie's *Peter Pan* and R. L. Stevenson's *Child's Garden of Verses* prolonged this way of expressing the delights of childhood. It was not until 1923–4, when her first novel had been published and the family had been back in London for six or seven years, that Margery bade farewell to the fairies she had found at Layer Breton.

'I would not go into that meadow now
Lest all I found when pressing back the bough
Of that old oak was long rank grass grown wild.'

As well as their physical space, gardens offered Margery a lifelong refuge. In *The Oaken Heart*, which was written with her time at the Old Rectory much in mind, she claims; 'I spent much of my childhood alone in a garden, and I have never lost the habit of hanging about one in times of stress waiting for a comforting thought. I do not mean anything fancified, of course;

no visions or voices, naturally; but I do expect to get in that sanctuary a momentary clarity of mind which will give me a definite lead at least to the next step in whatever I may be about.'

Quantitively, of course, she had spent much more of her childhood in London, at school, with nursemaids, relatives, her brother Phil, or indoors busy at a desk. She always spoke of her Layer Breton childhood as quiet and lonely. Letters from former members of Herbert and Em's staff suggest that there was considerably more romping at the Old Rectory than stayed in Margery's memory. They mention dressing up, acting and singing in the evenings. The Allinghams possessed a donkey which Margery thought of as her own. Its exploits were evidently notorious and outings with it harnessed to a tiny cart produced hilarity and disaster. For Margery in retrospect, the special quality of imaginative space discovered alone in the garden outweighed these other activities.

The reality with which the adults had to deal in their first years at the Old Rectory was less aesthetic. There was trouble with the drains. A surveyor's report presented to Herbert in 1911 made matters clear. 'At the present moment the premises are insanitary and dangerous to health and there is no doubt whatever that cesspool gas enters the house – which you have frequently noticed in your hall and dining room of late.' The surveyors suggested 'at the very minimum ' that a dry earth closet and an earthenware urinal be installed. They lobbied hard for the addition of a bath, 'which is required badly for a house of this kind, though it necessarily can only be a cold-water one . . .' But there was little money to spare, and their landlord, the Rev. Luard, was unwilling to expend the £50 that the surveyors estimated would be necessary 'to do a proper job'. That sum would have represented the entire annual rent that Herbert was paying for the lease of the house.

Margery caught typhoid at Layer Breton and became dangerously ill. The family believed that her life was saved only by Granny's devoted nursing. She was fed assiduously on white of egg. A baby sister or brother did die. No details are known though Margery as an adult had not forgotten the happening. The child was buried in the old churchyard (now a wood) but her name does not appear in the scanty parish registers. It may have been a stillbirth. Though the Allinghams and their friends always spoke of the Layer Breton period as a happy one it had not been without its moments of drama and sadness. The tensions latent in Margery's parents' relationship as well as her mother's abrasive personality were more than sufficient to make Margery glad to seek sanctuary.

Aged about six, when they were settled in their new home, Margery may not have been an easy child to manage. Although with one part of her self she loved the solitude of the garden, she demanded human attention too. It was Margery who, said one letter-writer, made all the household dress up for her, Margery, with her brother Phil, says another, who persuaded an unsuspecting governess onto the donkey then rolled on the ground screaming with laughter as the animal careered around the field.

By the time she was seven Margery had learned to read and write though she had initially found the process baffling and frustrating. Even in Herbert and Em's relatively 'modern' Edwardian household there was a separateness between the children, whose day was assumed to revolve round lessons, Nurse or Cook, and their parents, who put social and professional obligations first. In her poems of childhood, Margery appears to accept this essentially Victorian well-ordered security – but only as a literary convention. In life it was different. She resented her nursery isolation and was determined to assuage it on terms that suited her.

She does not, for instance, appear to have sought, or found, substitute-mothering from the staff. An Irish nurse is once mentioned in a letter but only Arthur Fletcher, who looked after the donkey, seems to have made sufficient impression to be remembered unprompted later in life. There was Granny of course but Granny was not always there and was perhaps more of a comforting than a stimulating influence. The companionship of her brother Phil, two years younger, is silently taken for granted. Nor did she find many opportunities for friendships with local children. In her various autobiographical statements, written in maturity, Margery makes it sound as if local segregation had been her parents' choice. 'We were a successful Edwardian family living in the edge of the salt-marshes, taking no notice of our neighbours and keeping our own peculiar hours.'

It was as likely to have been the other way round. In *The Love Story of a Colchester Girl*, an anonymous tale published in 1922 in *The Girl's Cinema* which was edited by Em's sister Maud and to which Em, Margery and Richard Starr all contributed, the heroine comes to live 'between Layer de la Haye and Wigborough' (which, for those not versed in Essex topography, can only be Layer Breton). Stories and series in magazines like *The Girl's Cinema* were sometimes given particular geographical location as a circulation-boosting device. Usually the barest minimum of local detail is involved. This story has a ring of actual experience. 'I remember Mother complaining that no-one but the clergyman's wife came to call when we first got there, and Father answering that "twopence couldn't speak to three ha'pence," not in that part of Essex anyway, and Mother complaining that it was deadly dull.' The mother 'had been a belle in her time', she 'liked a bit of style'. 'We soon discovered that we had neighbours, but they were awfully stuck-up folk. We wouldn't have minded if they had ignored us but they didn't. They had that peculiar way that people have of letting us see that they were making remarks about us to each other.'

Margery's teenage diary records a similar occasion when she was sitting unnoticed on a train among people who were making 'snobbish' remarks about Em and young Phil. The qualities in Em which turned heads in London might well have raised eyebrows in Essex. Margery could certainly have written *The Love Story of a Colchester Girl* with its indictment of East Anglian unfriendliness. And if it were not she, it was someone who had been very close to the family at that time.

Layer Breton is not a large village now. In 1909 it had about 250 inhabitants. The heads of six households, including Herbert, were listed by Kelly's directory as 'private residents' and a further eight as 'commercial'. The gypsies came sporadically and parked their painted waggons on the Heath. The rest were lesser tradespeople, farm labourers and domestic servants. Though Herbert would have been interested and curious to know more about their lives – the gypsies particularly were promising 'material' – he did not have the knack to win acceptance among people of other social classes in that class-ridden era. Sybil Fletcher who worked at the Old Rectory and married Arthur ten days before he had to go to war remembers how surprised they both were by his kindness and his genuine concern for their situation. Yet when Margery described Jeffrey in *Dance of the Years* as 'a man who was for ever trying to make friends with working folk, only to have them touch their hats at him and turn away uncomfortably', she was also describing her father.

The Allinghams did become friendly with their landlords, the Luards, and with the local doctor, John Henry Salter. Both relationships would influence Margery's development. More frequently, like cousin Grace, Herbert and Em peopled the house with other members of their family and with Fleet Street colleagues who used the Old Rectory as a haven to get on with their work. 'Father, mother, aunts and uncles, weekend visitors and novelist guests who stayed the whole summer, all sat down with a pen and paper after breakfast as a matter of course . . . There was always some extra person closeted upstairs, working to a press date or finishing some long speculative task.'

It could be dull for a child, especially for one who could too easily feel unwanted or insecure – and who had the strength of character to resent this. Shyness and the need for refuge were engrained early in Margery but equally present were a yearning for recognition and affection, a clear head and a passionate, if camouflaged, curiosity. 'My clearest recollection,' she wrote later, 'is my own frustration. I was energetic, affectionate and lonely, and all the interesting people in the world appeared to be on other side of glass.'

Physically they were on the other side of the green baize door. The Glebe, which had housed the housekeeper and her staff in more affluent days, was where the children now lived. It represented an intangible barrier imposed not solely by convention, but by the adult demand for solitude and concentration. Margery, writing forty and fifty years after the event, and as an author with a reputation to maintain, makes the solution of her difficulties seem willed and simple: 'There was nothing for it but to join the club.' She 'explained' this, she says, to her parents. They were sympathetic and provided her with a room in which to write, a plot on which to work and the means thereby to earn their adult acceptance. Summarised thus, it sounds extremely unchildlike.

There is one novel, *Dancers in Mourning*, written immediately after Herbert's death in 1936, in which Margery may be felt to be exorcising herself of certain memories from Layer Breton. In this work she brings a six-year-old's frustration vividly to life. Little Sarah Sutane is the first child to appear in Margery's mature fiction and contributes nothing to the murder plot of *Dancers in Mourning*. She is a 'nervy' child, a lonely child, a child who must constantly be kept apart from her father and his friends because of the nature of their work. She takes refuge in the garden, lavishes affection on her dog and has, in fact, many of the qualities of her creator at that age.

Sarah Sutane tries to explain her problems to the understanding Mr Campion. She does not do so in the calm, rational manner of Margery's autobiographical account – and the fiction rings much truer than the fact. 'I'm Sarah Sutane. I live here. I'm not allowed to talk to you or to anybody, but I want to. I want to. I want to.'

'She flung herself sobbing into his arms and rubbed a wet, unhappy face against his tie. He sat her up on his knee doing his best to look as if he were not pushing her away from him, and felt for a handkerchief.'

Campion attempts some soothing conversation but is interrupted by Sarah's nurse. 'Sarah shrieked and clung to her link with the outside world who rose embarrassed and dishevelled. In the end the nurse took her and carried her off kicking. Her angry screams echoed more and more faintly as a succeeding procession of doors closed after her.'

Margery possessed a strong will and a temper which she had to learn to control. 'Sceans' between her mother and herself, into which Herbert could also be drawn, were a commonplace throughout their life. However it was that she 'explained' her frustrations, aged six, to her parents, they did respond. According to the family memory, they prepared their surprise for Margery's seventh birthday. 'I was allotted a room in the Glebe . . . One morning it had been transformed into the complete stage set of a small outer office with a desk, a calendar, a waste-paper basket and at least six polished wooden chairs set round the walls.'

Margery described this room on more than one occasion and there are variations in the detail given. In the draft version quoted, she seems disposed to make it the subject of a slightly bitter humour. The chairs are a new feature. Had the room been a storeroom before it was allocated to Margery? She projects through them a feeling that she was both destined and inadequate; that her yearning for human companionship had lured her into a place where she would spend most of the rest of her life alone endeavouring to please an invisible and insatiable audience. They set a blight upon her human development.

'These chairs gave me a complex that I have not yet outgrown. There they waited day after day, hopeful and empty, while I sat in the middle of them with my stone bottle of blue-black ink . . . and faced the first of the two great problems of my trade: *How to say What*? However the second half of the spell, also a question, *Why say Anything at All*? did not occur to me then and so my initiation passed successfully and I was In.

'Looking back on it the picture has an absurdity not at all noticeable at the time, and I can sympathise with the exasperated housemaid who once snatched a ragged notebook from my hand and exploded, "Master, missus and three strangers all sitting in different rooms writing down lies and now YOU startin'!" '

In the opinion of this fiction-producing household, the first necessity after paper, pen and ink was something almost as tangible – a plot. Plots were craftsmen's items, capable of being 'given' by one person to another (or 'lifted' or 'stolen'), then 'written up'. 'In one of her off-hand bursts of magic', Em had stage-managed the room; Herbert, says Margery, contributed her first plot then directed her efforts to write it up to perfection. 'I wrote that same fairy story five hundred and forty five times while the leaves on the chestnut tree outside the window turned from golden-green to golden-red, from red to nothingness and re-appeared yellow-white in opening buds.'

Certainly she had lost something – the time for active experience. Her capacity for observation was intensively developed from this early age, and channelled towards literary expression. Life was turned into 'material'. 'I have been trained to remark since I was seven and must always be watching and noting and putting experience into communicable form.'

Her perspective had had to change. Is there, in this account, more than a hint of adult regret that the seven-year-old chose to be closeted inside working at such an arid and unending task while the seasons passed in the life of the garden? On other occasions Margery had expressed some pride in having been 'trained' and 'apprenticed to the writer's trade'; how disturbed did she become privately by the 'absurdity' of the picture?

Considering such questions reveals more about the attitudes of the ageing Margery – more tired, more disillusioned, less disposed to self-celebration – than about the child whose experience around 1911 provided its kernel. The alacrity with which young Margery settled to work, still forming her letters laboriously, blotching her fingers and clothes with Stephens ink and digging scratchy pen nibs through the rough paper of exercise books offers sufficient evidence that she found an early fulfilment at her desk. Most children growing up in such a household would at some time or other have played at writing. Phil collaborated with Margery on a handful of tales when they were both teenagers, and even Joyce, least ambitious of the Allingham children, found nothing extraordinary in selling her first article to a newspaper almost as soon as she was out of school.

Neither of the younger children found their lives shaped by a need to write. Neither succumbed to the potent blend of intellectual, imaginative and emotional satisfaction which kept Margery ever after in this room of her own.

III

Editress of *The Wag-Tale*

1911–1917

The first reward Margery received for her persistence and industry came from her father. From this time and throughout his life, Herbert took an ever-increasing interest and pride in her efforts. When they lived in Ealing he had always been busy, commuting to the city, out in the evenings, shutting himself up to write on the days he spent at home. Babies were traditionally women's business and, while Herbert was too open-minded to be dogmatic on that subject, he is likely to have been sufficiently influenced by his own upbringing to feel ill at ease if he had been asked to come and watch little Margery splashing in her bath.

Even at Layer Breton the gulf between Herbert and his children remained perceptible. In *Dancers in Mourning*, the novel of Margery's most strongly permeated with memories of Layer Breton and thoughts of her father, she attacks a situation 'where a man might love his child and have literally no time to think of her'. She was reluctant to risk such a situation occurring in her own adulthood. Herbert was a 'preoccupied' man. Later Margery offered all credit (sometimes more than his due) to her father for guiding her writerly development but she cannot help revealing, between the lines as it were, how inattentive he could be if other matters were not directly pointed out to him. Once a problem was made obvious, he would take it on his shoulders and do all he could by worry, discussion and surprisingly belligerent letter-writing to alleviate it. Em's scathing tongue and propensity to criticise those closest to her taught all three children to take their troubles to their father first. As time passed, the same factors encouraged Herbert to find increasing solace in his children's company, particularly in his working relationship with his elder daughter.

Certainly he had every reason to be preoccupied while at Layer Breton. Leaving London and regular employment in order to live solely by freelance fiction-production must have been a risk, however industriously he had prepared the ground. This was augmented by the size of the establishment that they had taken on. They were living, for the last time in Herbert and Em's married life, as gentry. Cultivated Edwardian Fabians might debate domestic servants as an issue but they did not usually expect to do their own washing-up. Herbert and Em had quite a staff at the Old Rectory. At one time or another there were Arthur Fletcher, Sybil (probably the housemaid) whom he later married, another maid (Florence Pudney), a cook, a gardener, a rapid succession of governesses when Margery and Phil were at home and a nursemaid (Cis Blackwell). It was not long before there were school fees to be found for the two older children as well as the money for family holidays and the entertainment of their London visitors.

Em contributed. 'My mother, who wrote in the drawing room across the hall . . . was one of those remarkable women who can always succeed at the thing everyone else is doing and with very much less effort than they. She did not write for as long as the others but she did do it, and sold the products, reaping a sort of awed unpopularity in consequence.' Em's enthusiasm for writing fluctuated and she was by no means as confident as she appeared to her children. Her writing depended on Herbert's encouragement and she produced nothing at all after his death. Their household income came from Herbert's hours of effort.

There is a certain neatness in the fact that, once he had resigned his editorship of *The New London Journal*, Herbert effectively settled to writing, and re-writing, modern versions of the Victorian melodramas on which the fortunes of that magazine and its companions had been founded. Mrs Henry Wood's *East Lynne*, for instance, had an immense popular success in the 1860s. Herbert extracted its most memorable plot-motif, the disguised mother watching over her children, wrote it up in ever more lurid detail and was still selling it to women's magazines in the 1930s. He reared his elder daughter on this theory of plot as a cerebral, detachable thing, a notion frequently attacked by his friend McFee and one which Margery eventually discovered to be quite alien to her own organic, intuitive approach.

The weekly serial in the penny comics and mass-market family magazines, for which Herbert wrote and towards which he was, whether consciously or not, directing Margery, was an area where the editor's word was law. Instalments had to be submitted in advance and could be altered almost at will. All must be set out plainly for the reader, nothing entrusted to the imagination. The very word 'suggestive' was used with pursed-lipped horror and was quite sufficient reason for an editor to reject Herbert's work. In one of her last discussions of her writer's technique Margery revealed that ever since these childhood days at her desk, she had been haunted by the editorial presence of her father standing over her as she worked. ' "What does it mean?" he would say, looking at the inky thing. "What does it mean?" '

Censorship was as rigorous as the editor's prejudice and if circulation figures dropped, the serial would probably be dropped forthwith. The success of Herbert's first major serial story, *Driven from Home*, which ran from November 1909 in the Amalgamated Press paper *The Butterfly*, gave him a useful bargaining tool to win contracts from editors. These included some guarantees of minimum length as well as per thousand word payment. Better still, the success of *Driven from Home* opened new markets for his work. He described it to Anne St John Cooper, a woman's magazine editor, in 1934:

'This was the first of my drama stories. It sent *The Butterfly* up over 100,000 and owing to this success, Sir Harold Harmsworth (Lord R.) permitted Mr Cordwell to start three other papers – *The Favourite Comic*, *Merry and Bright* and *Fun and Fiction*. Each of these papers started with a story by me. They all ran a year or more.' The most usual length for his stories to run was six to nine months (though one, *Human Nature*, continued for two years and had to alter course midway to become a tale of the First World War). It was not unknown for a paper to amalgamate or change its name with Herbert's saga in full spate. An instalment a week, four to five thousand words at a time, the reader's pleasure and editor's prejudice constantly to be catered for – it was not easy money.

His family equated Herbert's skill and flexibility in plot-construction with his skill at chess. In these sensational adventures he manoeuvred the wicked step-mother, the master-criminal head of a secret society, the husband or son returned from the dead, the gallant, lovely heroine through all manner of entanglements over, regularly, 80–100,000 words. He developed a technique of offering editors over the same period, week by week, a secondary serial story of a plucky working lass or lad making good. Not one but two extended games of chess – and possibly a school series also. Craftsmanship was what Herbert had to offer – concentration and staying power was what he needed. Time meant words and words converted directly into money, usually at the rate of 2–3 guineas per 1,000 words.

Although six-year-old Margery (like the six-year-old who seems to represent her in *Dancers in Mourning*) may have felt excluded and a stranger to her father, the seven-year-old who had showed both her interest in writing and some of the same tenacity that enabled Herbert to survive professionally, was frequently allowed to slip through the green baize door and into her father's study. In a poem, *The Study Fire*, she brings her fairies in from the garden with her.

'Vast red caverns, glittering hills,
Castles tall and fair,
Pitch black boulders, gleaming streams,
And grottos wild and rare.

'Land of wildest dreams untold,
Goal of strange desire,
That's where all the fairies live
Down in Daddy's fire.'

Initially, Margery's place by the study fire was a privilege that had to be earned by utter silence. It was not a hardship. The walls of the study, she recalled, 'were lined with an impressive glazed bookcase containing volumes which were incomprehensible to me . . . but the shining mahogany cupboards beneath were crammed with the coloured "comics" which were my father's files and my delight. I could look at them if I did not speak, sing or mutter and if I never took one out of the room.'

What did she find in the cupboard? Joyce has several boxes of their father's manuscripts, typescripts and complete runs of clippings from the ha'penny or penny papers in which his stories appeared. They have been kept methodically for business purposes but much of their original page-turning pull remains, hovering dustily around them. Only a few survive from before 1909. Piles of 'inessential' paper, including, it seems, almost all Margery's own juvenilia and the many thousands of words of hack-work which she too produced, were destroyed in the mid-1930s when Margery and Pip moved from Chappel to Tolleshunt D'Arcy and when Herbert died. Em travelled light after that event and had no more contact with the Fleet Street world.

Em's earliest stories seem to have been fairy tales for young children or sentimental stories with an improving religious bent. Herbert's, written primarily for boys and the adventure market, were more robust and very much more to his daughter's taste. His own favourite magazine had been *Young Folks*, the paper that first serialised *Treasure Island*, *The Black Arrow* and *Kidnapped* in the 1880s. It ran regular literary competitions for young writers. He had referred to them with nostalgia in his own editorial column and perhaps he kept some early issues. Stevenson was a seminal author for Herbert and his fellows, many of whom wrote pirate adventures in respectful imitation. These were certainly a major part of Margery's early reading.

Then there were the boys' school stories. From Uncle John's *The New Boy's Paper* Herbert had progressed to write for the Harmsworth market leader *Puck* as well as *Union Jack*, *True Blue* and other periodicals from the Aldine Publishing Company. Boys' school stories could grow into detective adventures. Herbert's hero, 'the Duffer', moved on from schoolboy exploits to escape, dramatically, from Cambridge University and embark on a career of unobtrusive detection. (Or at least, of adventure – the

Duffer is no Holmes.) Those critics who suggest that Margery's Albert Campion was created in imitation of Dorothy L. Sayers' Wimsey of Balliol might care to consider the likeness of both to her father's Duffer (and in turn, to his prototypes).

If Margery developed a taste for these light tales of detection as a child, she could have found whole series in the study cupboards compiled by both parents from 1901 onwards. Herbert's sleuth, the Irish journalist Michael Power, is a particularly engaging character. 'We were all smart men on *The Daily Record* but beyond a doubt Michael Power was the smartest of the lot . . . The most characteristic thing about him however was his colossal impudence and it was to that I think that he owed much of his really astounding success.'

Herbert produced the occasional 'girl detective tale' to please the female readers of *Puck* and he wrote 'bloods' for Thomson's of Dundee. By 1916, Em (with Herbert) had abandoned the 'charming fairy-tales' which she had been producing for *The Christian Globe* and other magazines from 1906 in favour of short stories for *Woman's Weekly* featuring the exploits of Phinella Martin – 'the beautiful and famous lady-detective'. (Margery imitated these in 1930 with her forgotten series of feminine detective adventures, *The Darings of the Red Rose*.)

The 'comics' which published Herbert's long-running and sensational serial stories were just that – comics. They had names like *Merry and Bright*, *Fun and Fiction*, *The Jester*, *The Firefly*, *The Butterfly* and *The Favourite Comic*. Strip cartoon series running rather strangely alongside the main melodramatic story made them accessible to readers of widely varying ages. These too must have played their part, not only in Margery's professional development as a writer of magazine serials herself, but also in her lifelong appreciation of a good cartoon or caricature.

Margery did not simply curl up by the study fire with these treasures; she showed her appreciation characteristically by attempting to produce her own. Her writing room in The Glebe became 'Ye Olde *Wag-Tale* Office' and, apparently aged seven, she produced the first issue of a 'family' magazine that was a faithful imitation of *The New London Journal* in its last days of prosperity. It may look like part of a tatty exercise book with a picture stuck on the outside but it is ruled into columns (for the better selling of advertisements) and the handsome illustration on the front cover (another important selling point) portrays a moving incident from one of three stirring serial stories within. (The fact that the story in question has had to be distorted slightly to suit the picture only increases its authenticity . . .)

The Wag-Tale contains: a school story (serial); 'The Crows' (a poem); 'The Change' (a short fairy story); 'The Coming of Miss Gregory' (a domestic adventure serial); an advertisement for 'tamarters' – ('Oh, by them! by them! by them!'); 'Fancy Work Corner' (instructions for making a horse- shoe pen-rack); a 'wanted' advertisement for lavender; 'The Pearl of the Sea' (a romantic adventure serial); 'The Fairy Queen' (a poem); 'Cookery Corner' (how to make jam buns); and a long advertising feature which tells the story of a farmer who tried in vain to rid his trees of hornets. The message to readers is 'By Sinite of Pottassium!'

The paper closes with advertisements for fresh blackberries (delivered at once), two requests for silk cigarette cards and a mysterious appeal for 'A thoroughly reliable person wanted to kill cats privately. Apply in secrecy to the kitchen, Layer Breton Rectory.'

The Wag-Tale was enjoyed by the family. Joyce, who was possibly not born when it was written, recalls the exhortation to 'By Sinite of Pottassium!' as a family joke in her childhood. Both Margery and her writing endeared themselves to William McFee when he spent the summer of 1912 at Layer Breton and (during the family holiday) on Mersea Island. For years to come, long after it had ceased to be a joke and become an embarrassment, he referred to Margery as 'the editress of The Wagtail' and to himself as her 'foreign correspondent'. In the irritating way of older family friends, he never seemed to notice that he got its title slightly wrong.

McFee ('Mac') was at Layer Breton to complete his own first novel. This was *Casuals of the Sea*, an ambitious book, dealing with questions of ethics and existence and the making and unmaking of souls. Already his impressions of life at sea (*Sketches from an Ocean Tramp*) had achieved publication and *Casuals of the Sea* had been commenced in long dull periods off watch. Mac worked at it over that summer at Layer Breton, filled with artistic aspirations and idealism, urged on, in his own view, by quite other considerations than the commercial imperatives which bound Herbert to his desk. He planned to emigrate to America when the book was finished and relished the security of knowing that he could always go back to sea if his writing proved unsuccessful. While he admired Herbert and his fellow hacks for their professionalism, Mac disapproved of their sheltered lives and detested the compromises they were forced to make.

The distinctions between his way of living and his host's were sharp in Mac's mind as he wrote the second and third sections of the novel. *Casuals of the Sea* is a passionate indictment of Fleet Street and the City. It ends in tragedy; a revelation of the actual human damage inflicted by those who lie for a living. Advertising copy was the villain of this piece – and advertising copy was what Herbert wrote for 'J. G. Francis' as his final resource when money was short. On board ship, Mac was prepared to keep his opinions to himself: he felt no such constraints on land. There must have been plenty of soul-searching and even acrimonious discussion during the evenings at the Old Rectory.

Fortunately the friendship between Herbert, Mac, Em and another journalist-writer, George Mant Hearn, had always thriven on discussion. 'Many an hour we had spent, all of us, downstairs in the ABC smoke-room in Fleet Street', as Mac wrote in his memoirs. When Mac was abroad, he and Herbert wrote long ('twenty-page') letters to each other. From 1911 Margery joined in the correspondence 'in letters an inch high'. Margery wrote on after Herbert died until Mac outlived her also. Clearly nothing unforgiveable was said. From America William McFee paid Margery Allingham, by then aged ten, the compliment of dedicating to her his next book, *Aliens* (first published in 1914). Though this was set in Manhattan it contains many references to the small patch of Essex with which he had become acquainted. It considers aspects of the artist's life – how to reconcile necessity and inspiration, commercial and artistic imperatives – almost as if he were sending the young Margery a message.

William McFee sometimes thought of himself as Margery's literary godfather. He kept her photograph in his cabin, sent her books (*Rewards and Fairies* was one such gift) and enquired solicitously about her doings and her progress. 'I often think of you all,' he wrote from Essex, New Jersey in 1913. 'Margery must be a giantess by now! Dear Margery! If ever she becomes a suffragette . . .' Mac warmed to Margery because he found her 'combative' as well as 'charming'. He joined Herbert in hoping great things for her – and did not hesitate to express his displeasure later. 'Margery is spending too much time on murder mystery stories which are only a passing fad and of no significance whatever.'

Some remember Margery at Layer Breton as a serious, even a severe little girl; others caught moments of foolery, these usually in conspiracy with Phil. She remembered herself as precocious in the narrow sphere of writing and literary conversation, excruciatingly shy and awkward elsewhere. However advanced ten-year-old Margery seemed to Herbert's childless friends, the message of *Aliens* must have been beyond her comprehension. Much as she may have craved adult attention, the lavish expressions of regard which she received from Mac were sometimes difficult to cope with.

Margery felt more at ease with the third member of the ABC/Clifford's Inn group, George Hearn. He too visited Layer Breton and, some years later, holidayed on Mersea Island. 'One of my favourite brother-quills at this time was an elderly Irishman named George Richard Mant Hearn. He was a great friend of the family and often stayed with us. He was bald and surprised looking with a stiff leg which gave a great stride to his walk. He came from Cork and was witty and gentle and poetical . . . He worked with care and precision, his basket full of spoiled pages. I used to accompany him to the post-office and, as he always enquired very politely after my work, I used to ask after his.'

According to Margery it was George Hearn who encouraged her to seek a middle way between McFee's purist notions of Art and her father's commercial craftsmanship by making use of a popular form (in Margery's case the murder mystery) as both vehicle and disguise for essentially personal statements. 'I learned many of the hazards of my profession from his accounts of his crises . . . and then, like one of the witches in his own fairy stories, he gave me a riddle to remember. "They never mind you putting all you've got into this sort of stuff. They never pay you any more for it, but they don't stop you." '

Herbert, in his editorial capacity, recommended Hearn as 'clever, cheap and not a hack' but Hearn made no literary mark. Mac did. During his lifetime he built up an impressive reputation in the United States where he was regularly compared to Joseph Conrad. His knowledge of the world was wide and definite, his reading profoundly intellectual. Arguing with Mac was like taking on a ship of the line from the deck of a privateer. George Hearn's admiration was less demanding. He could and did criticise Margery's work but in a gentle, intelligent fashion that contained no offence. He gave her confidence at some critical junctures in her adolescence. It was not until Margery was an adult, able to admit and to achieve her own ambitions, that she could feel equal to McFee.

As Herbert became more involved in fatherhood, he may have worried that Margery's friendship with his friends could be forcing the pace of her development. If it didn't occur to him then, it occurred to her later. One of the reasons that Jimmy Sutane in *Dancers in Mourning* is said to have for forbidding his daughter Sarah to 'run loose' with his own circle of artistic friends is that he believes she would 'get spoilt and precocious and pick up I don't know what words. Mr Sutane has a horror of her becoming what they call a stage child.' The narrator at this point is a frighteningly dedicated secretary, of the type who speak their minds with bleak candour throughout Margery's novels. She adds ominously, 'I keep telling them that she ought to go to boarding school.'

Margery did go to a weekly boarding school, the Misses Dobson's (later Endsleigh House) in Colchester, probably at the age of seven. After a year or more she suffered her serious attack of typhoid and the local doctor, Dr Salter, advised that she should be left to 'run wild' for a time. She then remained at home, taught by governesses until 1915 when she returned to the school as a full boarder. Margery mentions that she and Phil 'wore out' a succession of governesses. A letter written by Miss Fegan, the last of them, does suggest they were quite a handful. 'Little bears' agreed Margery ruefully. Miss Fegan's letter was written many years later, and paints a rosy picture of her happy existence at the Old Rectory. Phil, when Margery told him of it, remembered only that Em had been 'more than usually foul' to her. After Miss Fegan had left in January 1915, he was dispatched to a boys' preparatory school in Bognor Regis (which he loathed) and Margery back to the Misses Dobson's in Colchester.

The Wag-Tale contains a school story which conveys the quick-fire of questions from fellow pupils which any new girl might undergo: ' "What is your name?" "How old are you?" "What is your father?" ' A teacher appears, scoldings and order marks are given out, then the child is left face to face with this unknown and alarming adult. 'She had expected a very kind person, rather like her old governess but Miss Walford was very different. Miss Walford was a tall, thin person with dark brown hair and dark sparkling eyes which gave cross looks at her.'

'My education was rather odd,' wrote Margery in later life, 'unconventional to begin with and rigidly so afterwards; not a very comfortable progression.' Neither she nor Phil possessed the confidence to cope successfully with life away from home. Herbert was summoned several times to deal with Phil's educational crises and by the end of Margery's first term in Colchester she had developed a stutter which remained a handicap for many years. She later explained this as 'something to do with the noise and the people'. Her need to read and write seemed odd, she said, to those outside the Layer Breton Rectory and she was nicknamed 'Inky', not in kindness. There was once, apparently, an unpleasant scene when a teacher publicly tore up Margery's English essay and accused her of cheating. It was too good to be a child's unaided work. If this tale is true, the teacher may have been partially misled by the disparity between Margery's handwriting and spelling, which were certainly immature (and much carped at by McFee), and her language and ideas, which had been so intensively developed at home.

As an adult Margery managed to speak of her first teachers, the Misses Dobson, with tolerance at least. They had, she said, 'taught me some of the things that they had found useful to them but, as it happened, remarkably little which was to be of great value to me. I learned to read aloud in a quiet voice, to make raised roses on black satin cushion covers and how to enter a drawing room and sit down at a piano.

'I could do this last today if need be, but since all the other ladies in the Dobson employ who attempted to teach me to play the instrument failed in that endeavour, I doubt if the performance would be of great interest.'

It is likely that she subconciously wouldn't, rather than couldn't, learn to play the piano. Margery's school career was shaped by her blank refusal to be pushed in the 'wrong' direction. She 'couldn't' learn to spell correctly, to pass exams, to be dainty, neat or tidy, to construe Latin prose or to play games. Though the other pupils may not have been actively unfriendly, Margery did not feel at ease with them. She considered herself an outsider both at this young ladies' academy and at the more modern and academic Perse School in Cambridge to which she was moved, with high hopes, in 1919. She frequently describes herself as 'stubborn' or 'obstinate' as if in echo of some exasperated teacher, angered by this child who wasn't lazy and who wasn't stupid but who seemed, at some deep level, uninterested in the subjects school was there to provide.

Margery also dubs herself, more kindly, 'persistent' and 'tenacious'. Throughout her time with the Misses Dobson, she says, 'dirty little scraps of paper covered with nonsense continued to flow from me.' She does not entirely conceal her pride that the child remained true to herself. She learned too that she could win a measure of acceptance by amusing others. 'I had discovered a vast volume in very small print. The gothic letters on the cover misled me into thinking it was called the Gomplete Works of William Shakespeare. Noting that I could make older people laugh by reading it, I persevered and as far as I remember, my major achievement at that period was a play in uneven lines which saw production in the kindergarten. It was the sequel to Peter Pan which I had seen in London and one of the new characters was called Macbeth.'

There is no proof that this delightful playlet actually existed. It is only mentioned by her in this late, unpublished draft – 'as far as I remember'. No family or admiring friends tell of it and elsewhere Margery claims that it was at her second school, The Perse, that her first play was acted. Yet if it didn't exist, it deserved to be invented. Margery was deeply influenced, always, both by Shakespeare (particularly *Macbeth*) and by the fairy stories of her childhood. It was at school in Colchester that she discovered the relief drama could offer. A letter from a schoolfellow (also received late in life) mentions a game, devised by Margery in which they were 'the Bishop' and 'the Canon'. Shortly before she left Colchester Margery told Herbert of the fun she had had in the town performing a pierrot-show with one of the younger mistresses. 'I enjoyed myself so much that I even forgot to stutter!'

By this date, however, Margery's passive resistance could no longer insulate her from the demands of her teachers. The Misses Dobson had retired in 1917, handing on their school to a more ambitious pair, Miss Griffin and Miss Sharp. They, not unnaturally, wanted greater academic success from their pupils and spoke disparagingly of the previous management. Margery was entered for the Junior Cambridge exam, failed it and disliked them very much indeed. She probably became angry and overtly defiant. There were rows and finally she persuaded her father to take her away.

A letter written to 'My Dear Old Daddy' after Miss Griffin had been told of this decision in 1918 shows her flushed with triumph. Miss Sharp, she reports, 'doesn't exactly flare up and row but she says catty little things perfectly unnecessarily and it makes me feel simply mad but of course if I said anything to her there would be a wearisome row and it isn't worth it so I preserve an aggravating beam.' The hint of smugness is dissipated by an anxious P.S.: 'You aren't cross are you – dear Daddy?'

Two of the assistant teachers, Miss Saint and Miss Holt, had attempted to protect Margery from Miss Sharp and had given her friendship and support in her last months at Endsleigh House. They were not so very much older themselves and Margery remained in touch with them for many years. Miss Saint came to London in the mid-1920s to join the staff of *The Daily Sketch*. After Endsleigh House Margery's attitude to the race of school mistresses remained obdurately sour. Her first impression of her fellow detective-novelist Dorothy L. Sayers was that she was 'school-mistressy'. It was several years before Margery learned to feel at ease with her. Even in her sixties she rejected a prospective American publisher because there was 'something of the head-mistress' about her.

Margery was at school in Colchester for much of the First World War. Apart from the food shortages and some blackout restrictions, pupils at such a school were insulated from the emotional impact of the conflict. For country-dwellers, like Herbert, who needed to visit London to sell their work, travel became more difficult. His regular editor joined up and from 1916 paper shortage forced the closure or amalgamation of several of the cheap papers which had constituted his regular market. This as he put it later 'somewhat disorganised our little fiction-factory'. Their time of relative affluence at Layer Breton came to an end. Herbert and Em relinquished the lease of the Old Rectory in 1917 and moved back to London to a flat in Bayswater.

The children had been hurried back to town once already. During the first years of the war people in the coastal districts of Essex feared invasion. An entry in the diary of the Allinghams' friend and family doctor John Henry Salter made in November 1914 reads, 'Five or six submarines observed at the entrance to the Blackwater and an attempt at invasion thought probable. It is believed that the submarines put in there being quiet and snug out of the storms and probably for repairs. They were seen putting out this morning. Then a gunboat, torpedo boats and mine-finders came and dragged the bottom of the sea. The whole country is alive with soldiers and entrenchments are being dug all across the county.'

Dr Salter, who lived in Tolleshunt D'Arcy, three miles away from Layer Breton, was in an unrivalled position to glean every scrap of both official and unofficial rumour. When war broke out, he had already been practising in the district for fifty years. His extraordinary combination of professional and sporting activities had given him intimate knowledge of both the countryside and its people. Salter wielded official power on scores of County committees and was characteristically one of the first to volunteer to serve as a special constable when war broke out. Soon he was Chief Special Constable for the district. By early 1915 he had enrolled Herbert into his company, as unhesitatingly and inexorably as he had earlier compelled him to join his Freemasons' Lodge at Kelvedon.

The Doctor was a personality of extreme arrogance and forcefulness. Born in 1841, he had won praise and prizes during his medical training and looked set for a brilliant career as a surgeon – until he lost the sight of his right eye in a 'mill' (provoked by himself) between gypsies and swells at the Derby of 1862. Undeterred, he had married in 1864 and purchased 'a practice down in Essex [which] sounds exceedingly well'. On October 29th of that year he had reached Tolleshunt D'Arcy 'and sat down to dinner in the most cosy dining-room in the world'. His address was D'Arcy House. In 1964 Margery, who chose to keep that dining room almost exactly as it had been in the Doctor's day, celebrated one hundred years of their joint (virtually) continuous occupancy.

The secret of Dr Salter's career of success upon success both locally and nationally derived from something more than his quick brain, physical skills and determination. It stemmed from his completely unselfconscious certainty that he was right. For Margery he was the epitome of bulldog Englishmen and she planned, at the end of her own life, to write about him. She had already left a sketch of him as Dr Bouverie in *Dancers in Mourning* and though, in the novel, Margery's detective, Albert Campion, has only just met this fictional character, there is a revealing moment when the sequence of time is jolted aside and Campion offers a child's impression of the man. 'That half contemptuous tone which yet carried such absolute conviction reminded him of a time long ago when he had first heard it, and the thought "That's how God talks" had come to him with the awful certainty of truth.'

Another entry from Salter's diary on the subject of invasion shows this quality to perfection. 'I was rung up last night after I had got to bed and told that the soldiers were expecting an invasion during the night, and asked what provision I could make as Chairman of the Emergency Committee for getting the people away. I told my informant to go to bed and rest quietly – that with neap tides there was only 45 minutes to unload an army and it couldn't be done in the time.'

Not all alarms could be so easily dismissed. The authorities were worried and a more recent article quotes the then Chief Constable of Essex as saying, 'On more than one occasion reliable information was obtained that the Germans were on the point of making a raid and a "stand-by" order was issued. Had a raid been made during the early stages of the war, I fear it would have been a case of *sauve-qui-peut* as the preparations were far from complete.' The enemy reached Essex by air as well as sea. Bombs were dropped and in September 1916 a zeppelin was brought down at Great Wigborough only a few miles from Layer Breton. The day came when Dr Salter himself visited the Old Rectory in his tin hat and his medals to warn the Allinghams that the 'second warning' had been issued and invasion was believed to be imminent.

Margery was at home and remembered that occasion vividly. From her window in The Glebe she could glimpse the Blackwater Estuary, source of so many scares and sightings. At ten she was quite old enough to understand the reality of the East Coast threat but too young to be included in discussions as to the best means of coping with it. She remembered how afraid she had felt. 'The Old Doctor . . . had called to see the grown-ups and there had been a hasty conference in my father's study. I had gone nosing round, sniffing excitement in the wind, and had gathered from the muttering in the kitchen that the threatened invasion which had been talked about for months was actually upon us . . . Every responsible person had duties at this time and I was very much in the way while they made up their minds what to do with us children, so I returned to my desk where I was at work on one of my interminable poems and was frightened stiff.'

She had read the propaganda reports of sensational atrocities in Belgium and, if she had thought of it, she would presumably have regretted that she had ever been 'rather a one for calamities'. Her fear took shape as an imagined crisis of conscience. How well could she behave in an invasion? Would she have the courage to attempt resistance and risk seeing her baby sister, Joyce, bayonetted against the coach-house door (her mental horror-picture) or would she spinelessly fraternise and 'sidle up to the first Hun who appeared'?

Margery's fantasy of the 'right' way to tackle the enemy was an exploit any Stevensonian lad would have been proud to undertake. 'I should get up into my secret hiding place where the japonica and laburnum hung over the road, and drop a chunk of the broken stone pedestal from the Glebe garden on his head.' But she had few illusions about her actual capacity for heroism. Though she was sure she would have to do something ('the notion of doing nothing did not occur to me at that age'), she doubted, despairingly, whether she would have the mental strength to do right. 'The responsibility of making the choice reduced me to a state of abject misery and when I heard that the grown-ups had decided to bundle us children off to London there and then . . . I was more relieved than ever in my life before or since.'

The three children were evacuated to Em's sister Maud. They were sent in the care of their young nursemaid, Cis (a protégée of Aunt Grace's from Chappel), and left behind their country home, their parents – and Margery's donkey. It was the beginning of the end of her childhood.

The Red Rose
by A. J. Gregory (c 1930)

IV

'In a Sealed Dovecot'

1917–1920

After the first relief at leaving the possible dangers and practical difficulties of First World War life in Essex, the return to London was not a happy one for the Allingham family. Even as a child, Margery had been shaken by the extent of her fear and was left nervously aware that a challenge to heroism might only have been postponed. She was scarred too by the scale of bereavement she had witnessed in the small community of Layer Breton. Twenty-five years later when the shadows of war were again closing in, this childhood vision of sorrow returned vividly to her.

'War simply meant death to me; a soldier galloping up on a fat white horse to kiss my tearful nurse goodbye over the wall under the chestnut trees, and then death.

'It was not ordinary dying either, nor even death in its more horrible forms, but death final, empty and away somewhere. I had a sudden recollection of women and old people all in black, as country people were in those days on a Sunday, standing about in the village street reading enormous casualty lists in very small type which seemed to fill whole pages of the paper; a boy on a bike with not one telegram spelling tragedy but two or even three at a time; and long sad services in the small church which had been a barn and still smelt of hay.

'It was a dreadful picture of annihilation, of ending off, of the hopeless destruction of practically all a whole human crop. I remembered names I had not thought of for twenty-five years: George Playle and a big cowman that they used to call "Long 'un". I remembered the food shortage at the boarding school I went to later, and the miserable darkness too; but the principal thing was the hundreds and hundreds of far-away deaths.'

She believed that her father was left maimed by emotions of a different kind. 'My father hated the Germans. Long after the last war it used to astound me that such an extraordinarily tolerant and logical man should grow so coldly savage when he spoke of them. "They have the gift of offence" he used to say, and I think it may be that there is more in that than I realized. My father believed in Tolerance. It was his particular version of the Christian liking of mankind that is the simplest key to the comprehension of the universe, and in his case I think it was probably this that the 1914 Germans had attacked, all but destroyed, and he hated them for that.'

As a child trained to be observant, she had noticed 'the intolerable condition of strain against which our elders struggled irritably'. It was not only the day to day anxieties that oppressed Herbert but his awareness that the conduct of the war, the sacrifices being made so gallantly by so many, could be jeopardised by intrigue and incompetence in high places. He was rising fifty and therefore too old to fight himself. His youngest brother 'Tod' joined the Royal Flying Corps, another brother (probably Arthur) was wounded at the Dardanelles. Mac hurried home from America to volunteer for the Royal Navy but was rejected for active service because of his poor hearing, so joined a merchant ship that was promptly commandeered as an R.N. Transport. Herbert's brother-in-law, Wal Hughes, came with the Canadian forces to die at Ypres.

Unlike Dr Salter, Herbert could not find relief by flinging himself into committee work and paramilitary activities, drilling or being drilled across the country. His only implement was his pen and that was bound by necessity to continue producing feuilletons. Early in 1915 he erupted in a burst of rash fury directed against Lord Northcliffe, founder of the Amalgamated Press on which he largely depended for his living. The issue was conscription and Northcliffe's attacks, through *The Daily Mail*, on Lord Kitchener's policy. Herbert, with many others, considered that this was disloyalty and suspected that it sprang from discreditable motives.

'With respect, but also with all possible emphasis, I declare that if you are preventing your newspapers from conducting an energetic recruiting campaign owing to a personal prejudice or wounded amour propre, you are incurring a very grave responsibility indeed.

'If I had your papers I would raise a million new recruits in a month simply by telling them the truth and letting them know that they are really wanted.

'But the worst of all you men of outstanding ability when you get to the top, you lose the common touch. You lose faith in the masses and entirely underestimate their great qualities.

'I know the common people – I get my living from studying them as you once did – and I tell you that if this war lasts ten years, it will not be their courage and resolution that will be the first to slacken.'

He received a broadside of a reply from Northcliffe but no professional retaliation. The episode illustrates something characteristic of Herbert, his idealism fanned into anger by a realisation of his own impotence. 'If I had your papers . . .' Perhaps there is some bitterness there, a wish that he too had risen to wield real editorial power. Margery described her father's existence as 'exasperating'. Even in her grief after his death she would not, she claimed, have condemned him to live his life again.

This adult feeling of compassion finds expression in the brief fictional portrait of Jeffrey, a man 'whose idols had crashed round him . . . a man who had been trained and bred to be a gentleman, and who had come to believe that gentlemen were ungentle; a man who had been taught to believe in God and who had come to believe that God was hypocritical.' In Margery's opinion the last rags of Herbert's Victorian family optimism and his confidence in his role on earth were consumed in the moral chaos of the Great War.

Her parents did not return to London on the same terms of unity and partnership in which they had set out to live in the country. By 1917 they had been married for fifteen years. Both had changed, developing in ways which accentuated their antipathetic qualities. Herbert had moved further in his rejection of the class and attitudes with which he had been brought up; Em had become devoted to a man who exemplified so many of these in their most extreme form – Dr J. H. Salter.

She described Dr Salter, after his death, as 'a Master of Men'. He was almost seventy when the Allinghams arrived at Layer Breton yet his vigour and vitality for the next twenty years remained sufficient to put younger men in the shade. It is hard to over-emphasise the extent to which he stamped his personality on Tolleshunt D'Arcy and the surrounding villages. Today, more than half a century after his death, he remains a local legend. If Em longed for colour and excitement in 'the dull but pleasant dream' of their early years at the Old Rectory, the Doctor could hardly fail to attract her. With his supremely confident style of living – big house and garden, devoted retainers, wealth, status and success in so many activities, he was a figure from romantic fiction.

Herbert shared her respect for Salter. The Doctor delivered their younger daughter, Joyce, in 1913 and was consulted in various family crises thereafter. To Em, he was of pre-eminent importance for the rest of his life. It was not overtly a physical passion. Both Em and Salter prided themselves on their own righteousness and would have been shocked by any blatant admission of carnality. Dr Salter had been a widower since 1904 and was sentimentally devoted to the memory of his wife. He felt quite at liberty, however, to admire a fine-lookin' woman and there were several in the neighbourhood who were flattered by his attention. His diary shows that he was naively susceptible to admiration in return.

Em liked to perform small services for the Doctor. She chose his library books, assisted with his memoirs, and, later, attended him in illness. Even after the Allinghams returned to London, Salter would call at the flat unexpectedly or summon Em to D'Arcy in times of need as casually as he roused his gardener in the middle of the night to display a choice bloom to a passing guest. Herbert stood back, never dissenting, painfully aware of his unimportance to his wife. Em later explained '– her husband was part of herself, he did not come into the picture at all . . . The Doctor was a materialist, a man of action – the husband intellectual, interested mostly with ideas that found an outlet in his plots.'

The family polarities changed as they settled to life in Bayswater. Where there had been adults to one side, children to the other, there grew a tendency for Herbert to seek Margery's companionship and Em to find their son Phil most congenial. They paired off thus to theatres and cinemas and in the case of Margery and Herbert, for long walks through the capital, either at weekends or at night after his day's writing was done. The foundation of Margery's intimate knowledge and love of London was laid during these walks. And as they walked, Margery often made up brief stories about the people who might live behind the blinds or lighted windows. Although the family still visited Essex for holidays on Mersea Island, the return to urban life was not easy for any of them. 'We felt like pigeons in a sealed dovecote,' wrote Margery. Joyce, the youngest, spent much of her time with Granny, Em's sister Maud, or Aunt Grace at Pope's Hall. Aged seven she too was sent to boarding school, New Hall Convent, near Chelmsford in Essex.

Money was a problem. Even from the school in Colchester, Margery had noticed the sudden (and temporary) boost given to Essex agricultural incomes by supplying the needs of the Army. 'Everybody at all the farms round us had grown very grand indeed and there was a great blossoming of furs and gaily coloured tweeds and motor-cars . . . The strain and anxiety were there under it all of course, but on top there was a veneer of tremendous gaiety and extravagance.'

While there were new rich, the war also created new poor. Many families who, like the Allinghams, had been comfortably off, found themselves hard hit by taxation and rising prices. In 1916, Herbert's income was £1,054, an amount which was increasingly inadequate to support the 'successful Edwardian' style to which they had become accustomed. The Allinghams' move to Bayswater was a move to a more economical way of living. Their flat was one in a large mansion block, only a daily maid was needed for the housework and meals could be eaten out quite cheaply. Very little cooking was done at home. The change may have been hard for the teenage Margery to accept. Looking back later she commented, 'We were not alone in this sort of experience by any means, and it is an agonising business to be jerked out of one scheme into another when one is thirteen or so.'

Neither was the outlook promising. The newspaper industry was suffering both from the paper shortages, and from the crisis in manpower. George Dilnot, historian of the Amalgamated Press, wrote that 'before the end came, some twelve hundred men – directors, editors, managers, sub-editors, book-keepers, clerks, printers and office-boys – had left their desks for the trenches.' It was an unexpected stroke of good fortune for Herbert and Em that the ensuing shortage of competent staff necessitated the employment of more women – 'feminine assistants', as Dilnot calls them, 'whose devotion and energy enabled a very critical period to be passed, with the firm in a stronger position than ever when peace came.'

Among those 'feminine assistants' was Em's sister, Maud Hughes. She had been working for the Post Office when Herbert heard of a vacancy on the Northcliffe newspaper, *The Daily Sketch*. Cousin Grace came up to accompany Maud to the interview. They amused the family afterwards by recounting how they had changed skirts on the way there in the taxi. A telegram, 'Got it!', arrived at the Old Rectory and Maud was set for a career that was to be of benefit to all. She didn't stay long at the *Sketch* – though long enough to meet and marry its sports writer Edward Wood. This had to remain secret as women were dismissed automatically on marriage.

'It was in 1916 that two determined women journalists, Maudie Hughes and Winifred Johnston, first climbed the stairs of the Amalgamated Press. Between them they were to run a newer-than-1917 feminist paper, *Woman's Weekly*.' Thus ran the Fleetway Publications house magazine on Maud's retirement from the company more than forty years later. The writer may be misleading if not wrong about the senior editor of the two, Winifred ('Biddy') Johnston. According to Cynthia L. White's history of women's magazines, Biddy had edited Alfred Harmsworth's very first periodical for women, *Forget-Me-Not*, and was transferring on the strength of that success, to rescue *Woman's Weekly* from a shaky start.

Fiction and knitting were to be the *Woman's Weekly* recipes for success. While it seems odd now to see it described as 'feminist', the magazine broke new ground after 1916 in the extent of its success as a properly practical magazine run by women for women. Articles like 'The Business Girl As Wife' appear among the recipes for rice-pudding and advice on child-health, and one of the new management's first acts was to commission a series of detective stories from Em, *The Exploits of Phinella Martin*.

Maud was the family's most committed supporter of women's rights though she was not politically active. According to Joyce, the female members of this section of the Allingham family tended to take their independence for granted and to focus their attention on the work that earned their livings. Maud's considerable personality and her passion were poured into her job. The writer of the Fleetway article had been impressed by 'her flaming red hair and unquenchable vitality' but admits, 'she was a tartar to work for [though] the kindest woman on earth'. Much later in life Margery, who was very fond of her aunt, pays a notably candid tribute to Maud's manipulative skills. 'Aunt M. was a power and an authority who had learned how to be popular by using her head: she was used to making money and spending it and getting her own way.'

In 1916 all this was to come. While she remained at *Woman's Weekly*, Maud made full use of her family contacts in the job of regenerating the paper. Herbert discovered that his style of serial writing was as appropriate for the women's market as for the boys' and in January 1918 he noted 'am booked to do Maud's new serial'. *Mother and Home*, which published Margery's first offering, a fairy story, in 1917, when she was aged thirteen, was also from the *Woman's Weekly* stable. In 1919 Maud founded a magazine of her own for the Amalgamated Press. This was *The Picture Show* for film fans which ran until the 1960s and remained distinctively her creation. The family found themselves taking new interest in Mary Pickford, Tom Mix, Houdini and Charlie Chaplin.

Margery had left Endsleigh House at Christmas 1918 and in the following term moved to Cambridge to attend The Perse High School for Girls. The choice of school had been made on the advice of their former landlord in Layer Breton, the Rev. Edwin Luard. One of his sisters, Rose Luard, was a teacher at The Perse and had recently re-opened a small boarding house nearby in partnership with a second sister, Georgina. The house was named Sarum and the Luards had twenty-eight girls in their care. Looking back from a distance of thirty-five years, Margery saw much to commend in this arrangement: 'Sarum did not merely present us to school on time every morning in the term, but succeeded in giving us an approach to the ordinary domestic side of life which was compatible with and complementary to that special version of modern education for women for which the Perse stood at a period, just after the catastrophe of the 1914–18 war, when drastic change was in the air and all manners and morals temporarily in the melting pot.

'At Sarum we girls escaped from social upheaval into the cool, classically formal world of Jane Austen, entirely intelligent but always feminine . . . the code was not a hard one but it was absolutely rigid, and from this distance it is possible to see some of the little pieces of inspired machinery by which it was so adroitly enforced.'

She remembers their evening dresses of velveteen, the formal seating plans for their evening meal, and drawing room sessions with Miss Luard when the girls took their sewing 'and drank coffee and listened to a book just as if the world had never been on fire or the lovely, secure, dull domesticity of the nineteenth century had never known a rift . . . Afterwards we each shook hands with our hostess, that tiny ramrod maiden aunt who brought us up as she was brought up, to be emancipated, to be intelligent and to be gentlewomen without the sneer, and we learned not to break her wrist nor to touch her wetly. Not a bad first lesson as it has all fallen out.'

She had not responded so appreciatively at the time.

Margery entered The Perse with high hopes. The school was then under its second headmistress, Miss Kennett, and consolidating a somewhat daunting record of academic achievement. Margery's friend Miss Saint at Endsleigh House had herself been a pupil at the school and tried to reassure Margery that, although 'I'll be very scared of Miss Kennett when I get there because she's so ugly . . . she's really frightfully decent'. The official history of The Perse describes Miss Kennett as 'A brilliant teacher, an indefatigable worker . . . she would not tolerate the second rate in scholarship or anything else' and Rose Luard as 'highly intelligent, absolutely uncompromising in her standards for herself and for those in her charge'.

Both teachers are said by the school's historian to have possessed a sense of humour; to Margery at fifteen this was not sufficiently evident to outweigh her instinctive recoil from their code of austerity, from ceaseless academic striving and from the inflexibility of their admirable system. In some material ways Margery was recognisably Em's daughter – the intellectual qualities of her headmistress and housemistress failed to compensate for their dowdy appearance. Or Margery might unconsciously have assumed that her new teachers' looks were the necessary result of their intellects. Miss Kennett was quite frankly 'above clothes', and Miss Luard a dried-up little lady who put the coal on the fire one lump at a time and grudgingly. (She was in fact ill for much of the time Margery was at Sarum.)

In the first chapters of her unpublished autobiographical novel, *Green Corn*, written in 1923, three years after she had left The Perse, she describes the housemistress and headmistress of 'The Mar' school in Cambridge from a pupil's perspective. Two girls have been paying final, formal visits to their housemistress. Their impressions differ widely. Those of the first speaker, Mary, come close to Margery's own. ' "Well, look at Cherry," she said at last, "and our respected Head – Can you imagine either of them laughing until they were helpless, or, moved by some calamity, weeping?"

' "Of course not!" Betty was genuinely shocked.

'Mary shrugged. "Well, quite a lot of nice women are capable of both," she said.

' "But not in school!" Betty stared at her.

'Mary spread her hands in a gesture of helplessness, "Of course not in school, sea-cook," she said, laughing at the thought. "What I mean is – all the staff of The Mar don't appear to be capable of being anywhere else but in school – they're not a bit like ordinary women." '

These teachers are unremittingly chalk-and-dustery. They are idealistic predators, poised to capture bright young girls and mould them, with the best of motives, into the same dessicated, dedicated creatures as themselves. Margery's heroine feels both threatened and misunderstood.

The first section of *Green Corn* represents a school-leaver's revenge. Though she had entered The Perse with enthusiasm, contributing immediately to *The Persean* magazine, joining its committee and producing the form notes for the Middle and Upper Fourth, she stayed in Cambridge little more than a year and departed convinced that she could never be, and didn't want to be, an 'intellectual'. Betty, the school 'highbrow' in *Green Corn*, is drawn with wit and anger. She considers that Mary has wasted her time at The Mar because she obviously hasn't *worked*. Getting up at six in the morning day after day to make props and costumes for the house play (as Margery did) doesn't count – despite any contribution this may have made to the common happiness. Mary hasn't used her Brains. 'After all, anybody who isn't an idiot can learn to construe prose.'

Again she may have been criticised for the presentation of her work and for her spelling. If so, it had little effect except on her confidence. Ten years later (in 1929), Mac was still thundering from America, 'I never, never shall understand how she can have any real feeling for words when she doesn't even look at them for long enough to remember how they are spelled.' The 'phonetic' quality of Margery's spelling may suggest that she *heard* rather than *saw* words. This was never more than a minor blemish but she frequently apologises for both spelling and handwriting in her letters and, as soon as she could, found secretarial help to compensate.

Margery particularly disliked the teaching of Shakespeare by these academic ladies. 'Their method I remember was to plant the baby fully dressed in the bath, throw away the child with the suds and try to reconstruct the whole thing from the wet clothes.' Her own response to Shakespeare was immediate, 'almost physical' and oddly protective. As a student in London she would write after seeing a poor production, 'the old boy would turn in his grave' – personal sympathy from one artist to another. Arid fourth-form analysis could have been unexpectedly distressing to this emotional adolescent.

Margery describes herself when young as 'a nervy, big-boned exciteable child who trailed her coat and changed colour easily; I was quick to rage or laughter, self-conscious, over-aware and altogether about as restful as an unbroken mule'. This memory, set down many years later, is supported by a contemporary from The Perse who remembers her as 'tall and lanky', 'a somewhat volatile type with a tendency to stammer. I don't think she was outstanding academically, but she was creative.' Those photographs of Margery which survive from her teenage years show her shooting upwards, head and shoulders taller than Phil at this age until she was almost as tall as their father (though he was not a tall man). She looks slightly discomforted by this fact. The impression that she was 'volatile' gains somewhat melancholy confirmation from a record of her medical and emotional history which she produced for doctors during a period of crisis in later middle age. She says that 'temperamental difficulties' began about 1919–20. Possibly as well as being 'nervy' and 'quick to rage or laughter' she also found herself liable to sudden despondency – but this is supposition only. Her spurt of upwards growth over, she began to put on weight.

Margery wrote two plays while at The Perse (*Fairy Gold* and *Soldier of Fortune*) and saw them performed by her fellow-Sarumites. She was not unpopular with the other girls. Even the student who must have provided the model for Betty in *Green Corn* was in occasional touch with her several years later. Margery nevertheless left The Perse convinced that creativity counted for nothing and that she would always be 'odd man out' in a community which placed its highest value on academic excellence or, as a secondary quality, prowess on the games field. The school magazine confirms this impression which was not at all uncommon among such schools at that time. Although Miss Georgina Luard (and, independently, a fellow-pupil) pay tribute to the huge amount of effort Margery had put into the production of her two plays, Miss Luard regrets that 'in a crowded term' time could only be found for one performance. *The Persean*, alert to every examination entry or inter-form hockey match, did not mention either play until two years after Margery had left the school.

Margery believed that the achievements which were important to her were irrelevant to the The Perse. When, in *Green Corn*, a pupil suggests that Mary (Margery) has been in the wrong place 'for her type' at the Mar, highbrow Betty counters, witheringly, that there is then something wrong with Mary's 'type'. The things Mary cares about are essentially frivolous. They are not things which 'really matter'. She finds Mary 'charming' (a doubtful compliment) and has enjoyed her plays – but 'I don't approve of her that's all . . . The Mar is a modern school and turns out girls with the right stamp. Mary isn't stamped, somehow.' Just as she may have done at the young ladies' academy, Margery set out to avoid being 'stamped'. She may have been precocious or even, under her shyness, conceited. She certainly seems to have known what she did and didn't want. She didn't want frumpy teachers, stifling tradition and a set of selfless aims which in her view could be reduced, even for the university-bound girls, to the basic 'either to have or to teach kids'.

Those who knew Margery as an adult say with conviction that she possessed 'a first-class brain'. She was an acute observer but although she became an original and interesting thinker, she never excelled at expressing herself in abstractions. It must have been hard for her teachers to see how best to help her. Miss Rose Luard taught Ancient History to the Middle Fourth, only to have its facts gaily dispensed with in a poem contributed to *The Persean*, 'So Said the Blackbird'.

'When the garden of the Perse was a prehistoric fenland
And where the fourth form classrooms are, a pond used to be

The Dodos and the Jabberwocks and creeping things that
  scrunched up rocks
Mid verdant ferns and waving docks did sport and make them
  free.

'When the garden of the Perse was the home of furry cavemen
And over where the Hall is now a chief's hut used to be,
The children killed with granite flails the angry things with
  slashing tails
And fiery eyes and shining scales for folks to come and see.

'When the garden of the Perse was the scene of morning break,
  friends,
A sound was heard among the trees and I looked up to see,
The blackbird with his yellow nose and sparkling eyes and
  turned-out toes
Who tells but half he knows, told this mad tale to me.'

However reasoned and mature her decision to leave The Perse – and neither Herbert nor the Misses Luard seem to have argued strongly against it – Margery may have felt some sense of failure at the brevity of her stay. Her self-confidence, never secure, had taken a knock and she had developed a limiting prejudice against the intellect. Her view of the dichotomy between intelligence and the intellect forms a strand of thinking that runs throughout her work. Wider experience and increased awareness of her own capacity modified the teenage judgements of *Green Corn* but one belief stayed constant. The tendency of the intellect to shut itself off from normal human experience did not cease to perturb her. *Police at the Funeral*, World War II writings, *More Work for the Undertaker, The China Governess* all present groups of dangerously cloistered 'intellectuals' attempting to live according to books or tradition, failing to see life as it is and incapable of adapting to change. Among the schoolgirls of *Green Corn*, Betty is formed and fixed and daunting in her certainty; her success at school has left her institutionalised. Mary, intelligent, not intellectual, is just starting out, ready for whatever adventure life has to offer.

Even the architecture of Cambridge oppressed Margery. Her heroine, Mary, attends a last service in King's College Chapel. The place is glorious and monstrous, devouring the fresh young voices of its choristers, generation after generation, to kindle its cold stone into momentary life. The great west doors are open; Mary pauses for a moment, half-enthralled by the sacrifice of words and music, the over-arching gloom, the dusty, greedy beauty. She looks out towards 'the little stone bridge and the shadowed avenue to the road, all dancing and trembling in the sunlight . . . The girl on the steps smiled to herself and sighed. Then she walked down the wide aisle, out of the chapel and into the sunlight.'

Not that walking out into the sunlight, or setting off to seek one's fortune, is quite as uncomplicated in life as the adventure novelist likes to make it. 'What about the Board Of Trade regulations?' McFee used to enquire, crushingly, of any pulp-writer who allowed his school-boy protagonist to 'run away to sea'. Margery, aged sixteen, remained bound by the expectation that she would continue with her studies in London. 'Margery needs more education of course,' wrote Miss Georgina Luard, decidedly, to Herbert, 'and *higher* education later, in English at any rate, if she is to do the good work in future which I think it is in her to do.'

Miss Luard had a recommendation to make, an old friend, Miss Barbara Harper, who held a fellowship from Queen's College, Harley Street – 'the pioneer college for women's education,' said Miss Luard. 'She is a very clever, cultivated and charming woman, and I am sure that Margery will enjoy working with her and that she would be a sound and stimulating teacher.'

Margery and the Misses Luard liked each other more than an autobiographical reading of *Green Corn* alone might lead one to expect. They remained in touch for life. Margery took lessons from Miss Harper regularly and willingly for three years. They studied a broad range of literature including a steady trek through Plutarch's *Lives* and Carlyle's *History of the French Revolution*, French language practice, and *The Divine Comedy* in Italian. In the book reviews which Margery later wrote for *Time and Tide*

(1938–44), it became obvious that she had acquired an extensive knowledge of both English and European literature – and that she had continually under-valued, almost deliberately concealed, her real educational attainment.

In her late memoir she also obfuscates the question of who, exactly, was in charge of her life when she left school, and what her ambitions were then. 'I left school,' she says, 'and came to London to learn to write under my father.' This diplomatically glosses over the fact that she had left school because she was not happy there – and allows the reader to assume that she began some almost formal apprenticeship as a writer of adventure fiction, Herbert's staple commodity. In fact, before she was seventeen, she poured most of her effort into drama, a medium Herbert never attempted.

As well as the lessons with Miss Harper, Margery signed on to study elocution, stage-craft, drama, eurhythmics and fencing, at the Regent Street Polytechnic. Older Margery gives thanks to Herbert for all this. 'When I got to London . . . my father, who was a preoccupied man, noticed suddenly that I was almost unread and also, which he found curious, unable to speak. He arranged forthwith that I should go to a tutor to read English and to a Polytechnic to put the other little matter right.' Her husband, Pip, also stated that Margery was sent to the Polytechnic by Herbert 'to cure her of stammering and snobbery' – depressingly negative objectives for what were two of the most fulfilling years of Margery's life.

But such high-handed action would have been quite un-typical of Herbert. He was never a father who attempted to dictate his children's lives. In 1919, while Margery was newly arrived at The Perse, he had prophesied that 'in a year or two she will take her life into her own hands and poor pa will have to grin and try to pretend that he likes it.' This is more credible. Herbert's 1920 diary states 'Margery wants to leave the Perse' – he was only required to listen and acquiesce – and in the same year Herbert reports to McFee that Margery 'chaffs her mother and cajoles me'. (Mary, Margery's heroine, chaffs her mother and 'sweedles' her father, 'sweedling' him most importantly into allowing her to arrange her future studies exactly as she likes, while preserving the feminine pretence that all is done on his initiative.)

The year 1920 was a busy one for Herbert. Both his parents died and there were family matters to be arranged down in Sible Hedingham. Maud's magazines were doing well but although he and Em had almost more work than they could handle, cash was worryingly short. Joyce started school in the summer, then Herbert searched for a Public School prepared to take Phil who had been removed from Bognor in 1918 and had been working since then with tutors – 'backward but a good boy' was their summing-up to Herbert in 1920. Haileybury and Tonbridge turned Phil down but in 1921 he entered Forest School in Chigwell which proved unexpectedly congenial. Throughout all this, Herbert was trying to keep up his 2,000 words per day. He may well have been glad to let his elder daughter have her head.

Mary, Margery's fictional persona, is honest enough to feel guilt at her manipulation of her father, and some shame at her own expertise. She employs it nonetheless so that she is not forced to admit her real ambition. Mary's ambition is to become an actress – and so was Margery's then – possibly a playwright, like Robin, the hero of *Green Corn*, a novel which is explicit about the difficulty of admitting teenage hopes, especially to one's family.

It was much later in life, after the stage doors had closed, that Margery reinterpreted her student career as one of 'training' to be a writer of fiction and placed the responsibility for its direction firmly on her father's shoulders. But though she needed Herbert's approval he was probably as unsure as she was as to which path she would finally take. 'One feels she may "go off" in any direction,' he wrote. It was not, in fact, until the composition of *Green Corn* itself that he attempted to influence her decisively towards the novel –and then she resented his interference.

Autobiography tends to be a filial genre – whether for or against the parental influence. Margery loved Herbert and was glad, later in life, to depict herself as the dutiful daughter, his most 'industrious apprentice'. As she grew older, and a more formidable figure in her sphere, she grew paradoxically less inclined to take the credit for her achievements. She laid increasing emphasis on the extent to which she had been 'trained' to write and was merely following family 'tradition' by so doing. She tended to dismiss or to mock her personal, perfectionist drive towards original expression. (Mary, in *Green Corn*, had been more candid. Whatever the methods she employed, she recognised that she was demanding 'something to take up the whole of my mind' and that she needed this for herself, for her own satisfaction and ultimately, perhaps, for her own glory.)

Margery went to the Regent Street Polytechnic School of Speech and Drama, albeit with Herbert's approval and support, because it was what she wanted to do then. It was a sad progression to the later Margery, who so often felt slow and fat and tired, who hid behind her workload and professed total inability to open her mouth in public. Despite the professional success she had achieved, her confidence was far less than the teenager's had been when it came to admitting in print that once she'd dreamed of taking centre stage as Charlotte Corday, Lady Macbeth or Dido, Queen of Carthage.

V

Mersea Island

1921

'I thought I was somebody alright but was not at all sure who it was going to turn out to be. Considering it dispassionately from this distance, my state of mind appears hyper-sensitive to the point of absurdity.' In these words Margery recalled her initial session among the crowd of students waiting to be assessed by Miss Louie Bagley, principal of the School of Speech and Drama.

It was an ordeal that remained fresh in her memory for many years. The Regent Street Polytechnic, 'The Pioneer Institute for Technical Education' as it styled itself, was quite unlike anything she had previously known. Now renamed the Polytechnic of Central London, it was founded in 1882 as the Youth's Christian Institute 'where every reasonable facility shall be offered for the formation of a steadfast character and of true friendships, for training the intellect and for leading an upright and useful life.' Education was at the heart of the enterprise: 'to train and fit young men and women for their life work and to make them more efficient in the trade or occupations they have adopted.'

The range of activities offered by the Polytechnic had been curtailed during the First World War. By the winter of 1920/1 when Margery enrolled, the institution was regaining its momentum. There were no formal entrance qualifications; anyone over fifteen was eligible. The fees were low – and 25,000 students were registered. The Speech and Drama School was expanding with particular rapidity. Students of different ages, classes and nationalities applied to enrol; some hoping to improve their current job prospects by learning to speak more clearly, others training to teach drama or elocution in L.C.C. schools, a few, like Margery, nursing dreams of the stage. They were all at the preliminary session.

Miss Louie Bagley, the principal, was a daunting personality, 'a Boadicea of a woman', as Margery's fellow student Josephina de Vasconcellos recalls her. All Margery could remember, forty years on, were 'those bullet eyes glowing with amusement, know-how and uninhibited merciless drive'. One by one, her prospective pupils stood up in the large first floor room to say their piece. 'Each would-be student rose smartly, read, or attempted to read, a couple of lines from book of verse and received in return a brief brilliant caricature of his performance delivered with relish . . . Even if I had not been about to be a victim I should have found the experience agonising. Dog ate dog without qualm. Sycophantic laughter followed each excruciating performance and the casualty rate was high.'

Margery waited in the grip of terror – hyperconscious of herself, her middle-class looks and accent, the Cambridge élitist background – and her paralysing stutter. She expected either to be hated by her fellow-students or humiliated before them. 'Then, when the moment came and I stood up and looked at the words before me, my whole mind panicked and shuttered and appeared to explode. I do not know if there is any kind of baby bird that bursts from its egg like a bomb but if so, I know what it feels like. My speaking voice shot out naked and new and angry in a very cold and hostile world.'

Her 'ingrowing hobble', as she called her stutter, had dropped from her. The School of Speech and Drama ran special sessions or recommended extra private tuition for sufferers from speech defects. Margery did not attend them. She practised her elocution exercises diligently and for once in her life she passed exams and collected praise, certificates – and a medal – for the excellence of her tragic and comic renderings. Josephina found it hard to believe that Margery had ever stuttered. 'She had a beautiful voice, like a cello.' Margery was among those most favoured students taken by Miss Bagley to participate in her own public performances. At Poly Open Evenings and elsewhere Herbert was frequently able to report proudly 'Marge the only one to get a call.'

Mechanically what seems to have happened is that she had

acquired a technique of fluency. Some friends noticed a certain hesitancy in her ordinary speech but recitation sent her into a different gear. This may have demanded some abdication of conscious control. Safe enough in a monologue where the words had been learned and the actions practised; not quite trustworthy when delivered unscripted. On the few occasions in later life when Margery failed to avoid speaking in public – a Foyle's Literary Lunch, for instance – she was open to criticism for reading every word of her address. Among her more revealing excuses for turning down invitations to speak was that she was frightened not of what she could not say, but of what she could, 'freely, audibly and without a thought'.

Speech therapists today suggest that the achievement of mechanical control may not always be enough to convince a former stammerer that he or she has nothing to fear. They suggest that the wider area of social relationships requires consideration; the stammer may have been but a symptom of more subtle difficulties, feelings of inferiority perhaps, problems in sustaining relationships, unease in specific social situations. Margery's new-found skill did enable her to approach her fellow-students with greater confidence. From her initial conviction that they would hate her for her young lady's upbringing, she grew convinced that she was accepted at the Poly as she had never been at school. As she shed her self-consciousness, the cheerful, practical, enthusiastic aspects of her personality received an airing and she 'joined in' as never before.

To Margery and her peers in the Speech and Drama classes, the recitation was the stuff of life; it was a drawing-room accomplishment, a charity concert turn or an essential item in the portfolio of any aspiring actress. Browning, Longfellow, Shakespeare, forgotten verse dramatists like Stephen Philips, all were regularly mined for material. Though students could and did recite lyric poetry, Margery almost invariably preferred to take on a personality other than her own and gave dramatic representations in verse. Empathy with the character was the quality for which she excelled beyond the technical skills of voice production, phrasing and articulation. A notable tribute comes from her future sister-in-law, Betty Carter, whom she met in the autumn of 1921.

Betty was the daughter of Lilian Carter (née Robinson) whom Herbert had known at Cambridge. Though Herbert and Lilian had exchanged no more than a handful of letters in the thirty-five years that had passed, the family connection had been kept alive by Florence Allingham, the wife of Herbert's brother Arthur. She was a close friend of Lilian's and a frequent visitor to the Carter household. Lilian's son Pip had enrolled in the School of Art at the Regent Street Poly and it was decided that the young people should be introduced to one another.

As Betty Carter, like Margery, hoped to make a career on the stage, it seemed a good idea to ask both girls to recite. Florence, unfortunately, had for many years been over-zealously praising the achievements of each set of children to the other, thus an undercurrent of uneasy rivalry already existed between them. Betty, who did succeed in earning her living as an actress, describes herself on that occasion as articulating and gesticulating with conscious correctness, just as she'd been taught. 'Betty recited very well,' commented Margery in her diary. Betty remembers waiting, with some anxiety, to hear what the large, still almost-stuttering Margery would produce. As soon as she began, any sense of impediment vanished and the identification of speaker and character seemed complete. 'She got up and became . . . a peasant girl watching the execution of her lover. It was heart-rending.'

Soon Margery began to compose her own recitations, often making use of historical or legendary personalities. These were popular with her fellow-students and she continued to provide her friends with suitable 'pieces' for several years after she herself had left the Polytechnic. Her notebooks bear witness to her interest in metrical scansion and the patterning of rhymed and unrhymed verse (taught by Miss Bagley on Friday evenings). The subject-matter of Margery's compositions was red-bloodedly romantic – hauntings, hangings, revenge and remorse fired her teenage imagination. To this day Josephina remembers the last lines of Margery's monologue *Tib Merryweather* written especially for an older fellow student.

Attending her classes at the 'Polly' (as she usually spelled it) and studying with Miss Harper did not consume all of Margery's week. She had plenty of time to write at home and began 1921, her first full year out of school, by sending a clutch of plays and short stories away to various editors – they were as speedily returned. Margery also began to keep a diary in 1921 – perhaps an earnest of the new purposefulness with which she was tackling adult life. She admitted no disappointment at the rejection of her work but was clearly delighted to receive, in March of that year, an encouraging letter from her father's hero George Bernard Shaw to whom she had sent a play entitled *Without Being Naturally Qualified*.

The play, which is by far the most interesting of Margery's surviving work to that date, describes the final experiment of a professor who has discovered that he can 'transfer a certain number of people, you, from this world to the next. Send your ego, personality – soul, if you like. The casket which contains the self remains.' The souls go and – after moments of tension – return. But they leave without speaking. Such was the nature of their experience that they have no words and no desire to describe what they have seen. The professor realises that his life's work has necessarily ended in failure and the audience's expectations are similarly dashed. 'If you "sell" your audience,' said Shaw, 'you won't sell your seats.' He thought that, if she persisted, she might 'do something' someday. Twenty years later, after the publication of *The Oaken Heart* in 1941, he remembered Margery and sent his congratulations.

As well as reading, writing and studying drama, she was also watching a wealth of productions – of Shakespeare above all. During 1921, she saw *Julius Caesar, Midsummer Night's Dream, Romeo and Juliet, The Tempest* (twice), *Hamlet* (twice), *Pericles, Much Ado, Merchant of Venice, All's Well, Richard II* and *Macbeth*. She went to at least five plays by G. B. Shaw during that year, plays by Ibsen and Strindberg, as well as numerous silent films and other shows. Her most regular visits were to the Old Vic where she nourished a passionate hero-worship for the actor Ernest Milton.

Though she read the drama reviews keenly on a Sunday to

reassure herself that Milton was allotted his due praise, her attitude was not that of the critic. She did not seek to tease out subtleties of meaning or relate the performances to external standards. Her concern was with their impact on herself. Her diary for this period gives the impression that she is consciously using herself as a sounding-board for experience – and observing her reactions with interest and occasional surprise. After an uncut (five and a half hour) performance of *Hamlet*, she confesses dramatically, 'I am too young to see such stuff and keep my head.'

Herbert, her most usual companion until late in 1921, described her as 'a curiously sane girl'. Her characteristic response to an overwhelming performance was to attempt to write something of her own. One short story, *Romeo Domino*, written after a performance of *Romeo and Juliet*, deals regretfully, though firmly, with the unwisdom of letting stage romance spill over into 'real' life. The potency, indeed the magic, of being Juliet to an unknown Romeo is fully felt – though there were as yet no hints of romance in her own life. She encountered her fellow- students only during lessons and rehearsals and did not know anyone else of her own age in London. Her social life centred on her family.

Sunday afternoons were usually spent at Aunt Maud's flat in Rosebery Avenue. Margery, who had inherited her mother's deftness with a needle, was often asked to trim a hat or embroider a frock for Maud. She spent a great deal of time making dresses for herself or costumes for the Polytechnic shows. She dressed simply and cleverly, almost always in dark or royal blue to detract from her plumpness. She was fashion-conscious, the first in her group of students to wear her hair 'anhedral', later one of the first to have it bobbed. Years later she described how excited she had been by the cheapness and brilliant colours of a material known as government silk 'which burst on our world in a range of colour hitherto unknown save in explosions'. With this she could pour her dress-making creativity into her costumes. Required wear for lessons with Miss Bagley was 'a short, simple undergarment allowing perfect freedom for the body, bare feet and a straight tunic of any soft-falling material held in at the waist by an elastic girdle'. The long velveteen dresses that had prevented the

Sarumites from romping were folded away with the rest of the decorous past.

Other family visitors foregathered at Maud's on a Sunday. Granny was usually there and Maud's husband Ted – who was rather often 'squiffy'. Aunt Phoebe (the Hughes' half-sister) came, and 'Big Phil', Herbert's favourite brother. Mac paid a visit in 1921 and there was once a 'foreign countess' at Maud's. Margery found it all 'most boreing'. When Phil was home from school they squabbled and made up and went to the cinema together; when Joyce was home, Margery helped look after her and indulged herself with long sessions reading *Alice Through the Looking Glass* to her little sister.

William and Louise Allingham, Margery's paternal grandparents, had both died during 1920. Herbert and his brothers decided that Christmas of that year should be spent, probably for the last time, at Bakers, Sible Hedingham, Essex, where William and Louise had lived. There was a need for entertainment and Margery suggested a session with 'the glass', a pastime she had learned at The Perse. This was a most rudimentary type of seance, an experiment with 'automatic' writing conducted, as many former schoolgirls may remember, with an upturned tumbler and a set of alphabet cards.

The Allingham family (at least Herbert and Em's family) were at ease on the outer fringes of the supernatural. While the children might, as they grew older, laugh privately at Em's increasing interest in auras, Madame Blavatsky and the vibrate-to-colour school, Margery later admitted that she had found her mother's apparent ability to read her secret thoughts 'uncanny' and was driven to take mental precautions to block this intrusion. They all accepted telepathy as a valid means of communication, certainly within the family. This was not as eccentric as many will find it today. The need for comfort felt by countless families after the deaths of loved ones, whether in the slaughter of the Great War or the flu epidemic which followed it, had precipitated a resurgence of interest in spiritualism. The caretaker of the block of flats in which they lived frequently hastened to impart her premonitions to Em. On the most frivolous level Margery admitted that she had ordinarily expected to win card games by simply willing her opponent to discard the number or suit she required.

Playing the glass in such a family – and in the house where her grandparents had recently died – was patently not the same as playing among her friends in Sarum. Some notes survive which may, just possibly, date from this session, colourful jottings of violence and bawdry apparently from 'historical' Colchester (some fifteen miles from Sible Hedingham). This attribution remains speculative. What is certain is that something happened to upset Margery in this holiday game. As soon as the family returned to London she settled down to write *Without Being Naturally Qualified.* Its central character, the professor, is seeking 'authentic evidence concerning the after life. Not from a set of poets or lying spirits, unsatisfactory planchette boards or ricketty tables . . .' The play was written at speed and could well have been a method of exorcising an unexpectedly disturbing experience. Herbert reported that 'she would have nothing more to do with it [the glass] – until August 3rd 1921'.

When Margery and Phil were very young, the Allinghams, like so many Londoners, had been used to spending happy summer days on Clacton beach. During their time at Layer Breton, they switched their seaside allegiance to the less-frequented Mersea Island. The Island, which lies between the mouths of the Rivers Colne and Blackwater, was their nearest approach to the sea from Layer Breton. It contains two quite separate villages, farmland and stretches of sandy beach as well as the characteristic miles of Essex salting. Mersea Island is connected to the mainland by a causeway, The Strood, first built by the Romans, which is often covered at high tide. There has never been a railway to the Island and, until the early years of the twentieth century, it remained very much a world of its own with a largely indigenous population. One elderly resident, Sybil Brand, born late in the nineteenth century, described the scene of her childhood before The Island was discovered by 'the Londoners'.

'Our world was Mersea Island, the world of Baring-Gould's *Mehalah*, with its long sandy beaches and brown seaweed, its salt-marshes covered in sea-thrift and purple sea-lavender.

Golden sea-asters bloomed on the island and always, every day, the tides of the Blackwater and the Colne flowed round it . . .

'We had no cars and no buses and no planes. The *East Anglian Daily Times* might arrive by carrier in the evening or be posted on from Colchester but the news had lost its urgency. We were comfortable and enclosed in our island world.'

There was a sinister aspect to this isolation. The Island was a place where Miss Brand's uncle put metal beneath the threshold to ward off witches; where there were fierce feuds between the 'uplanders' and the 'downlanders' (agricultural and sea-faring families); where rumours of ghosts and tales of smugglers were not far to seek. The most famous literary monument to these days was *Mehalah*, 'the Essex *Lorna Doone*', a tale of death and treachery written in 1880. *Mehalah* was not written out of love but out of hatred for The Island. Its author, the Rev. Sabine Baring-Gould, trapped in his draughty rectory in East Mersea, longed to return to the kindlier countryside of his Devon home. Another South Coast man, John Fowles, who wrote an introduction to *Mehalah* in the 1960s, shared this view of Mersea Island as a 'bleak wasteland'.

'The vast God-denying skies, the endless grey horizon, the icy northeasterlies, all these belong to the Arctic tundra of northern Norway. The whole area is set to the key of winter – it is for the dour, the taciturn, the obstinate, the solitary mussel-picker, the wild-fowler, the anachronisms of our age . . . It is not English, though it lies so close to the termite heart of England; but spiteful, anti-human, a Beckett nightmare waiting for the world to grow desolate again.'

An odd place to choose for a holiday? Yet the Allinghams were among the earliest visitors to rent the newly furnished houses that sprang up in West Mersea from the early years of the century. They could be there at Easter, occasionally at Christmas and always for three to four weeks in July and August. For Margery, unlike John Fowles and Sabine Baring-Gould, this was the essential England and she grew to love it as a native. She responded to its characteristically East Anglian beauties of sea and sky in juvenile poems such as 'Sunset over Mersea' and

'Moonlight over the Island', and to its social idiosyncrasies in *Mystery Mile*, written in 1929 and named for an island where the twentieth century is barely skin deep. Mersea Island encapsulated the landscape pattern of field, mud and marsh, the mix of puritanism and eccentricity, buried violence and dour humour that fascinated Margery throughout her life.

Evenings on Mersea Island, for those used to the London theatres and restaurants, could seem somewhat slow – 'smuggling was all one could do there except graze,' wrote Margery later, dismissing the island scene of her first novel, *Blackerchief Dick*, with a contempt she did not feel. In her surviving fragments of autobiography, Margery omits to offer any account of the method they chose to amuse themselves in the summer of 1921, but it led her to write her first novel, and may have influenced her beliefs and reactions throughout her life. Fortunately Herbert recorded events in detail. Transcripts were made as the game progressed, and afterwards he produced a formal account. The brief entries that were made by Margery in her 1921 diary give exact confirmation.

On August 3rd, twelve days into their annual holiday, the Allinghams had been entertaining a large party of relatives and friends over from Sible Hedingham. When Big Phil, Bill, Toots, Grace, Tunk, and Aunt Hat had left, the house in Seaview Avenue felt a little dull. Only their friend George Hearn remained with them. Joyce had already gone to bed when, according to Herbert's account, 'Margery suggested that we should amuse ourselves by "trying the glass" '. Phil, Hearn, Herbert and Margery, but not Em, agreed to play. 'The glass began to move as soon as we touched it and we found ourselves apparently in communication with a person who called himself Joseph Pullen. Pullen is a common name on the island familiar to at least three of us. We therefore attributed this early success to auto-suggestion. We asked Pullen how long ago it was since he lived on the island. He replied two hundred years. After one or two unimportant questions and replies, Hearn asked Pullen if he knew anything about smugglers. This proved a happy suggestion. Pullen was an old smuggler and after this he spoke freely.'

Herbert's narrative continues: 'Then someone' (elsewhere he says that this was Margery) 'suggested asking about the old Ship Inn. On a previous visit to Mersea we had heard a story about the Ship. The building is now demolished but it was once a notorious smuggling centre. A murder is said to have been committed there and the place was reputed to be haunted. There are still old residents on the Island who will tell you they have seen the ghost. This much we knew when we asked the question that led to such surprising results.

'Pullen knew all about the Ship and nearly all about the murder. He gave us the names of the various characters who figured in the drama and in reply to our questions supplied us with all sorts of information about their lives and his own. He told us of Anny Farran, the girl who served rum at the Ship; of Blackerchief Dick, the Spaniard who loved her; and of Nan Swayle the woman who was ducked as a witch.'

'It is difficult to describe our sensations at that first sitting,' wrote Herbert. 'We all had a feeling amounting to absolute conviction that we were receiving an account of actual incidents which had occurred and of actual people who had lived in Mersea Island over two hundred years ago.'

The four tried again at the same time on the following night. This time, to their surprise, they discovered the villain of the tale, Captain Dick Delfazio, apparently waiting to tell them of 'my greatness and her madness'. His victim, Anny, frightened and unhappy, was there too, and Nan, foul-mouthed, vengeful – yet also obscurely afraid.

'We questioned these about the affair at the Ship and they all gave their evidence just as though they had been witnesses in a police-court case. As the story unfolded itself new facts came to light and new actors in the little drama were mentioned. At subsequent sittings we called up all those who seemed to have any bearing on the story and questioned them in turn. Nearly all of them answered freely and during the eight sittings . . . we had communications from twelve different spirits, everyone of whom had a distinct and strongly marked personality.'

In this 'official' account, written to arouse interest both in the experience itself and in the book which sprang from it, Herbert makes all four participants, himself, Hearn, Phil and Margery, equally answerable for the truth or falsity of the experience. Privately he knew that whatever was going on had been initiated, somehow, by Margery. 'My daughter is, or appears to be, a medium,' he wrote to fellow seekers after paranormal truth. As a caring father, he expressed worries about her health and the possible risks of such dabbling in the occult. He could not quite conceal how keenly he was interested both by the revelations themselves and by the possibilities they might open up for Margery. Herbert was the closest to being convinced that they were truly in communication with persons long dead.

Phil, then aged fifteen, was apt to scoff and make saucy remarks to the 'spirits'; George Hearn could become 'politely ironical'. They were all sufficiently intrigued to visit the site of the old Ship Inn over at East Mersea. Phil also travelled into Colchester to ask the museum curator there whether he had any knowledge of these seventeenth-century crimes. Margery's diary shows her as 'amazed' as the others – yet it was only she who could start the glass, and when she was away from the table the question and answer sessions soon petered out. She tacitly accepted responsibility for the story that was spelled out over their thirteen sittings by using it as the plot of her first novel, *Blackerchief Dick*.

She had never attempted a novel before. Perhaps Baring-Gould's tale of Mehalah, the older Island girl done to death by her wicked lover, encouraged her to try that form; perhaps the professionals, Hearn and her father, suggested it as the most obviously commercial use of the material 'given'.

People interested in extrasensory perception differ widely in their interpretation of material produced through 'automatic' writing or speech. Does it imply the intervention of other personalities, perhaps long dead, or the limitlessness of the individual personality? What is the nature of the reality involved? Is the truth verifiable? Margery kept her beliefs private – at least until she approached the subject of extrasensory perception again in her experimental 1960s novel, *The Mind Readers*.

As an adult, she was embarrassed by *Blackerchief Dick*, by its style, its content, and the circumstances of its conception. Brushing it aside as her first, teenage novel, she allowed people to assume that she had 'made it all up' in the 'normal' way of fiction – yet she was never quite sure whether it had come from within or without her. There was a magic about imagination; her inspiration seemed to her a fragile gift – not unlike a medium's. She was awed, but not entirely surprised, when stories she thought she had invented turned out to be true elsewhere. The experience on Mersea Island of apparently discovering the plot of *Blackerchief Dick*, involuntarily spelled out for her, could scarcely have been more formative.

Charlatans have always existed in the fringe E.S.P. world – Dorothy Sayers' Miss Climpson strapped hooks to her wrists and soapboxes to her knees to dupe an elderly spinster – but there was no such conscious deception in Margery's seances. Aged seventeen, she was left confused and somewhat troubled by the apparition of these latent 'powers'. Her father, Herbert, had his account printed and became involved in correspondence with a bevy of E.S.P. enthusiasts and eccentrics. He was convinced that Margery could not have known many of the arcane words and historical details that were spelled out by the glass – and must therefore have been the mouthpiece for something Other.

The transcripts made at the West Mersea sessions still exist. They contain nothing that Margery could not, at some level, have known. Herbert made great play, for example, with the word 'ronyon', which he claimed not to recognise. His correspondents offered him etymologies with various degrees of accuracy and crankiness, but no-one mentioned Shakespeare. Herbert, who had watched *Macbeth* at the Old Vic with Margery, must have heard it said on stage – on the heath in the third scene of Act I: ' "Aroint thee, witch!" the rump-fed ronyon cries.' And she who had been studying the play with that absorption which 'was almost physical' said nothing to enlighten her father.

There was a linguistic prudery in the situation which was not uncommon in the earlier spiritualist circles. The degree of relationship between 'controls' who used foul language and the lady mediums who would blush to hear such words was, to say the least, problematic. George Hearn, at West Mersea, was shocked by the vigour of one character's, Pet Salt's, curses. The transcript reads: ' "May the skin of her melt and many flies kill her" (Hearn protested at the language and told Pet to behave herself whereupon apparently she went off in a temper. The glass stopped . . .)' When *Blackerchief Dick* was finally accepted by a publisher, it was only on condition that Margery delete the phrase 'blasting, wilting swine' – another sub-Shakespearean coinage. She confided to Pip, her future husband, that she thought this was a pity as 'I don't know any oaths and buccaneers ought to be allowed to swear – don't you think?'

Her illustrious predecessor Robert Louis Stevenson would have agreed, 'Buccaneers without oaths – bricks without straw'. His problem was that parents would not allow their sons and daughters to buy the serialisation of *Treasure Island* in *Young Folks* if the language was deemed unsuitable; hers was that young girls couldn't admit, even to themselves, that they might know such words. Margery's writing in her conscious teenage person is banal – 'ripping!', 'rotten!', 'frightfully bucked!' In fact she was concealing a vigorous and inventive vocabulary – 'By'r lakin!', 'joskin', 'hell-kite', 'scooning', 'delf', 'quean', 'filcher' and 'scabby wanton' have all crept into the published novel though they have no 'authority' from the transcripts of the spirit-speech.

Stevenson, interestingly, learned to rely upon the workings of his subconscious in dreams to push his adventure stories on. Any study of the 'anatomy' of inspiration reveals the diverseness of the ways by which artists seek access to their own creative powers. Though Herbert Allingham is said to have been excited by the future possibilities of plots from the glass, Margery lacked the confidence to make any such systematic inroads into her own imagination. She was too uncertain of the nature of what she was attempting. Back at the Poly, Josephina de Vasconcellos remembers a rumour that Margery Allingham experimented with spiritualism, whispered as something daring but not quite right.

Notes remain from subsequent occasions when Margery 'tried the glass' (or the 'improved Planchette' which her father bought her). There is nothing as lengthy or coherent as the 6,000–7,000 words of transcripts that provide the plot of *Blackerchief Dick*. Two ingredients that sparked her creativity were absent from the other attempts – the atmosphere of place and the stimulating presence of a friend like Hearn. When they tried a session at Mersea using Em in Hearn's stead, a spirit named Mab appeared, only to refuse to answer questions; when the sessions were resumed in London but with Hearn also present, there was first a disruptive spirit named Yorick Onions, then, briefly, Nan Swayle who declared 'I do not like this place' – and left.

When, in 1964, Margery finally wrote a novel, *The Mind Readers*, that took telepathy (widened into extrasensory perception) as its subject, she offered some speculations of her own. People, she thought, were continually giving off intangible sparks of emotion – fear, exasperation, glee, (presumably also desire). The image of electricity was a way of making the concept comprehensible but this power was not electrical. It was some sort of life force, a 'creative energy'. All were constantly bombarded by these sparks and flashes from others; a sympathetic person, or in more esoteric terms a 'sensitive', could differentiate them, could even develop 'techniques of reception' for sorting out which came from a source that mattered to them. In *The Mind Readers* Margery postulates a mechanical device that amplifies such signals. This seems akin to the 'glass' of her youth. She also, in the later book, describes how frightening it might be to find oneself suddenly open to a welter of perceptions and messages over which one could exercise no control.

This theory could be extended to explain manifestations such as haunted buildings. The emotion generated at the moment when, say, a crime was committed in the historic past, could – if this force is understood to be something actual, though intangible – permeate the fabric of a building or a site. A 'sensitive' might then receive some flash of insight into the original happening. Herbert tended towards this type of explanation when he considered *Blackerchief Dick* and the old Ship Inn at East Mersea. He queried it when seances with Margery wandered into wilder regions of ahistoric time.

Together with the linguistic daring, the lurid inventiveness and mimetic ability revealed by the Mersea transcripts, there is some underlying sexual anxiety. Later in life, in a private letter, Margery refers to the feelings of surprise and acceptance with which she had learned the 'facts of life'. 'It was an astounding tale, and a shock, but obviously inescapably true.' She does not say when this was. A letter from William McFee to Herbert Allingham dated 1925 discusses the wisdom, or otherwise, of talking frankly to 'the children' about sex. Margery was twenty-one by then! Aged seventeen on Mersea Island she looked physically mature and it seems safe to assume that she had some basic biological information. Emotionally she may well have been troubled by the conflicting impressions gleaned from Em's attitude to matters of the body, and the intensity of her response to the love-scenes in Shakespeare for instance. She had not long been at the Poly and there were as yet no friends close enough to giggle with over matters sexual and so keep them in proportion. She may even, but this is pure speculation, have had a holiday 'crush' on George Hearn.

Assuming that almost all the material in the transcripts does come from Margery's personal subconscious – not from Herbert, Phil or Hearn – it seems relevant to mention the sense of female fear evinced. This is patent in the heroine's, Anny's, responses and even in those of Nan Swayle, the suspected witch. As well as the shootings and stabbings among the smugglers, there are inessential incidents bleak with the cruelties of men to women. How did jolly Joe Pullen and his neighbours celebrate the Restoration of King Charles?

A. 'We drank and ducked Mother Swayle.'

Q. 'Did the ducking kill her?'

A. 'No, not quite.'

In the transcripts of the sittings, Nan Swayle lives in fear that this could happen again if she does not take care to be conciliatory. Her fellow-character, Pet Salt, in both transcripts and novel is about as venomous an old hag as one might choose to avoid. Ben Farran her lover is drink-sodden and incapable. Nonetheless, in the transcripts their 'spirits' appear to think it quite in order that he should beat her to death for a trivial offence. When Margery wrote these incidents back into the novel – using, presumably, her conscious intelligence – her women regain their confidence. Nan is brain-damaged by her ducking but not essentially subdued; Pet is beaten by Ben but not to death. Though Anny, the heroine, is shocked by her condition – 'Oh Hal, how he has beaten her!' – the reader is aware of little more than a temporary hiatus in Pet's execrations. Ben, who needs her to fuel the alcoholism she has induced, is shown soon crawling back for favours. Anny, the seventeen-year-old, consistently timorous in the transcripts, is blithe and even pert in the published book.

Blackerchief Dick's killing of Anny at the climax of the novel is described in language over-charged with the symbolism of defloration. It is their wedding night. Dick has come to demand 'the jewel that is mine by right.' This jewel is a 'flowered ring' which he has given her at the ceremony. Anny, who is transparently ignorant of her conjugal obligations, takes it out of her pocket and hands it to him. Dick slips it on the blade of his dagger (regularly described as 'a part of himself'). 'It slid up to the hilt and there stuck, a band of gold and gems around the blue steel.' Recklessly innocent, she chooses this moment to tell him that she loves another. 'The Spaniard's smile returned and the blue knife with the gold band on it seemed suddenly to have become part of his hand as with a deft movement he laid the bright steel against the girl's bosom.

' "Oh! my sweet one, how fair my blade looks against thy white breast," said Dick, his eyes holding Anny's. "You gave me back my ring, but I am generous; see, I give it back to you." With these last words the knife seemed suddenly to quicken and spring from his hand, and Anny staggered back from the table, her hand clasped to her breast.

' "Oh! how you hurt me, sir," she said simply, the smile still on her lips and her eyes still bright with the excitement of a moment before. Then her eyes closed and she dropped to the floor . . . and the knife Blackerchief Dick held in his hand was red blood up to the hilt.'

The poetic dramas that so fired Margery's teenage imagination do treat the simultaneity of sexual union and death almost as a commonplace. The book was an embarrassment to her in adulthood. It was often omitted from her list of published works, never reprinted in her lifetime and bookseller gossip has it that she was willing to buy up second-hand copies in order to remove it from local circulation. She tended also to exaggerate her youthfulness at the time of its composition.

Blackerchief Dick remains an achievement as well as a phenomenon. The essence of the Island – its windswept beaches, swathes of sea lavender, the constantly changing colouration of the light and the water – is conjured up, though not with Margery's mature skill. A portrait is left of a bleak little community, prey to feud and superstition, its sole focus of companionship the rum-fumed timbers of The Ship, its only excitement the coming of the silk-clad smuggler. The language, though often obscured by what Stevenson would have termed 'tushery', has, in places, an alcoholic vitality that comes reeking off the page.

The novel could have benefited immeasurably from discussion with an editor. There are repetitions and inconsistencies that could so easily have been corrected. For Margery *Blackerchief Dick* was an imaginative outburst; an experience which she did not fully understand and over which she felt she had scant control. Herbert makes much of the claim that Margery 'wrote up' the story exactly as it had come to them. This is disingenuous. Some 6,000 words of transcript growing to 50,000 words of novel gives plenty of scope for art. The book was published almost exactly as Margery wrote it, in haste, during the autumn of 1921. If Herbert was too close to the material to wish to tamper, it seems surprising that the experienced literary agent, A. P. Watt, and the publisher, Sir Ernest Hodder-Williams, who brought out the book in 1923, offered so little guidance. Editorial attitudes were different then. It was Margery's misfortune that she was left exposed and vulnerable by the relative success of this, her first novel.

Maldon
by P. Youngman Carter (c 1960)

VI

Sentimental Adventures

1921–1923

Blackerchief Dick did not appear until the late summer of 1923. When it did, in Margery's words, 'it sold a few copies and irritated quite a lot of people'.

She had set to work to write up the transcripts as soon as the Allinghams had returned to London from Mersea in September 1921 and had completed this within four months. Once again, as with the play, *Without Being Naturally Qualified*, Margery may have been given some extra impetus by a desire to rid herself of the experience. Her diary suggests that she discussed the events of her summer holiday with her teacher, Miss Harper, but does not elaborate on this. After Christmas, which was spent with Aunt Grace at Pope's Hall and included a visit to her father's friends the Starrs, she sat up late 'talking and reading about Essex'. Dick Starr was interested in local history, George Hearn in archaeology. Both may have reinforced her awareness of past events, landscapes, habits of mind so thinly, in country places, skinned over by the present. Folklore, superstition – and witchcraft – fascinated her throughout her life.

The composition of *Blackerchief Dick* did not convince Margery that she wanted to become a novelist. Writing was by now her domestic habit, neither exciting nor sufficiently challenging. 'Sewed, wrote, read. To Maud's, not very lively. Am a little sick of living but I guess I expect too much.' Stimulation came from evenings at the theatre; energy and ambition found their focus at the Poly. She was beginning to make friends. As the new term opened Margery spent a considerable amount of her leisure time 'practising with Miss Scarlett'. Miss Scarlett's Christian name was Hilda. Margery remembered that this custom of addressing one another as Mr or Miss had 'struck a chord of unbearable loneliness in me' at that first enrolment session. It took rather more than a year before Christian names re-entered her diary but she began to feel at ease sooner than that. She and Miss Scarlett practised their recitations and talked together. One evening Miss Scarlett told Margery about her romantic affairs. Margery was dismayed: 'Dear oh me, I must be a very uncommon freak.'

Three days later, with the novel at chapter 15, 'she with her head full of vain imaginings' wrote, in a month, a five-act drama in blank verse, *Dido and Aeneas*. This carried the full freight of her hopes and brought her suddenly into far closer intimacy with her peers.

Margery's play was a response to her reading of *The Merchant of Venice* (due to be performed at the end of that term by Phil's schoolmates at the Forest School). She may have read the *Aeneid* with Miss Harper. The status of Carthage as a trading centre is given prominence and a group of non-Virgilian Jewish characters has a significant role. Margery was sympathetic to Zionism and may have been writing with a Jewish fellow-student in mind. Several of the *Dido* parts were cast even as they were composed. The characterisation is original and Margery's play reveals a high degree of technical skill in its verse-making. Her parents' reaction was disappointing – 'Mummy and Daddy not very interested'. When she read *Dido* at Aunt Maud's however – 'Caused a sensation, quite. So that's that.' The discriminating Miss Harper was pronounced 'in love' with *Dido* and her fellow drama--students were unreservedly enthusiastic.

In the spring of 1922 Miss Bagley, applied to with much trepidation, gave Margery and her friends permission to produce the play for semi-public performance. The busy-ness of the next few months placed them among the happiest in Margery's life. She could put behind her the rows at home, the days when she had written, 'If I cry so much I shall be ill,' or 'Mother worried at Daddy and so nagging me. I think I shall go mad, may the Lord help me.' At the Poly she could use all her skills, not only as author and actress (she herself played Dido, described in the stage directions as 'a not necessarily beautiful lady') but also as costume designer and seamstress, organiser and persuader of others. 'It was a pleasure to be organised by her,' says Josephina who played Cleon. She remembers Margery at this time as very quick, very vital, seeming to take notice of a multitude of people and conversations at once. She was light on her feet and her eyes which were her most distinctive feature were dark and round, the whites, Josephina noticed, showing more than is usual round the iris. Margery looked, and was, alert, intelligent, exuberant, always ready with a comment or a joke.

The central happening in *Green Corn*, Margery's autobiographical novel (written 1923–4), is the student production of a verse play. This play, 'The Phoenician Queen', is *Dido*, and Margery becomes both Mary the actress/producer and Robin the playwright. Mary reassures Robin that 'we're not just kids having a game. The play ought to do us all good – both as far as training goes and – well, advertisement. I mean . . . it's no use us practising and practising if we never show what we can do, and it's no use you writing and writing if you lock all your stuff in a cupboard, is it?' Robin underwrites the scheme financially. ' "I'm not rich you know. In fact," he went on with explosive frankness, fixing them both with his bright narrow eyes, "I've got about seventy-two pounds in a bank, but I work," he added as though they had questioned him, "and that's mine – that's mine, apart from expenses." ' He refuses to say more and the fictional students are left to wonder what kind of work he can be doing which allows him to attend The Straker (alias Regent Street Polytechnic) three and a half days a week and accumulate such riches at the bank.

Margery had an answer. From early in 1922 she had regularly been able to earn between six and nine pounds for a couple of days' work (though she never succeeded in saving so much of it!). The first reading of *Dido* in November 1921 had finally convinced Aunt Maud of her niece's ability. Immediately after the 'sensation', Maud had suggested to Margery that she try her hand at viewing a film (they were silent, of course), and writing it up for publication in her magazine *Girl's Cinema*.

Maud's enduring mark on the Amalgamated Press was made through her conception and successful editing of the first British film-fan magazine, *The Picture Show*, in 1919. 'Devised on ingenious lines and produced by the most modern methods . . . it was an instant and enormous success,' wrote George Dilnot. *Girl's Cinema*, founded in the wake of this success, appealed to a younger readership which possessed an apparently insatiable appetite for romance. Margery would attend a private showing, usually in Wardour Street, make notes of the film's plot and main characters then write it up at home into a 5,000 word short story. It was a tough, uncongenial discipline but it provided her with regular income for more than a decade. The titles of some of the stories which Margery was paid to write up during 1922 are eloquent of their content – *Love's Pay-day, The Path She Chose, Gilded Dream, The Dawn of Love*. Margery may well, like her fictional Robin, have been somewhat cagey about admitting to her idealistic contemporaries that such were her sources of income.

The students in *Green Corn*, written 1923–4, are based on the seventeen-, eighteen- and nineteen-year-olds who became Margery's friends from the end of 1921 onwards. Josephina de Vasconcellos, outwardly demure, inwardly bubbling with high spirits, became 'Chelly' and others of Margery's friends are equally identifiable. As well as Hilda Scarlett, Margery's diary frequently mentions Millicent Reed who was considered 'an outstanding pupil' and for whose young pupils she later wrote the playlet *Water in a Sieve*. Angela Doubleday with whom she became emotionally involved and Mary Orr, a slightly younger contemporary who was the gold medallist in her year, also feature in her diary. Mary (always known as 'Cooee') gave recitations of Margery's pieces with great success and, a decade later, came to live with her in Essex.

Meeting Pip Youngman Carter towards the close of 1921 brought Margery her first male friend of her own age. He, like his sister Betty when she had been asked to recite with Margery, approached his first meeting with this unknown 'cousin' with a distinct reluctance fostered by their well-meaning 'Aunt' Florence. 'All our lives my sister and I had been threatened by this pair,' wrote Pip (meaning Margery and Phil), 'for the aunt we had in common was a persistent visitor . . . a garrulous artistic lady who emphasised that nothing we did came up to our cousins' brilliance.' At their first encounter Margery was unimpressed: 'Pip came. Not much of a chap.' He is remembered in his Poly days as hopelessly spotty and callow, tall, bending, a sort of second-rate Noel Coward and almost a joke to some of their fellow-students.

He and Margery discovered however they had certain matters in common. They were the same age, seventeen (Margery a few months older), they attended the same institution and they both wrote poetry. To their next meeting Pip brought some of his verses, and Margery soon reciprocated. They began to go to the theatre together and when scenery was needed for the production of *Dido* in the following spring, it was natural for Margery to turn to the art-student, Pip.

They also discovered that they were not cousins. Florence Allingham was an aunt-by-marriage to Margery and Phil; an 'honorary' aunt only to Pip and Betty. 'The true connection was an unfulfilled romance between my mother and Margery's father . . . when my grandmother's home at Waterbeach was open house to literary-minded students.' 'You and I would not be human,' wrote Herbert affectionately to Lilian in April 1927 when Margery and Pip had finally announced their intention to marry, 'if this engagement did not carry our minds back over the years . . . It so fell out that we both found happiness apart from one another but tonight I like to feel that perhaps the qualities in us which made us sympathise with and understand one another were transmitted to our children and have been the means of bringing them together.'

The man whom Lilian did marry became headmaster of Watford Grammar School. He was highly regarded, an innovator in his profession, but in 1914 he contracted meningitis and died with terrible suddenness before his son, aged ten, 'could know him as a human being'. Pip, an asthmatic child, remained uncomfortably at his father's school until he achieved what was for him his crowning good fortune – a scholarship to Christ's Hospital. 'I was no longer the son of a widow, a child whom it seemed improbable would live up to his father's reputation, but a person in his own right. I was a Bluecoat boy, an inheritor of real education – a commodity I understood – and I had achieved this for myself.' If there are strokes of luck which mark a character for life, this single happening shaped Pip.

Not that existence at Christ's Hospital in 1917 had been without its problems; there was the seemingly inevitable bullying, the usual hierarchical tyrannies and a shortage of staff. There was grief for all those, only a few years older, who lay dead on the battlefields and there was the daily, dismal lack of food. Nevertheless Pip's experience of school was considerably happier than Margery's. He did not doubt that he fitted in. He was content to feel himself 'a tadpole' in this 'great luxuriant pool' and treasured the camaraderie of Bluecoat boys for the rest of his life. He lost his asthma in 1917 and also the brief academic brilliance that had gained him his place. He found discriminating and expert encouragement for his talents as an artist and, at the end of his schooldays, was given the small grant which enabled him to study at the Polytechnic.

Pip arrived at a moment when Margery's confidence was high. She was writing both *Dick* and *Dido* and knew she had found her feet at the Poly. He remembers her as 'a big, bouncing schoolgirl . . . elated with the champagne of success'. After her initial hesitation she accepted him cheerfully as an honorary member of the family circle and as a personal friend. Their interest in one another's work was an immediate and lasting bond. Early in the spring of 1922, they formed a small group of 'poets' – possibly in imitation of their parents' Cambridge circle. These were fellow-students who came to tea on Mondays at the Allinghams' Bayswater flat to read and criticise one another's verses. Margery's circle of acquaintances widened further to include some of Pip's art-school friends and then the dearest of all their friends, A. J. Gregory ('Grog'), who left Christ's Hospital a year or two after Pip and also made his way to London to study art.

They were invaluable material for *Green Corn*. Playing up slightly to the newspaper image of Bright Young Things, yet inwardly uncertain and bereft of direction, this first generation to have escaped decimation in the Great War were intent on maintaining their personal facades of sophistication. Poetry, current art exhibitions, Shavian drama and clever comment were 'in' ('1911!' exclaims one of Margery's characters before a performance of *Fanny's First Play*. 'Will they do it in costume?'); notions of conventional love and marriage 'out'. 'Sentimentality' was a pit to be avoided at all costs. And sentimentality of course was what Aunt Maud's film-fans, source of Margery's income, wallowed in.

Neither was Margery as immune from the afflictions of sentimentality as she hoped. Although at seventeen she listened to Miss Scarlett's love-stories without a trace of sympathy, her diary from the age of eighteen shows her, or at least a part of her, in the throes of utter soppiness (whilst another part observed this process with both interest and just sufficient anxiety to add a touch of piquancy to her emotional experiments). The production of *Dido and Aeneas* in the early summer of 1922 precipitated Margery into a floridly romantic relationship with apparently complete sexual safety. She fell in love with the leading man. There were few talented male actors among her group of friends. Margery played Dido and the part of Aeneas was taken by her friend Angela Doubleday, a tall, pale girl with matt-blonde hair, ivory skin, blue eyes and the classic profile of a Roman youth – an obvious physical contrast to sturdily-built Margery with her rich, dark hair, brown eyes and quick facial colour. Margery called Angela 'Charles' and made the most of being 'in love'; 'Charles kissed my hand after my last speech. I was very happy. I love her very much.'

She threw herself into their 'sentimental adventures', 'sentimental interviews', tiffs, doubts and reconciliations. The physical element, such as it was, kissing and hand-holding, remained unfrightening. If Margery was suppressing secret fears of male dominance and possession (as suggested by both *Blackerchief Dick* and two other stories of this period) there was nothing to arouse them in this affair between two girls. They could play in the shadow of the classic romantic lovers without, in 1922, feeling the subtle guilts of lesbianism. And all the while Margery was observing her own behaviour, wondering, not uncomfortably, what it might portend. 'I love her I'm afraid. I'm in for it again. I love her more than anything just now. I think she likes me. I hope so. It is funny that one woman should attract another so much. Perhaps all this work is unhinging me?' 'Got up late, sewed, walked wrote letters thought about Charles. I am not sure that I am not being an ass. I hope she is true with me.' Margery's alter ego Mary in *Green Corn* was often inhibited by 'the peculiar clear-sightedness with which she saw all matters concerning herself', and it's hard to resist the conclusion that Margery knew perfectly well that she was being an 'ass' and was determined to make the most of it.

The first performance of *Dido* at the end of June 1922 was a success and attracted a certain amount of newspaper attention for the 'clever young Bayswater dramatist'. The students were asked to repeat their performance in aid of the Middlesex Hospital. In 1923 the same group put on *Through the Windows of Legend*, sixteen dramatic monologues written by Margery for her friends, then a fortnight later, Gilbert Murray's translation of Euripides' *The Trojan Women*. Dresses were designed and executed by Miss Margery Allingham, scenery painted by Mr Philip Carter. Margery played Andromache. Again those who noticed, wrote favourably.

Phil Allingham had left school by this time and joined in easily with Margery's friends and schemes. Perhaps the most ambitious was a plan to form a small touring company to spend a summer holiday in 1924 playing round villages in Essex and Kent. Margery explained to Mac, 'We would take a farce, a drama, a harlequinade, a one-act shocker, a one-act comedy (all written by our noble selves) and then one or two really clever highbrow pieces to make it all worth doing. I think it will come off because you see it will simply be a tramping holiday with the shows thrown in. It will be good acting experience for everyone and an interesting adventure anyway.' 'Daddy,' she said, 'seems a bit bewildered by the idea . . .' There were ambitious plans too for Millicent Reed's child actors. Margery apparently wrote two other plays for them, besides *Water in a Sieve*, and settled to concoct plots for the 'farce, tragedy etc.'. It was all 'very jolly'. But first she and Angela, who had been practising their Beatrice and Benedict, decided to enter for the L.R.A.M. diploma.

Imperceptibly their friendship had been waning. From Margery's 1923 diary it appears that she was beginning to grow tired of Angela's emotional demands and tearful recriminations. 'Charles came in the evening to tea. She still very weepy. Makes one feel a pig but it is so difficult to talk with her.' By this time *Blackerchief Dick* was scheduled for publication and Margery was under some pressure to leave the Poly. Her heart was still in the theatre but the same letter to Mac that outlined her plans with such enthusiasm also contained the undertaking 'to get well on with another book' first. The context suggests that this was intended as a reassurance to her father. Josephina remembers Margery saying she felt 'trapped' by her parents' demand that she must write for her living, no longer according to her inclinations. Tension between the necessity that she should start to earn her keep, and her own desire to continue acting and having fun with her friends, may have taken a toll on the relationship with Angela.

After they had taken the exam, 'Charles' joined the Allinghams for the first week of their 1923 summer holiday on Mersea Island. Though she is described as a 'dear old pal', Margery also remarked that she was 'a bit of a mollycoddle to have about one but gets on alright with Mummy'. They corresponded and met only occasionally after that holiday. When they attended a Poly reunion the following spring, Margery remarked, 'Saw Charles. Can't think what I ever saw in her.' Unfortunately Angela, seen again during the following year, 1925, remained 'tragic' and wouldn't speak to Margery. 'Oh lord,' reflected Margery then, 'how hard it is to do anything really right.'

Margery was nineteen in the summer of 1923. She attended the weddings of friends and wrote two stories during the Mersea holiday that suggest she was coming to terms, slowly, with her imaginings of male sexuality and the deeper levels of human nature. Her stories, *The Sexton's Wife* and *The Hill of His Ancestors*, imperfect and immature, happen on the borders of reality. *The Sexton's Wife* is a ghost story, set in the Essex fishing village of Tollesbury, to which Margery, her brother Phil, and friend Pip had enjoyed sailing trips during the holiday. The narrator is one of Margery's old, wise women who wonders 'what it would have been like to have married for love'. She herself, misled by girlish vanity, apparent commonsense and the desire to please her family, had married a man who found his pleasure in tormenting her both mentally and physically. It takes on, beyond the wedding night, *Blackerchief Dick* themes of the terrifying strength of the male will to possess, men's latent brutality – and the hopeless vulnerability of young women, betrayed by their ignorance and their fatal misunderstanding of what marriage means.

Though Margery by this time had an agent, A. P. Watt, who was among the best-known in the trade, *The Sexton's Wife* did not find a publisher until 1932. And the second and more extraordinary of these two stories was never published at all. *Hill of His Ancestors* was written at Mersea. It is a comic/tragic tale of a modern man, timidly celibate and sensitively vegetarian, a traveller, appropriately, for fire-extinguishers. He takes pride in his superiority to the 'animal' country folk with whom he finds lodging. One day he is compelled, by forces deep within himself, to ascend a curious hill. As he achieves the summit he is transported back in time, far beyond the historical past of *Blackerchief Dick* or *The Sexton's Wife*.

It may have been that George Hearn, who spent some time with Margery on this holiday, drew her attention to the burial mounds which are visible in the area. What Margery's Mr Juniper experiences is less a rediscovery of ancient history than of his 'true' barbaric nature. When he stamps on an earthworm purely for the joy of seeing the whitish, slimy body explode and flatten beneath his foot, the reader feels that he is more essentially himself, and a man, than when he smugly helps a bluebottle to fly free from the cottage window. Alone on the hill Mr Juniper tears off his constricting clothes and succeeds in catching a young rabbit which he skins and eats raw. Towards evening he is gripped by loneliness and sexual longing. He comes down in search of a mate unaware that, in the valley, the twentieth century still holds sway. When he leaps out on a short-sighted village girl cycling home from the town, clad only in his vest and uttering imperious bellows of desire, he is consigned to an asylum. In a nicely ironic touch his male captors take time to reflect admiringly on the fight he has managed to put up despite his puny physique, while leaving the girl, his intended victim, lying disregarded in a ditch.

The story is surprising, ridiculous, over-written and oddly moving. After he has been 'cured' and returned to vegetarianism and the sale of fire-extinguishers, Mr Juniper has lost his old conceit. The story's alternative title is *Back*. 'Back?' says Mr Juniper, on a trip with a historically nostalgic friend. 'Take it from me, you don't want to go too far.' The fragmentary seance notes that survive from late 1922–23 are similarly revealing. The 'spirits' evoked come not only from the time of costume drama, but from occult, ahistoric spheres. 'Ferdal of the Dark Hills' who had lived 'north of the great river', 'Abenden, Son of Tor' from 'the Hill of the Bull'. Notes from this sitting, dated December 6th 1923, begin a tale of human sacrifice and may represent the last time Margery agreed to use 'the glass'. Whether she accepted that these bizarre fragments were coming from within herself or whether she feared she was losing control of her own mind, Margery grew increasingly alarmed. Finally she presented Herbert with a pointblank refusal to explore any further.

Only one of the sittings, other than those which produced *Blackerchief Dick*, had attracted her to try to write it up – a session with a 'Pan' spirit, an 'elemental', named 'Lobot of Gleet'. Nothing came of her attempt but the seance notes which Herbert kept may shed some light on the nature of Margery's ambitions towards the end of her teens. 'Lobot' claims to have identified Margery and her companions as 'poets' by their characteristic combination of 'unrest and bitter thoughts and yet gay'. He offered three useful axioms to those who 'would sing the songs of the gods',

1. 'Love none unto one third part so much as thou lovest thyself.'
2. 'See with thine own eyes and have care that thou seest all.'
3. 'Tell what thou must and not that thou wouldst hear thyself say.'

Sound advice – and a significant emphasis on the selfishness necessary for artistic success. Margery's fictional students in *Green Corn*, commenced in the same period, are clear that success is something they want, intensely, for themselves alone. Her heroines, Mary and her actress friend Jane, want to make people listen and to have success in their own right. Marriage is all very well for 'girls who haven't anything else to do'. Significantly, the third person with Herbert and Margery at the 'Lobot' sitting was the young man who asked her to marry him in the summer of 1923, Pip Youngman Carter.

Their relationship had developed happily from their first meeting in 1921. For most of that time Margery's emotions had been centred on her love affair with 'Charles' and she seems scarcely to have considered Pip as a member of the opposite sex. He had slipped in under the camouflage, as it were, of their supposed cousinship and soon began to replace Herbert as Margery's regular theatre companion. Frequently Pip took his sketchbook with him and drew the leading actors. Two trips to Whitechapel to see Ernest Milton as The Witch in a play by John Masefield and then in Zola's *Thérèse Raquin* were especially memorable. Pip admired Sybil Thorndike and Margery met her brother Russell at a *Picture Show* dance which she attended with Phil. They shared the widespread grief of their generation when the actress Meggie Albanesi died suddenly in December 1923.

In May of that busy year, Margery discovered that 'Granny thinks I'm going to marry Pip!' She treated this, initially, as a joke. Nevertheless Emily Jane's assumption may have jolted Margery into observing their friendship more self-consciously. A newly analytical note creeps into her diaries; her entries, unusually, spill over into a notebook for more space. Pip is a 'funny boy' she thinks on 10th May and on 19th June she admits that she is disappointed when he fails to turn up. 'I don't know if I have scared him off. I hope not. I like him in a way. He is honest-hearted if a bit conventional on top.' She admires his drawings, commiserates when he fails to win a medal and stays in to keep him company before an exam. She is puzzled by him – and often less than complimentary, 'We talked. He is a funny, warped or rather retarded little boy.' Nevertheless she goes as far by 30th June as to record that she has 'thought about Pip a lot. I hope I don't fall in love with him.'

'Falling in love' with Pip may have appeared a more attractive possibility as the relationship with Charles/Angela waned. When Margery made this entry, she had returned from a somewhat difficult afternoon at the Doubledays'. She was uncomfortable at purely social gatherings. She had little small-talk and worried that her family background left her indefinably odd. On this occasion she had felt that Angela's mother disapproved of her so was both bored and uneasily defiant. Aged nineteen, Pip's public school 'conventionality', his attempts at social savoir faire, had tended to count against him in Margery's pantheon of virtues. As her own youthful bravado began to wither, these very qualities she had at first despised, grew steadily more attractive.

She was taken completely by surprise when, two weeks after Angela had left Mersea in the summer of 1923, Pip told her that he wanted to marry her. 'I told him to forget it.' Two days later he approached the subject again. 'More talk with Pip. Promised to marry him someday if have not anyone else before.' Next day, she notes, 'Poor chap must be potty,' and the next, 'Pip left'. Two days after this Margery began *Hill of His Ancestors* and completed it within a week.

Pip gave his own account of his proposal and their 'secret engagement' in a memoir written shortly after Margery's death. It is suffused by his sorrow and nostalgia and makes uncomfortable reading alongside the blunt bewilderment expressed by Margery at the time. Says Pip, 'We became secretly engaged on an August night at Mersea. It was a curious courtship because we were both naturally shy and completely inexperienced. We neither kissed nor held hands, but walked arm in arm like children: yet between us there was that complete understanding that makes sex of minor importance and mutual interests so paramount that other considerations appear remote and mildly funny.'

Betty Carter remembers the feeling of affinity that existed between Margery and Pip from early days as being an almost tangible thing, despite their glaring dissimilarities of attitude and temperament. She found this quality hard to define then, and it is impossible to assess now. Though Margery's diaries of 1921–24 offer no indication that she felt 'in love' with Pip, they do confirm that he was the only male of her own age, apart from her brother, that she spent any time with alone. In the two years before Pip's 1923 proposal of marriage their mutual interests had forged a durable bond. Pip was not as confident as his poses suggested. He felt at home in the Allingham household where the uncritical man-to-man friendship offered from the first by Herbert was especially welcome.

Unfortunately his premature declaration made the friendship less easy and there were occasions when Pip's arrival at the flat brought an awkwardness with it. Immediately after his departure from Mersea, he had written to her and she to him. Their relationship seemed set to continue as before. Back in London, however, Margery felt burdened by an increasing load of anxiety and guilt and some need to make a decision. In November she wrote, 'Pip's awfully in love. I unhappy about him,' and in January 1924, 'I am not fair to Pip . . . I don't know what to do about him. At present I'm simply being silly . . . Have sent him away for three weeks. Feel it is best but am very uncertain about it. I won't love him.'

Absence did nothing to clear her confusion. In February she wrote, 'Asked Pip not to stay next Monday. He waxed sentimental and I let him kiss me out of pure idiocy. Told him I'd never marry him and felt very unkind . . . Sad in my heart still because of Pip . . . Poets came . . . Pip very awkward. Feel I've been a pig but not as bad as all that.'

The months of easy companionship had left their mark however. With the benefits of hindsight, a rueful acceptance, as well as exasperation, may be read into another diary phrase which Margery was to find herself repeating at intervals for the rest of her life, 'Pip quite impossible.'

Pip
by A. J. Gregory

VII

'Miss 1925 Confesses'

1924–1927

At the end of August 1923 Margery's first novel, *Blackerchief Dick*, was finally published. Hodder and Stoughton had accepted it for the British market, Doubleday & Page for America. Pip had designed the jacket for the British edition and it was of lasting satisfaction to them both that her first book appeared with his first commissioned cover. Mac, in America, was delighted by Margery's success and eager to assist her. He contributed an enthusiastic preface which was something of a mixed blessing. The first copies arrived while the Allinghams were still in Mersea and first notices appeared in the *Observer* and the *News Chronicle*. A photographer from the *Daily Sketch* paid two visits to the island to interview and photograph the 'Novelist at Eighteen'. (Margery was then nineteen and three months.) Before Margery was back in London, the reviews had begun in earnest. Herbert used 25 pages of a large leather scrapbook to paste them all in. He was patently thrilled by Margery's success. There is no record at all of Em's feelings. Much later Margery said that her mother had always treated her work with 'an extraordinary indifference'.

Among the critics, those who saw the book as a direct descendant of *Treasure Island* or (particularly in America) of Rafael Sabatini's *Captain Blood*, were complimentary though most regretted the lack of a happy ending for Anny. They concentrated on the tale itself and ignored the account of its supernatural origins given by McFee. The reviewer in the *Yorkshire Post* liked the book as adventure story so much that he doubted the identity of the author. 'The book is so well done that it leaves one with the uneasy suspicion that the authoress who is said in an introduction by William McFee to be a girl of 17 is herself as fictitious as Blackerchief Dick himself . . .' Another agreed it was 'uncanny that a girl should write like this' but a third explained helpfully, 'She must be the possessor of a blood-thirsty disposition, probably developed through playing at pirates with boy chums.'

Those readers who looked for more than a stirring tale were the more often disappointed. There was some stylistic criticism of the 'sham archaic diction' and 'crudities of composition'. Rose Macaulay called it 'heavy, wordy and conventional' though the *Glasgow Evening Times* was more encouraging: 'Certain passages indicate that Miss Allingham has the ability to paint vivid word pictures and has a sense of humour though rigidly suppressed here.' Much dissatisfaction was expressed with McFee's preface by those who thought about its content rather than simply reproduced the information. Mac's affection for Margery had led him to produce an over-enthusiastic piece, full of quasi-avuncular anecdotes and jokiness about Margery as a representative of 'modern youth' which she found thoroughly embarrassing. He also appeared to believe wholeheartedly in the reality of the 'ethereal spirits summoned from the vasty deep'. The reviewers were almost unanimous in stating that the book showed promise and wishing the young author well. 'If Miss Allingham leaves spiritualistic communication alone, and admiring friends leave her alone, then she ought to write a really good novel some day,' said *The Englishman, Calcutta*. Perhaps *The Guardian* took the long view most successfully: 'It seems almost a pity that a book like this which might more suitably perhaps have been published in serial form in a magazine for boys, did not remain in obscurity until the young lady above mentioned became famous, when it might have been given to the world as a literary curiosity among her juvenilia.'

Feeling that she was encompassed by high expectations, yet without definite plans as to how they might be met, had been a problem to Margery for some time. After a visit to the Luards at Layer Breton at Christmas 1921, she had written, 'They made a great fuss of me. I wondering what will happen if I don't do something some day.' *Blackerchief Dick* was not a great sales success and was the only one of Margery's books to sell almost as well in the Colonies as in England. To be lauded publicly as 'something of a child wonder' and simultaneously subjected to criticism from Calcutta to Oklahoma did not increase her confidence. Secretly she was aiming high for herself, but such a degree of exposure to the literary and media world was premature and only convinced her of her ignorance and inexperience. Her stutter threatened to reappear when she was being interviewed and, worse, she discovered she had nothing to say to the journalists. 'Good God, girl, haven't you done anything in your life except write!' was one comment she remembered with a wince into adulthood.

She was invited to a P.E.N. club dinner in November 1923 – along with such established figures as H. G. Wells, Georges Duhamel, Lloyd Osbourne, and May Sinclair. A family friend, Edith Heald, also friend of W. B. Yeats, accompanied her. Though they were 'all very nice to me' Margery referred to the dinner later as something of a nightmare experience. Her childhood precociousness had long since dropped from her. While she had learned to feel accepted and at ease working with her friends at the Poly, she was very immature socially and lacked either small-talk or the poise to deal with unexpected sallies such as her dinner companion's sudden, 'Have you been painted by Augustus John?' Margery never did learn to enjoy literary occasions. When she was invited to join the Detection Club almost a decade later, memories of that P.E.N. dinner flooded back together with the old panic that made her tongue-tied and painfully self-conscious. She attended one or two of the Detection Club's functions in the 1930s and scuttled home to Essex feeling inadequate.

Margery remembered her youth as a time when she was always indefinably frightened (she assumed indeed that this was the general experience of people in their late teens and early twenties). Occasionally, when she was reciting, her very fear had given an edge to her performance. 'I so frightened I did my piece better than ever,' she once wrote in her diary. There was no obvious reason why she should not steadily build up her confidence in the friendly Poly atmosphere. She wanted to like and be liked and as Pip said, remembering her then, 'I do not think that anyone who ever met Margery could be immune from her infectious, exhilarating charm.' Gradually, however, the very intensity of her desire to succeed became another 'ingrowing hobble'. Because she had come to believe that she would only be valued for achievements, she had no fall-back position – of safe domestic love, for instance.

She failed her L.R.A.M. and was slowly forced to realise that there was no future for her on the stage. It was apparently Pip who persuaded her she had not the figure for it – where in all the performances they attended were the fat actresses? And the stultifying terror that gripped her as she tried to talk to newspapermen about *Dick* convinced her that she had not the temperament either. (Oddly enough she seems to have managed perfectly well when she was interviewed about her productions of *Dido*.) She left the Poly in July 1923 and by autumn she knew she had to start another novel. There had been rows that summer over money, an extension of Herbert and Em's constant arguments on the subject. Margery had reached the sad conclusion, 'They seem to see me as some kind of cuckoo in the nest.'

Herbert found it increasingly hard to make ends meet in the middle years of the 1920s. He was often in debt, to his bank, to his agents, to his relatives. Though Em did earn something on her own account (she sold a string of inexpensive novels through this period, as well as writing for Maud), her contributions were erratic and she could be very demanding. Responsibility for financing the family remained squarely on Herbert. There were school fees to be found for Phil and Joyce and while Margery was living at home they were still, to some extent, supporting her. The money she had begun to earn by writing the fortnightly film stories provided her with spending money only. It was generally mortgaged against money borrowed from her parents to buy material to make costumes for the Poly. These shows became sources of domestic friction as well as parental pride. They brought brief glory but earned nothing.

Among her autobiographical jottings, Margery mentions a

childish desire to paint. 'This was discouraged. I hesitate to write "put down" but the other family characteristic, second only to this passion for the written word, is, to put it plainly, force.' The little story serves as a parable for those other occasions when she felt bereft of the opportunity to stretch her wings a little and try her talents beyond the confines of the desk.

In 1923, her father thought she should get on with some 'serious' work; her mother thought she should earn some money. Margery did not stand out against them. She did not have the confidence. She was even glad to escape London for a while and go away with her father to a cottage at Lyminge in Kent where there was 'nothing but hills and sheep and ugly villas' to distract her from settling to the new novel. The resentment she was suppressing eventually found its focus on Herbert's choice of subject for the novel itself.

Left to her own devices one guesses she would have continued to experiment – she spent the early months of 1924 evading her obligations to *Green Corn* by writing a libretto for an opera to be composed by Donald Ford, a friend of Pip's. She remained involved with those of her friends who were still at the Poly and was always ready to make costumes or compose recitations for them. Her ballads had a regular place on Miss Bagley's programmes and she tried, without success, to persuade 'Daddy' Watt that French's or some similar company might be prepared to publish a collection of them. In 1925, they did publish the playlet, *Water in a Sieve*, with music by Donald Ford, but it was not a money-making venture.

As it was she was persuaded to exploit her most obvious asset, her youth, and undertake a novel of manners, a survey of her own generation. Her father, she says 'was bitten with curiosity concerning one of the most controversial subjects of the day, degenerate teenagers or Bright Young People as they were called'. Herbert ordered, she says, 'a factual truthful account of the Inmost Thoughts, Aspirations and Actions of the Young as You Know Them'. All this aged nineteen in her second full-length book! Her diary shows that from the first she was doubtful and unhappy about the project. 'Started my synopsis. Pray God it'll be alright . . . Wrote some more of my synopsis. Let it be alright dear God.' She described Herbert, years later, as 'one of those born editors who are able to inspire almost anybody to write anything but whose decisions are in any case final'. Her imagination refused to be coerced. She never was a writer who liked to write in an orderly fashion to a plan. But she could not know that then. It was the way her father and mother always worked; the detailed outline of the story was settled and approved, then it was 'written up'.

Writing the synopsis cannot have been either easy or particularly interesting. There was no genre for the adolescent novel as there is today, no mould into which Margery could pour her observation. The only young people she could write about were herself, Pip, and their friends who, for all their posing, were generally young craftsmen and women trying to establish themselves in their chosen artistic trades. Not at all the iconoclastic young revellers whose antics made the newspapers. Herbert was becoming increasingly worried by Phil's tendency to wildness and by some of the company he kept. Margery shared his anxiety. 'Phil came in at 8.30 this morning after a hectic time but all on the level – thank God!' She was loyal to Phil and covered up for him when necessary. She made no copy at this stage from his adventures.

With only limited material at her disposal, the autobiographical value of *Green Corn* is considerably more straightforward than the subconscious revelations of *Blackerchief Dick*. As well as allowing Margery to articulate many of her own hopes and observations, it is the vehicle for a notably bitchy portrayal of Pip. The change which his proposal effected in their attitude towards one another, coming at the same time as the pressure put on Margery by the publication of *Dick*, placed another demand upon her which she was not ready to meet. Far from this being the period of the 'secret engagement' of which Pip liked to speak in later life, there is tangible hurt and dislike in several of Margery's diary entries made during 1924 and 1925.

Specific causes are not clear. Pip was instinctively attracted by the razzmatazz of success and Margery may have come to suspect that it was her potential achievement rather than her personal qualities that had precipitated his Mersea Island proposal. (In 1925 she damns him as 'a sucker-up after people'.) Though she joked about her size, 'I had the family figure only fitted for hours of endurance at the desk', she minded bitterly that she was not slim and lovely for the stage. When she put her hair up, it was obvious that she had a beautiful bone structure and most expressive eyes. She moved gracefully, had a sense of style and could speak. She did not then know that her inexorably increasing weight was determined by a malfunctioning thyroid gland. It would not be surprising if she found it hard to forgive the person who pointed out how effectively this debarred her from the career she had wanted. She vents her feelings in *Green Corn* on the minor character, Noll.

'His face was negligible; it was the last part of him one noticed. It had nothing that was at all peculiar to it and served simply to prevent his appearance becoming startling by its absence. However, what he lost in natural distinction he strove to recapture by his clothes.' Wickedly though Margery's pen runs away with her, much of the detail supplied about Noll is recognisably teenage Pip – even to the Campionesque horn-rimmed glasses with which he seeks to disguise his insignificance.'Product of a famous school', and struggling to escape his suburban background, Noll chases sophistication at all costs, through tedium, embarrassment and humiliation. His natural perceptiveness is minimal and his few insights have been laboriously achieved. Fortunately for him, his bourgeois politeness and well-brought-up manner (the 'bright artificiality' which Mary initially finds both ludicrous and repellent) does succeed in extricating him from situations where more 'bohemian' attitudes would have foundered. Mary's older sister takes a more tolerant view of Noll's idiosyncrasies. 'She knew him. She understood pretty well how much was sincere about him and because she knew more or less all his impossibleness was bad bluff, she forgave him most of it.'

Slowly Mary comes to realise that, though Noll is rarely other than supremely irritating, he does have a genuine kindliness and desire to be helpful. The biggest surprise of all is the admirably clear, decisive quality of his poetry and drawings. Under all the affectations lies a good heart and a real artistic talent. As *Green Corn* progresses, Noll becomes a more likeable character and the reader may even feel, with Mary, a tendency to protectiveness when 'Chelly' is making the group laugh with tales of Noll's experimental wooings. Margery's feelings for Pip fluctuated. A month after the evening in February when she let him kiss her, told him she'd never marry him and felt very unkind, she was reasoning herself back into friendliness: 'I don't know if he is quite such a little beast as I thought . . .'

She continued to go out with Pip at intervals, often seeking Herbert's advice before she accepted an invitation or answered a letter. There was certainly no 'secret engagement' as Pip claimed after her death. He frequently enraged Margery by his 'lordly' or 'off-hand' manner but when she heard gossip about him, from mutual art-school friends, she was sorry. 'Hear they've kicked Pip out. Apparently he's picked up with a lot of rich folk and is dancing instead of working. I was sorry to hear it for though I believe him to be a fool I don't think he's really bad.' Friends in later life discerned a powerful streak of protectiveness in Margery's attitude towards Pip. This startled those who knew him as a formidable and intolerant, if also witty and charming, personality. Its roots must lie in this period of their late teens and early twenties when both were trying to discover the attitudes and ways of living that would see them through their personal uncertainties.

Theirs, thought Margery later, was a generation who had to find out how to live 'through trial and error' in the period of exhaustion and disillusion that succeeded the Great War. '. . . To those of us who were green and rather frightened, as all people are at that age, there was nothing but broken planks wherever we trod. Nobody knew anything at all for certain. The most elementary morals were in considerable doubt. Every formula for behaviour whose use was not immediately apparent had been thrown overboard . . . We were given doorkeys and the freedom of a shambles.' When she expressed this view in 1940–1, it was endorsed by several of her contemporaries. Aged twenty in 1924, she had written, 'the fragments of the world's deceptions and sentimental weatherproofs were lying around like broken glass in a hot-house after a tempest and great jagged holes were letting nature back into culture again.'

Although *Green Corn* offered Margery an outlet for her emotions and an opportunity to record her experiences both at The Perse and at the Poly, she had few illusions about its quality. 'Read *Green Corn*. I think it is *awful*!' she wrote in March 1924. Phil professed admiration and, though she remained doubtful, she continued working at it for some weeks longer. It is not quite clear whether she ever actually finished the novel. However it was sufficiently complete for Hodder and Stoughton to decline it in June 1924 and Doubleday in August. Margery was 'rather sad'; Herbert was incredulous. 'It only needs a real man of letters to read it.' But even then, as George Hearn gently suggested, the novel had no obvious market; it was too old for those who might be expected to enjoy school stories, and too young for the adult reader. Margery should put it aside and return to it later. The Doubleday reader had criticised the book's structure and like *Blackerchief Dick* it is hopelessly unedited – a fact which again seems astonishing given the hours she and Herbert spent working together, either in his studio (a room in Delamere Terrace, Bayswater, not far from their flat) or at Lyminge. She frequently read sections aloud to Herbert, Em or Phil. From the evidence of her diary, none of them were able to give any guidance and nothing was ever polished or revised. One hundred and twenty thousand words were written straight through and dispatched to the publishers just as if they were a serial for *Merry and Bright*.

All three Allingham children experienced feelings of inadequacy, of failure, of the hopelessness of pleasing their parents. Margery was generally the most robust of the three, and usually the most successful. Her father's disappointment over the failure of *Green Corn* may have been even harder to bear than her own – especially as she did not then feel any saving anger at having been set such an impossible task. As an older woman, she came to realise the extent to which Herbert's romantic tales had coloured his world for him. Speaking of the publication of *Blackerchief*

Dick she said, 'My poor father was bitterly disappointed by the mess I made of it all. He was the kindest man alive but in one of his stories I would have been beautiful as well as industrious, witty, resourceful, and above all, lucky.' Of *Green Corn* she said only, 'The book was a very great disaster.'

Within twelve months all the confidence, and perhaps the little piece of conceit, she possessed when she rejected Pip on Mersea Island in August 1923, had gone. She felt cast down creatively and socially. After a visit to some art-school friends she wrote, 'Find I am an unsociable clumsy person. Very sad at that.'

The following day – to cheer herself up? – she completed a short story, *The Barbarian*. It is the story of a girl who has discovered, at nineteen, that she is 'too big' for the men who wish to marry her. She is hampered not only by her five foot eleven inch body, but by her large Wagnerian personality and her Olympian brain which is too 'wide-meshed' to catch the little modern brilliancies. A crook-backed poet who loves her hopelessly and in secrecy explains, 'Just as the gilt chairs in her mother's hideous drawing room are all too small, too dainty, for her to sit upon comfortably, so the ideas, the wit, the fashions, the cynicisms of the men who love her are all too dainty, too exquisitely intricate for her to grasp. She's too big for them, that's all.'

Elfreda is certain that somewhere there is a man who is her 'complement', who will make her 'a perfect whole'. The notion that man + wife = a complete human unit was a belief which Margery was coming to hold more strongly, even within *Green Corn*, but which remained difficult to reconcile with her concept of the solitariness of the artist. Elfreda finds a Guardsman, a magnificent physical specimen. She loves him hugely and they marry. After the honeymoon she realises that he is spiritually small, blind and pitifully weak, unfitted to be her 'lord and master'. So, in her simple Northern way, she murders him – in order that he may become again the man she had thought he was. Only the poet comprehends what she has done. ' "No, she didn't kill him, Meyers," he said. "Don't you understand – she gave him birth!" But though he acquiesced Meyers never did understand, for he is twentieth century through and through.'

Margery began another novel, *The Lover*, but abandoned it at the beginning of 1925, after nine chapters. Here the possessor of the strong will and powerful idea is unequivocally the villain. Savernake (a favourite Margery and Herbert name) is a collector of fine china who stalks his unwilling bride with the same ruthlessness as he does a Dresden shepherdess. He is a mental sadist whose acquisitive pleasure is whetted as much by his perception of the anguish of the old man who must lose the porcelain he has loved, as by his young bride's reluctance. The hero is small, Gallic, all that is civilised and charming. The heroine has even less nous than her china counterpart and the plot loses its way.

Though those pieces of Margery's serious writing which have survived from 1924 illuminate her intellectual preoccupations and reveal the germination of some ideas which are important in her mature work, they are not successful. *The Barbarian* did achieve publication (in *The Allingham Minibus*) but it would need both more confidence and more refinement for such a parable to work. Margery *tells* the reader too much. In *Green Corn*, she is too close to her background material – and in *The Lover* too far away from it. All the time she had continued turning out film stories for Maud at increasingly regular intervals. After she had set *The Lover* aside in the early months of 1925, her ambition to be anything more than a hack writer went underground while she tackled the unfinished business of her personal life.

Living at home with Herbert and Em was not comfortable. They were not a harmonious couple. 'I wish I had a contented mind, wrote Em to Mac in 1919. But she had not. Throughout the 1920s she sought to assuage her dissatisfactions with a variety of religions and causes. Pip, who did not like her, wrote that she 'embraced the beliefs of the Church of England, Christian Science, Mrs Baker Eddy, Madam Blavatsky and the vibrate-to-colour school with alternate impartiality'. It became rather too easy for her children to reject Em, secretly, as a sanctimonious crank. A friend of Joyce's coming upon Em unexpectedly remembers being hissed at 'Be Quiet! I am thinking *Purple*!' Em's work for the Girls' Friendly Society, however, was a long-standing and worthwhile commitment. Herbert did not laugh at Em's enthusiasms though he did feel excluded by them. Possibly he understood, as the children did not, the insecurities for which she may have been overcompensating. To McFee he explained that Em 'very often says more than she means'. She was unaware, he thought, of the way in which she could be misunderstood by others. 'She is appalled sometimes when I translate a remark of hers into plain brutal English.'

One area of potential misunderstanding lay in Em's continuing friendship with Dr Salter. On his trips to town Salter had called occasionally at the Allinghams' flat and when she was in Essex (staying at Mersea or Pope's Hall) Em visited him. She usually took one or other of the elder children with her to his annual garden party at Tolleshunt D'Arcy and during the 1920s she spent quite a considerable amount of time helping the Doctor put his papers in order. A note in Herbert's diary says that he 'corrected Em's Salter stuff'. It therefore seems likely that she assisted with the actual writing of some of Dr Salter's *Recollections*. Herbert raised no objection to the friendship but Margery seems to have resented it. She sent the Doctor her books and wrote politely, but later admitted to feeling furiously bored as she trailed round the garden in her mother's wake. In 1931, after what would be her last visit, she concluded that he was 'a wonderful old boy spoilt for us by mother's obsession with him'.

'Things not joyous at home,' wrote Margery in the summer of 1924, 'think I shall leave.' She was twenty years old. Herbert and Em agreed that the time had come for her to be independent and self-supporting and by the turn of the year, the means to both were at hand. In February 1925, Aunt Maud brought out a third magazine in addition to *The Picture Show* and *Girl's Cinema*. This was *Joy*, 'the love and laughter weekly', a magazine costing twopence for the would-be 'flapper', the typist or shop-girl who was eager to be up-to-date. Effie Rowlandson in Margery's 1937 short novel *Death of the Late Pig* is an archetypal *Joy* heroine – lower class, dressy, clawing her way through the social jungle by her own red-painted fingernails, her vulgarity redeemed by her self-reliance and pragmatism. Some verses contributed by

Margery (as Louise A.) to the magazine's first issue set its characteristic tone. '*Not Hard-Hearted – Wise!* Miss 1925 confesses:

'I lost my sweetheart one fine day
He said "So long" and went right away
I had a little weep, oh! I had a little cry
But that didn't kill me, I didn't die
Other girls laughed but I didn't mind that
I bought a little frock and a smart little hat
I bought a little powder, and I bought a little cream
I made myself look a chic little dream.
I found a sweetheart the very next week
I love him very well and he's very fond of me
If you lose one fish there's more in the sea.'

Maud had involved Margery from the first and, after her unhappy experiences in the literary world, Margery was glad to find someone who welcomed her ideas, however trivial. Maud offered regular employment and Em pressed Margery to accept. She could earn £40 – £50 per month and it was the obvious way to gain her independence. Every week Margery contributed 'Claude's criticisms – always witty and sometimes wise'; powder-puff jingles of advice to accompany cartoons. She also wrote 'Little Scratches', brief tales of office in-fighting between a plain and a pretty girl, eternally competing for the attention of their male colleagues. Margery's narrator is mean, conceited, scheming 'Tabby' (a brunette of course) who is defeated and comically humiliated, week in, week out, by sweet, blonde, silly 'Kitty' and her band of male adorers.

Margery invented the 'Little Scratches' to a formula and it shows her level of journalistic professionalism that she could turn out these and the verses week by week for the two years that the magazine appeared. She also supplied a film-story for *Girl's Cinema* weekly; contributed verse and occasional features to *The Picture Show* – and helped her uncle, Maud's husband, Teddy Wood, write his Wild West or boxing assignments when he was too drunk to manage them himself. For most of 1925–26,

Margery was the complete hack – writing much and saying nothing in the trade to which she had been born. It was an admission of defeat. After the failure of *Green Corn*, said Margery later, she 'tasted the Dead Sea fruit of authorship'.

Nevertheless, she set out in 1925 with a burst of energy. In the garden of Hurlingham House, the mansion block where the Allinghams' flat was situated, there was an unused building, large enough to be converted into a space for Margery to both sleep and work. It was available at a reasonable rent and Margery delightedly began to redecorate it and to furnish it with whatever she could pick up cheaply, or with whatever other members of the family were prepared to discard. A kitchenette was fitted. She began to experiment with her cooking. Among the first visitors she entertained were Miss Holt and Miss Saint from long ago days at Endsleigh House. Margery's 'studio' was almost too convenient. Phil and his friends called in late at night for coffee and once or twice Margery was forced to take her sleeping things and return to the flat to escape the revelry.

She was ready to have some fun herself. At the beginning of the year she was still struggling with *The Lover* as well as writing for *Joy* and the film magazines. Almost all the free time she had was spent making elaborate costumes for a show at the Poly. 'Don't know whether I'm a potential saint or a b.f. – fancy the latter,' she said to herself. She took some more elocution lessons from Miss Bagley (which she paid for herself) and 'gave' Medea and Magdalen. Then, like one of her own *Joy* heroines, she had some new rubber corsets made and her hair waved for the first time. Phil was currently keen on her friend Cooee (Mary Orr) from Polytechnic days and Margery began to look at Phil's friends with a new interest. By the summer of 1925 she was falling in love with Reggie Goode.

Reggie was a motor mechanic, a big, freckled, Viking type with curly reddish hair. He seems to have been as physically attracted to her as she to him. Though they enjoyed occasional visits to the theatre (to a performance of Ibsen's *Wild Duck* for instance) they spent more time in Margery's studio or out in Phil's GN car. With Phil, Cooee, a gramophone and some drink the four of them drove gaily from London to Mersea at weekends or bank holidays, as often as not with Margery at the wheel. 'So, Marge has a love affair on, eh?' wrote Mac to Herbert in November 1925, and her diary leaves no doubt that she was very fond of Reggie – in a domestic, womanly way. 'I believe him to be a good, honest, kindly old boy who will be good to me . . . I feel I would chuck up everything and look after him.' She was a practical person, ready to take her share of the household chores, to sew, cook or redecorate a room. She found a satisfaction in such activities and later was to use them, quite deliberately, as therapy when she had overworked herself writing. She may unconsciously have been doing something similar during 1925–6.

At the same time as she was enjoying being 'made love to' by Reggie (the phrase does not have its explicit modern meaning) she was uneasy. 'I hope and pray I be not seeing another mirage.' She expected to be hurt and, every time he failed to ring or had to cancel a visit, she was. 'No phone from Reg all week . . . What a fool I was. I knew it would hurt when it started and yet I went blundering into it.' She was also troubled that it was 'silly' to be so in love, 'absurd' to contemplate abandoning her literary ambitions. Cooee remembers Reg as being everything Margery thought he was: big, kindly, a straightforward working lad who would, as Margery hoped, have been good to her. But he would never have fitted into a literary life, or enabled her to do so. Margery left no record of the reasons why they parted. It was, apparently, her decision. After that Reg disappeared from her life as completely as Angela Doubleday.

They separated during the summer of 1926. Cooee remembers that they said goodbye in the pouring rain, 'tears tearing them both to pieces'. By the autumn Margery was discussing the synopsis of a detective story with Herbert. He also 'talked Pip' to her. By the following spring the detective story, *The White Cottage Mystery*, was ready for serialisation in *The Daily Express* and she and Pip were officially engaged to be married. 'He's not as awful as you think,' she reassured Josephina. Like her own Mr Juniper she had suffered a chastening bout of self-knowledge since the day at Mersea when she promised to marry Pip only 'if I haven't found anyone else first'.

Herbert and Em had left London in 1926 to rent an old vicarage at Letheringham in Suffolk. During the General Strike in May of that year Margery was both frightened and lonely. After living in London for the best part of a decade since Layer Breton, she was highly sensitive to its atmosphere. Later she compared the mood of the city in 1926 with the time of crisis after the 'Second Fire of London' – December 29th 1940. 'In some ways the two were alike. There was the same quiet stoicism and the same spontaneous gallantry, but in the strike there was menace and danger, and if I may say such an odd-sounding thing, evil in the air, hatred and anger which I certainly did not feel at the fire.'

The General Strike tested many people's political attitudes. Pip had, until then, been sufficiently pragmatic to accept design work from Hamilton Fyfe's socialist paper *The Daily Herald* and make some effort to conceal his own political opinions. During the strike, however, he was exhilarated by Churchill's extremist right-wing stance. He left *The Daily Herald* and dashed about the town, busy, like many others of the middle-class young, 'keeping things going'. He never afterwards deviated from a Conservative position. His social and political attitudes hardened as he aged – to such a degree that one wonders how Margery, taught by her father that all -isms and opinions would reduce her powers of observation and understanding, could have lived with him – or why she had agreed to marry him in the first place.

Joyce, Margery's sister, who often asked herself the same question, believes that part of the answer lies in Margery's lack of social and personal confidence. She possessed an enduring confidence in herself as an artist and an ambition which survived even fallow years such as 1925–26. Pip's quality of savoir-faire took care of life's surface for them both, enabling Margery to mine her own depths more safely than she could alone. In 1926–27 she also, Joyce suggests, needed to establish her independence from her family. So far she had merely exchanged Herbert's tutelage for Maud's demands. Pip could give her both the support and the freedom she needed to aim high creatively. She respected his artistic talents; he was inventive, witty and kindled a responsive spark of gaiety in her. Josephina remembers the quality of their conversation as they joked and scored points off one another; she likens it to figure skaters giving a bravura performance.

Pip's sister, Betty, thinks that Margery and Pip shared an ability to bring their minds to bear on their experiences; not merely in intellectual self-analysis, but to bear on their emotions. Consciousness of sharing such an attribute could constitute a powerful affinity. It could, says Betty, make both of them appear slightly cold. Perhaps this was what Pip meant when he spoke of 'that complete understanding which makes sex of minor importance and mutual interests so important that other considerations seem remote and mildly funny'? Margery described their love more simply as 'bread and butter stuff'.

Margery and Pip's engagement in April 1927 took both families by surprise. They gave a month's notice of their wedding date and were married quietly on September 29th in 'the costers' church' of St Giles-in-the-Fields. Margery pressed a four-leaved clover in her otherwise blank diary.

'Two Little Birds' –
Margery and Pip (c 1927)
by A. J. Gregory

VIII

Enter Albert Campion

1927–1929

Margery and Pip could only afford a brief honeymoon. In two letters to Mac, describing her 'future husbeing', Margery introduced him as 'an etcher on copper by trade', also as 'a worthy young man and not at all likely to beat me'. She did not, she added, think that Mac would approve of him.

Mac wrote to Herbert that he was appalled by Margery's lack of sentiment. 'Of course I ups and defends myself at once,' replied Margery. 'I can only plead the conventions of the age and group in which I live. I love my sweetheart as much – I make bold to say – as ever you did yours but to admit such a fact is as indecent today as appearing without a bustle would have been forty years ago, and about as serious.' Herbert wrote temperately that Pip had 'no money but some talent', that he and Margery shared interests in common and that 'they should do well in double harness'.

In his diary Herbert recorded rows between himself and Margery during the months of her engagement but gave no account of their cause. He wondered whether she was 'not altogether happy'. He himself liked and supported Pip and had acted immediately to reassure Lilian Carter who worried that Pip was too selfish to make a good husband. According to her daughter Betty, Lilian feared that Pip had built such a formidable barricade of cynicism and toughness to shield his own sensitivity that he had effectively excluded the rest of the world. The enduring strength of the marriage may have rested solely on Margery's continuing ability to see Pip as he was behind his defences.

'At the time of our marriage Pip was six months younger than I and neither of us possessed much except our talents. Our older friends and relatives were mildly sceptical of the wisdom of such a step.' *Joy* had folded in the spring of 1927 but Margery had achieved a significant success in selling *The White Cottage Mystery* to *The Daily Express*. She still wrote up film stories for Aunt Maud and, since the days of *Blackerchief Dick*, Pip had continued to receive regular commissions to design book jackets.

They spent the first week after their wedding in northern France. Returning thirty-five years later to the Hotel de France at Montreuil-sur-Mer, Pip remembered how unconvincing they had felt as a newly married couple. 'Madam Virginie kept the hotel in those days, a hard sharp-eyed old lady who taught my wife to make an omelette in order to show that she at least was a good Christian even if we were, as she suspected, pagans living in sin.

'Madam conducted her domain with rigour as a good bourgeois eating house and at dinner we ate in the kitchen surrounded by bright copper pans as she cooked and presided. Her other guests were usually locals, the deputy Mayor, the horse breeder and farmers in for the Market. They discussed us and our probable relationship with an amiable bawdy gusto, certain that we understood no French. My poor dear wife, though seldom dismayed, has never been back.'

Margery's failure to revisit Montreuil stemmed rather from the gradual changes in herself and in the nature of their married relationship than from memories of an evening's embarrassment. She and Pip returned to France for a second, longer honeymoon in the following September – a holiday for which they had worked hard. Pip claimed that Margery had dictated 70,000 words to him in a single week in order to get sufficiently far ahead with her *Girl's Cinema* stories to earn them the leisure and the money to travel down to the Riviera. They stayed for a month and may also have visited Italy.

In the Mediterranean area Margery's opulent looks attracted some appreciation. Betty Carter relates an old countryman's comment to Pip as he stood sketching a stone bridge over a stream with Margery nearby. 'Monsieur,' said the man, 'you are an artist. How you must *glory* in your wife!' It is curious that Pip, who drew men well, did not ever attempt more than the most childish sketch of Margery. Did he think she was beautiful? It seems not. Some of his friends thought that she was, admiring her eyes, her skin and her surprising gracefulness. Pip has left it on record that he loved her for her charm and gaiety, her generosity and kindness. He says nothing about her appearance.

In what ways Pip and Margery found each other desirable in these early days is another unanswerable question. Though Pip later claimed that 'sex was of minor importance' in their relationship and Margery emphasised their compatibility as working partners, they probably did not view one another quite so dispassionately in 1927. As Pip explained, they belonged to a generation that had been 'talking grandly about vice and living in sin but had done very little about it'. They were the first of their closest circle to marry and an unsubstantiated rumour persists that their friends discovered seven different types of contraceptive with which to present them. The tone of Pip's honeymoon reminiscences suggests that it had been fun to be married and in France while trailing the innuendos of 'sin' along behind them. Sparse chinks of light through the bedroom door reveal Margery in these early years of marriage as robustly physical, releasing tension in a knock-about fight with Pip, 'hitting each other really hard'.

In the third summer of their married life they went to Belgium taking Joyce with them. After that 'Frogland', for Margery, became somewhere 'the boys' went for holidays. She chose, or felt obliged, to stay at home herself.

Margery's early notebooks contain several pages of continental recipes but no impressions gathered for her writing. She had, after all, set episodes of *The White Cottage Mystery* in Paris and Mentone before she had ever crossed the Channel. Later, in wartime, she recalled some of the ordinary folk they had met on their first and second honeymoons: 'Virginie in her pub in the Pas de Calais . . . Paul, *très sérieux*, . . . who drove P.Y.C. and me all round the Alpes Maritimes. The nice people in St Malo, who still always showed their youngsters with the old, proud, "another son for France".' One or two of her short stories used a Riviera background but elsewhere her literary interest remained reserved for her own 'manors' of East Anglia and London.

The Carters returned from honeymoon to their first home, 1, Middle Row Place, High Holborn, a flat in the heart of London, which they had rented shortly before their wedding. Although Middle Row Place, like Margery's birthplace in Ealing, was obliterated during the Second World War the area is preserved in several of her stories. She described the flat itself in *The Lieabout*. 'We had a small flat in a courtyard leading off High Holborn, right in the city. The courtyard was really only the foot of an airshaft striking down amid enormous office buildings. There were only two doors in it; one belonged to a printing works and the other one was ours. When you opened our door you found yourself at the foot of a flight of steep stairs, at the top of which were our three rooms and a sort of corridor called a kitchenette-bath.'

The publisher, Robert Lusty, a friend of Margery and Pip from this time, remembers the flat made pleasantly chaotic by its clutter of books and artists' materials and possessing a welcoming, happy-go-lucky atmosphere which swiftly set visitors at ease. Margery described herself as 'fat and furry' with contentment and Herbert was cheered to report Margery and Pip 'very happy and snug in their little home'. He liked those of their friends whom he met in the flat and took to calling whenever he was in London.

Middle Row Place itself was interestingly different from either Bayswater or from 'the Hovel' off Shaftesbury Avenue where Pip had previously lived. It could be deathly quiet and deserted late at night and at weekends when the City businesses closed down, or the whole flat might shake 'like a power-drill morning, noon and night, by the vibrations from the printing-presses beside and below it'. Margery spoke of 'the surprising intimacy and friendliness of it all . . . as I walked down the crowded pavement with my shopping basket on my arm, I found I had as many people to nod to as if I were in a small town street which had suddenly been overrun with half a million foreigners.'

During the first year of their married life Margery and Pip shared their small floor-space with a bookmaker's office. From their first weeks and for the next thirteen years, they shared all their homes with an old school friend of Pip's, Alan Joseph Gregory, 'Grog'. 'He came to tea,' they used to say, 'and never left. . .' Grog and Pip had been in the same house, Maine 'B', at Christ's Hospital, and had shared 'the Hovel' from 1926. Grog, who was slightly younger, had trained at the Slade School of Fine Art and was a gifted caricaturist. Like Pip at this time he had no regular employment but unlike Pip he had no special desire to better himself or be Someone. He would happily spend his days in bed, or watching cricket, decorating the Hovel door as a *trompe l'oeil* stained-glass window or painting cardboard effigies for a fancy-dress party.

Those who noticed Grog in Margery and Pip's household grew very fond of him. Christina Carter describes Grog as 'a nice little man, very quiet. He had a habit of seeming to shy away from you as you talked to him.' Underneath this veneer of timidity his close friends discovered deep sensitivity to both art and music – and a fund of bawdy wit. Pages of Grog's portfolios are filled with collages made from disembodied female legs flaunting suspenders and fancy stockings, or torsos encased in the frilliest of camisoles and knickers, all painstakingly cut out from lingerie catalogues and re-arranged. Caricatures poured from Grog's pen when there was no need for them. When his talent was once 'discovered' and he was given an office and paid to draw, he found himself completely unable to oblige. Pip had practised the cartoonist's art on unsuspecting masters at school and for years he and Grog kept up a private skit on pompous army aw-fficers. These were of the 'pig-stickin' in Poon-ah' variety and were known collectively as the Featherstones. Their adventures ran in tandem to Grog's, Pip's and Margery's lives and it is not surprising to find one or two of the cast, 'Towser of the Foreign Office' and 'Lieutenant Stukely-Wivenhoe', slipping across into her fiction.

Pip had made new friends since leaving the Poly. He invited some of them to a party at Herbert and Em's house in Suffolk in the July before they were married. Afterwards Margery admitted to feeling somewhat out of her depth. 'I think I must be one of the old-fashioned type of young women – this crowd although, I swear, perfectly innocent in deed, had a range of dinner-time conversation that seemed to be confined between free love, sex and obstetrics – all very interesting of course . . . but I had some difficulty keeping up with it.' By the spring of 1928, she claimed, she was 'getting quite good' at keeping her end up in such conversations 'but the strain on a respectable high school girl is terrific – purity of everything except style is apparently such bad taste . . . "all damn silly" as the old boy says but I find it interesting because it's so universal and such a change.' There was 'no repression' and they were 'not all fools'.

Those of the Gang who can be identified from this distance certainly were not. There were new friends in publishing, like Robert Lusty, whom Pip had met as he sought book jacket commissions; there were old friends from the Poly like Josephina, in London only briefly between scholarship study in France and Italy. The future keeper of the Royal Academy, Henry Rushbury, 'Rush' to Pip and Margery, and later his wife, 'Birdie', were close friends from these early days. There was a core of former Christ's Hospital pupils, some following conventional professional paths, others seeking to establish themselves as song-writer or poet – as Edmund Blunden, slightly older, had already done. During the General Strike Pip had met the medical student Ronnie Reid. He became a friend for life.

Several other durable friendships arose through the Amalgamated Press. These were the children of Lord Northcliffe's 'bright young men'. Barbara Gowing (now Barbara Muir, bookseller and writer) whose father, like Herbert, earned his living through magazine serials, and who herself was then working for the A.P., remembers two who were central in setting the tone of the Gang. They were Robert St John Cooper and T. E. B. Clarke. 'Coop', as Margery usually referred to him, was a gifted cartoonist who later became widely known for his creation of household characters like Tate and Lyle's 'Mr Cube'. His step-mother Anne St John Cooper was, in the early 1930s, Herbert's editor, and his wife 'Pippa' Gee was the daughter of another former Northcliffe employee. Pippa too had been a student at the Slade and, thirty years later, married again to Grog. 'Tibby' Clarke, a journalist, held the post of 'Mr Answers' for a while. He travelled the country performing outrageous stunts to gain publicity for the magazine and found fame himself in the 1940s and '50s writing screenplays for films such as *Passport to Pimlico*, *The Lavender Hill Mob* and *The Titfield Thunderbolt*.

Barbara tells of the constantly inventive quality of their fun. Coop and Tibby would accost anyone and bet on anything. They enjoyed setting up elaborate hoaxes into which Barbara was frequently drawn as a stooge. Another friend was Jack Hargreaves, later a founder director of Southern T.V. He was then 'the essence of bright advertising', says Pippa Gee's younger brother, Bill. 'Ideas simply poured from him.' Despite the cleverness of individuals within the group, however, there was a certain non-intellectual feeling amongst them. They read Aldous Huxley but wrote for the pulps mainly because they were always broke. They used to foregather at various cheap eating places or cram into one another's flats. Margery and Pip had 'barmy nights' when any of the Gang was welcome for a meal. The Gang was the audience for whom she wrote her first 'Campions'.

The first years of marriage stayed in Margery's memory as a time of exhilaration and gaiety but also of dogged hard work. Her continuing employment by *Girl's Cinema* made her the only member of the Carter household with a regular income. Herbert wondered whether this was a new social trend: 'Today the young woman can often earn a bigger income than the young man of the same age. Later he may go ahead and leave her behind but when they are both young, he is often in a position of financial inferiority.' Earnings were pooled and Pip and Grog were willing enough to take Margery's dictation or type up her stories when every thousand words accepted brought in a definite sum of money. As Pip explained later, 'In those comparatively tax free days, a party for a dozen friends could be paid for by what was called "a splendid long complete" for Sexton Blake or a "Special Love Story" for the Christmas number of a film fan paper.'

Margery's name does not appear among the chroniclers of Sexton Blake but that in itself proves little. As her literary reputation grew more important to her she glossed over her early hack work. While it is possible to extract from her diary notes many of the film stories which she wrote for *Girl's Cinema*, and while Louise A. still signed some of her jingles for *Picture Show*, scant trace of her other writing during this period has remained. If she kept a diary at all from February 1927 to January 1931, it too has vanished.

As well as writing for the Amalgamated Press, Margery, like Herbert, often wrote for 'The North' – the Allinghams' name for the group of newspapers and periodicals owned by Thomson of Dundee. Pip speaks of 'an epic serial' written for them 'dealing with the adventures of The Society Millgirl and the Seven Wicked Millionaires'. This does exist. It was not a serial but a series of short stories, *The Darings of the Red Rose*, written for *Weekly Welcome* early in 1930. They detail the step-by-step revenge extracted, Robin-Hood style, by a beautiful, if mysterious, society girl on eight wicked financiers who have brought ruin on her family. She leaves a small red rosebud as her trademark. In achieving the redistribution of the financiers' ill-gotten gains, The Red Rose runs rings round her gentlemanly admirer, a Scotland Yard detective named Thomas Kempis. The last of the eight stories brings an admission from Kempis which should please all lovers of feminist adventure. "My dear," he said, looking down at her, "I wish you'd take me seriously. I admit I'm not much good as a detective, but I'd make a wonderful husband." '

Stories of adventure and detection were in fashion at all levels of the literary marketplace towards the end of the 1920s. 'The present vogue for books of this sort is indeed extraordinary,' said *The Bookseller* magazine of January 1927. And from the academic standpoint, Q. D. Leavis singled out its popularity among the 'educated' section of the reading public for particular disapprobation. The genre was diversifying. Full-length novels were gaining ground over short stories, and tales of detection were becoming more self-consciously distinguishable from the adventure stories or 'thrillers'.

This latter was, at first, the style to which Margery was instinctively attracted. Her *White Cottage Mystery* was written in instalments and prizes were offered to readers who guessed the correct solution. Although the puzzle element was there, the action, shifting from Kent to London, Paris, the Riviera and back, was closer to E. Phillips Oppenheim and Edgar Wallace than to Agatha Christie and Dorothy Sayers, the authors with whom she was later associated. *The White Cottage Mystery* was published in 1928 by Jarrolds (then part of the Hutchinson publishing group) as a novel at 7/6.

Pip as well as Margery could see the opportunities which lay ahead. He too had been nourished on boys' comics and enjoyed stories filled with incident and action – 'a surprise every tenth page and a shock every twentieth', as Margery glibly explained the form. After his first visit to Middle Row Place, Herbert reported that 'Pip is starting to write.' In fact Pip wrote little, if anything, in this period. What he did do was take on Herbert's role of supporting and encouraging Margery. Her father had given her some help with the synopsis of *The White Cottage Mystery*; Pip was soon working with her on her next book, *The Crime at Black Dudley*, destined this time to be published immediately by Jarrolds as a novel and serialised later.

His influence was good. Even allowing for some retrospective idealisation, Margery's account of this first collaborative effort (and the help both he and Grog gave her with the film stories) tells of merriment and the release of something that was essential in her creative self, her sense of humour. 'Hitherto, I had always assumed that utter solitude not to say boredom was the only condition in which fiction could be produced but now I learned to work anywhere at any time with anything from a party to a dogfight going on in the same room. Better still I grew gay myself. For the first time I ventured to encourage the humour which until then I had always tried to keep out of my work . . .

'We had been married two months when we decided to write *The Crime at Black Dudley*. The world was our oyster and a good one. I dictated it to Pip who took it down in longhand and we argued over every word. It took us three months of hilarious endeavour. Never was writing more fun.'

A letter from Margery to McFee written in July 1927 indicates that she had had the idea for *Black Dudley*, also possibly *Mystery Mile*, well before her wedding day. Nevertheless the rapid development evident within these books offers ample testimony to the value of Pip's (and Grog's) contribution.

Humour had not been entirely absent from Margery's earlier work. The students of *Green Corn* had their moments of 'witty' conversation and the young sophisticates in *Black Dudley* are only as far ahead of them as Margery's friends aged 24 were from her friends aged 19. A casual joke in *The White Cottage Mystery*, written before her marriage, may be a more significant pointer towards Margery's growth into a seriously comic writer than all the slightly dated hilarity of *The Crime at Black Dudley*. An elderly detective, W. T. Challoner, is interviewing a gaunt, resentful nurse, Estah Philips. She is stubbornly unimpressed by his affability and he hazards a guess that she comes from the Essex coast, Colchester way.

' "Yes," she said at last, her tone sullen and begrudging. "I was born at Goldhanger near there. My folks lived there for lifetimes."

' "So I thought," said W.T. "Do you want to know how I told?"

' "No," said she.

' "That's how I told," said W.T. and smiled to himself with pardonable pleasure.'

And in the oddity of Estah Philips' personality lies the psychological key to the mystery. There is no such structural humour in *The Crime at Black Dudley*. That its authors enjoyed writing it is obvious and attractive. Unfortunately the impression that the bright young things are laughing at their own jokes and heaping on the action beyond the point of parody, leaves the reader at times uncertain whether she has hold of a thriller or a farce.

Black Dudley remains notable as the first book in which Margery introduced the character ever afterwards associated with her – Albert Campion, the 'lunatic', the 'inoffensive', 'silly ass', 'the fresh-faced young man with the tow coloured hair and the foolish pale-blue eyes behind tortoiseshell-rimmed spectacles' whom some thought they recognised, but whom nobody knew. 'The slightly receding chin and mouth so unnecessarily full of teeth was distinctly familiar. "Albert Campion?" he repeated under his breath, "Albert Campion? Campion? Campion?" But still his memory would not serve him . . .'

George Abbershaw, the fictional character first puzzled by Campion's identity, had been cast as the hero in *Black Dudley*. He was a precise, fastidious pathologist, chubby and solemn with an 'amazingly orderly' mind. His name was well-known at Scotland Yard and his opinions respected. He failed however to amuse his creators. Campion was intended as a minor criminal, a mere muddying of the waters of plot. A passage describing his unsavoury activities as 'Mornington Dodd' had to be excised from all later editions of the novel. To Abbershaw alone Campion whispered his mother's name: 'a name so illustrious that Abbershaw started back and stared at him in astonishment.

' "Good God!" he said. "You don't mean that?"

' "No," said Mr Campion cheerfully and went off . . .'

Margery enjoyed teasing those people who pressed too insistently for the 'real' identity of her Campion. On one occasion she told Pamela Hansford Johnson that he was George VI and gave up detection when he came to the throne. Some friends wondered whether Campion was a version of Pip, they wore similar spectacle frames at least. Barbara Muir remembers that her friends in the late 1920s thought the 'inoffensive' 'unobtrusive' Grog more likely to have been Margery's model. The Campion of the early novels was however a type, not a personality. *Black Dudley* had been dedicated to the Gang and Campion had ousted Abbershaw as its central character just because he was the goon, the zany, 'the private joke-figure of we smarter youngsters'. In a generation still laughing off the effects of the Great War, she was not the only writer who relished fatuousness.

Of more practical import was the fact that Mr Maule of Doubleday, who had accepted *Blackerchief Dick* then, gently but firmly, rejected *Green Corn*, liked Campion. He took *Black Dudley* onto the list and asked for more of the character in Margery's subsequent novels. Over the eighteen 'Campions' that followed, the character developed and his relationship to Margery herself changed and deepened. 'As the only life I had to give anybody was my own,' she wrote as she neared the end, 'we grew very close as time went on.'

Most of the writing, as opposed to the planning and discussing of *Black Dudley*, took place in Suffolk at the Old Vicarage, Letheringham, which Herbert and Em had rented since 1926. However well-accustomed Margery had become to sitting down to write 'with anything from a party to a dogfight going on in the same room', Middle Row Place was not conducive to anything more than work for *Girl's Cinema*. Daily life in Letheringham was very different. 'There are only a few cottages in the village,' wrote Herbert to Mac, 'and the nearest pub is a mile away.' They had a telephone but no car so 'Nothing to do but work, read and potter about the garden.' Margery had spent several weeks as well as weekends working there before her marriage in 1927. Between April and June of 1928, she and Pip exchanged houses with her parents, giving the older couple an opportunity to spend time with their relations and business contacts in town, and the younger, a chance to concentrate.

Letheringham survives remote and little changed today, a tiny cluster of houses far up the valley of the willowy Deben. What was once an abbey there has become part of a farm, Tudor brickwork incorporated into field walls and the tiny church nestling quietly among scenes of agricultural busy-ness. Water meadows, hayed in early summer and grazed at other times of the year, infuse tranquillity to the gentle landscape. When Herbert and Em lived at the Old Vicarage, the red-brick house was welcoming but shabby, its garden half-choked with nettles. Though smaller than the Old Rectory at Layer Breton, and certainly attractive, the house was draughty and old-fashioned, too awkward to be managed efficiently by a single maid-of-all-work.

Margery used elements of this landscape to set the scene for *Black Dudley*, though she brings the sea very much closer (as it had been at Layer Breton) and introduces an appropriately sinister note. From one of the upstairs windows at the Old Vicarage, it may have been possible to see across the valley to Glevering Hall, the most likely original for *Black Dudley*, a forbidding stone-clad house from which a park slopes away. 'In the centre of this desolation, standing in a thousand acres of its own land, was the mansion, Black Dudley; a great grey building, bare and ugly as a fortress. No creepers hid its nakedness and the long, narrow windows were dark curtained and uninviting.' For the secondary dénouement of the novel, Margery brings her characters home – place name by place name – to the saltings beyond Layer Breton.

A month after Margery, Pip and Grog returned to London, *The Crime at Black Dudley* was in the hands of Mr Maule of Doubleday Doran. Their success at achieving American publication was of great benefit, at this stage, to Margery's development as a crime-novelist. Doubleday had prospered by its energetic and skilful build-up of book series – such as its Crime Club. Margery and Pip became personally friendly with Doubleday's London representative, a vivacious youngster named Mary Leonard Pritchett. She was cheerful and congenial, ready to join the gang for meals and parties in London or appreciate the flippant tone of their letters from the country. Her brief was to spot British titles and authors to help supply the market for crime-fiction that had been created in America. Later Margery would rebel at the pressure to step up her production and shape her plots to a Crime Club mould. Initially it was exciting to discover a ready market and a friend.

In 1929, the process that had created *Black Dudley* was repeated. Margery, Pip and Grog went twice to Letheringham, between March and May and then during July and August while Herbert and Em took over the flat. The result was *Mystery Mile*, a far better novel than *Black Dudley* and with a correspondingly more interesting and important sense of place. Rural Margeland, a personal mix of Essex and Suffolk country and coastal scenery, is thoroughly established in *Mystery Mile*. The place itself, linked to the mainland only by way of the Stroud, is clearly reminiscent of Mersea Island – at least of the island's undeveloped eastern part with its tiny village straggled around the 'Dog and Pheasant' pub and the bare mediaeval church of which Baring-Gould had once been rector. The death of the villain in this new novel derives both atmosphere and specific vocabulary from the smuggler's burial in the sucking mud of *Blackerchief Dick*.

According to the map drawn by Grog for the frontispiece,

however, the island of 'Mystery Mile' is located in the River Orwell (possibly on the Sholtey peninsula, the border between Essex and Suffolk) and is said to be only an hour's indirect drive from 'the narrow awkward old town' of Woodbridge. Even heroes in a borrowed Bentley could not have reached Mersea Island itself in that time. There was no shortage in 1929 of tiny, semi-enclosed communities comprising a Big House (often impoverished), a vicarage, post-office-cum-shop, pub, and a scatter of cottages housing inter-related, ill-educated inhabitants. Letheringham could have matched that specification – as could many East Anglian villages in the depressed 1920s and '30s. Nevertheless the impression remains from *Mystery Mile* that Margery is charting her territory with exactitude. Heronhoe, Redding Knights, Kepesake, recurring names in her 'Suffolk' scene, seem as securely mappable as the actual places mentioned – Debenham, Monewdon, Woodbridge, Yarmouth, Bury St Edmunds.

The novel gives space to the country people as well as the landscape. Margery had had a 'bucolic' novel in mind ever since the completion of *The White Cottage Mystery* and the respect with which she views her villagers and farm hands is rare among her detective novel peers. George and 'Anry Willsmore are 'bokels', an Allingham word meaning 'half a barmy, half a yokel', comic characters who can neither read nor write ('the Education Act hasn't been in very long really'), but it would be a mistake to underestimate their ingenuity and inventiveness. The old women, Cruddy and 'Al-us' (Alice), have a special dignity. Alice, the rector's devoted housekeeper, makes light of Campion's scruples at leaving her alone with his headless and bloody corpse. 'She looked at him, faint surprise showing in her small eyes. "I shan't be afeard o' him," she said. "What if there's blood? 'Tis his, ain't it? I looked arter him since I were a young woman, but no doubt you meant well. Good night." '

Margery, like others in her family, was impressed and somewhat in awe of an old countrywoman called Jessie Bacon, Dr Salter's housekeeper in Tolleshunt D'Arcy. For years Jessie expended her failing strength unstintingly to meet the Doctor's demands, nursing him through his bouts of illness, waiting up to all hours of the night for his return or trudging miles without complaining of her own bad legs in order to glean news of a patient that the Doctor was unable to visit himself. The 'scrappy' (Margery's description) and occasional letters which Em wrote to Margery in London frequently contained news of the Tolleshunt D'Arcy household and it is possible that Jessie had an influence on the conception of 'Al-us'. Her fictional employer, Swithin Cush, shares Dr Salter's fondness for an unusual variety of apple tree, the D'Arcy Spice, but is not otherwise a portrait. Cruddy and Alice, though minor characters, are early examples of the line of dour, dependable working women that Margery creates with such frequency in her fiction, and for whose ministrations her more 'nervy' characters yearn.

The routine of *Mystery Mile*'s composition at Letheringham in 1929 differed from that of *Black Dudley*. Pip's contribution was to the planning of each day's work. Grog recalled that in the mornings Pip and Margery used to walk or sit together in the vicarage garden discussing the next episode. Pip sometimes jotted down notes on the development of the action. Margery would then spend the day writing and finally dictate to Grog who was now 'employed' to do her typing.

Pip was still ambitious to make his own name as an artist. He had had various small exhibitions in London throughout this period and some success at the Royal Academy. Etching remained his usual medium but he was also much influenced by the watercolours of Sir William Russell Flint whose courses he had attended and with whose son, Francis, also an artist, he and Margery remained friends for many years. As Pip sat at his work, he listened to Margery reading aloud or dictating her story to Grog. 'And any word, let alone incident, to which he took exception was commented on there and then at the top of his voice. It has always seemed a miracle to me that our marriage let alone our collaboration survived this baptism of cross-fire, but it did and even flourished.' Grog as well as Pip had decided views on what Campion would or wouldn't say. The verbal repetitiousness and the 'unedited' quality that had marred Margery's early work largely vanished under this ruthless treatment.

Working alongside two such opinionated artists may also have sharpened her visual sense in a 'painterly' way. Herbert had taken her to the National Gallery as a child and now the names of great painters and illustrators begin to run through her writing as if she is learning to see figures and landscape through their eyes as well as her own. In the context of *Mystery Mile* it is possible to sense a response to the gloriously wide East Anglian light which inspired not only Constable but Cotman and the Norwich School–painters whom Margery and Pip are known to have admired. 'The sun was dropping behind the house, the last blaze of yellow light shone over the garden, gilding the green leaves and warming the pale browns of the tree stems. The old house looked mellow and resplendent in the haze. The air was very warm and clear and the sound of clanking water pails and the lowing of cows sounded distinctly from the yard on the other side of the stables a quarter of a mile away.'

Mystery Mile exudes confidence. Characters from her two earlier books, W.T. from *The White Cottage Mystery* and Guffy Randell from *Black Dudley,* are effortlessly included and Margery's style allows her to play frivolously with people and incidents from her own life – 'in' jokes abound and do not, this time, detract from the action. Campion mentions 'the putting away of Joe Gregory, a gentleman who crossed the Atlantic unspotted by anyone or anything save his own dirty soul and myself', and asks, 'Who trailed Palmer the Poisoner? Who brought Jack the Ripper triumphantly to Justice? Who stopped mixed ping-pong in the Polytechnic?' The novel is inscribed to P.Y.C. and A.J.G. 'Partners in Crime'.

Although their help had been so valuable – and would be missed when it ceased – one character above all stamps *Mystery Mile* as Margery's own: Magersfontein Lugg, Campion's manservant. Named for a discreditable encounter in the Boer War, Lugg is first introduced in this novel as 'a hillock of a man, with a big pallid face that reminded one irresistibly of a bull terrier. He was practically bald but by far the most outstanding thing about him was the all-pervading impression of melancholy which he conveyed.' He is large and lugubrious, Margery's archetypal

Lugg appears in most, but not all, of Margery's ion' novels. Unlike his employer he does not age or change. later Margery, noticing this, rationalised Lugg as 'part of Mr Campion's personal accoutrements'; the Sancho Panza to his Don Quixote, Watson to his Holmes, the fat man within the thin man, perhaps. Margery discovered that she never had to try to think up dialogue for Lugg. He almost wrote himself. Pip, with uncharitable acuteness, suggested that Lugg was in fact the representation of Margery's own 'unconscious' – an interesting theory when one remembers the assortment of characters who had manifested themselves from that area when she used to try 'the glass'.

The inclusion of Lugg within a novel came to say much for the level at which it was written. He was certainly a touchstone for reviewers, the more fastidious of whom disliked him intensely. In modern parlance Lugg is something of a 'subversive'. His comments on Campion's behaviour are too apt, his treatment by Campion frequently too bad. His unattractive qualities are harped upon, his good ones for ever unrewarded. Lugg represents the stubborn, anarchic part of one's self that remains unsatisfied, uncheered and unconvinced by moments of success. The character may well have given expression to potential qualities within Margery herself which she would not choose to acknowledge – vulgarity, sentimentality, perpetual dissatisfaction, irreverence and gloom. She considered herself, she often said, 'a peasant at heart', not born to be as smart, witty, and sophisticated as the circles in which she and Pip were taking their place.

Mystery Mile, however, ends with a sense of elation, a promise that Margery and her partners are on their way to more adventures, even to fame and fortune. ' "Lugg," said Mr Campion, joyously, "you may kiss our hand." ' The book closes quickly before Lugg has a chance to reply.

'Uncle Grog'
by A. J. Gregory

'Uncle Grog'
by A. J. Gregory

IX

Donning the Deerstalker

1930–1931

Mystery Mile won the Book of the Month recommendation in America and achieved three times the subscription sales of its predecessor, *The Crime at Black Dudley*. It did adequately well in Britain and those reviewers who mentioned it were complimentary. In her next novel, *Look to the Lady* (in America, *The Gryth Chalice Mystery*), Margery clearly intended to offer more of the same. Unfortunately – at least, unfortunately as far as planning and financial security was concerned – Margery was not particularly good at writing to a formula. She could do it, of course, she had done it on *Joy* and week by week she turned in her allotted number of words for *Girl's Cinema*. This, though, was 'front of the mind' writing, the sort she called 'left-handed'. As soon as she let herself and her preoccupations in, as she did increasingly in the novels which featured Albert Campion, the operation was in jeopardy.

As she grew more used to working within the outline of the detective novel, she also discovered that her books had a tendency to fall into groups of three: 'one to break new ground, one to consolidate it and one to convince me that I must push on again.' *Look to the Lady* turned out to be just such an unsatisfactory third book. Margery later described her first three books as 'constructed on the Plumpudding principle. One collected as many colourful, exciting or ingenious inventions, jokes, incidents or characters, as one could lay hands on and simply crammed them into the box as tightly as they would go. This,' she continued, 'is no construction at all.' The books succeed through their brisk pace and agreeably frivolous tone. They cannot comfortably include matters that give the reader pause for thought.

Part of *Look to the Lady* was written in London, most of it in

Suffolk, at The Dairy House, Shelley, to which Herbert and Em had moved in the autumn of '29. The owners of the Old Vicarage at Letheringham had needed to sell it and Herbert's own finances were in a parlous state that year. He sold the cheap book rights of some of his serials (always a sign of desperation in his arrangements). He used Mac to sell some 'Shaw items' in America (these may have included the comments on *Without Being Naturally Qualified*) and, in partnership with Mac, sold some of the many letters he had received from him over the years. He and Em looked for a smaller, more manageable house to rent, something more suitable for two or three people (and a maid) and with room for occasional visitors.

Except during Joyce's school holidays their children were rarely at home. She had moved from New Hall Convent School to The Perse in Cambridge where she had settled more happily than Margery under the care of Miss Rose Luard at Sarum. Meeting her termly fees regularly sent Herbert to his relatives or agents in search of a loan. In the same year that Margery was married, Phil, aged twenty-one, had 'gone on the road'. In his own words, 'I had tried my hand at practically everything it was considered dignified for a son of my family to do, but although my heart was willing, my hand, or possibly my head was weak.' He had attempted journalism (as a cub reporter on *The Cambridge Evening News*), advertising (with Uncle Phil at 'J. G. Francis'), 'business' (working as a copywriter at Selfridges and on some slightly nebulous marketing jobs), and writing (a 'blood' for Thomsons of Dundee is mentioned by Herbert and part of a detective story written with Margery in the earlier 1920s survives). None of these ventures had proved successful and in 1927/8 he had put his top hat firmly on his head and set out to earn money as an itinerant fortune-teller. When in London he often stayed with Aunt Maud but he rarely spent long in the country with his parents.

The Dairy House, Herbert and Em's new home, was a low, compact building, a former farmhouse with about four bedrooms and disused outbuildings. It was some distance away from the village of Shelley which was reached by a walk across the fields. Shelley is slightly to the south of Hadleigh, not far from the

Suffolk–Essex border. The surrounding countryside is comparatively wooded and, to East Anglian eyes, hilly. The village lies in the valley of the Brett which flows into the Stour which runs on down to Manningtree, home of the notorious Matthew Hopkins, Witchfinder General in the seventeenth century. More than half the seventeenth-century men and women hanged as witches, were hanged in Suffolk. Margery read books on folklore and magic and later told Joyce that she would not wish to live in Suffolk again. She thought it most beautiful but 'fey'. Troubled memories and superstitions lurked too close to its picturesque surface. Her sensitivity to such occult survivals disrupts the tone of *Look to the Lady*.

The novel is set in countryside very near Hadleigh. As in *Mystery Mile*, Margery's description is of the sort that leaves readers convinced that the place exists precisely as it is said to do – if only one could find it. 'The village of Sanctuary lay in that part of Suffolk which the railway has ignored and which motorists have not yet discovered. Moreover, the steep-sided valley of which it consisted, with the squat Norman church on one eminence and the Tower on the other, did not lie on the direct route to anywhere, so that no-one turned down the cherry-lined lane which was its southern approach unless they had actual business in the village. The place itself was one of those staggering pieces of beauty which made Morland paint in spite of all the noggins of rum in the world.

'A little stream ran across the road dividing the two hills; whilst the cottages, the majority pure Elizabethan, sprawled up each side of the road like sheep asleep in a meadow.'

To Margery's understanding, the rural past came whole. 'After all, if you find these country folk sitting on three hundred year old chairs and using Elizabethan horn spoons to mix their puddings, why shouldn't you find them – very, very rarely I admit – practising the black rites of three or four centuries back?' The squalid authenticity of Mrs Munsey, Margery's village witch, jostles uneasily against her pseudo-Arthurian romance of the Gryths and their Chalice. As in *Black Dudley* the moments that are obviously intended to be of High Seriousness can too easily produce a giggle not a gasp from the reader. The question who or what caused Mrs Dick to fall to her death fails to achieve the frisson of ambiguity that Margery clearly intends. It looks vulgarly like a cop-out for Campion.

'Find The Lady is a mug's game,' commented Lugg sourly towards the end of *Mystery Mile*. Margery often had the germ of her next novel in mind before she had completed the work in progress. It may have been so in this case. The title of *Look to the Lady* came from *Macbeth*, the play which had gripped her imagination from early childhood. She had often 'given' Lady Macbeth at the Poly. Shakespeare's character goes mad and dies offstage, a fact obviously convenient for the good Macduff. It is he who speaks the line, he who would otherwise have had to kill her as he kills her husband. Margery wonders what would have happened in that case – how does the Hero cope when the Villain is a Damsel? It was not a question she was personally well equipped to answer.

In *Look to the Lady* she posits a situation where a national treasure on which depends not only the fortunes of an ancient family but even, obscurely, the wellbeing of the country, is desired by a powerful group of international collectors. They will only relinquish their quest if the agent they have set to steal the treasure is killed. And Campion discovers that the agent is a woman. Every authorial card is stacked against the character Mrs Dick. From the first she is cast as 'one of these damn women-with-a-personality'. Margery had grown up with two such women, Em and Maud, and even as a married woman with a home of her own, she did not feel quite free from their influence. She was also a 'woman-with-a-personality' herself and may already have been uneasy with her leading role as the main provider as well as potentially the most dominant character in her household.

On the one hand, in *Look to the Lady*, she considers that if women behave like men they should be treated as such and lose the protection of chivalry. She piles on the loudness, the rudeness, the sheer awfulness of Mrs Dick. But on the other hand Margery retained her longing that gentlemen should be gentlemanly, whatever the provocation. There is a great deal of authorial feeling in the novel, not quite enough clear authorial thought. Behind the action may lie Herbert and Em quarrelling and whether he should have 'allowed' her to browbeat him so. Should someone prevent Maud from behaving as a termagant in the A. P. office? And was that what Margery herself was like when she and Pip had a blazing row? *Look to the Lady* shirks its central question – could Albert Campion, gentlemanly goon, kill a woman in the line of duty? Margery's attitude towards the women in her fiction could provide some of its most uncomfortable, as well as most revealing, moments. It was thirty-five years after *Look to the Lady* before she again risked anyone as active and assertive as a female villain; never, in her mainstream work, a heroine to rival Campion.

The novel was, nevertheless, well received. None of Margery's first three 'Campions' sold more than around 1,000 copies on first U.K. publication but in America both *Mystery Mile* and *Look to the Lady* had sold 9,000 and 10,000 on subscription. Both were Doubleday Crime Club 'Books of the Month' and even Mac who continued to disparage the murder genre and to criticise Margery for wasting her time with it, allowed that there was 'a robustness about Marge's writing that is both engaging and refreshing'. When Mary Leonard told Margery that the novel had won its 'Book of the Month' award in America, Margery was at Shelley and was duly thrilled: 'Hurrah! Oh my! Oh my! Oh my!' Yet on only the previous day, she had completed *Police at the Funeral*, her fourth detective novel and a book so different in style, setting and seriousness as to offer its own comprehensive criticism of its predecessor.

Police at the Funeral was also written at The Dairy House, Shelley – in between *Girl's Cinema* stories *Hell's Island, Sinner's Holiday, Sisters, Midnight Mystery, The Love Waltz* and *The Gay Nineties*, and two sets of cartoon verses for Maud. Margery's diary, which covers only the first part of the year, makes her dislike of this work patent; 'awful job', 'impossible task', she says of *The Gay Nineties*. With *Police at the Funeral*, she and Pip were hoping to achieve a more literary readership. It was, she explained later to Malcolm Johnson, her Crime Club editor in

America, 'a deliberate attempt to capture the higher-browed murder mystery fans', i.e. those in Great Britain who were choosing to read Agatha Christie and Dorothy Sayers in preference, perhaps, to Edgar Wallace.

At the time she wrote to Mary Leonard that the book was 'less wild and more plausible as befits the dignity of our advancing years'. She and Pip were twenty-six but on the evidence of the handful of letters that have survived from this period they seem more rather than less inclined to foolery. The efforts of Pip and Grog to grow beards during their three months in Suffolk provided good copy for Margery's letters to Mary. For instance,

'Touching beards. The scores at present: Philip 40 (hairs) Grog, in play, 90 (hairs) Neb (rec. 5000) 4992 – a bad break.

'Grog, copper tip and red sleeves is keeping well to the fore making good going over coarse stubble. Expects to reach the standard (Joe Davidson) in about six weeks.

'Philip, heather mixture tip, pepper and salt sleeves, is not proving the dark horse as was at first hoped, but promises to turn out a pretty little Philly.

'Neb disqualified for early starting and going off the rails, has been put back to scratch.

'Want to buy a doormat lady?'

Neb was a mongrel dog who had followed them home one night in London and become the fourth member of the household. He was the first of several canine misfits who would keep Margery amused and exasperated over the next decade by their propensity to rove, to injure themselves and to return home smelly, flea-ridden and pursued on occasion by the wrath of the local gamekeepers. She worried for their safety but relished their 'appalling' anarchic exploits.

Her change of style in *Police at the Funeral* involved a move away from adventure and towards detection. This demanded a parallel development in the character of Albert Campion which was accomplished with characteristic flippancy. In the first scene of the novel, Campion is introduced wearing an ostentatiously Holmesian deerstalker – and asks to be taken seriously – 'Am I a serious practitioner or someone playing the fool? I know that feeling. But I assure you I'm a first class professional person.' As Campion evolved, he grew closer to his creator. Margery too was asking to be taken seriously. A legal 'Featherstone' has initiated the case, and Lugg is kept out of all but the first and last pages. Her bow to the tradition of Sherlock Holmes has no room for a character who yearns only for 'a tinned 'erring and tomato sauce'.

The debt to Conan Doyle goes beyond the flaunting of a deerstalker. The method by which the first murder is faked is lifted directly from one of his short stories *The Problem of Thor Bridge* and there are several other details reminiscent of the great detective – his penchant for measuring footprints for example. They have an air of having been mugged up for the occasion or being included as a subfusc joke. Although the deadly serious, fast-paced action of the thriller was not Margery's most congenial métier, neither was the painstaking sifting of theories, clues and alibis demanded by the cerebral detection of the early 1930s. Murder as an intellectual puzzle, à la Dorothy Sayers and the Detection Club, was, Margery found, 'a chastening ride for any aspiring writer of Comedy'.

For, although *Police at the Funeral* (working title *A Murder in the House*) was Margery's conscious attempt to capture the 'higher-browed fan', it was also the first, or second if the unpublished *Green Corn* is included, of her satirical portraits of the 'highbrow' breed. Kindly George Hearn had been sure that there was much good material particularly in the Cambridge section of *Green Corn*. He suggested that she keep it and return to it again when she was ready. In a sense, that was what she did, though not a sentence or a character of *Green Corn* appeared in *Police at the Funeral*. The two books share their attitudes towards 'intellect' versus 'intelligence' – and their picture of a bleak, comfortless Cambridge, where ordinary human life is relentlessly stifled by the rigid legacy of Tradition. In *Police at the Funeral*, the fictional household at Socrates Close, where Lugg cannot be allowed, is caught in a Victorian time-warp. ' "I suppose this must be the last household in England of its kind?" The girl shuddered. "I hope so." '

Police at the Funeral was dedicated 'To my seven paternal

uncles'. Herbert's parents, William and Louise, had now been dead ten years. The final disintegration of their Victorian family was not far away. A gap of sixteen years separated the eight boys and though this was not itself unbridgeable, a gulf of education and attainment threatened to divide the older from the younger. As there were no daughters, one of the younger boys had been kept at home dependent on his parents – deliberately, Margery and Joyce believed, so that there should be someone to minister to William and Louise in their old age.

Of Margery's 'seven paternal uncles' few were able to manage their lives and their livelihoods successfully in the difficult years of the 1920s and '30s. The eldest brother Will, who had been the first to move to Essex, endeavoured to build up country property at Sible Hedingham and Southey Green and was engaged in constant litigation; Phil and Tod who had taken on the advertising agency seemed (to Herbert at least) often and alarmingly on the verge of ruin; Arthur and Claude picked precarious livelihoods, untalented, unmotivated, as artist and actor and there is little mention in either Margery's or Herbert's diaries of the other two, Walter (Tub) and Albert. Joyce remembers her distress as a child when she opened the door of the flat in Bayswater to someone whom she assumed to be a rough working man, and afterwards discovered that she had utterly failed to recognise one of her younger uncles.

Although Margery and Pip were an independent married couple of some three and a half years' standing when she wrote *Police at the Funeral*, they were still caught up in the web of relationships and personalities that formed the extended Allingham clan. While *Police at the Funeral* was not (unlike Andrew Seeley's biography of the Master of *Ignatius*) a book written for the purpose of annoying one's relations, the situation postulated within it allowed Margery to express the dismay she felt at the dangerous claustrophobia inherent in family life. It tells the story of a household whose spirit has reached a stage beyond disintegration, that of putrefaction. Five adults who have only degrees of consanguinity to link them are forced by their individual ineptitudes and by the iron will of the head of the household to live in close proximity and states of dependence. There is, in such a situation, 'no vent to the suppressed hatreds, petty jealousies, desires or impulses of any living soul under that roof'.

If *Police at the Funeral* is somewhat irreverent as a detective story, it does offer serious portrayals of character. The squabbles and sulks of the elderly brothers and sisters are so well done that some of the detail of the detective plot seems unnecessary – except that the murderer is characterised as a practical joker run mad. His motivation is psychologically in a different class from the jewel thieves and international master criminals of the previous books.

Occasionally Margery's mysteries have twin solutions; one person has committed the crime and is guilty but someone quite different and in the terms of the plot 'innocent' has caused it. Great Aunt Caroline Faraday keeps her household in a state of dependence because they have failed to fend for themselves and because she considers them too hopelessly incompetent and stupid to take their chance in the world at all. This is both justifiable and wrong. However lightly it is glossed over, the exquisite grande dame, who has lost her capacity for emotion, and wields her power with such refined arrogance, is as responsible for the eventual murders as their insane perpetrator.

Caroline Faraday is a period figure. Behind her, dimly, lie the Victorian ladies in Margery's life: Granny, the tiny, black-eyed lover of fine lace whose 'refuge was in manners and in God' and who, like Great Aunt Caroline, had lost her only son at Ypres; Pip's unknown Grandmother in whose Cambridge drawing room of the 1880s Herbert Allingham and Lilian Robinson had met, and above all, Grandmama Louise, mother of those eight Allingham boys, who had brought them up as gentlemen, given them the ill-founded belief that they were special and seemed somehow to have disabled them for effective living in the twentieth century.

Police at the Funeral was written in two months at The Dairy House. The exchange, this year, had not been entirely trouble-free. Granny was with Margery and Pip for some of the time.

Margery found her 'very, very trying – bless her'. Local relationships were not easy either – 'gamekeeper threatening to shoot Nebby' – and in London Em had complained about Mrs Lawrence, Margery and Pip's daily help at the flat. Then for the final three weeks, Margery, Pip, Herbert and Em were all at Shelley together. The atmosphere could be tense. 'Daddy rather snappy and Mother a disturbing element as usual. Pip complaining that he isn't fed enough. Mother very silly not to see to the housekeeping better. Have promised PYC to get back as soon as possible. Anxious to get back as soon as I can.'

Their stay had been productive. Pip had produced some etchings which Margery thought 'very fine' and she had produced at least six film stories and two sets of verses for Maud as well as the novel – probably 170,000 words in just over two months. 'Consider myself quite hard-working,' she comments with satisfaction. If she had looked forward to some time for relaxation or fun with their friends on their return to Middle Row Place, she was disappointed. For March 3rd 1931 her diary reads, 'Came to town. Maud in bed ill and tight and Ted drunk as a lord. Very nasty. Old cousins in charge drunkish too. Rather scared. Trying to manage Ted and persuade him to Grace's. Rang Grace. She says she'll have him.' She coped. 'Phil and I packed Ted down to Grace's. Got in two trained nurses. Think it will be okay. Maud principally tight.'

Though this storm had blown itself out in a couple of weeks, it was, sadly, not untypical. Margery and Joyce both regarded Ted as a favourite uncle, 'the old pirate', someone who always had time for them and was generous with his affection. Too often however the company of his fellow-journalists and the amenities of the Press Club caused Ted's downfall. Margery grew used to completing his assignments for him, and for a while it was a sufficiently rare event to be noted in Herbert's diary – 'Ted sober'. There was an ugly scene when Ted, drunk, alarmed Granny in some indescribable respect. On that occasion it was Em who hastened to the rescue. His drinking became such a problem that Maud, who still could not tell the A.P. that she was married, occasionally resorted to locking him in their flat. She returned home from work one day to find him blithely on the fourth-floor window-ledge, climbing unsteadily round to make his escape through the flat next door.

Another favourite uncle, 'Old Phil', was seriously ill in hospital, the Allingham brothers were alarmed and his wife Amy seemed 'unhelpful'. They found Margery and Pip's small flat a convenient place for meeting and worrying. Betty Carter had a part in a London play so she and 'Mater' were also, unusually, in and out of the flat. So was Phil. Mary Leonard was introducing Margery and Pip to new literary friends and there was a flurry of lunch and dinner parties. With *Police at the Funeral*, Margery moved to a more prestigious publisher, Heinemann, then under Charles Evans as managing director. Margery had a great and abiding respect for Charles Evans and was delighted to be taken on to his list. She knew that this could mark an important step forward in her career and was sufficiently anxious to please that she hesitated before deciding not to attend some of the larger literary functions to which her new publishers invited her.

She did not shun London social life, however. Apart from the accustomed meetings with members of the Gang, she became friendly with fellow-Heinemann novelist Kate O'Brien. Of fellow-detective novelists she knew and liked John Dickson Carr (published by Heinemann as Carter Dickson and by Hamish Hamilton under his own name) and Philip (Pip) MacDonald. From the evidence available she neither met nor mentions Agatha Christie, Dorothy Sayers and Ngaio Marsh, the writers with whom she is usually linked, until the middle of the decade – the last not at all. She spent whole days cooking and cleaning up the flat in order to give small dinner parties to literary friends such as Robert Lusty, Sir Philip Gibbs and Mary Griggs. Eighteen friends crammed in to celebrate Grog's birthday in April. She and Pip began to eat in more fashionable (and expensive) restaurants and were invited to private views in art galleries. They went to Sir William Russell Flint's studio, and knew the sculptors Jacob Epstein and Jo Davidson and the Jersey artist Edmund Blampied.

Charles Evans was pleased with *Police at the Funeral* and encouraged Margery to look ahead towards mainstream novel writing rather than remaining narrowly in the crime genre. This was exciting. She wanted to say something, be someone and, at this time, was still influenced by Mac's and probably also Herbert's view that the detective story was only an entertainment genre, a passing fad. 'If a girl can't write a detective story to buy herself a trousseau, when can she write one?' she had written defensively to Mac. She did not believe that she could manage more than hack work in London and thought back with nostalgia to her childhood years at Layer Breton. As early as 1929 she, Pip and Grog had considered renting a farmhouse in Kersey, Suffolk. In May 1931 they looked again in Bures and Chappel and decided to take Viaduct Farm, 'a pretty, rat-ridden house on the river' in the same village as Dick Starr and Aunt Grace and just a few miles over the county border from Herbert and Em at Shelley. They moved there on August 27th 1931.

Margery's diary falls virtually silent from April of that year. There are indications that she underwent some sort of mental or physical crisis during the summer or early autumn. These hints are few indeed. There are two references in Margery's 1931 diary to Molly (full name unknown) who 'came to do my neck'. A solitary, significant prescription has survived, from one of their friends, Dr Doyle, for thyroid extract. Herbert paying his first visit to Viaduct Farm in October reports, 'Marge still a bit nervy but she has a sound brain which enables her to make a quick recovery.' From what he does not say but again, in December, he thought she seemed 'restless and not quite happy'.

Such scattered and uncorroborated allusions would be meaningless indeed if it were not for the evidence – and that, too, sparse and confusing – from moments of medical/emotional crisis much later in Margery's life. Molly must have been the first (remembering, however, that there are no diaries from 1927–1931) of the succession of masseuses and physiotherapists from whom Margery sought relief for her stiff neck (and, later, blocked sinuses). One of the causes of discomfort in her neck was the area around her thyroid gland which, later, was often swollen, and occasionally cystic. Dr Doyle, also, may be the first of the various doctors who sought to treat Margery's weight gain, if nothing more, by supplementing her natural production of thyroxine.

Thyroxine is the hormone secreted by the thyroid gland to control the body's rate of metabolism. Later in the 1930s when Margery's diary offers fuller evidence, some symptoms characteristic of myxoedema, under-activity of the thyroid gland, may be detected, but not at this early stage. As far as may be understood, Margery at the beginning of 1931 appeared a physically healthy woman just passing her mid-twenties, able to work hard when in the country and play with enthusiasm when in town. Only her weight was outwardly unusual. She was now more than plump; a contemporary describes her as 'billowing' with fat, but Aunt Maud, too, was a big woman and Em was not slight. As long as she felt well, she could have assumed that she had simply 'been blest by Providence with the family figure'. Photographs suggest that her weight fluctuated, or that she was more successful at some times than she was at others in camouflaging her shape with clothes and corsets. In the country she now wore long, comfortable, concealing dresses. A secret unhappiness with her appearance may have contributed to her decision to move out of London.

There may also have been a moment of emotional turmoil when Margery suspected Pip of involvement with another woman. In an autobiographical story, *The Pioneers*, written in 1937, the heroine remembers 'a scene in the studio in the third year of their marriage. She saw herself trembling, angry and excruciatingly jealous.' The encroaching female was seen off and, in *The Pioneers*, the incident was significant merely as a pale precursor of trouble to come. Seven years later, in a letter to a friend to whom she confided her deepest problems, Margery mentions 1931 as a year in which a personal disaster was only narrowly averted, when unnamed outside circumstances combined to stop her making 'a complete ape' of herself. The context suggests that this was emotional. She says no more than that.

Inwardly, she was aware that she had 'temperamental difficulties'. She had seen herself and been seen by others as 'volatile' ever since school days. Instead of stabilising in adulthood, this trait developed towards potentially more extreme bipolarity of mood. She could appear, as Betty Carter described her, 'supercharged', full of energy, enthusiasms and dynamism. Joyce found her slightly alarming in this elated frame of mind and Em, whose personality caused others to quail, once wrote of Margery to Mac, 'Her personality is too strong, it exhausts me.'

Temperamentally mother and daughter were more alike than either wished to recognise. Em claimed to Mac that she had 'always been so very fearful and frightened of life'. Her flights to various religions were attempts to understand existence and thus confront it more calmly. This is so completely at variance with the impression she made on others, her family above all, that one might dismiss it as a fabrication if it were not that her elder daughter also suffered from phases of uncertainty and downright fear that passed unsuspected by those around her.

Marriage had given Margery an initial lease of energy, confidence and contentment. With Pip she had set out on a gregarious, ambitious existence which she largely abandoned after they went to live at Chappel. Her writing benefited from their move to the countryside, her life as a social being and happy wife did not. When Margery's diary is again available in 1934, depression and self-doubt mark a sad contrast to the cheerful, even 'cocksure' tone of early 1931.

Dr Russell Barton, the psychiatrist who attended Margery in her last months, suggested that Margery's mood swings (far more extreme and distressing by that stage) were characteristic of a personality type shared, or suffered, by many creative people. Phases of energy, self-confidence and intense awareness of life's potential alternate with depressive periods which can be hard to bear. Such a clear outsider's diagnosis did not come Margery's way for forty-five years. In the interim she struggled, for the most part alone, to make sense of herself, her family and her life.

Margery had unquestionably worked and then played hard in the early months of 1931: 170,000 words in the two months at Shelley is two average-length novels. She may unwittingly have set herself a standard of productivity that she expected to be able to maintain more consistently than was to be the case. Much of the anxiety in her later diaries comes from her feeling of inability to meet the targets she had set herself and to discharge the financial responsibilities she had taken on when she persuaded Pip and Grog to move with her to the countryside. An attack of nervous exhaustion, some form of minor breakdown during the summer months when her diary is silent and there are no letters, would offer an appropriate explanation for Herbert's comments in October. She does not appear to have written anything at all significant in this period.

Within Margery, matters of body and mind were in finely balanced interdependence. The relationship of thyroid activity to her mental and physical condition was intricate and almost certainly not understood by her, or her doctor, at this time. In later life an occasion of great emotion or a change of medication were equally capable of triggering the hormonal activity which precipitated her into states of elation or despondency which she had to struggle to control. If Dr Doyle's prescription of thyroid extract in March 1931 was the first of its kind, it could certainly have affected her in ways which she could not have anticipated. Nevertheless, in 1931, the hints of trouble in her neck, her equilibrium, her productivity and her marriage remain no more than scattered straws in a light and fitful breeze.

Margery
by A. J. Gregory

X

'Unbalanced Companionship and Furniture in Every Room'

1931–1934

'Are you afraid of institutions?' began a circular letter from 'Carter's County Homes and Gardens, Ink.' to Pip and Margery's London friends. 'How do you pronounce cubbin'?' 'Have you ever had a pet wallah?' Recipients were urged to reassure themselves by paying a visit to 'CARTER'S HOME FROM HOME, where the bell rings every time: a visit to this establishment will provide you with just that final touch of assurance, just that ultimate soupcon of je ne sais quois, that will enable you to move in the hautest of mondes with complete sauve-qui-peut and sans-chemise.'

The writer, W. A. Smallcraft (Pip in a Featherstone guise), further promised 'Unbalanced companionship, furniture in every room (nearly), two staircases, three elevators (moral), coal scuttles at pithead prices, musical bathroom, every likelyhood of ghosts, fauna in the park – (porcine, bovine, ovine, equine and allah rest of them) river in, and at times over, the garden, herbaceous borders and spacious potato plantations. Rough shooting: hunt the rabbit, stalk the rabbit, badger the rabbit and —— the rabbit. Billiards, if own table brought. Imaginative inmates may fish in the pond.'

Behind its wide facade, built of the same Victorian stone as the railway arches, Viaduct Farm was a timber-framed Tudor house of considerable charm. It had suffered, as had so many farmhouses, from the slump in agricultural incomes after the First World War. Its owner wished to sell and the house was almost as devoid of modern conveniences as Layer Breton Rectory had been. There was virtually no plumbing at all – the only lavatory was an Elsan type, the contents of which had to be regularly 'dug-in'. (The 'musical bathroom' to which Pip refers was the false chain which when pulled set off a system of loud bells and incurred a mock £5 fine.) The River Colne wound gently past and the footpath beside it led on to Wakes Colne water mill, an impressive late-Georgian building three storeys high in white weatherboard.

The mill (home for the Fittons in Margery's *Sweet Danger*) was worked by the Ashby Brothers, stalwarts of the village cricket team. Pip soon established good neighbourly relations, not only on the pitch, but in mass forays against the rats who infested the mill, the river bank and the farm's outbuildings. These outbuildings were at a distance from Viaduct Farm house. Beside the house lay a small fourteenth-century church and a cluster of picturesque cottages. And beyond them, by the bridge that crossed the river, stood the local pub. Further down the broad valley, the many-arched railway viaduct was visible for miles.

During the winter of 1931/2, after Britain had abandoned the Gold Standard, many people feared that the nation was in a state of crisis. Margery was glad to be living once again in the Essex countryside 'where every tenth person appears to remember the hard times in the '60's, the bad winter in '74 and the time Mr Gladstone made such a mess of his Chancellorship. The present trouble seems a long way off and the mild winter is the real topic of the day. It is very heartening after London where the evening paper headlines seemed to matter.'

In the same letter she reported herself busy on a new story. Though her ultimate aim was to 'try a novel' as Charles Evans had suggested, the work in progress was to be another Campion in the same 'realistic' style as *Police at the Funeral*. Margery explained that she was 'reserving only the murder plot as a sort of balancing pole until I get really steady. I think I shall do it eventually.' By the end of the month, the story, *Death of a Ghost* was sufficiently advanced for Margery to read Herbert the first 15,000 words. He found it 'very promising'.

Shelley was only a few miles over the county border and Margery was glad to be closer to her father again. After she had abandoned *The Lover* and moved out of her parents' flat in 1925, she seems to have kept Herbert at a defensive distance from her work. Reviews in 'the better papers' and the encouragement she was receiving from Heinemann had done much to restore her artistic self-respect, dented after the failure of *Green Corn*. She was the better able to acknowledge the help Herbert had given her in the past and to discuss her present work with him without feeling obliged to accept direction. She could even use her achievement to bolster Herbert's much-battered confidence. *Death of a Ghost*, the book she knew was her best yet, was dedicated 'to H.J.A. by his industrious apprentice'. But this was not for another two years.

Police at the Funeral was published in America in the spring of 1932. It was not a Doubleday Book of the Month and was not the success it had been in England. Very soon Margery was writing agitated letters to Mary Leonard. 'The sales figures for *Police at the Funeral* have come to hand and are so appalling that I am only just sitting up and taking notice . . .' She was hurt, she said, that Malcolm Johnson, the Crime Club editor in America, had not warned her that this effort 'to capture the higher-browed mystery fan' was not likely to succeed in the States as it had in Britain. She claimed that she was not 'sensitive' about her work, 'I only want to send him what he can sell.'

Both Mary and Malcolm tried to reassure her with talk of the trade recession and reminded her that the figures she had been sent were only the subscription figures. She was unconvinced. 'Consider,' she replied, '*Black Dudley*, not a very good story, which was the first book I ever wrote for the Crime Club, published at $2 and not a book of the month, sold nearly 3,000 on subscription. *Mystery Mile* published at $2 and Book of the Month sold nearly 9,000 on subscription. *The Gyrth Chalice* at $1 nearly 10,000 on subscription, but *Police at the Funeral* at $2 only 2,083.'

She proposed a complete change of plan. She did not want to abandon *Death of a Ghost* but she no longer felt confident that it would suit the Crime Club. The move to Chappel was stretching her financial resources to the limit and sales in America still counted for more than prestige in Britain. She proposed therefore to write, especially for the Crime Club list – and at high speed – 'a Campion thriller of the adventure type'. The timetable she set herself (completion by the end of July 1932) proved impossible. May brought family trauma at Shelley and *Death of a Ghost* had to be put aside completely. It was autumn before she had completed the substitute thriller, *Sweet Danger*. This was published in the Crime Club spring list of 1933. And in the following year, Doubleday published *Death of a Ghost* – as Book of the Month and to a warmly appreciative readership. It had been no more than a sales 'blip' all along.

The degree of panic caused by the disappointing figures for *Police at the Funeral* is indicative of the financial strain Margery was under. Though Pip continued to visit London to collect commissions for book jackets (and was held in high esteem for his work) the 8–10 guineas he earned for each one did not go far towards meeting the expenses of their household. In January 1932, for instance, he earned 16 guineas, Margery about 44. Some months he earned almost nothing whereas she always had at least the film money. Grog had moved with them. He took Margery's dictation and did some of her typing. He drew maps and designed endpapers for her books. Occasionally he received commissions from publishers to provide lettering for book covers but otherwise brought in no money independently.

They employed a cook, a housemaid and a handyman. It was generally Margery's responsibility to pay the wages and the bills from local tradesmen. Any slight upset, even a slowness in payment by one of her publishers, soon assumed the proportions of a disaster. This was to be the situation for several years as the cost of their chosen way of life seemed always to rise slightly faster than her increasing earnings. Even at this moment, in the spring of 1932, some of her disappointment stemmed from the fact that the Old Rectory at Layer Breton was for sale and she had cherished secret hopes of re-possessing it. Its more advanced state of dilapidation would have made such a purchase extremely risky. The relative failure of *Police at the Funeral* with the American public may not therefore have been entirely unfortunate.

Margery had made plans to cover their expenditure at Viaduct

Farm. She wrote herself a timetable, 'Thursday, Friday, novel; Saturday, Sunday, film; Monday, day off; Tuesday, Wednesday, thriller.' The 'thriller' mentioned was a new venture, a serial for *Answers*, the original Northcliffe family paper. Robert St John Cooper and another young London contemporary, the publisher Robert Hale, had arranged this promising commission for Margery and the paper announced her first offering *Dangerous Secrets* with something of a flourish as the first woman to follow in the tradition of Edgar Wallace.

Answers regarded their serial stories 'with passionate seriousness' as she later recalled. There was no longer direct proprietorial control as in its early days but the magazine remained the flagship of the A.P. and enjoyed a wide circulation. Margery was initially excited by the possibilities offered by its editors' interest in her work. 'They pay generously and promptly,' she wrote to Mary Leonard, 'and really take one on the staff for the duration of the work.' She had to submit every instalment in advance and endure what she later described as a bombardment of criticism and advice as to its future development. 'The only two men who mattered sat one behind the other. The editor had definite views but so had his second in command, a much older man called Yates for whom I conceived a great respect. They never agreed. Old Mr Yates negatived each point in dumb show from behind every time something was settled. He used to take me down in the lift afterwards and shake a finger at me and say "Humanity, Miss Allingham. Humanity! Get a little humanity into it or you'll never get anywhere." '

Margery wrote three melodramatic serials for *Answers*: *Dangerous Secrets* (later published as *Other Man's Danger*) in 1931, *Rogue's Holiday* in 1933, and *The Devil and Her Son* (later published as *The Shadow in the House*) in 1935. They were subsequently brought out by Collins in cheap book form under the authorial pseudonym Maxwell March. They are humourless and somewhat undistinguished productions sporting helpless heroines and handsome heroes, international super-villains, secret societies and impenetrable disguises. The fear that they play to is the nightmare fear of insanity, the white powder in the coffee, the prick of a needle, drugs which render Margery's heroines incapable of acting for themselves. The cruel tricks and substitutions perpetrated against them make it almost impossible for them to believe the evidence of their senses. All they can do is hang on to their minds and wait for the heroes to win through.

In the spring of 1932, Margery's mother, Em, suffered a nervous breakdown. Dr Salter, ninety years old, had been ailing through 1930–1 and Em had made frequent trips to Tolleshunt D'Arcy to visit him. The Doctor enjoyed walking round his house, and his garden especially, pointing to the mementos of his long and vigorous lifetime: there was the wolf he had shot in Siberia with Prince Galietsyn; there the astromeria with which he had won the Royal Horticultural Society's Gold Medal. He talked to her about the future, how he wanted the house and garden managed and his dependants cared for after he was gone. Em was flattered, dangerously so, by the impression he gave that he was looking to her to carry out these wishes for him.

When the Doctor died on April 17th 1932, Em believed that she had been appointed an executor of his will. She also thought he planned to leave his house to her. Poor Em had been living in a romantic fiction. Though Dr Salter confirmed in his will that he had intended to appoint Mrs E. Allingham among his executors, he had been advised that this would exceed the statutory number. He could only urge those whom he had appointed to attend to her advice and offer her a place if anyone among them could not act. He had left her, with ten other major legatees, the sum of £500, but it was to his partner, Dr Arthur William James, that he bequeathed the freehold property known as D'Arcy House.

Em was devastated. She could not believe that the house was to go to Dr James – or that her dear friend had not told her that he had changed his plans. On April 27th she wrote requesting a copy of the will. On the 28th Herbert described her as 'very nervy'; on the 29th as 'abnormal and fanciful'. The solicitors refused to send a copy. On April 30th 1932 Herbert, feeling quite unable to cope, took Em over to Viaduct Farm. She grew rapidly worse. Margery turned for help to their friend, Ronnie Reid, who had moved out of London to practise in Colchester at about the same time they themselves had come to Essex. He summoned a specialist. 'Immediate action under proper medical treatment' was advised and on the same day, May 3rd, Em was taken to a private mental hospital in Northampton. Herbert reported that 'she was willing and eager to go'.

He then gave way briefly to the strain. Grog and Pip rallied round to cheer him up and Phil made one of his periodic appearances in his much-travelled car. He was able to take Herbert to Northampton to reassure him that Em was in good hands. A month later she was out and able to seek traditional refuge with Grace at Pope's Hall. There were anxious months ahead and Herbert decided to effect a change of scene. He gave up the lease of The Dairy House and moved to Thorpe Bay (near Southend-on-Sea) to which Maud and Ted had also moved.

The reverberations of this crisis had shaken several members of the family more deeply than they may have realised at the time. Em's problems were believed to have been compounded by a protracted and difficult menopause. She became susceptible to extreme agitation of manner and oscillation of mood which could quickly panic her family into assuming she was again on the verge of mental illness. When Margery at a similar age displayed similar symptoms, it was all too easy for those close to her to suppose she too was menopausal and hysterical. Margery and her mother shared a more pervasive problem within their personalities. This inherited resemblance was the aspect of herself that Margery did her best to suppress.

During these months Margery set to work on *Sweet Danger*, the adventure story that she had promised Malcolm Johnson in place of *Death of a Ghost*. Many years later she reintroduced it as a favourite. 'This purely "right-hand" tale was written as a private celebration because I had achieved an ambition and got back to the countryside where I belonged after ten years of exile in the city. I like to think that a trace of the march hare ecstasy that I felt all that enchanted summer has been caught in it.' Rather a different motive for its composition than the anxious desire to produce something quick and commercial for the Crime Club list! That itself may have been in part a smokescreen to disguise the fact that Margery wanted to put *Death of a Ghost* aside and spin something more frivolous. The character of Donna Beatrice in the former book is a little too close to unkind caricature of Em's mystical mannerisms to have been comfortable writing at such a time.

Sweet Danger is full of 'alarums and excursions, bamboozlements and frolics' – and few deeper meanings. It carries the reader along at the level of a sophisticated treasure hunt and includes all the trappings that American admirers of *Mystery Mile* and *Look to the Lady* might be supposed to enjoy: bizarre remnants of folklore, colourful pseudo-history, idyllic scenery, rural eccentrics, and the fairy-tale appeal of aristocracy in rags. 'People like a title,' said an old duke to a socialist M.P. in one of Margery's romantic short stories. 'It cheers 'em up.' The Lady Amanda, Albert Campion's future wife, made her first appearance in *Sweet Danger*. He discovered her sitting in a darkened room, her best dress homemade from village shop curtaining.

Much of the reading pleasure given by *Sweet Danger* stems from Margery's defter, lighter touch. The moments of seriousness do not lurch into portentousness. At the end of the book, in place of *Look to the Lady*'s Very Important Personage arriving with Official Plaudits, the establishment is represented by Colonel Featherstone and Stukely-Wivenhoe. This is typical of its tone throughout. Margery's family trouble, financial uncertainty and private self-exploration make no mark on it – except insofar as it exemplified her much later view that escapist literature represented 'an escape from insanity into sanity'.

Her ambivalent view of the countryside had not changed. There is enough brutality, ignorance and overt hostility among the villagers to lend convincing support to the experiments of the local necromancer who sees himself as the follower of Elizabethan Dr Dee. In America *Sweet Danger* was retitled *Kingdom of Death* or *The Fear Sign*. This dark side of the rural coin, however, remains subordinate to the atmosphere of comedy, holiday and Margery's patent affection for the village she had known since she was a child.

For most readers of *Sweet Danger*, the distinguishing feature of the book is the character of Amanda – potentially Margery's chance to create a really satisfactory female heroine. Sadly, Amanda with her wit and initiative, her thoroughly practical grasp of electronics and engineering, never quite fulfils her teenage promise. Even in *Sweet Danger* her freedom of action is limited, both by Campion's taint of kindly condescension, based on age, and the claims of her younger brother Hal, based on gender. Hal has really nothing to recommend him – beyond his unshakeable confidence in himself as the male member of the family and therefore 'head of the household'. This has little to do with Margery's relationship to her own younger brother Phil, but may be linked to the gradual claims of inequality that began to creep into her relationship with Pip throughout the decade. In *Sweet Danger* Hal is (irritatingly) physically stronger than Amanda and relies on this to impose his will on her. Though she is as determined and far quicker-witted than he, the book offers no challenge to this view of the basics of male–female relationships. There is even felt to be something rather right and attractive about Hal's young pomposities. Margery was not confident of women's freedom to act on their own and by the end of the Campion novels Amanda has had to be content with the status of 'Mr Campion's yard-stick and ideal' instead of being able to participate fully in the action, experience set-backs and develop, fictionally, in her own right.

There was a sense of fear, an awareness of vulnerability at the core of Margery's view of womanhood that she only rarely allowed to surface in her work. From *Blackerchief Dick* and *The Sexton's Wife* to at least *The Beckoning Lady*, there exists a half-hidden, uncomfortable acceptance that, however clear-sighted, pragmatic and conscientious the woman is, the man has the final advantage that he can, if he wishes, beat her up. This is not really connected with the rough and tumble of brothers and sisters or even with the disparities of strength between men and women. It has to do with Margery's understanding of the power lines of sexuality and is not a politely discussable subject. In *The Beckoning Lady*, the child, Rupert Campion, plans to marry the fattest little girl of his acquaintance. 'And I shall shout at her and put her across a bed and smack her until she cries and then I shall kiss her until she laughs, and we shall go downstairs and pour out drinks for a lot of visitors.' He is forcefully and unanimously shushed by all the adults present. They realise he is describing their hosts, the characters Minnie and Tonker, versions, it is said, of Margery and Pip. In his autobiography Pip comments on the solidly deaf ear turned by neighbours and police to the Saturday night yells from the flat adjacent to his and Grog's 'hovel' in Neal Street as the scrawny, mild-mannered tailor routinely belted his hulking wife and son, 'Aw Gawd, Pa! Not the buckle end!'

There is one single, sad entry in Margery's diary, 'Cocky beat me up.' Made in a moment of misery during 1935, the contrast to her earlier 1931 comment 'had a fight with Pip, hitting each other really hard' is shocking and could suggest that her secret fears of male violence were to some extent confirmed in her marriage. This would be a mistake. It is a single entry only in a relatively well-documented period and receives no confirmation from those who lived with Margery and Pip. What may fairly be said is that the mid years of the 1930s were years in which the balance of their working relationship and their human relationship was unstable and that, as both were aware of the darker strand in sexual relationships, it is possible that such exaggerated forms of male dominance and female submissiveness were an occasional, even an enacted counterbalance to the greater degree of artistic success and household responsibility that was falling to Margery. 'If you have to hold a man up,' she said bitterly in later life, 'you might as well make sure you hold him up the right way.'

Meanwhile *Sweet Danger*, written over the summer of 1932, is romantic and escapist and written at a time when romance in Margery's life was just beginning to come under pressure. It was the last book produced overtly to please Malcolm Johnson and the Crime Club. Good sales were always financially vital but she grew more sophisticated in her efforts to achieve them. Only two years after assuring Malcolm that she 'only wanted to send him what he could sell', she was strongly resisting the wholesale editorial changes through which he wished to bring *Flowers for the Judge* (published 1936) in line with the generality of the list. That book was taken out of the Crime Club and published with Doubleday's general fiction. 'Margery Allingham,' she asserted proudly, 'thinks of her reputation.'

As Margery faced the reality of living, not holidaying, in the pre-war countryside she found herself beset by problems. This was her first attempt at managing a household of any size. She was twenty-seven when they moved to Chappel and she was not entirely successful. It was not easy to find or retain staff who would work willingly in the Carters' somewhat chaotic household. Viaduct Farm was inconvenient in itself and made more so by the litter of artist's materials, books, papers, casual visitors, dogs (an unexpected litter of pups brought the total to fourteen at the end of 1934) and scraps of Margery's sewing.

Her servants were local people in the main and brought their own troubles, incompatibilities and amorousnesses with them. Margery could not remain unaware of these. One older female servant was distressed by village gossip that she was secretly pregnant. 'Promised airily to fix it all up. Poor old Marge.' Neither was she an effective disciplinarian. A grandmother complained about the licence allowed her granddaughter as Margery's housemaid. The girl had imported a 'follower' to the household. Margery had tried to be tolerant but when the girl's family discovered the situation they insisted that she leave.

The staff argued and flirted amongst themselves, were threatened with sacking and reprieved, left and were replaced with some difficulty. Pip was unhelpful. He was quick to complain if meals, for instance, were not to his liking, but he regarded domestic matters as Margery's responsibility, vented his vexation on her and did nothing to support her various attempts at kitchen discipline. Where, she wondered, was the sustained working and thinking time for which she had come to the countryside?

It may be that Pip and Margery's quarrels about household problems were a cover for more serious differences. One quarrel, for example, apparently his expression of anger at her decision not to sack the cook, occurred the morning after a night when she had refused to go to dinner with a woman whom she suspected of being his mistress. 'Do not want to see A– definitely and obstinately.' Pip's determination prevailed and Margery remained on terms of social friendship with this woman until the end of her life. Those who suffer, as Dr Barton, the psychiatrist, believes both Margery and her mother did, from a 'manic-depressive' personality, are sometimes prey to unfounded suspicion of those closest to them. A vivid imagination or the facility for spinning plots can be an additional curse in this respect. But Pip's reputation among his friends and his later open infidelity suggest that Margery's jealousy in 1934 was likely to have been justified.

The code of conduct among their friends was relaxed in matters of sexual morality. They had moved on from the age when they had 'talked grandly about vice and living in sin but had done nothing about it'. Late night, occasionally all-night, parties of the Gang at Viaduct Farm were unrestrained affairs at which married and unmarried couples behaved with little inhibition (by the standards of the time). They were not orgies but tremendous opportunities for the young professionals, almost all of them ambitious and working hard in London, to let off steam, play bawdy jokes and drink copious amounts of beer. No-one could admit to being shocked and those who might be hurt in the process were expected to pretend that they didn't care.

Pip and Margery's annual cricket parties dated from this time and became something of a tradition. They started quite casually. Pip and Grog enjoyed the game and collected a team of London publishing and ex-Christ's Hospital friends to play a team from Chappel village. This gave occasion for a party and grew year by year into the major event of their summer. After they moved to Tolleshunt D'Arcy (in 1935) the parties became both more formal and more exciting. The match was usually on August Bank Holiday weekend and the meal became a 'Feast'. Other parties spawned from this to coincide, for instance, with the village flower show and fete. There was sometimes a theme for the evening and guests arrived in fancy dress. Grog's inventions decorated the house. Conversation sparkled and it is for the sheer fun of these events that many people who knew Pip and Margery remember them best. Bill Gee, who was younger than most of the guests, recalls that his first anxiety when he received one of Margery's invitations was always that he would never manage to express his delight adequately when he came to write his thank-you letter afterwards.

As Margery's household organisation improved, she grew to love the preparation for such weekends. For one thing it gave her an undeniable excuse, to herself, to stop work and plunge into domesticity. For another, she was good at it, just as she had been good at making costumes, finding props and planning the staging of their Polytechnic productions. In the early days at Viaduct Farm she may have been less at ease during the parties themselves. She was curious about others and found plenty of scope for observation. She had great charm, could be gay and set her guests at ease. Bill Gee remembers her as formidably able and amusing, seeing and doing so much at once. However, when the fun grew more boisterous, the conversation more outrageous, Margery remained privately unsure of her ability to keep up. She was glad to find an older, quieter man with whom to sit aside and talk.

This was Leslie Cresswell ('Cressie'), tall, lean and prematurely grey. He was a technical draughtsman and the only one of the group old enough to have served in the First World War, when he had suffered from shell shock. 'Like all these war-blokes, there's something odd and missing about him (half a dead thing),' wrote Margery in her diary after an early meeting. She found him blessedly easy to talk to and interested in her opinions, 'doesn't seem to think I'm so dumb as most people do'. Pip, Grog, Coop, Tibby, Ronnie and the rest never considered her 'dumb' in the sense of stupid but there were certainly areas where they were cynical and she was credulous and they were sophisticated and she naive. She felt silenced by their readiness to scoff at the matters she took seriously.

Cressie was an attractive man. Margery is said to have 'looked over her shoulder at him' at parties when Pip's attentions were engaged elsewhere. He had several girlfriends but never married. His First World War experiences had left their mark. Though he was quiet, polite and a sympathetic listener, he was also prone to outbursts of anger that were completely unpredictable. As he grew older these became more violent. He might quarrel with a guest and storm out, write a letter full of passionate reproach with no clear cause. Margery was untroubled by his difficult temperament and smoothed the ruffled feelings of their friends where she could. He remained devoted to her for life. The appearance if not the character of Mike Barnabas in *Flowers for the Judge* (written 1934–5) may owe something to Leslie Cresswell.

One of the more frequent, and anarchic, visitors to Viaduct Farm was Margery's brother Phil. He had found life 'on the road' congenial and after his initial experiments with fortune-telling had branched out into a variety of fairground occupations. He was 'a lad', emancipated and unconventional. He would have been so much more at home, his sister Joyce thought later, in the culture of the 1960s than he was in the age to which he had been born. Robert Lusty remembers Phil in the 1930s claiming with great relish that he had been officially classified as a 'rogue and a vagabond' – and was therefore exempt from taxes! He could be described with even more arcane accuracy as a 'Grafter, Knocker-Worker and Mounted Pitcher'. This description was written by Margery for the blurb of Phil's single book, *Cheapjack*, an account of his adventures 'in the Market-Places and Fairgrounds of a Modern but still Romantic England'. *Cheapjack* was published in 1934, only three months later than her own 'up-market' novel, *Death of a Ghost*, and by the same firm, Heinemann.

Although Phil had turned his back on the family way of life and London with it, setting out for Southend Pier, Newcastle Town Moor and Llandudno, he had not lost his taste for brief intervals of metropolitan living or his Allingham ease with a pen. Brief accounts of his experiences made saleable articles for the London evening papers and it was not surprising that he began to think of a book – perhaps something along the lines of W. H. Davies' *Autobiography of a Super-Tramp*. The family were enthusiastic and Margery undertook to help Phil present the book for publication. She spent a considerable amount of time during 1933 helping Phil with the structure and verbal detail of his work. She and Pip persuaded Heinemann to publish and Margery toned down Phil's riskier sexual passages. Even so, some booksellers returned the published version as being 'not quite nice' and The Book Society was thought to have 'fought shy' of recommending it on grounds of taste.

In her editing of *Cheapjack*, Margery showed herself more prudish in word than in deed. For Phil's 'fanny' or 'spiel' as a 'mounted-pitcher' selling heated wavers, he needed an assistant, preferably a young girl with long, resilient curlable hair. Margery cut the section of *Cheapjack* where Phil teased the reader by suggesting alternative motives for his tramps through the slums of South Shields in search of young female assistants. She knew there was nothing improper in his relationship with Jenny, Nancy, Susannah and Fanny but did not assume the public would be so trusting. The girls were usually only twelve to fourteen years old. Among the other passages which Margery excised from *Cheapjack* was the account of his relationships with a gypsy woman and his frank statement of the pleasure of a relationship without commitment, 'having sex when one felt like it'. In life Margery looked after several of Phil's protégées at Viaduct Farm, made clothes for them, struggled with their problems of fleas and headlice – and even babysat them. Phil's entourage, and thus on occasion Margery's household, also included a likeable itinerant called 'Three-fingered Billy'. Not all her Essex neighbours viewed this with charity.

Margery functioned as a 'poste restante' address for Phil, who was not easy for editors or newspapermen to contact, and took on pre-publication chores such as proof-reading. She came to feel that *Cheapjack* was, in some sense, also her own, and would have liked to accept some credit for it. At the time this was out of the question – the authenticity of *Cheapjack* might have been called into question if involvement of a fiction-writer was admitted – and its subject matter could have impeded Margery's own pursuit of the higher-browed. In a single diary entry, Margery writes, 'Phoned Phil. Emphasised importance of saying stuff had not been tampered with by me.' Then, 'Wrote Phil's article on gypsies. Hope it will do.'

In the latter part of 1933, Margery's extraordinary flow of work continued. She was working simultaneously on *Cheapjack* and *Death of a Ghost* and planning a second serial for *Answers* – as well as keeping the film-stories flowing. Towards the end of that year she again suffered some sort of nervous collapse, 'temporary depression and nervous debility' as she explained it to Mary Leonard. 'When I started writing the same letter twice over in the same day, I got the wind up and realised something had to be done – So I ate a lot of bread and made a patchwork quilt – a whole one – very elaborate – you'd be suprised. However it worked in about six months and if ever you think you're going crackers . . . you try it . . . N.B. You have to make the quilt by hand. It's the steady monotonous sewing that does it – I don't know why the bread is so good but it's important –'

Though Margery did not have the detailed medical knowledge that might have made her, in this instance, consider the vitamin B content of brown bread, she was interested in natural, slightly folksy remedies. Her housemaid, Christina Carter, who joined the Viaduct Farm household in the autumn of 1934, remembers the efficacy of Margery's belladonna plasters – and her comforting authoritativeness. 'If she told you to go and lie down with the plaster on, and the backache would be better tomorrow – you did, and it was . . .' Sewing, or any practical household chore, always provided relief. She liked to plunge into something big. Christina remembers the pounds of apple jelly left behind when the household moved from Chappel, relics of an unappreciated burst of domesticity.

Margery's diary for 1934 shows her feeling irritable, nervy and put upon through the first half of the year at least. The sewing and eating of bread may have restored her authorial energy. 'I have written 19,000 words since Tuesday,' she says in the letter to Mary, written at the weekend, but her underlying anxieties could only be eased by better physical health, not dismissed.

Chief among these was her relationship with Pip. The move from London to the country slowly changed them both. Pip grew more socially confident and found a whole range of new pleasures and new friends to share them with; Margery, with her health imperceptibly worsening, grew less and less comfortable beyond her own domain. The uninterrupted writing time for which she had come to Chappel was too often purchased by leaving Pip to go out by himself. If she had imagined that he would stay at home and work at his drawing as she worked at her writing, this hope was disappointed. The two 'boys', he and Grog, took up cricket and ratting and dances and cocktail parties. Pip was much in demand as a partner in the county round of Hunt Balls and other similar functions.

The summer party of 1934 brought a new member of the household. Margery's Polytechnic friend, Mary Orr, 'Cooee', came for a cricket weekend and was persuaded to stay on. She was small and vivacious with an upturned nose, wide smile and a figure which offered endless temptation to Grog's teasing and lascivious pen. Since leaving the Poly, Cooee had been working as an actress with a repertory company, taking plenty of work, particularly in comic roles, but travelling constantly and seeing no prospect of improved conditions in the future. In her travels she had acquired a pony and a passionate love of animals. The sight of Viaduct Farm, its dogs and outbuildings, so suitable for stables, decided her to change her career. She would settle in Essex, take on oversight of the household from Margery and work for her horsemaster's examination.

Cooee was, thought Margery, 'a sport', 'capable and intelligent', 'splendid'. The extra money that Margery would have to earn to support her would surely be well spent if Cooee could relieve her of daily domestic anxiety. In fact it was Christina Carter hired as housemaid on a temporary basis six weeks after Cooee's arrival who fully effected this change. Cooee swiftly acquired a thoroughbred hunter mare and poured her energy into horses and fun. Pip bought a horse himself and rode out with her. Margery tried not to mind. Their country way of life had been her choice and she rarely expressed doubt that it was therefore she who must stick to her desk and earn the money to pay for it. In the back of her mind may also have been the feeling that Pip was safer with Cooee than with other of the local ladies.

The central character in *Death of a Ghost*, the novel which

Margery had finally completed late in 1933, has the graciousness to accept and indeed care for her husband's mistress. Her success enhances her standing as his wife. If Margery had been trying for the same sang-froid it was not to be easily won. In July 1934, for instance, she took a message from one of Pip's friends and commented in her diary, 'Eve – isn't coming but would like to meet the old man in town sometime to "go dancing" – am getting aggrieved. Must be just an ordinary person after all.' She was considerably more irritated by another of Pip's partners. 'A– is just a little whore, don't even feel 'tis pity.'

The local lady doctor was among Pip's regular dance-partners and references to her in the diary have a frosty tinge. Margery nursed a secret dislike for 'these Colchester ladies' and took private revenge by labelling them in her diary 'suburban'. Only once, on diary evidence, does she seem to have risked an overt confrontation with Pip over his pursuit of pleasure. 'Had a scean with Cocky – he doesn't (won't or can't) see that he ought to behave a bit like a married man since he makes me look so bloody cheap if he doesn't.'

Still she didn't insist on her 'right' to accompany him to the Hunt Balls or parties. And when she was dragged 'after fierce protestations' to the lady doctor's Hogmanay celebration, she hated it. 'One of the horridest shows I ever went to. I haven't the temperament, I'm afraid . . . not a good finish to the year.' And the less frequently she went out, the harder it became to feel relaxed in the company of semi-strangers – and the deeper ran the gulf from Pip, consistently at his happiest when the life and soul of a party. Margery sat alone in the evenings, was woken by his tipsy return in the early, or later, hours of the morning and often saw little of him, or Grog, as they lay 'in a torpor' for most of the following day. Her diary shows her confused and dispirited until she reached the conclusion, 'Cocky has no time for me and I can't think of anything to say to interest him. Hope I haven't bitten off more than I can chew.'

Death of a Ghost also makes a distinction between the Great Artist, who may be allowed to possess both wife and mistresses, and the talented potential artist who expects the same privileges but has sold his soul to commerce. 'Do you realise he's brought that girl over here to make wrappers for patent medicines?' says the outraged Linda Lafcadio of her unfaithful lover, Tommy. Pip did little work in 1934 other than for publishers and that year was the last that anything of his was exhibited in the Royal Academy. Slowly his name disappeared from the registers of practising, exhibiting artists. This was difficult for Margery to accept. Since student days she had sincerely admired Pip's drawing and been prepared to work and wait for him to make his creative mark. Linda Lafcadio continues, 'I've got nothing against commercialism. But it puts a man on a different plane. It's insufferable of him to expect the same sacrifices.' There is considerable authorial sympathy for Linda's point of view.

As she began to see her own achievements outstripping Pip's she grew increasingly concerned lest this damage the equilibrium of their marriage. It seems unlikely that she confided her unease to anyone other than her diary. Her standard press release for this period stated, 'In private life Margery Allingham is a happy, domesticated person, the antithesis of the conventional idea of the horror-monger. She lives in a rambling 450-year-old farmhouse in Essex overrun with dogs. Practically all her spare time is spent on her hobbies which include cooking, needlework and interior decoration. Her husband, P. Youngman Carter, the book jacket artist, is exactly her own age and his first cover adorned her first book when they were both seventeen. They work together in an incredibly untidy studio which looks like an old fashioned playroom and is littered with books, masses of papers, a shove ha'penny board and scraps of material. Youngman Carter sits at one window drawing while Mrs Carter dictates her most exciting stories from the fireside sofa as she finishes the household darning –'

And how satisfactory that would have been.

'Cooeyism!'
by A. J. Gregory

XI

The Old Doctor's House

1935–1937

In the autumn of 1934 the Old Doctor's house, D'Arcy House, came on the market – and Margery and Pip's landlady at Viaduct Farm gave them one year's notice to quit. Viaduct Farm house was due to be sold together with its land and buildings. This had been expected for some time but purchase of the entire farm, even at 1930s land prices, was quite beyond the Carters' means. They had gone to look round D'Arcy House some weeks before formal notice was given them at Chappel. 'Fell for it utterly,' said Margery, 'and wanted it badly – £2,000 and seems hopeless but am somehow confident that a miracle will occur and we shall come by it (very odd feeling).'

In Dr Salter's bequest of the house to his partner, Dr James, in 1932, he had expressed, as he had done to Em, his 'wish and desire that the said Arthur William James will, as far as possible, not alter the existing arrangements made by me in and about the said house, gardens and meadows and that so far as regards my servants, things shall be carried on after my death as they now are.'

D'Arcy House in the Doctor's day was dark, inconvenient and elaborately furnished. As well as the good solid furniture, rich flock wallpapers, trophies and memorabilia from literally hundreds of sporting events, the house was also home for the Doctor's vast collection of stuffed animals and birds. Three large wolves shot before the Russian Revolution sat with the Doctor in his drawing room and Joyce remembers the shock it gave her as a small child to pass a lifesize brown bear at a corner of the stairs. The kitchen range consumed a ton of coal a week and too many of the other systems in the house were correspondingly expensive and inefficient. 'The Old Doctor', the local plumber was heard to remark later, 'made more bad improvements in that house than anyone he ever knew . . .'

The beautiful garden, in which the County had been entertained and from which prize-winning exhibits, hooded and specially crated, had been dispatched to the Chelsea Flower Show and innumerable local events, required two or three men and considerable expertise to maintain it. Now it curled and crept and spread its tendrils to block the light from most of the downstairs windows of the house. Dr Salter had made generous provision for his staff, for Jessie Bacon especially, for his gardener William (Bill) Bullard, William's son Herbert and for his chauffeur William Miller. It would nevertheless have been virtually impossible for any legatee to have fulfilled the Doctor's wish 'that things should be carried on as they now are' – and equally impossible to make a single significant change without the whole village commenting.

The imposing Queen Anne facade of D'Arcy House stands in the centre of the village. Opposite it, in the 1930s, was the meadow where Salter had drilled his volunteers during the First World War and where events like the annual village fete (and the annual roughhouse with the neighbouring village of Tollesbury) were traditionally held. The cricket meadow lay behind.

Three roads meet at the centre of Tolleshunt D'Arcy, from Maldon, Kelvedon and Colchester. A maypole stands at the hub of this intersection and in those days before the Second World War, 'the Square' was ringed by the village forge, the post office, a pub, a baker's, the saddle maker, newsagent and the grocer's shop. Adjoining D'Arcy House, though reached by a separate entrance, was the surgery. In here, the villagers had been used to undergo medical examination, exhortation and treatment, and even minor operations. In whatever manner Dr James had proposed to manage his bequest, he could not hope to pass unnoticed. On the day he began to lop an old oak tree that was threatening a wall, the conservatory roof fell in – and people said it was a sign that the Old Doctor was angry. Dr James undertook the crucial task of seeing to the roof of the house but had little time to make many more changes before he was killed in a car accident early in 1934.

His death left a vacancy among Dr Salter's executors into which, at last, Em stepped. Em's devotion to her 'master of men' had survived unscathed. In an emotional account of her first visit to his grave after she had been discharged from the Northampton nursing home, she recalled how she had written to him daily for ten years, how he was the only person who listened to her, appreciated her, took her advice. She continued to believe that she had been 'meant' to have the house and retained her vision of it as it had been when in the Doctor's possession – and as she was convinced he had intended it to be kept.

The solicitors administering Dr James' estate put D'Arcy House, its meadow and gardens on the market. In September 1934, Margery, Pip and Grog, with Grog's brother Robin and their friend Pippa St John Cooper, came to look round. Pip came again a few days later with Robin and Joyce. 'Decided for it and I wrote bank manager,' said Margery. 'Have odd feeling that these things are ordained somehow'. Neither the bank manager nor the building society shared Margery's feeling. Herbert and Em proposed various schemes by which they might help but nothing which approached the £2,000 asking price. Margery began to 'get the wind up' about the cost. She was, as usual, short even of the wherewithal to pay their normal outgoings at Viaduct Farm. They took more friends over to D'Arcy House: Cooee, who was, said Margery, 'hysterical with delight' at the Old Doctor's stables, and Arthur and Betty Underwood, a London solicitor and his wife who opined that at anything under £1,500 it was 'a snip'. Only Phil of all the family was frankly appalled at the idea of buying 'Featherstone's House' and said so.

Pip was determined to have it. He grew angry with Margery for hanging back on the grounds of expense. Once again, there were 'sceans'. Although Margery had determination of her own and was well used to managing life in her own way, she never quite found the confidence to stand out against Pip when he really wanted something, nor to proceed with anything that he definitely didn't like. Suddenly Lilian Carter stepped in with a promise of Pip's inheritance in advance – £750. Pip offered Dr James' solicitors £1,000, half the asking price. And to their amazement, after the briefest of negotiations, their offer of £1,075 was accepted. (Earlier in the year the house had been privately on offer at £3,500.) There was scarcely time to give more than a cursory thought to the implications of all that they were taking on. 'I suppose we shall manage,' wrote Margery doubtfully. 'Pip still has no work. Rather scared. Hope to God it's going to work'.

When Margery reached a certain pitch of worry, the streak of fatalism in her, which she may have inherited from Granny, took over. She abdicated mentally, trusting God to see them through. (Pip in his turn left all such anxieties to Margery.) Her diary shows that she often felt put upon and resentful but rarely made a firm stand in her own defence. She was too conscious that she was responsible for their way of life so tended to suppress her doubts and carry on working. 'Have uncomfortable feeling that it's my fault,' she had written at Viaduct Farm. 'Have either taken on more than I can chew or else am trying to do a he-woman's job and do it nicely and in a feminine fashion. However there's not enough thinking time to worry about it all so I shall muddle on . . . The Lord will fix it, he always does.' Time after time Margery and Pip did come through, but opportunities were lost *en route* that clearer thinking and proper discussion might perhaps have salvaged.

In her periods of tiredness and depression Margery had felt that she and Pip needed some 'joint project' to pull them together again. She wondered whether a child might be the answer. The lady doctor in Chappel advised her to go ahead and try for one but in her heart Margery knew it was 'just not in his line'. She and Pip had arguments, 'kid v. car really', and too often the car, or whatever 'necessity' was under discussion, won. Even at Viaduct Farm the focus of their partnership had shifted from one founded on work to one which had a lifestyle at its heart, a lifestyle which Margery, not Pip, felt she was committed to maintaining. It seems obvious, in retrospect, that the move to D'Arcy House delivered the *coup de grâce* to any hopes Margery might have entertained of being able to step back far enough from her work to bear and bring up children.

Such hopes were probably never more than passing wishes. Cooee remembers the years before the Second World War at

Viaduct Farm and D'Arcy House as among the happiest in her life. 'We had such FUN!' she says. She, Pip and Grog were as one in their zestful enjoyment of horses and parties, light-hearted flirtations and practical jokes. She remembers Margery as devoted to her work, pleased to see them dressed up and setting out, apparently quite content with her responsibilities. In her diary, Margery sometimes calls the three of them 'the kids'. It was not, says Cooee, a way of life in which the inclusion of a real child could ever have been seriously considered.

Other friends have wondered since whether Margery's health, her large size and hormonal imbalance would have allowed her to conceive. As it was, her fertility was never put to the test. No impediment of that nature was recognised by Margery (or her doctor) at the time. She may have been afraid of the act of giving birth. Em's stories of travail had bred a lurking squeamishness in her daughters. Margery's increasingly frequent periods of depression and sense of deep exhaustion may have taken their toll on her initially adequate, rather jolly, physical relationship with Pip. She was 'too tired' at bedtime, 'ungracious' when he woke her in the night. Once past the age of thirty, she felt old. 'I must be ill,' she says to her diary, yet she appears to have done nothing to discover what was the matter.

More fundamentally still, it was not only Pip about whose parental instincts she was uncertain; she was not convinced that she had the necessary qualities to make a good mother herself. She was determined to succeed as an artist, and believed that the single-mindedness necessary to do so was just another form of selfishness. Children needed to be given time and attention from their parents, to be wanted and made to feel wanted. Margery's inclusion of the neglected little figure of Sarah Sutane in *Dancers in Mourning* (written 1936–7) is eloquent of the way memories of her own childhood in her parents' writing household may have contributed to a disinclination to insist on her right to bring up children of her own in a similar establishment. By 1937 when she was thirty-three years old, she seems to have decided finally that her novels were to be her children. She speaks of her 'maternal exuberance' over *Dancers* and later in that year announces to her close friend Louisa Callender (Charles Evans' secretary at Heinemann and a power there in her own right) that she is 'pregnant with book again'. The moment when actual children were a possibility had gone, mentally if not physically. It was a decision – or an indecision – that she afterwards regretted.

The financial strain imposed by D'Arcy House must have been conclusive. Lilian Carter's generosity meant that they had only had to meet a part of the purchase price from their own resources but these were already overstretched. The extra expenditure required just to keep the kitchen range alight, let alone maintain the garden, was not covered by any automatic increase in Margery's income. In fact, quite the reverse was true. They stayed at Viaduct Farm until June 1935, then moved to Tolleshunt D'Arcy with Grog, Cooee, Christina, two horses, a pony and several dogs. Once there, they hired a cook and re-employed Herbert Bullard who had worked since boyhood in Dr Salter's garden. 'Talkies' meanwhile had ousted silent films from the cinema and, as soon as they had settled in, Margery's employment, and income, from Aunt Maud came to an end.

She compensated as best she could by stepping up her short story output. *Strand* magazine, chronicler of Sherlock Holmes, offered a fairly steady market for detective adventures of a certain type – written, said Margery, 'for lonely exiles overseas who wanted to be reassured that London was "just the same". They realised that the petrol engine most have replaced the hansom cab, presumably, but did not want the news rubbed in.' Though she used the character of Albert Campion for some of these stories, she did so reluctantly and as sparingly as the editor would allow. Several such *Strand* stories were collected during 1939 in *Mr Campion and Others* and it is noticeable in them that the character does not have the personal, authorial significance that increasingly he was bearing in the novels.

The Evening News was another outlet for short stories and their friends Roger Pippett at the *Daily Herald* and Robert St John Cooper at the *Express* were able to put occasional reviewing opportunities in Margery's way. She began her third serial for *Answers*. Serial and cheap book rights from her earlier novels could occasionally raise £50 – £60. Heinemann's royalty rates were generous and the extra advertising they had given *Death of a Ghost* pushed its sales beyond anything she had so far achieved. In the first nine months after publication, it had earned her almost £250 with which she was delighted. Nevertheless she was far from expecting her Campion novels to support a household such as theirs. Although the film work had been a thoroughly uncongenial chore, both for her and for Grog (to whom she dictated), there was nothing yet to compensate for that trickle of regular money.

She was in the midst of *Flowers for the Judge* when they arrived at D'Arcy. Arguably the most classic of her detective stories, at its end it springs out of detective story routine with an acrobatic ease. Joyce has always felt sure that Margery was thinking of Phil when she wrote *Flowers*. Not in any exact sense – the description of Ritchie Barnabas could not be a description of Phil Allingham – but in the relationship between two worlds; between a London publishing house and an address c/o the World's Fair, which provides the key to the plot. As in *Police at the Funeral* and *Death of a Ghost*, the reader is left with a surprise perspective on a character as well as the solution to a puzzle.

Margery had dedicated her earlier novel *Look to the Lady* to Phil, under his nickname of 'Orlando'. Its *mélange* of full-blooded gypsies, fairground characters and race touts is vigorous, colourful and unextraordinary. The discovery made during *Flowers for the Judge* (dedicated to her publishers) is the essential otherness of the world that Phil had chosen. In *Flowers*, one person cannot live comfortably at both The Sign of the Golden Quiver (publishers since 1810) and the travelling show.

After *Cheapjack*, Phil could have established himself in a more conventionally successful manner. He discovered a talent for broadcasting and gave several talks for the B.B.C. His articles were in demand and there was talk of him and Margery writing 'Lavengro' stories together. But the pull of the road was too strong for Phil. A reading of *Cheapjack* beside, for instance, *Jeremy's England*, which was Tibby Clarke's second volume of autobiography (also published in 1934), makes plain the difference between them. Tibby was sowing his wild oats and gleaning journalistic copy from low company while remaining essentially a Cambridge chap; Phil, far more deeply identified with the vagrant life, was discovering his true self within its distinctive culture. In the 1930s at least, Herbert's children cherished the belief that there was gypsy blood in their family. As Margery became better known, she was sometimes asked whether she was related to the Irish expatriate poet, William Allingham. She had 'always understood', she replied to one especially formal enquirer, 'that the common ancestor was a James Allingham of Ireland who had two families of which the poet was descended from the first and herself from the second.' She did not see fit to append her belief that the ancestress of this second family, theirs, was a gypsy woman.

The Allinghams had accepted Phil's chosen way of life without great difficulty. While Em took Joyce to Oberammergau with the Girls' Friendly Society in 1934, Herbert, in his mid-sixties, went on the road with Phil and Three-Fingered Billy for a month. He remained interested and uncensorious throughout – though he was glad to return home to his and Em's seaside villa at Thorpe Bay. Margery found herself more anxious about the company Phil kept when he was having 'stupendous' times in London, than when he was safely off to Hull Fair or Wakes Week in Ashton-under-Lyne. Towards the end of the decade, however, when Joyce announced that she was leaving her job in publishing to go on the road with Phil, Margery was far from acquiescent. Joyce went all the same and her career as Phil's assistant was interrupted only by the outbreak of World War Two.

Pip's reactions were ambivalent. He had enjoyed the publishing excitement of *Cheapjack* and had spent enough time promoting the book with Phil in London to begin to irritate Margery who had been left on her own in Chappel to ghost Phil's articles. 'Suppose he's only young once,' she mutters in her diary. Once Pip and Margery had moved to 'the Featherstones' house and had begun to behave accordingly, Pip's personal friendship with Phil waned. Phil visited D'Arcy House only rarely and friends of Pip's gained the impression that he would have preferred to disown his vagabond brother-in-law. For Margery, however, Phil's arrival 'was always an event'. She was delighted to see him and his over-laden car and was equally ready to store his grafter's gear or lend him a fiver as required.

In the days when they had lived at home together, Phil and Margery had been both devoted confederates and occasionally enraged adversaries. 'Phil a very unbearable young puppy nowadays,' wrote Margery aged sixteen. Phil retained the ability to upset Margery in a way which she seems to have thought of as peculiar to blood-relations and about which she makes several slightly cryptic asides in the brother/sister scenes of *Fashion in Shrouds* (1938). He admired his older sister but was not in awe of her, as Joyce certainly was. His quick wits and alert sense of humour might have made him a tease to be reckoned with – particularly if she appeared at all sanctimonious. Though they remained personally close and available to each other in times of need, *Flowers for the Judge*, commenced at Viaduct Farm and completed at D'Arcy House, represents Margery's instinctive recognition, almost before the event, that their ways, as literary lady and successful grafter, had parted.

Before their arrival in Tolleshunt D'Arcy, Margery had felt some nervousness as to whether they would be accepted by the local community. A diary note from December 1934 reads, 'Went over to D'Arcy to see about pond. Saw Jessie and Bill. Both seem to be pleased to see us. Let's hope they still feel like smiling this time next year – Hope we don't disgrace ourselves.' As it transpired, Jessie Bacon, a self-contained and independent old lady, had no wish to interest herself in the doings at D'Arcy House. She lived out her last years in the cottage that the Doctor had left her and only had anything to do with Margery when Em visited on the congenial business of The Salter Relief Fund. Bill Bullard, the elder of Dr Salter's surviving gardeners, was long past retirement age and adequately provided for. His son Herbert continued, partly at Em's insistence, to be employed in the garden.

Margery's apprehension was not unjustified. D'Arcy House was far more prominent in its village than anywhere she had lived previously and the village was a more demanding community.

There were invisible networks of service and obligation that ignorant newcomers disregarded at their peril. There was plain unfriendliness too. One small boy, from the upper echelons of the D'Arcy social scale, remembers his first sight of 'this fat lady' crossing the Square. 'Go away,' he said – echoing those at home? – 'we don't want you here.' Margery, he recalls, took this calmly. He was soon devoted to her and is generous with his praise for the part which she came to play locally – giving such effective service to the community that some ladies in his own family, accustomed to being Ladies Bountiful, were quite frankly jealous.

Initially it was Cooee whom the people of Tolleshunt D'Arcy saw most frequently. Born a townie in Maida Vale, she was utterly absorbed in her new-found love of horses. As well as going hunting, working for her horsemaster qualification and giving riding lessons to the children of friends, as she had done at Chappel, the facilities of D'Arcy House encouraged Cooee to dream of breeding horses – as the Old Doctor had done there before her. The local blacksmith, Norry Emeny, took her and her friend Valentine Crittall in hand almost as a matter of course, and excited them with tales of the turf. Horse shows and point-to-point meetings became key events in their lives.

While Grog crept out, sketchbook in hand, to capture Cooee and Valentine tumbling off at enormous fences or hacking home disconsolately through the rain, Margery observed them curiously and from a distance. Preparations for a horse show seemed 'a hell of a set-out' to her and she was horrified by the dangerousness of the point-to-points. She used Cooee's new world as background for one short story, *Sweet and Low* (1937), but it was not successful, and was declined by Reeves Shaw at *Strand* magazine. Only the travails of horse-breeding made an enduring mark on Margery's imagination.

What the neighbours saw was an attractive young girl, who was also an ex-actress, riding through the village high on a thoroughbred hunter, not only with Valentine, but regularly with Margery's husband Pip. They drew their erroneous conclusions but were not unduly shocked. Tolleshunt D'Arcy was a hierarchical society and they were used to 'characters'. Many of them had grown up under the despotism of the Doctor's religious counterpart, the Rev. Bobby Graves, who lived there still in retirement with his younger second wife. His handsome profile, it was whispered, had been reproduced in several other families within his parish. 'Goings-on' were nothing new; neither were certain types of eccentricity. The 'boxing baronet' Sir Claude de Crespigny had been prominent among the Old Doctor's cronies and a fruitful focus for tall tales locally. The farming community outside the village kept their characteristic distance – and edged up to Valentine Crittall for details once it became known that she was friendly with this new and odd household.

Pip liked Tolleshunt D'Arcy. He ranged himself immediately on the side of the squirearchy and grew rapidly less bohemian. Here he was a man of property. The annual cricket matches which had formed the basis of their raffish summer parties at Chappel were re-established on a more formal footing at D'Arcy. The local cricket team were granted permission to use what was now 'Mr Carter's meadow' and he was soon active in local affairs. Margery hung back, nervously aware, like her character Linda Sutane in *Dancers in Mourning*, of the multiplicity of ways in which households such as her own could offend against the hidden conventions of a rural community. Pip felt no such inhibitions. Within the narrow scope of old-fashioned village life, he was at ease. Far more at ease than the open-minded Herbert had managed to be when he had lived three miles away and a quarter of a century earlier at Layer Breton.

There were, in fact, several professional families residing locally. The village was then served by the railway (the 'Crab and Winkle' line which ran on across the marsh to Tollesbury) and some businessmen found this convenient for work in the City. Pip became friendly with Edward Terrell, member of the Middle Temple and Recorder of Newbury; with John Hortin, businessman and wine-lover with whom he took gourmet trips to 'Frogland', and with other members of the Hortin family who lived in post-Edwardian splendour at another Big House, Guisnes Court. The friendship with Ronnie Reid and his family continued and was supplemented by close links with the Carters' local doctor, James Madden.

As he settled into this new way of life, delicately sprinkled with titles and Old Money, Pip forgot his own meritocratic, Watford origins and became more confidently intolerant. Where he could, he 'cut' those people of whom he did not approve; socialists and homosexuals were automatic victims. Valentine Crittall's father, head of a notable Essex family, a rich man – and the first Labour Member of Parliament for the (local) Maldon division in the mid-1920s – tried his self-control. Such people, Pip and some of his friends maintained, were 'traitors to their class'. Valentine, very much younger than he, resented his continual gibing at herself for her father's achievements. She felt powerless to retaliate and learned to avoid Pip as she would any other bully.

Margery, Valentine thought, was invariably kind and cheerful. She called everybody 'ducky' and loved to make generous gestures. On hearing that Cooee and Valentine were establishing their equine business together, Margery made them a gift of ornately-headed, high quality business stationery with which they were to impress potential customers. Valentine remembers her wearing the long dresses in which she was most comfortable at home and with 'a young face on an old body'. She wheezed slightly, Valentine noticed, if she came down to watch them with the horses in the paddock. Cooee sometimes hinted to her friend that Margery was not as carefree as she liked to appear but there was never any mention of a specific health problem. If there was, it is likely that Valentine would have remembered. Like many others she had wondered idly why Margery was so overweight; unlike those others, she would have understood completely if thyroid deficiency (for which Margery had been prescribed the remedy in 1931) had been mentioned. Her own father was being treated for the condition throughout the 1930s and was struggling against feelings of lethargy and depression similar to those which dogged Margery throughout the decade.

Beneath its blithe surface, Margery and Pip's household was not a happy one in the later 1930s. Domestically, Christina, who had been employed merely as the housemaid, was steadily taking control, thus freeing Margery from many practical anxieties. Christina 'liked to see jobs done properly' and had been scandalised by the indifferent service Margery had been given at Chappel. Emotionally, however, the lively personalities of the 'white-collar' members of the household could brew up disturbing storms.

There was an episode when Dr James Madden, then a bachelor, received an anonymous letter written on D'Arcy House paper suggesting that he marry Cooee. He promptly brought it round demanding to know who had written it. Accusation and counter-accusation flared, Margery tabulated each person's motive and opportunity, but found herself reduced to hysterical weeping by her inability to detect a culprit as neatly in real life as she regularly did in fiction. She referred to the episode briefly in a short story (*The Mistress in the House*) written early in 1937 – the hero's advice there is unequivocal, 'sack 'em at once, sack 'em all or you won't have a moment's peace'. More relevant perhaps is the convincing manner in which Margery shows utterly petty, slightly unkind practical jokes poisoning the life of a household in *Dancers in Mourning*, the novel she wrote during 1936–7.

Before the commencement of that book, she had a true crisis to endure. On January 10th 1936, barely six months after Margery and Pip had set up home at Tolleshunt D'Arcy, Herbert Allingham died. He and Margery had had their quarrels. Mac wrote to her on one occasion begging her 'not to be so hard on that fond parent of yours'. Herbert, fortunately, had known when to step back from his children's lives, waiting patiently until they needed him again. His marriage had had to be conducted on the same un-possessive principles.

When Pip was working closely with Margery on their early adventure stories, Herbert took little part. He noted their successes in his diary and listened when sections were read to him at house-changeover times. The proximity of Shelley to Chappel had provided him and Margery renewed opportunities to enjoy one another's company and it is clear, from his diary, that they continued to write to one another frequently. The single letter that survives is written to Herbert by Margery from Viaduct Farm, and is full of the trivia of her daily life as well as news of her writing and pen-portraits of the editorial offices that were known to them both. It's a spontaneously amusing as well as affectionate letter. As much as shared experience, shared jokes formed the vital bonds in Margery's view of family relationships.

Herbert had supported the move to D'Arcy House and during 1935 was more closely involved with Margery and her work than he had been for ten years. Pip had little to do with *Flowers for the Judge* whereas Herbert not only listened to sections regularly but felt able to comment at some length. He gave her a present – several pages of a well-worked-out plot for a new novel which she never seems to have used. Scarcely a week of 1935 went by without some mention of Margery in Herbert's diary – until November when he succumbed to his last illness. His final entry, made on November 13th, 'Read Margery's story,' trails off the page exhaustedly.

The new year, 1936, opened with Herbert dying in a Colchester nursing home and Em staying in D'Arcy House with Margery and Pip. It was a dreadful time. The gradual slipping away of Herbert, at every visit weaker and more speechless, was counterpointed by extraordinary and unpredictable displays of temperament from Em. She was 'vague' about Herbert's condition, made a scene when she thought Pip had not acknowledged her in the passage, talked of her own 'extraordinary virtue' and Margery's 'sinfulness' and continually returned to the theme that she was 'destined' to live at D'Arcy House.

Even when she was more normally 'nervy' and upset, Margery dared not feel too sorry for her. Conscious that 'one of the two supports of my world is going', she feared that she had somehow been 'caught' by Em and the Old Doctor. She knew, too, that Pip's forbearance was being pushed to its limits. A typical diary entry for January 5th 1936 reads: 'A terrible, terrible day. The old boy much worse. Did not see him. Joyce and Phil went together – not anxious to intrude or, more honestly, to share. Em horrible over the book. Dreadful scene, just like her. Kids thoroughly frightened of her. Seems to have come down and taken possession of our house. Kids off to Town. Pip amazingly good. Frightened myself. Em talking of Old Doc.'

On one occasion Em returned from the hospital wearing a ring of Dr Salter's which she had taken off Herbert's semi-conscious hand. Margery could scarcely bear it. With Pip's support she went over to Pope's and poured out her problems to Aunt Grace and her husband Steve. Granny, Em's mother, now aged 86, was also there and a welcome for Em was assured – if, said Grace, she could possibly contribute something to the household funds – ? Her own days of affluence were long gone. Margery returned home and managed 'a long, reasonable talk' with Em. She offered a room in D'Arcy House always and storage of any furniture or personal belongings, but she was adamant that Em could not live with them permanently. It helped that the house was, at this stage, officially Pip's.

This seemed to work. Herbert's last few days of life passed away with no dramatic scenes being enacted among his family. After the funeral, Em went to stay at Pope's, returning only to discuss financial matters with Margery. 'Mother over to see about insurance. Talked carefully to her. Feel she understands me. She is radiant and very important. Feel horrible – I do miss the old man – but its much better she should take it like this. Oh dear, I don't know what I think. Life is very complex.'

The King, George V, was also dying. The D'Arcy household was rocked by another emotional tempest, this time over a horse of Cooee's. Cooee decided to leave. The King died. 'Death seems to be everywhere,' wrote Margery. The newspapers were lined with black and a six month period of public mourning was announced. Cooee visited her mother and returned 'chastened'. Margery had suffered the 'awfulness' of sorting through all her father's papers and was struggling to return to normal, and start writing again. She had finished the third of her 'Maxwell March' serials (*The Devil and Her Son*) in the weeks before Herbert died and now dashed off a short (and not very good) story, *The Beauty King*, simply in order to get pen to paper. 'Frantically anxious to begin something.' The project which finally engaged her attention was her 'new Campion story', the novel, *Dancers in Mourning*.

Taken as a detective story, *Dancers in Mourning* is good enough. When it was published in 1937, it quickly outsold anything Margery had written previously and was exceptionally well-reviewed. In the opinion of those critics who indulged in comparisons, it was the moment at which Margery decisively outstripped her contemporary, Dorothy Sayers, who that year published the disappointing *Busman's Honeymoon*. In retrospect it may be seen that both writers were coming to terms, in their separate ways, with a disillusion with the scope of the 'classic' 1930s detective novel. Both had produced excellent examples of the genre with *Death of a Ghost* and *The Nine Tailors* in 1934, *Flowers for the Judge* and *Gaudy Night* in 1935. Both would be seeking new directions after 1937.

Margery's strength at this point in her life was as a domestic writer. Taken as a novelist's portrait of a troubled, disintegrating household, *Dancers in Mourning* is a better book than it is a crime story. There is too much complication and petty sub-villainy for a satisfying puzzle. This becomes obvious if the bare plot of *Dancers* is compared with either of its predecessors, *Flowers* and *Death of a Ghost*. Margery was at her best when using the small world of home to focus powerfully on the trivial but revealing interactions between people. If someone in a household will regularly help himself to anyone else's coat, neither asking permission nor feeling any obligation to return the garment; if he has no thought of helping in a family emergency, or the vestiges of tact at a time of grief, he may be a 'genius' but he is a bad and dangerous person.

Her novels had moved on from offering definable qualities such as greed or revenge as motivating forces for crime, to more generally applicable questions of ethics, and the exploration of 'types of mind'. The essential question in *Dancers* that Campion must ask is not who did what? where? when? or how? but 'Who was the little god of this circle?' Who was it 'who was flattered and cozened and protected until his opinion of his own importance had lost all touch with reality?' A good question.

Margery had learned much about households since their move to Essex. Now she had further adjustments to make: to life without Herbert, to a measure of responsibility for Em, to the community within which they had come to live. *Dancers in*

Mourning helped her express her problems but could offer few conclusions. Its leading characters decide that emigration is the only solution to the pressures they face. The novel may have provided Margery with one small, personal exorcism. The character of Dr Bouverie is an unusually exact depiction of Dr Salter.

Margery was in general careful that her identifications of real people with her fictional characters should be imaginative rather than accurate in every detail, Salter, though, was dead – and Margery was left feeling threatened by his spirit and by the house which he had made so particularly his own. The details of Campion's midnight visit from White Walls to Dr Bouverie's home (covering the same distance as The Old Rectory, Layer Breton, to D'Arcy House) are meticulously correct – even down to the Victorian porch which Dr Salter once had on the house.

Margery's diary for January 21st 1936 reads: 'Tried to work out some of the new story . . . went over to see Jessie. She showed me a snap of the house when it still had its original porch. Interesting. Always a barracky place.' And in Chapter IV of the 'new story': 'Campion discovered that the dark wall which he had taken to be the side of a rural factory was the front of a bleak Georgian house. A Victorian porch, fastened with solid wooden doors, stuck out into the road at an angle no modern council would dream of sanctioning.'

Despite Dr James' occupancy, D'Arcy House remained littered with Dr Salter's paraphernalia when Margery and Pip moved in. These and Margery's memories of the 'God-like' figure of her childhood are incorporated into the figure of Dr Bouverie. In the novel, however, Campion views Bouverie/Salter as a comic figure for all his autocratic impressiveness. He is shrewd, but not quite shrewd enough to understand the modern world. It is to be hoped that Margery gained some personal relief from thus limiting the Old Doc's ghost.

Margery's diary is blank after the end of January 1936 and no letters have survived to describe how she coped with her great bereavement. Later she said she had gained some comfort from knowing that her father was at peace. She also said she felt some of his qualities (the sense of responsibility perhaps) continuing within herself. She was, nevertheless, 'horribly miserable'. The note that rings truest is the comment after Em's 'radiant' post-funeral visit, the heartfelt, exhausted admission, 'Oh dear, I don't know what I think. Life is very complex.'

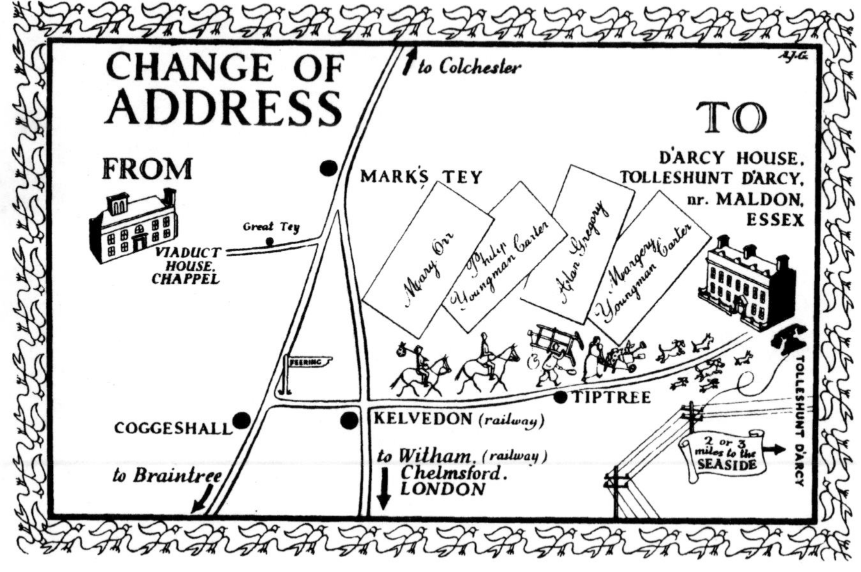

Change of Address card
by A. J. Gregory

William and Louise Allingham with six of their sons and four daughters-in-law

Phil and Margery Allingham, c 1909

Em and Herbert Allingham on their engagement, c 1902

Layer Breton Rectory

William McFee and Herbert Allingham with an unidentified child

Margery at the Miss Dobsons'

Margery, Em, Joyce and Phil, c 1919

Maine B House, Christ's Hospital, c 1919 (Pip is standing fifth from left, second row from back. Grog is second from left, middle row)

Dr J. H. Salter in his drawing room

Dido and Aeneas, 1922. Margery and Angela Doubleday are seated centre (both bewigged), Millicent Read is gesticulating, Josephina De Vasconcellos far right *(Harry Smith, Fleet Street)*

Photograph of Margery taken for *Blackerchief Dick*, 1923 *(HANA)*

Miss Louie Bagley, c 1926

Herbert and 'his most industrious apprentice'

In 'The Half Nelson' at Viaduct Farmhouse, c 1932

'Partners in Crime', Pip and Margery working in the garden at Letheringham, c 1928

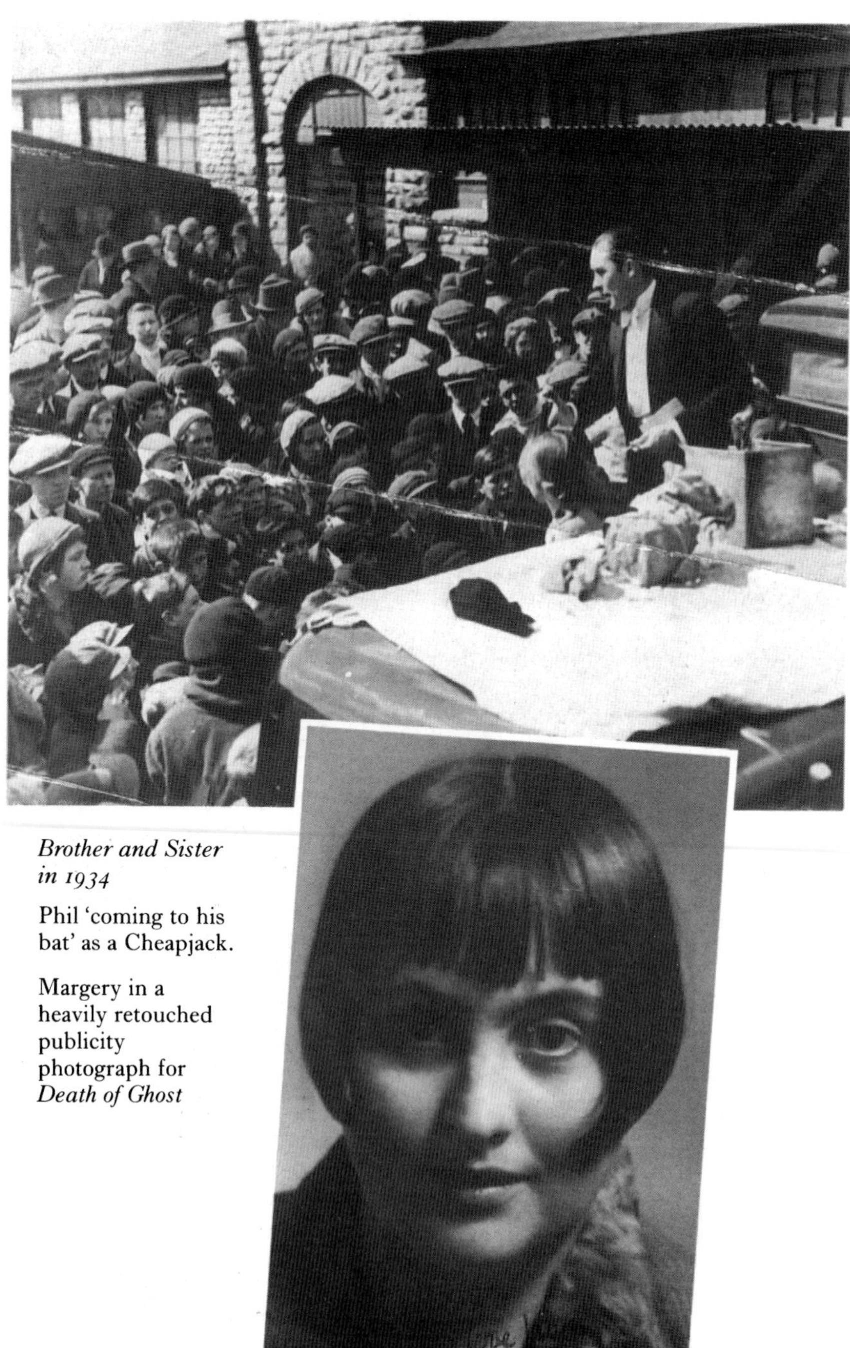

Brother and Sister in 1934

Phil 'coming to his bat' as a Cheapjack.

Margery in a heavily retouched publicity photograph for *Death of Ghost*

D'Arcy House *(Essex County Standard)*

Margery in her drawing room, c 1937 *(Bertram Park)*

Russell Meiggs in much later life

Margery with her new 1940s hairstyle *(Howard Coster)* surrounding her clockwise from top r.h. corner: Joyce in the WRNS, Betty Carter in the ATS, Pip in the RASC, Phil in the RASC and Grog in the RAF

XII

'What is the Reason for Me?'

1937–1938

'Thought for the year,' wrote Margery wryly at the commencement of her 1937 diary: 'We like your heart's blood, bleed away.' This and the following year, 1938, would bring her a higher degree of public recognition than she had achieved so far – and a more mature awareness of the cost of her success.

Diary entries for January '37 are somewhat monotonous: 'wrote all day', 'wrote all day', 'worked all day'. She was completing *Dancers in Mourning* with one of her characteristic late bursts of energy. She was also refusing to consider their 'alarming' financial situation until the book was done. Pip was shooting, Cooee hunting, Grog up to Town and all three out to dinner as usual. Margery had some difficulty persuading Grog to find time to help her with the typing. Hours at her desk made her neck and shoulders stiff. She employed a masseuse to keep her limber and carried on. Blocked sinuses were a problem. She promised a friend that she would visit a pathologist or endocrinologist 'when the book is done' – there is nothing to say whether or not she did so.

Grog was there to take her dictation of the long final section of the novel. By this stage in her writer's development Margery spent much longer re-drafting and polishing her work. It was correspondingly important, or so she believed, to be able to re-dictate the final version to this trusted friend, in order that the book should retain a sense of spontaneity. She was glad of his support too and never more happy than when Pip was working simultaneously on a design for the novel's cover. They sat up into the early hours of the morning to complete *Dancers*. 'Quite an emotional finish. Like old times again. We're very sanguine.' As she looked back over the novel, Margery felt most satisfied with her portrait of Sutane 'the worker, the man who recognised his responsibilities and was secretly appalled by them'. So many livelihoods rested on Sutane's dancing feet as they did on Margery's inspiration.

She dispatched the novel to Dwye Evans at Heinemann 'with a careful letter' and waited anxiously for his response. Dwye was Charles Evans' eldest son and had been a director of Heinemann since 1933. He was a few years younger than Margery, a fact which may have accounted for some of the tension in their relationship. She was more at ease with men older than herself – a legacy from the days when her father was her editor. She remained grateful to Charles Evans for his initial support of *Police at the Funeral* and his advice to 'try a novel next time'. The older Evans was one of the outstanding publishers of fiction within his generation and was particularly proud of his reputation for spotting and encouraging younger authors. Margery's exact contemporary Graham Greene owed much to Evans' financial support in the early stages of his career, as did her friend, Kate O'Brien, whose first novel *Without My Cloak* had been published by Heinemann in 1931, and had won the Hawthornden Prize. Charles Evans became Margery's editorial yardstick. 'Of course, he's no Charles Evans,' she said of her American publisher, Malcolm Johnson, when he tried to take his blue pencil to *Flowers for the Judge*.

This attitude posed particular difficulties for Charles Evans' son as he assumed greater responsibility for Margery's work. Dwye was financially astute and would later be a good chairman for the company in difficult times. Although he and Pip were friends and Dwye an occasional guest at summer cricket parties, he has said since that he found Margery difficult to deal with; she demanded praise, resented criticism and had, he thought, an inflated idea of her own abilities. With the advantage of Margery's diary, it is possible to see that she was at her most insecure when she had packed up her book and sent it out of the household to her publishers. The surge of optimism which she felt on actual completion – 'Bloody good story though I say it' – evaporated at once and she remained acutely uneasy until Dwye rang or telephoned. She then needed to ask, with cautious urgency, for whatever part of her advance might be due. In this case Dwye sent £90 in January (£100 less the commission for Margery's agent A. P. Watt) and the same sum again in February. Both amounts were hastened to the bank. 'So we go on. Another block of ice, Eliza!'

Margery's relationship with her American publishers, Doubleday, had been enhanced from the late '20s onwards by the character of their London representatives; first Mary Leonard, optimistic and full of high spirits, then, from 1932 to 1954, Winifred Nerney, an older woman, as ready to 'clown' and come to parties as Mary Leonard, but possessing a more down-to-earth attitude and an outstanding quality of kindness. Winifred (known to Margery as 'Nerney') had been secretary to Arnold Bennett until his death in 1931 and transferred the intelligent devotion from which he had benefited, to her new employers, Doubleday. Nothing, in Nerney's opinion, was too good for the Doubleday authors in her care. There was a motherliness in her attitude to Margery which bred a great affection, even dependence, in its recipient. Margery was the more irritated by Joyce's decision to join forces with Phil in 1938, because it was the position of Nerney's secretary that she would be relinquishing.

When she had received Doubleday's copy of *Dancers in Mourning*, Nerney wrote to America for some money for Margery. Meanwhile the D'Arcy House supply of coal ran out. 'Have faif!' said Margery to herself. In less than two months after she had finished *Dancers* and before she settled to serious consideration of her next novel, Margery wrote a horsy romance, a ghost story, at least two detective and three general short stories, and put together a collection, *Mr Campion, Criminologist*, for sale in America. Various small sums of money came in. Even so when Watt advanced £50 in May, it went straight out again to settle food bills run up in February.

Towards the end of April when there were ominous signs that Em might be heading for another breakdown, Margery's first reaction was panic. How could she meet the doctor's fees? 'I'm praying for a little money for without it I can't handle the situation at all and I am responsible.'

After Herbert's death in 1936, Em had sublet their house in Thorpe Bay, spent time at Pope's with Grace and Granny, and paid regular but brief visits to Tolleshunt D'Arcy. Early in 1937 she went as a paying guest to the Rev. Marcus Lawrence in Foulness Island Rectory with some idea of beginning to write again. She described Foulness, near the mouth of the river Thames, as being '1837 not 1937. You can't come onto the island without a permit as the Army are in charge. We have oil lamps and the roads except for the one cement road through the place are deep ruts and winding paths across fields – like Mersea used to be before the war.' The rector's wife had been in an asylum for many years and Em decided that he and his belongings had been 'shamefully' mistreated in her absence. Em liked a Cause and was immediately happy on Foulness. She did no writing but set to work to improve living conditions at the Rectory and was soon installed as the housekeeper.

Something in Em's exuberant behaviour alarmed her children. They remembered the spring five years ago when she had been taken to Northampton. Joyce wrote to Margery, Margery consulted James Madden and invited Em and Rev. Lawrence to dinner. During the evening Dr Madden seems to have been convinced that Em was suffering some mental disturbance. Margery thought she was 'ill not mad'. To make matters worse Marcus Lawrence made it plain that he disliked and suspected Margery. 'I am living in luxury, Em has to work for her keep and I won't have her here.' There was enough truth in this to hurt. Pip meanwhile was 'rattled' and angrily forbidding Margery to have Her in the house. There were rows. The doctor on Foulness Island had just managed to calm the situation and reassure all concerned when Phil went to visit his mother. He decided that Em was 'bad', drove to Tolleshunt D'Arcy and 'went off' at Margery 'like an antagonistic dynamo'. 'I disgraced myself by bursting into tears before he'd been in the house ten minutes.'

Despite this, Margery had made up her mind that there was nothing she could do. 'I'm taking it that I made a mistake and she was simply over-excited.' If her mother was in some way attracted to the parson, that was her mother's business. Margery felt she'd made a complete mess of the situation and was tired out. She missed Herbert, was irritable, weepy, in her own parlance 'thoroughly demoralised'. The forceful temperaments within her household were too much for her. 'Row with the boys. Find I can't even snap when I'm nervy without having an avalanche of fury descend on my head. Bloody miserable and broke. Started to make fair copy of story.' She had several places around the house where she liked to write including one tiny room off a back stairway to which she could retire and literally pull the steps up behind her. Next day she 'dictated story – Not so bad at all – Felt better at once!'

June, July and August passed cheerfully enough on the surface. Margery and Cooee began re-painting the back of the house, the more homely side away from the splendid brick facade. This was the aspect that Margery thought resembled 'a heap of up-ended egg boxes'. Architecturally, D'Arcy House consists of a Queen Anne dwelling superimposed on an older Tudor building and has thus a two-fold personality. The front rooms, that is the drawing room and dining room, are beautifully proportioned, panelled, corniced; not too large to be comfortable but well able to evoke an atmosphere of gracious living. The main staircase turns elegantly down between them and the bedrooms in the front of the house are poised and spacious. Margery's sense of style was expressed by the furniture and ornaments she chose. Even in the Holborn flat she and Pip had managed to include a pretty four-poster bed. In Essex she became (when money allowed) a regular buyer at local auctions with an eye for unusual as well as conventionally 'good' items.

The rooms at the rear of the house are more haphazard. Doors, steps and cupboards have been rearranged as if each generation of owners had a different idea of what suited them. Heavy beams from old ships' timbers are much in evidence and at the heart of the house is the small, square room with the stone-flagged floor that became Pip and Margery's bar. It has a high serving counter and a bench running round the walls. They installed the shove ha'penny board that they had brought with them from Viaduct Farm and were for ever adding to the collection of cartoons and souvenirs with which they decorated it.

There was plenty of work to be done to maintain the house and garden and throughout the summer of 1937 plenty of visitors arrived to enjoy them. Yet in Margery's mind there ran an instability and a niggling dissatisfaction with herself and her lot. For various reasons she was finding it difficult to work and unless she was working she was not truly at ease. It was not only their crying need for cash that made it so hard for her to take a holiday and have fun. Deep down she had not moved far from the belief, probably engendered in childhood, that only her work gave her any value as a person. During the summer of '37 she enjoyed friendships, parties and her lovely garden but made no progress with her new novel. Extracts from her diary towards the end of August give a picture of her state of mind in what was, for many reasons, an unsettled period. August 25th: 'Carter to Town. Line from S. Paws telling me to get on with story. Trying to. Still having bad time mentally. Suppose it's alright – have faif. Albert putting bog in big bathroom. Must work, must work, finding it very hard.' The 26th: '. . . Tried to work. Did a bit. In a funny mental state. Getting to dislike myself as a responsibility . . .' 27th: 'Still pottering instead of working. Infuriated with myself. Did a bit,' and 28th: 'watched a cricket match instead of working. Feel I'm losing my grip or something.'

Margery was naturally a seasonal writer. Late autumn was her best time for planning and beginning a new project and the new year gave her stimulus for intense periods of concentrated work. In late spring/early summer she could be at her most emotionally vulnerable – typescripts of the novels had often gone to her publishers at Easter time – and during high summer she 'conceived a nausea at the smell of ink and a great dislike of sitting indoors all day'. It seems a pity that she could not allow herself to be idle, to watch a cricket match and enjoy it. As her books became more serious they needed time to evolve and new stories had, using her characteristic expression, to be 'incubated'. It was not until she was a more mature and financially successful author that she was able to recognise the way her creative mind functioned and try to worry less about the length of time it took.

Reviews of *Dancers*, published by Heinemann in June 1937,

had been outstanding. She longed to write 'my novel' – but was not ready to risk the loss of her regular detective fiction sales. By November she had made some slow headway into the book, *The Fashion in Shrouds*, that was intended to do both; to be a 'formal novel of contemporary manners' and a whodunnit. 'A satirical comedy contrasting the careers of two young women who have fallen in love with the same man,' she explained, 'fits in neatly beside the straightforward detective story with its odd "hand of fate" motif.' This was later, in 1965. In 1937 as she struggled with the early chapters, Margery felt herself floundering – probably because she had not allowed herself sufficient time to mull it over during the summer. 'Having great difficulty with *Shrouds*. Am in one of those moods when I wonder if it's worth writing at all or if I ought to take up washing as a profession. Sometimes I feel it may be alright and sometimes it's just dead and bloody.'

Through the last months of 1937 and the first of the new year Margery remained 'frightened', 'nervy' and 'miserable'. She was desperate to 'get *on*' with the novel but found herself working very slowly indeed. Two bouts of sinusitis kept her in bed. She felt so ill at one point that she decided she had meningitis and was going to die. Her friend Dr James Madden told her firmly there was nothing wrong with her head, she was just run down. Whether she had been seeking reassurance, or whether the days in bed had enforced less conscious consideration of the book, after chapter nine (the point at which she had been taken ill) the story began to 'move'. *The Fashion in Shrouds* is unusual among Margery's novels to this date in that murder is not committed until the tenth chapter – the very point at which the book seems to find its momentum. 'Getting interested in the story at last.' Once the narrative begins to flow, the anxieties and opinions of the author, which can seem both obtrusive and contentious in the early pages, dovetail in behind the narrative bringing the book close to achieving its difficult, two-fold aim.

Comparing this first *Fashion in Shrouds* with the later, heavily-cut version prepared in 1965, emphasises the extent to which it was a novel of its time. James Laver, a distinguished contemporary writer with whom Margery briefly corresponded, describes the era of 'Between The Wars', which by this time was visibly coming to a close, as 'hectic, frivolous, frustrated, puzzled, frantic'. 'Whatever happens, whatever happens,' Margery promised herself after the declaration of hostilities on September 3rd 1939, 'never go pretending that things were going well before the war. Never deceive yourself that you could not foresee a dead end . . . I knew what I meant,' she continued, 'though I had not been able to nail it down before.'

With *The Fashion in Shrouds* she had come close to doing so. The novel marks a move out from her domestic world to offer a wider view of society. It is a crowded novel. Through it she conveys the very texture of pre-war success – the places to go, people to be seen with, the wines and foods for connoisseurs, the glorious cut and shimmer of choice fabrics. This last was especially congenial. Margery's personal notion of a binge, reminiscent of her costume-making days, was to go to town and buy yards of chintz, velvet, voile, satin, artificial silk. Some of it might lie unused for years – and was unexpectedly welcome in the period of rationing which lay ahead. She retained a keen appreciation of fashion, made or refurbished many of her own clothes and was adept at putting together a 'new' wardrobe for a stay in London without spending more than a few shillings. And 'she did look smart when she got herself up,' recalls Christina appreciatively.

Margery was encouraged to look beyond her house and garden during 1937–8. In the middle of her mother's springtime crisis, she was momentarily flattered to receive an invitation to list her achievements for *Who's Who*. (With a glance towards the Old Doctor's still-burgeoning conservatory, she listed 'begonias' among her recreations!) She had become pen-friendly with the novelist and influential critic Frank Swinnerton, a fervent admirer of her work, and on her trips to London she met A. A. Milne and the novelist Margery Sharp. She and Pip were already friendly with the thriller writer Francis Gerard and met Jan Struther, creator of *Mrs Miniver*. She attended a Foyle's literary lunch and in the autumn of 1938 organised and manned a 'Sleuths' Corner' at the *Sunday Times* National Book Fair.

She was invited to review new novels for the weekly magazine *Time and Tide*. On another trip to London she lunched with its owner and editor Lady Rhondda and her friend, the magazine's literary editor, Theodora Bosanquet. 'Wrong hat' was Margery's sole diary comment after this meeting (rather in the manner of the magazine's archetypal Provincial Lady, E. M. Delafield!). However the friendship initiated with Theodora Bosanquet proved lasting if somewhat distant. Their shared interest in parapsychology proved a bond and a few days later Margery 'lent Miss Bosanquet my magic books'.

She wrote her review column, usually covering five books in about one thousand words, once or twice a month. Her reviews are personal and characteristic. She damns, for instance, 'those earnest, cultured works which widen the gulf between the countryman and the educated town-dweller until one feels that the time will come when these two human species will look out for specimens of each other to stuff', and praises 'a fine, straightforward style based on the golden rule that the secret of good writing lies in saying exactly what one means, no more and no less'. Her approach to the world of her fellow-novelists is direct: 'to have read it is to have gone to the house in Suffolk, had trouble with the servants and met four women of this present generation . . . in my opinion all these four women are backing losing horses, but because I too am of their generation, I do not know.' In Margery's opinion bad writing and 'slovenly' construction rank as 'discourtesy to the reader'. She liked to balance and discriminate, to devise rules and then exceptions to those rules. Her reviews cannot help but throw light on her habits of mind and on her own writing aims. She contrasts, for instance, those books 'written to entertain or educate the reader' and those 'which appear to be written to do the author good'. For Margery, a first-class novel was almost always from the second category but succeeded also in achieving the aims of the first.

Time and Tide was never able to pay its reviewers lavishly but the small sums earned and the steady chore of considering other people's writing was of great benefit in helping her through this period of reassessment in her own life and work. There was a welcoming feel about the magazine. Politicians of all parties, artists, thinkers and explorers contributed to it. From radical beginnings in the 1920s, it had developed into a forum for humane, intelligent discussion in which even a writer as wary of public speech as Margery could speak in her own, not an edited voice. She felt 'at home', she said.

Fashion in Shrouds' broader outlook on society sprang primarily from observation of those closer to her actual home. Several friends from student days were starting to do rather well in their various professions. The surgeon, Mr Ronnie Reid, for example, had recently moved with his family into a large house in Colchester's Lexden Road – the sort of town house which possessed stabling, servants' quarters and a considerable area of garden. 'On to Ronnie's grand new house. He looks whacked too. I reckon we're both a bit too sanguine. However nuthin' comes wi'out a struggle.' She remained worried about all that she had taken on at D'Arcy House. The garden seemed to demand constant expenditure on choice plants as well as wages and she was secretly relieved when the last of Dr Salter's former gardeners handed in his resignation. Only a week after visiting the Reids, she acted on a sudden impulse and talked Pip into offering their house for sale in answer to a 'wanted' advertisement. 'No blame if we should sell at large profit . . . made Pip write (wrote letter myself). Extraordinary feeling of deep relief. Fond of house but feel it's killing me.' Some potential buyers looked round but it had only been a whim. Nothing came of it.

Later that year Aunt Grace with problems of her own talked of selling Pope's. Margery was tempted. 'I must say I felt like buying it and getting out of false position here if at all possible.' Merely living in the Doctor's House cast her and Pip in roles which she, at least, did not want. Tolleshunt D'Arcy was in ferment over the future of the Church School. The Vicar and the schoolmistress quarrelled and the school was scheduled for closure. Pip and Edward Terrell flung themselves into the fray. 'Grand meeting in dining room. I entertained Mrs T. while excitement waxed terrific – Vicar rude on phone to Edward. Edward out for blood. Idiotically amusing.' The canvassing and caballing went on for days and Margery's sense of humour was severely tested as her household privacy was repeatedly invaded and work disrupted.

Her attitude to village affairs would change markedly within six months and her attitude to her neighbours too. Initially however, the well-to-do professional families whom Pip had met socially repelled her as representatives of a 'suburban species'. 'They lead very dull lives,' she wrote to a friend, 'all amateur theatricals and behind the door flirtations with each other – also they never seem to get to know each other very well although they eat at each other's houses every week.'

The Fashion in Shrouds attains distinction as a portrait of the self-made man; the mechanics of achievement, the prices paid, the strain and watchfulness required to keep a hold of one's investments, both human and material. Murder is the device which turns the spotlight on. The brief portrait of a Harley Street specialist being persuaded to connive at the cover-up of a killing is tellingly satirical (and toned down in her later version). Circumlocutions and evasions mask the inner rottenness of this prosperous society. The atmosphere is so close that an unambiguous revelation of murder is greeted with relief. 'To the police a corpse is a corpse and murder is a hanging matter and the whole affair slid out of the shrouding mists of the fashionable world and the gossip of the bridge clubs and came under the glare of bull's eyes and the indelicate curiosity of the Press.'

Margery had long believed that the strength of the detective novel lay in its requirement that one small section of society be focussed upon and the knots and tangles of its intrigue shown up in the clear light of investigation. Murder was the spur by which she jabbed her readers – and herself – to attention. Although she might talk of the murder story as no more than a dispensable 'prop' and the 'mystery' as the 'box' in which she chose to pack her tales, the alchemy that this form of violence exercised within her imagination was considerably more subtle. Her diary gives evidence of the sudden acceleration of *Shrouds'* physical progress after the first and second killings. The middle section, after the death of Sir Raymond Ramillies, was completed in a month and the last third of the book (over 40,000 words) was completed in three weeks – a rate of working not dissimilar to her film story productivity. The diarist had lost all doubts about what she was doing: 'worked like a fiend', 'worked like hell', 'worked like forty fiends' (!), 'ploughing fiercely on', 'worked all day, nearly dead', 'Feel I'm conking out, slugging on', 'dictated for twelve solid hours and got it done'.

In February 1938, when she was, as it were, summoning her energies, she had taken a literary stock check. 'I find I have written and had published about eight million words to date. I am on my 15th thriller and the rest has been A.P. stuff and shorts. The figure does not include the unsold stuff or the 125,000 word novel *Green Corn* which never got published. It represents 17 years work. God only knows if it has been worth it. If I'd had 17 children instead at least my life would have been more exciting but I should probably still be disconsolate and even more overworked and tired. I'm so slow.'

Margery wrote later that throughout the 1930s she had seemed to herself to be 'running on the wrong force'. Periods of tremendous dynamism, to describe which she used the term 'ferocious' and which, it is said, could be quite alarming to those around her, had been interspersed with periods of lethargy which frightened her because she could not understand them. 'Not much guts left I'm afraid.' Depression came with the tiredness. Medically, had she but known, this was not surprising. Not knowing about 'bipolar temperaments' or 'thyroid-controlled metabolic imbalance', she frequently ascribed her depression to the complex strain of undertaking a 'he-woman's job'.

The Fashion in Shrouds has much to say about the emotional pressures on women who dedicate themselves to a career but who 'will not relinquish their femininity'. Val and Georgia are 'two fine ladies of the modern world' – aware both of their success and of inner dissatisfaction as they drive home alone to their bijou hard-earned houses. 'Their several responsibilities were far heavier than most men's and their abilities greater.' But their femininity, 'femininity unprotected from itself', is presented as 'a weakness not a strength'. At this point in the novel both women are single but have no wish to remain so. This introduces a volatility into their lives and into the fictional situation.

Margery has been accused of 'a bland instinctive anti-feminism' on the evidence of *The Fashion in Shrouds*. Seen in the context not only of her life but that of other gifted women of the 1930s who struggled to maintain a happy balance between their ambitions and their human need to be both cherished and cherishing, the novel is anything but 'bland'. Neither is it anti-feminist – though its conclusion may depress those who think that it is easy to achieve marriage, motherhood and a career at the top of any profession.

There are three women with careers and love affairs at stake. Georgia, the actress, has had three husbands, several affaires and a child – a pathetically insecure adolescent who must rank as one of Margery's finest minor creations. Georgia is emotionally voracious, she swamps those with whom she is in love – until she tires of them – and has no idea either of thinking before she speaks or considering the likely consequences of her actions. There is something of Em in Georgia – the something that Margery guarded against in herself. 'It's not what I can't say that worries me,' she wrote once, 'but what I could – freely audibly and without a thought.' Georgia is 'off the chain' of sexual or financial dependence but must be ringed by shadowy 'keepers' if she is not to bring herself and all around her to disaster. ' "Does she always say any mortal thing that comes into her head?" "Usually I think . . . it was the fashion to be daring some years ago . . . It's dangerous of course." '

There is something already slightly old-fashioned about Georgia. Amanda, however, reappearing from *Sweet Danger,* represents a younger generation, younger than Margery's own. Amanda works in aircraft design, is utterly clear-thinking, can weigh up 'bread-and-butter' against 'cake' love with perfect aplomb and make her own proposals of marriage accordingly. Too much aplomb perhaps. The younger girl can seem, in another phrase of Margery's, like 'one of those people who sail through puberty without a fear or a boil'. The third woman, Val Ferris, who is Campion's sister and therefore, as it were, Margery's contemporary, has been unhappily married and has worked singlemindedly since then to establish herself as a leading dress designer. She has 'made' herself but in the process the loving and giving aspects of her personality have been neglected and she is patently under strain. Though Val sets a high value on herself and her career, she continues to hope that she will meet a man she can love and admire. When she does so, she gives up her work without a backward glance.

The choice Val makes is not glossed over. Alan, her future husband, sets out his terms unambiguously. He wants 'a wife, not a mistress', and offers to assume 'full responsibility' for Val in return for her yielding to him 'your independence, the enthusiasm which you give your career, your time and your thought'. And she does so with a sigh of relief that is also an admission of defeat. 'Authority. The simple nature of her desire from him took her breath away with its very obviousness and in the back of her mind she caught a glimpse of its root. She was a clever woman who would not relinquish her femininity and femininity unpossessed is a femininity unprotected from itself, a weakness and not a charm.'

For Margery this was not a matter of sexual politics but a dramatisation of the problem as she saw it. Men and women, she believed, were designed as two halves of one whole, neither better nor worse than each other, but different. She considered that the conventional expectations and 'training' of women had fostered dependency and the capacity to feel rather than to think for so long that it required strenuous efforts of will for a working woman, like Val, to carry responsibility and bring her mind to bear on her emotional decisions. Margery thought that this was tiring – not that it could not be done. She took a farmyard look at the sexual act and wondered whether the whole 'muddle' about the equality of the sexes might be 'pretty elementary and mechanical. For in sex the female is designed to be both aquiescent and protective. It would be a laugh if this was the fact on which our fathers based their tall ideas of male superiority, the apes!' The secret was to discover 'exactly what one needs to make the world that place in which one's own particular temperament may thrive'. If one was constructed 'far from the norm' in one direction, one might have to go as far from the norm in the other to find one's complement. Choices had to be made, and choices involved sacrifice.

She had made a hard choice around the mid-point of *The Fashion in Shrouds*. In her diary on March 7th 1938 she records, 'Wrote and put M. off. Feel that's the last personal sacrifice I have to make. Now I have nothin'. Feel it's rather a serious and final step but it must be done.' A fortnight later she has received 'a letter' (the words 'at last' are erased). 'Feel resentful in my heart. Want to live.' And as soon as the novel was completed she 'sent note of invitation'. Two 'M's. Maud and Mac, visited D'Arcy House on April 10th and on the 12th 'Meiggs writes he's coming on Friday.'

Russell Meiggs, ancient history scholar and fellow, at this time, of Keble College, Oxford, was a slightly older contemporary of Pip's from Christ's Hospital. He had been known to Margery at least since Chappel days when his name appears on a list of players for Pip's cricket team. At some time during the intervening period he had become very important to her. Her capacity to fall in love – the quality that had led her as a teenager to make 'an ass' of herself over 'Charles' and consider 'giving up everything' for Reggie – was an attribute she suppressed. Meiggs (as she invariably referred to him) seems to have caught her unaware. His contemporaries were impressed by his striking 'leonine' appearance and evident, if (some thought) 'dry', intellect. Others speak of a 'magnetism' that attracted all types and ages of people. When Margery used a version of Meiggs in her novel *Traitor's Purse*, she introduced the fictional character as being 'a personality. That is to say he exuded a force and spiritual flavour as actual as if it had been warmth or a small electric current.' A warmth, a charm and an impression of special, personal interest, such qualities, from a man himself worthy of admiration, evoked a response from Margery that was born of need.

A fragment of a letter to 'my dear Mr Meiggs' survives drafted in one of Margery's notebooks during the early summer of 1937. It tells local news – the tale of the Coronation binge at the marsh village of Salcot, when the village elders laid in plentiful supplies of alcohol, barricaded their single road with hurdles, and were neither seen nor heard of for three days afterwards. The tone of the letter ripples with confidence that such anecdotes will be enjoyed. There are others of its kind, candid and delightful. Margery had met Meiggs only three or four times a year at parties. He had become the person to whom she could write with the most complete freedom, an invisible companion on occasions when Pip, Grog and Cooee were out and she spending a long evening alone. Later in 1938 her mood changed and she accused Meiggs of 'promising people (women I mean) much more than you are prepared to give them'. She wrote then with contempt of her own 'infatuation' which had sprung up and been nurtured, she said, 'in an atmosphere of moonlight and alcohol'.

In the middle years of the 1930s Margery was playing with extramarital affairs in her fiction as she did not do at any other period. Mike and Gina in *Flowers*, Campion and Linda in *Dancers* – these 'good' characters refrain from consummating their relationships. There are two stories, from the spring of 1937, where the heroines go further. *The Mistress in the House* ('difficult, emotional stuff' comments Margery), which was written for submission to *Cosmopolitan* magazine, reads as a wish-fulfilment tale. It describes a county lady who conducts her double life as wife and once-a-month mistress with an efficiency that is slightly chilling. Her affaire is described as her 'beauty treatment'. Margery professed scant sympathy with what she called 'the sex-to-do-you-good school' but there are moments of real relief and tenderness when mistress meets lover in this short story.

The Pioneers, written a few weeks later, tells of a husband and wife who have decided, in the politest possible way, to part and go to their respective lovers. They are saved from what will clearly be miserable consequences by the arrival of two young friends. This irrepressible pair recall the gaiety of the 'bohemian' days when the older couple set out on matrimony – before they attained recognition and the material rewards of success, their grand country house and its exquisite antique furniture. Those were the days when 'they had worked together in the dusty little studio littered with the paraphernalia of Jan's trade, miscellaneous belongings of their myriad friends and their own few household possessions.' In the story the strength of this shared memory is enough to hold them together and dispatch the alternatives – a brassy, 'suburban' blonde and 'Fergus Capet', a dreary scholar.

The starting point, at least, of this story was autobiographical. Two days before it was written, Margery noted in her diary that 'Box and Joan', members of the Gang from Holborn days, had paid them a visit. Local guests had been got rid of early and the household had then enjoyed 'a fine, old barmy night'. The visitors had been 'a salutary influence on us all. Even boys saw the light.' The next day Margery thought out *The Pioneers*, then 'stayed up late watching Cocky work'. A trivial, comforting episode.

There is much mention of the 'dangerousness' of love in the first version of *Shrouds*. It is, interestingly, excised in Margery's 1965 revision. In the version written during 1937–8, Val comes close to losing her balance. 'I am nervy, very nervy,' she explains in a passage later dispensed with. 'I had no idea I could behave like this. It's come rather late – I ought to be twenty-two to feel like this and enjoy it – and it's frightening me for the time being.' It seems beyond reasonable doubt that Margery was attracted to Russell Meiggs, believed that the feeling was mutual and wondered where it might have led. But, however potent was that combination of moonlight and alcohol, or perhaps of loneliness and the feeling that 'Cocky has no time for me', infidelity must be ruled out – and not only because Pip remained friendly with Meiggs for many years. Margery was, in her own orthography, a morally 'honnest' person, taught by Granny to be straightforwardly 'good' and trying her best to continue so. In a letter to Meiggs she described the sort of person that she believed capable of spiritual development, and, one guesses, the sort of person she hoped she was: 'a decent, sensative, frightened-of-hurting-people, innocent-at-heart person who is also honnest in the *head* and who is always being forced to do things because he really and intelligently feels they are best for everyone'. That was the 'good child' within her, and was central to her view of herself.

The most convincing reason not to believe that Margery had any illicit relationship after her marriage is that she was afraid that if she did so her work, so vital to her equilibrium, would suffer. She explained the theory behind this in a letter written to Dr A. D. Lindsay, Master of Balliol College (to which Meiggs moved as a fellow in 1939). Margery suggested that her generation talked about sex ad nauseam in order to stop themselves thinking about it clearly. 'The thing people are frightened of is seeing sex for what it is and that is roughly speaking creative physical energy – It's such a very transmutable power that it is easily used for purposes other than reproduction . . . what I mean is you can use your spare creative energy for the purpose nature created it or you can use it for something you'd rather do, like climbing Vesuvius or writing a book . . . That's why the blessed business has to be so attractive, people would use the petrol to do something else if it wasn't.'

Somehow Margery's relationship with Meiggs had reached a crucial point in the spring of 1938. Why otherwise would she write in her diary 'rather a serious and final step' of asking someone to put off (not to cancel) a visit for what was merely a matter of weeks? When, at last, he did come, all was not as overwhelming as she'd anticipated, probably because of the emotion she had already expended making the decision that this relationship, her chance 'to live', must come second to her work. 'Was just a tiny bit bored. (I'm barmy!)' she commented. 'Turns out to be more usual than I thought. Interesting facade. Very young. Highly relieved.' Later in that year this 'relief' turned to a resentment for which no precise cause is discernible. A degree of defensiveness, perhaps some remaining emotional confusion, is revealed in letters to her sister written four years later. There are five of them, newsy letters, written when Joyce was serving in the W.R.N.S. In each one of them Margery mentions Meiggs' name. Not for any pressing reason, rather as if she were fingering a scar, wondering still what it had been about him that had so attracted her and what might have been if she had acted differently. 'Maybe he wasn't so very extraordinary', perhaps he was even 'odd and difficult' but nevertheless 'there was no-one ever quite like him as far as I was concerned.'

Around the turn of the year 1937–8 Margery had written two

especially long letters to Russell Meiggs which are central to her understanding of herself and her life. They are certainly letters of love, love of the mind. Although Margery was not a church-goer, she was profoundly, idiosyncratically Christian. Meiggs took a historian's view of the truth of the New Testament and was aware of, if not actually involved with, the evangelical groups springing up in Oxford then. Margery could discuss her faith with him as she would never have been able to with Pip. Her respect for the quality of Meiggs' intelligence, and her anxiety to explain exactly what she meant, led her to draft and re-draft these letters – hence their survival from a period when she did not regularly keep personal material. Their importance to her is hard to over-estimate. After one particularly fervent justification of the 'human truth' of the Gospels, she adds apologetically, 'I don't think I have ever written so frankly about anything to anyone before and I have rather shocked myself.' She nags him too, provokes, and contradicts. Such insecurities seem born of an urgent desire to be understood. 'What is the reason for me?' she asks – and gives answers which are influenced by her reading but which are essentially her own.

Hidden behind Meiggs' academic exterior was a complex temperament to which Margery felt an affinity. She was able to describe to him, as to no-one else, the moments when she had been gripped by panic and despair. 'There comes a point when you suddenly realise you're sunk – you call on all those resources that you have never known to fail you before – your own guts, your intelligence and faith in yourself and you realise with a sort of sick feeling that they have an end and that the bag is empty and you can't do anything at all. You are always quite alone when it does come. People you've relied on for years are suddenly weaker even than you – there is nothing and nobody – You get long past the point when nothing matters – after that you know that there are two or three stages ranging from acute nervous pain to downright hallucination and then to a second apathy and a lot of dreadful fear which is like nothing I've ever read of.'

It is impossible to know when Margery suffered thus. Perhaps at the time of Herbert's death when she wrote in her diary that she 'had the horrors'? Or in the pendulum downswings of her 'bi-polar' personality? To find a faith, to be able to reassure herself that she had 'done her honnest best' was vital if the possibilities of suicide or madness were to be held at bay. 'One day in the middle of disaster, after weeks of wishing it were morning and wishing it were night, it will suddenly occur to you that you have done everything you could, that you have acted sensibly in every way and that by all the rules of the game you ought to be alright. Faith in the intrinsic value of good things, the eternal persistence and triumph of good over evil is the only thing there is left.

'At this point something happens, something quite small. You get a little trivial miracle . . . in the ordinary way you wouldn't notice it but because you are living so desperately close to the edge of sanity and everything else you seize on it and hang on waiting, doing all you can but not much because you are at the end of your resources, mental, physical and spiritual . . . Then you get another small miracle. Finally you notice that this web of small miracles continues and in the end you realise that it is a natural law, a right thing.'

This 'right thing' is pattern – not the impious machinery that reveals the manipulating villain in *Shrouds* but a personal pattern that must be sought out and worked for by each individual. 'Man,' she wrote later, 'is the raw material of God,' and God, the letters suggest, is the cosmic pattern, giving significance to the many struggling little patterns and to 'the terrifying web of coincidence and dramatic irony which', as Margery claimed in a *Time and Tide* review in March 1938, 'is the very stuff that life is made of.'

Margery's letters to Russell Meiggs, and presumably discussions too, begin to articulate a coherent, individual philosophy which was strong enough to underpin the rest of her work and experience. When Malcolm Johnson queried *The Fashion in Shrouds* Margery wrote to Nerney with complete certainty, 'I now know what I am doing and *what I am going to do*. I wrote the book intentionally not by accident and I am going on writing similar stories – Malcolm can't *cure* me, I'm doing it on purpose.' She remained however obscurely vulnerable to Meiggs and her use of some of his characteristics for the villain in *Traitor's Purse,* published in 1941, may have been a therapy for herself or even a revenge. When she heard that he had recognised the portrait and been hurt by it, she was not especially sorry. She again used the word 'relieved' to express her feelings when he married later in the year.

But whatever the less comfortable emotions he had aroused, it had been invaluable to find someone to whom she could tell those inner experiences which would not fit the detective 'box'. She inscribed a copy of *The Oaken Heart*, the book in which she abandoned fiction to speak out directly, 'for Meiggs, who taught me to write letters, this longest one of all.'

Margery managed the summer of 1938 rather more successfully than that of 1937. She was determined to enter the lucrative market of American magazine serials and worked straight through June to complete the first instalment of *Bring Out Your Rubber-Tyred Hearses*, the story that became *Black Plumes*. She sent it to her new American agent, Paul Reynolds, who cabled at the beginning of August that it had been accepted by the *Woman's Home Companion*. *Shrouds* was well received and elicited one review which Margery is known to have prized: 'To Albert Campion has fallen the honour of being the first detective to figure in a story which is by any standard a distinguished novel,' said 'Torquemada' of *The Observer*. She felt entitled to enjoy Pip's and her annual cricket party to the full. This was the moment when their household came into its own and the sacrifices made to possess such a place seemed justified.

'The August party was terrific that year,' Margery remembered afterwards. 'It reached a zenith, achieved a ripeness, which lifted it out of the class of "Good Times" and planted it squarely in the front row of "Life Experiences".' The weather was glorious, a multitude of friends were gathered from Chappel, the Poly, Christ's Hospital and the neighbourhood of Tolleshunt D'Arcy. The atmosphere was exhilarating. Then, 'a few weeks later when we were still clearing up and packing away things that might come in useful next year, the incredible descended upon us and we were suddenly required to take instant precautions in case of an attack on our lives by poison gas.'

XIII

Strangers at the Gate

1938–1941

Margery's diary remained blank from August 1938 to the end of the year. The crisis in relationships with Germany over her annexation of vital areas of Czechoslovakia made war frighteningly imminent. It had been received wisdom for several years that if war did come again it would bring massive aerial bombardment and widespread atack by poison gas. Lurid articles had been written, staggering predictions of slaughter made. There was a feeling of horror in the public imagination.

Suddenly, in September 1938, Great Britain's defence machinery swung into action. At Tolleshunt D'Arcy Pip was asked to chair an A.R.P. meeting in the village hall. The local policeman (nicknamed 'Me') called at D'Arcy House with a handbook for them to study. 'Phosgene,' Margery learned, 'filled your lungs with water and produced gangrene of the extremities. Mustard had scarcely any odour but blinded you and ate your flesh away.' She received detailed sheets of instructions for nursing 'blister/ non-blister/lung cases' etc. Those which followed on the decontamination of clothing, stretchers, buildings and vehicles were if anything more terrifying in their practicality. In the early hours of a September morning Pip received a telegram from the nearby town of Maldon. 'Collect seven hundred gas masks for your area and fit.'

Immediately problems arose: there was, at first, no protection available either for the very old or the very young and no hope of any for the animals. In an agricultural area accustomed to grazing its stock over the wide acres of marshland, this brought particular distress. 'The notion of a concentration strong enough to envelop half the county did not then seem absurd. Fogs and sea-wracks are a commonplace with us and it was only natural to assume that something like one of these, but possessing all the injurious qualities mentioned in "Me's" book was not really unlikely.' The threat that they thought they were facing had a nightmarish quality. And as Margery said, 'You cannot attempt to frighten folk off war for twenty years without your efforts taking some effect upon them and the sudden present of a gas mask will hardly wipe all that out in ten minutes.' She shared in the national feeling of respite when the Prime Minister, Neville Chamberlain, flew out to Munich to negotiate with Hitler.

Mac, writing from America, was furious. 'You will wake and find Handsome Adolf installed in Downing Street and being crowned in Westminster. Your papers apart from the *Manchester Guardian* have nothing in them about what is happening. Or do you want Germany to absorb Europe and make England a third class power? Ministers have been impeached and hung on gibbets for less than Chamberlain has done to sell his country to the enemy. I have never before felt so ashamed of being an Englishman.'

Margery who, in common she said with most people in her village, cherished few illusions about the durability of Chamberlain's 'Peace in our Time', replied with candour. 'Don't judge England too harshly before you get the low-down. On the face of it, it was, and is, a poor show, but the alternative to the Prime Minister's flight was a raid on an undefended country within five hours of two thousand bombers arriving in half hour waves, first with high explosive, then with incendiary and then with gas – phosgene mixed with mustard.' She detailed the measures they had been asked to implement: 'after putting six hundred old ladies, yokels and school kids into gas masks, explaining to horrified country folk that the food they eat, the crops they grow and the animals they are fond of cannot be protected in any way . . . Well, in view of all this, all I can say is temper your shame at being an Englishman with a modicum of relief that you live in the United States.'

Mac sent her letter straight on to the *New York Sun*. 'I regard Mr McFee's performance as an outrage,' spluttered Margery's agent, A. P. Watt. Once war proper had come Mac wrote cheerfully: 'My editor, Grey of the *Sun* . . . said "If you could get Miss Margery Allingham to write some more we could print it." ' Malcolm Johnson, Margery's editor at Doubleday, complimented her on 'that extraordinary little esseay on preparing England for war, a jewel of its kind'.

There were other defence matters to consider. Official plans had been drawn up for the evacuation of the most vulnerable members of London's civilian population to the surrounding countryside. In Tolleshunt D'Arcy, Mr Doe the village butcher was nominated billeting officer. Margery volunteered to act as his assistant. Together they evolved what seemed to them a workmanlike scheme for the reception and housing of one hundred and twenty unaccompanied children. She found this a congenial exercise. This first threat of war had revived, 'bright and bald', her childhood vision of 'the hundreds and hundreds of far-away dead'. The prospect of other people's children coming to her village offered some consolation. It 'almost mitigated the cold dread of the casualty lists that must lie behind the mind of everyone who has to stay at home'. She did not believe, however, that people should be forced to offer accommodation. 'I felt particularly vehement about this I remember, because I felt with a passion left over from my own childhood that the important thing was to put the youngster where someone wanted him first and worry about his living space afterwards.'

Even after this 1938 crisis was over, Margery continued to think about the potential problems of the evacuation scheme. It was not voluntary for prospective billetors and there had been vociferous opposition to it from certain county ladies. Margery did not contribute to Ellen Wilkinson's lively airing of the subject in the *Time and Tide* correspondence columns. Instead she prepared a report on their experience in Tolleshunt D'Arcy and submitted it to the headquarters of the Women's Voluntary Service.

The Chairman, Lady Reading, was appreciative. Margery's memorandum was copied and circulated to all their evacuation assistants. Lady Reading requested an article to be submitted to one of the leading daily papers. Margery headed it 'Strangers at the Gate'. 'In war,' she began, 'there are many terrors and the art of winning wars seem to lie in looking at each of them not so much with bravery as with practical and constructive common sense.' She showed sympathy with the countryside fear of strangers and suggested that the months gained before catastrophe finally came upon them should be spent in some form of twinning, encouraging town and country women's organisations to introduce themselves to each other. 'Let us meet them not as Government boarders, nor as invading foreigners but as ordinary other people who may, Heaven knows, in many cases be extremely nice.' She ended strongly, 'What about them? What about the mothers in the slums of London who rushed out in the crisis to pawn something needed to get a shilling or two to buy their children new nightdresses and a brush and comb each so that they should not arrive in the sanctuary of the hamlets ashamed . . . It was also a courtesy to us in the country. Our poorer folk responded to it with a magnificence which is all their own. The big houses must not snub it.'

The W.V.S. sent Margery's article to the *Sunday Times* who 'couldn't accommodate it', to the *Daily Telegraph* and to *The Times*, both of whom rejected it. 'As I have always suspected,' wrote the frustrated publicity officer to Margery, 'there seems to be a definite policy against publishing anything about this ticklish problem other than the actual notices sent out by the Ministry of Health.' Finally, rather sensibly, the article was circulated to provincial papers and published in the *Reading Mercury, Herts Advertiser*, *Crewe Chronicle* and a dozen others.

In Tolleshunt D'Arcy Margery and Mr Doe began a round of visiting and talking to likely billetors. Grog drew her a detailed map of the area with the addresses and occupiers of every house and cottage on it. She felt little inclination now to shut herself away in her writing room, except to compile lists of names and add her own assessment of each household's suitability to receive the promised children.

Others among her fellow-novelists found it hard to settle to work in the early months of 1939. As one contributor to *Time and Tide* put it, 'the mind wandered, hanging about for it didn't know what.' Many people shared this strained unease of waiting. Margery, in a review written in February 1939, spoke of 'the hopeless grief of the ordinary man at the prospect of the ruin of civilisation'. Those early months of 1939 were, she said, a period of 'peculiar wretchedness'.

Nevertheless, livings still had to be earned. The commission negotiated by Paul Reynolds in America for a serial story to be completed by Christmas 1938, had not been forgotten but neither had it been written. Margery had appointed Paul to manage her affairs during 1937. Previously any work for sale in the United States that had not been handled by the Doubleday London office had been sent to Mary Leonard. Mary had been Doubleday's London representative but had returned to live in America. Margery liked Mary but had become restive at what she felt was Malcolm Johnson's continuing pressure on her to conform to a Crime Club mould. She wanted someone who could get tough with Doubleday on her behalf and Mary, she felt, was too close to Malcolm. 'She writes as if she was in his office.' Her decision to appoint a new agent did not impair their friendship. Mary often visited D'Arcy House on her trips to England and among Margery's favourite treats were meals out in London with Mary, Nerney and Louisa Callender – four business women with a sense of humour and interests in common from book-trade gossip to cooking and sewing.

Margery's new American agent, Paul Revere Reynolds, was well-respected in his work. They rarely met but became friends by letter over the years. Paul 'is America to me' she wrote later. Margery placed complete reliance on Paul's integrity and was grateful for the extreme conscientiousness with which he attended to her affairs. The serialisation of her work in U.S. magazines such as *Collier's* and *The Saturday Evening Post* came to be of crucial financial importance to her. This was something Paul took seriously. When one of the influential editors was interested, air letters and cables flashed to and fro across the Atlantic detailing every stage of the negotiations. It was exciting and could be lucrative. It also made Margery's business affairs very much more complex as two sets of magazine editors and two sets of publishers on both sides of the Atlantic had to be persuaded by two sets of agents to cooperate over titles and release dates.

The first serial, *Black Plumes* (originally *Hearses*), was completed and delivered during 1939. When war broke out cables were received from *Collier's*, the eventual purchaser, asking permission to introduce a war background. Though this plan eventually came to nothing, it must have reminded Margery of her father being required to change the course of his long-running *Human Nature* in order to acknowledge the outbreak of the First World War.

A volume of *Strand* stories, *Mr Campion and Others*, was published in England during 1939. Otherwise it was a fallow year. In October 1939 Margery took the opportunity of a *Time and Tide* book review to take stock of fluctuations in the mood of the literary public. 'A few months ago there was a growing feeling among many of us that those who read at all were inclined to read too much. "Literature of Escape" was becoming a familiar epithet and I for one was beginning to feel that a little less reading and a little more constructive private thinking might do many people, myself included, a power of good.' By that date, October 21st, England had been a month and a half at war. Margery continued, 'In the last few weeeks however most people have done their share of thinking and a few hours escape into another, less personal world is not to be sneered at.' Not many more weeks were to pass before she was able to send Paul the first instalment and synopsis of her new novel, *Traitor's Purse*, a 'Campion' this time unlike *Black Plumes* but, she hoped, equally suitable for serialisation. She used the plot-device of inflicting partial amnesia on her hero to give dramatic prominence to the post-Munich and Phoney War 'shadows in the mind'.

Paul was initially uncertain of its potential. He explained disarmingly, 'As you know I had doubts about the serial probably because it was different from most stories and an agent is always scared of what's different.' Potential buyers were enthusiastic and Paul was soon urging Margery to 'go full steam ahead and not to monkey with the buzz saw'. The editors, he assured her, 'want you to continue the story the way you think it ought to be continued and as good as you can make it . . .' Stimulating advice for the daughter of Herbert herself accustomed to tremble before the editors of *Answers*, weekly instalment humbly in hand. Almost impossible to respond to amid the clamour of village duties.

Civil Defence procedures had been put in motion in advance of the formal declaration of war on September 3rd. It was feared that the air raids might commence even before hostilities officially existed. Pip was Chief Warden for the area with Grog as his deputy. D'Arcy House, in the centre of the village and one of the relatively few houses with a telephone, became the Warden's Post. The dining room was cleared, phone manned, rotas organised, a bomb map 'virgin and sinister' pinned up on the wall. Oilskins, wellingtons, a bucket and shovel to deal with incendiaries, all the pages of official advice on coping with gas attacks were gathered there. Margery commented that the smell of the brand new wellington boots stored in her sideboard was practically asphixiating in itself! As Deputy Chief First Aid Officer as well as Chief Warden ('Pooh-Bah' said Margery), Pip received a supply of First Aid materials from Dr Madden. Margery checked and stored it. 'The spectacle of all this medical stuff presented free to us, the ordinary public, by the local government, convinced us more than anything else that the danger of death or injury was more than just likely. I remember looking at a new splint and wondering involuntarily which well-known arm it was for, then getting hot under the collar for being so theatrical and then hoping suddenly that I was being theatrical.'

And then the evacuees arrived. By now D'Arcy considered itself well-prepared. Mr Doe, Margery and the village school teachers had billets ready and waiting for the ninety unaccompanied school children they had been advised to expect. Eight double-decker buses arrived. '*Eight* buses?' said Mr Doe, when he heard they were on their way. They brought the children – and their mothers, their toddler brothers and sisters, a scattering of grandmothers and single pregnant women. Three hundred souls to be accommodated in a village of six hundred and fifty.

Margery later reported on their problems to the County

Medical Officer. 'Among the number who arrived there was a single family of nineteen persons (a matriarch, daughters, daughters-in-law and their children) all vehement in their determination not to be parted; an expectant mother with three children under two years of age, including twins of eleven months; another expectant mother of twenty two years who had with her three children, the eldest of whom was four years old and the youngest seven months, and a particularly pathetic group who had not registered under any scheme but had "seen a bus and got in it". This family, a pregnant mother and three children including a baby in arms, afterwards turned out to be very verminous.'

The arrangements so carefully made for the reception of the children were useless in the new situation. Miraculously (or so it seemed to Margery) the villagers 'came up to the sunny playground with unwilling conscience-driven steps' and the visitors were accommodated – for the first night at least. Her report continues, 'The following morning after a very uncomfortable night much of the original emotional pity of the hosts had turned to alarm and exasperation and after an awkward interview with one of his clients who had inadvertently been given a verminous family, the billeting officer (the village butcher) resigned and I took over.'

Unexpected help came from two newcomers to the village, Mark Benney, an author, and his economist wife, Jane Degras. Mark, himself a child of the slums, had earned a sudden literary reputation, not to say notoriety, for his autobiographical account of a childhood of petty crime, *Low Company*. It had been praised by Rebecca West, slated by Malcolm Muggeridge. Margery, reviewing a later Benney novel for *Time and Tide*, remained uncharacteristically ambivalent. During the ten months they lived in Tolleshunt D'Arcy, she came to sympathise with and like Mark, though he always struck her as a 'little' man. Her association with Jane Degras was stormy from the outset. Jane was radically left-wing and did not trouble to disguise her conviction that Margery was 'some sort of female blimp'. This was disconcerting as Margery thought of herself as independent if not apolitical. She regarded Herbert's legacy of Fabianism as an essential part of herself but felt no need to quarrel with Pip's right-wingery. She had attended a couple of Conservative Women's meetings in the village and had found them rather comic. Although there was no time for party political argument in September 1939, Jane's overt antagonism shocked Margery into defining her own political beliefs more clearly later.

The evacuation procedures themselves challenged hazy notions of individual rights and privacies with compulsory national duty. The paradox of being required to enforce so many new state regulations, obligations and curtailments of personal liberty in the cause of a war for freedom and self-determination was obvious. Jane's convictions simply made it more so. 'The inhumanity of man to man scandalised Jane. Not only that, it infuriated her . . . It will probably startle her to say so, for she is Jewish and of Russian extraction, but she appeared to me to be bent on enforcing old-fashioned British Christianity with a mallet, while I who am East Anglian and middle Church of England, was equally vehement that nobody must ever be forced into doing good and must only be forcibly restrained from doing evil if he is actively harming somebody else.' It was a stimulating partnership (or 'battlegrip'). 'People like me need people like Jane to prevent us from seeing some things so much more clearly than others.' They worked together effectively during the critical winter of 1939/40 and achieved through it a sort of friendship.

The project which afforded Margery most satisfaction during this time was the 'Mamas' House'. One of the young mothers who had become their responsibility was ten days away from giving birth. Others had only a few weeks of pregnancy left. No arrangements had been made for them beyond a last-minute dash to hospital in Chelmsford, twenty miles away. Under wartime conditions and with winter approaching, this seemed hazardous. Margery decided that 'home' conditions should be made available in the village. Cynthia Tatchell, from Guisnes Court, one of a local family with whom Pip and Margery were on dinner party and cocktail terms, offered to loan an empty four-bedroomed house. The local Women's Institute found furniture and bedding and contributed some money towards medical supplies. Albert Smith, the D'Arcy handyman, colour-washed the rooms and installed a simple, but unorthodox, plumbing system ('called by its inventors on several official forms "the Buried Soak-Away" '). Jane discovered what grants, aids and reliefs could be claimed to finance the project ('Most of these schemes. . . had been fought for by people like her in the teeth of people like me, or so she said and I would not be at all surprised . . .') and a sympathetic County Medical Officer guided the project through official channels. For a few remarkable months Margery could, if she so wished, style herself 'an Authorised Matron in the County of Essex'.

The same talents that had brought the production of *Dido and Aeneas* into being, came out of hibernation. Margery felt refreshed. 'It's taken me some time to realise it and longer to admit it but so far the war has been my salvation. I've had my holiday and at last it has worked. I've recovered my health and my equilibrium. I'm all right. (Looking back I seem to have been a neurasthenic or something for the past five years.) I haven't felt so enthusiastic or glad to be alive since I was 16 or so. Anyway I no longer wake up every morning with a feeling of impending doom.' At some time during 1940 she found a doctor who was able to give her expert guidance on managing her thyroid condition. He prescribed a regular dosage of thyroxine and gave advice on diet. Photographs of Margery taken during the war-years show a loss of weight and of the puffiness noticeable in some of her 1930s pictures.

Their 'race to beat the stork' was won by the narrowest of margins and only because the first evacuee baby arrived late. Five healthy children were born in the Mamas' House during the first winter of the war. Margery felt her own childlessness acutely. When in the spring of 1940, the village was designated a Defence Area and soldiers instead of children were billeted on D'Arcy House, her feeling of regret was undiminished. Some of the ensigns were so young. 'To blunder into the back hall to find a smooth-faced, fair-haired child sleeping sweetly in the camp-bed . . . his rifle clasped in his arms like a toy, was one of those things you could wish not to have seen until you remembered how lucky it was for you that there were children to do it, and that if you had done your duty there would be your children growing up to take their places.' This is the draft version of a passage from *The Oaken Heart*. In the final version, she has changed 'if you had done your duty' to 'if you had had any sense'.

What she called her 'disgustingly exuberant' escape from the desk could not last. By March, Paul Reynolds, who had provisionally arranged for *Traitor's Purse* to be scheduled for magazine publication in October, was vainly trying to discover whether she had written anything. It had been a strange few months: the invasions, the annihilating attacks by air and poison gas had not come; the evacuees had for the most part gone home again. The winter had been among the most severe in living memory, even the salt-water estuary had frozen and the sea birds had come waddling hungrily inland. And Pip, exasperated by the inactivity of his Warden's Post, the lack of incidents with which to fill the columns of their elaborately ruled logbook, had applied to join the Royal Army Service Corps.

His appointment came through in March – to Margery's dismay: 'feel we're a three-legged stool with one leg going.' She was 'wildly relieved' to learn that Pip would spend his first months in the garrison town of Colchester and would therefore be able to come home when not required for duty. It helped accustom her to a parting which she found surprisingly hard.

She had minded intensely when Cooee had left the household on the day before the war broke out in order to join the A.T.S. There had been a quarrel which wreaked permanent damage to their friendship. Cooee remembers how shaken she was, how incomprehensible she had found Margery's outburst then. Looking back, she has come to believe that Margery saw more quickly and clearly than the rest of them that the youthful, irresponsible way of life that they had enjoyed was over – and this was her panicky reaction to the first one of them who chose to leave. There may have been more behind the quarrel – a culmination of the tensions between such dissimilar adults living closely together, memories of all the occasions when Margery had stayed at home to work while Cooee, Pip and Grog went out to enjoy themselves, suppressed jealousy even – but essentially Cooee is right. Despite, or because of, the strain and self-sacrifice that the others demanded from her, Margery was protective, even possessive of her 'family'. That one member should choose to leave at such a moment could have seemed worse than ungrateful – disloyal. Phil and Joyce had abandoned their grafters' life early in the war to seek Service posts but they were not of the household.

Similarly despite Pip's gadding-about, his possible infidelities and complete failure to share her burden of responsibility before the war, Margery felt dependent on him. It was an emotion she seems to have fostered somewhat artificially. As she achieved greater success outside the home, she became more anxious to build up his 'Head of the Household' status within it. Her combination of strengths and insecurities was complex and she clung to her belief that Pip was her essential complement. In a melancholy little poem scribbled in a notebook during a period of depression (probably in late 1934) she wrote, 'Without you I am half a thing, a butterfly without a wing.'

Nevertheless she also considered that 'Love is not a cement but a solvent' and, on Albert Campion's behalf, claimed that she had long dreaded the 'contented weldings', 'the placid partnership in which the protagonists grew closer and closer until they actually began to *look* alike'. In *The Pioneers* she had set out what may have been an early, cerebral, blueprint for their marriage. 'You proved to us,' say the younger to the older couple, 'that it is possible to be free, egotistical, sophisticated, unconventional and at the same time perfectly happy, both individualists and both experimenters.' But both in the context of the story and in the first decade of Margery and Pip's marriage it had not proved anything like as straightforward as that. There remained however the very simple streak in Margery's personality. Like her inarticulate gypsy girl in *Dance of the Years* she loved Pip 'because he was her husband'. In the stark atmosphere of a country at war, many people experienced the unacknowledged potency of such fundamental words and ties. 'There were no sudden changes of heart, of course, no miracles, but most folk did seem to give up pretending that they did not love their husbands and wives or that their children were mentally defective nuisances.'

Margery had grown used to thinking of herself, Pip and Grog as a team, with herself as the central worker. It had been a shock, she said, to return home after a hectic first day of the war as billeting officer to discover that 'the boys' refused to be interested in anything other than the problems of the Warden's Post. In the spring of 1940, as Pip became increasingly absorbed in his military duties, Margery expressed her apprehension at being 'off the chain' (the very expression she had used in *Shrouds* to describe the unfettered Georgia Wells). When she finally settled to work on *Traitor's Purse* she may have found an outlet for some such feelings of loss and fear in imagining Campion's emotions as he faces a life without Amanda.

Then prospect of parting drew Pip and Margery closer. Her diary for 1940 shows that they spent more time together, playing cards, talking and going out locally. They wondered what they should do if invasion did indeed come. 'Finally we agreed that Malcolm's office in America was the only safe address in the world. If we got irrevocably split up we would get in touch through that somehow, if we had to swim the Atlantic or wait ten years.' On his spells home from the barracks in Colchester Pip gave renewed encouragement to her work as she got on with *Traitor's Purse*. She had taken over his First Aid responsibilities in the village and shared the duties of the Warden's Post with Grog.

Uninterrupted time at her desk was hard to come by. Ever hospitable, Pip constantly brought fellow-R.A.S.C. men home with him to enjoy brief spells of civilian living. Local people came freely in and out with 'official' problems, personal worries or frankly seeking gossip. April 7th 1940 was fairly typical: 'A mad day. Constant interruptions. Just finished letters and getting down to work when hairdresser came. Hair all wet when Mrs T. came. Very worried poor soul, her boy with B.E.F. in Norway – hardly time to collect thoughts before lunch. Just back at desk when Margaret Willson came (all A.R.P.) stayed to tea. Went back to work and Mrs Seabrook came (school). Just back to work when PYC came home. Read a review book. Tired but managed to get a chapter clearer. Feel all this outside activity is stimulating although worrying.'

As the weather improved and the European situation worsened, invasion fears revived. Heavy guns could be heard from the Low Countries (only seventy-five miles across the North Sea from the Essex coast). Alarming tales of infiltration and attack by parachute came back over the water. Suspicion of quislings and of organised Fifth Column activity threatened to supply a sinister topicality to the *Traitor's Purse* plot. In May Margery wrote to the *Time and Tide* office 'hysterical' with the difficulty of fulfilling her commitments and asked to be excused from reviewing work until June. A note appeared in the Diary section of the magazine a couple of weeks later: 'One result of the parachute menace is to raise the possibilities of mere everyday life to a level of excitement that can't be beaten even by the wildest fiction. As one of our best detective story writers put it in a letter the other day, "you've no idea how difficult it is to finish a modest thriller when all your neighbours are mucking about in the dawn looking for nuns with sub-machine guns and collapsible bicycles to arrive by parachute." '

By May 25th 1940, when this issue of the magazine appeared, D'Arcy House had become local H.Q. for a hundred officers and men of the 9th Cameronians. Grog and Margery were 'secretly tickled' to observe the Featherstones at first hand. 'To see them in the flesh doing and saying all the things we had said they did was an experience. However, for the first time we began to see the sense of it . . . If there had not been this rigorous code of manner and thought everybody might have been dithering hopelessly, however brave he was and although that might have been more natural it would not have been so sound by any means. The idea was to win not to be clever.'

The men camped in the meadow, the officers and subalterns – 'polo and blood and can they see some action?' – slept in the house. Margery was hardly reassured to hear that they considered it a 'front-line' posting. 'Trying to work. Pip went off rather sad.

Nothing much to report until now, midnight. Went to bed at 10 and had been asleep for about two hours when heard a great rumpus and came down to hear that the Germans were attempting to land in *Kent*. I'm waiting to hear about messages etc. Have time to report that my reaction is pure astonishment and anger – cheek, absolute cheek.' It was a false alarm but brought vivid memories of the little girl who had been so frightened by the invasion scare twenty-five years ago.

Then Belgium fell and the fishermen and yacht crew from next door Tollesbury set out to help in the evacuation. There are still little ships at anchor round the East Coast bearing the proud, blue plaque 'Dunkirk 1940'. Margery's neighbour, Cynthia, lost her husband there. The Cameronians moved on from D'Arcy and a detachment of the King's Own Scottish Borderers took their place. 'It was an odd life,' Margery commented, 'I was always hoping that the end of one thriller would not overtake me before I had finished the other.'

'The Square' Tolleshunt D'Arcy
by P. Youngman Carter (1960)

XIV

The Inner Island

1940–1941

In a *Time and Tide* review published in April 1940, Margery gave her opinion that 'the thriller proper is a work of art as delicate and precise as a sonnet.' It was a tricky moment to give one's attention to a fresh and demanding genre. *Traitor's Purse* was written as the British public was buffeted by news of the Nazi invasion of Norway, the surrender of Belgium, the defeat of Holland and the evacuation of the British Expeditionary Force. It was completed in the week of the fall of France. Collaboration and treachery were in the air. Since Munich or before, the allied nations had sustained a series of blows crushing to their self-respect. It was a time to look askance at one's neighbours.

After their return from Essex to London in the First World War, the Allingham family had brushed briefly with direct betrayal. They had spent the Christmas of 1918 in their usual holiday house on Mersea Island. After returning to London in the New Year they were contacted by the police. A radio transmitter had been discovered in the attic of the house next door. It was beamed on Germany and had apparently been in use throughout hostilities. Herbert was interviewed by the Colchester police and felt sufficiently alarmed to appeal to Dr Salter to help him establish his honesty and clear up the matter.

For *Traitor's Purse* Margery was gripped by an idea that seemed to her good fiction. What a story it would make, she thought, if the quislings lurking in Great Britain planned to destabilise the country crucially before invasion by flooding it with 'Government-issued' forged money. Some reviewers considered this plot rather too far-fetched. Fifteen years later she was sent a newspaper cutting which confirmed that Himmler's S.S. had been planning something very like.

In contrast with the clogged and lavish style of *The Fashion in Shrouds*, the narrative of *Traitor's Purse* moves along swiftly (if somewhat bafflingly) from the outset. Margery demands attention and creates suspense, the first duty of any thriller-writer. The blow to Albert Campion's head is an effective mechanism to do just that. It is also at work on other, symbolic levels of meaning which make the comparison with the intricate sonnet-structure seem not so inept after all.

The physical blow that Campion suffers immediately before the action begins has included not only amnesia but an extraordinary sense of oppression; a nightmare feeling of urgency coupled with complete vagueness about what it is that must be done. On the evidence of journals such as *Time and Tide*, this found its equivalent in many people's emotional bewilderment through the eighteen month period from September 1938 to June 1940. Margery had used this same image of 'blows on the head' in her letters to Russell Meiggs, to describe the series of shocks and spiritual crises that had brought her close to the 'edge of sanity and everything else'. Through them she had learned to notice the 'little miracles' in life and had moved on thus to faith in 'the intrinsic value of good things' and the perception of a 'moving pattern'.

Albert Campion and his creator seem very close in *Traitor's Purse*. Wavering on the brink of consciousness throughout the novel, Campion is repeatedly close to disaster, then saved by the providential appearances of Amanda or Lugg. Much of the action takes place in darkness or underground. In a central scene, he realises that he has acquired something new. 'It had been something which so far he had entirely lacked . . . He saw it for what it was. It was a faith, a spiritual and romantic faith. That was the force that was driving him.' Acting on impulse, he leans forward into a patch of light. His true identity is revealed and the small-time villain who has been attempting to buy him off makes a run for it. Increasingly Margery's work asks to be read for its metaphysical as well as its physical action.

'The capitulation of France was a blow on a numbed head,' wrote Margery recalling the final shock of June 1940. The ordinary French people whom she and Pip had met on their honeymoon came vividly to mind then. 'They were alright. They would fight to the death just as we expected they would but there was something very funny about a High Command who would not defend Paris with six million men.' The events of May and June 1940 finally roused the instinct for battle in her. Previously she had felt part of a people 'elderly in soul, going to war stolidly as a duty to kill or to be killed'. After Dunkirk she identified unexpectedly with Dr Salter, 'the most uncomplicated, uncompromisingly English man', who had explained to her 'that one of the great joys of bare-knuckle prizefighting . . . was the agony when you first felt the other fellow's fist in your face, and every sinew and essence in your body boiled up in splendid rage as you plunged in to give him one better.' Margery was an ardent Churchillian. While he assured the country that 'We shall fight them on the beaches . . .' she and Grog looked out their weapons – a rifle from the funfair and a sword left by William McFee, intended for use on camel-back. All over the village, she discovered, people were considering rook rifles and homely basins of lighted kerosene to hurl at the invader.

Spiritual armaments were, she thought, equally important. Although German anti-morale propaganda appeared to be a powerful and destructive force, the National Day of Prayer, initiated by King George VI on May 26th 1940, promised something equally potent to set against it. With encouragement from Theodora Bosanquet, Margery nailed her colours boldly to the mast with a letter to *Time and Tide*: 'In the whole world God alone is neither neutral nor against us . . . with God we shall assuredly save ourselves and mankind from chaos, but between most of us and God there is the Church. In this desperate hour let it be a bridge and not a barrier.' As the Prime Minister took the lead and organised the physical defence of the country, so the Church should be seeing to its spiritual preparedness. 'Its material resources are enormous and its work is vital. What in Heaven's name is it doing?'

She had touched a nerve. There was a flurry of correspondence (some of it gently orchestrated by Theodora Bosanquet who sent copies of Margery's letter to likely respondents before its publication). Several writers doubted whether it was quite the thing to invoke God as an 'ammunition of war'. 'Sometimes it is God's Will,' suggested one correspondent, 'that the better cause should on the earthly plane suffer a defeat . . .' 'Christ,' wrote another, 'lived and worked in an occupied country conforming to the requirements of his conquerer with humble tranquillity.' Margery insisted that if they understood clearly what they were fighting for – and against – in the metaphysical conflict, and stuck to it, then they couldn't finally be defeated, whatever happened in physical terms. She came confidently to her own defence:

'I am in conscience compelled to state baldly . . . that for myself and for thousands of other simple, but not therefore I think, negligible or even unintellectual people, there *is* an aspect of the Christian God who is a military ally in this fight . . . the quarrel we have with the Nazi doctrine is also the quarrel of this particular aspect of God.' She had to be dissuaded by Miss Bosanquet from labelling these correspondents as 'academic'. She thought that they revealed 'as well as a fundamental niceness, a terrifying lazy-minded tolerance and indecision, certainly defeatist and almost decadent. It is all very well to put oneself unreservedly into the arms of God but it is insane to expect him to think for one.' (In her letters to Meiggs she had vehemently rejected what seemed to her the belittling notion that God 'has a brain'. 'He does not *think*!') Her reaction to her *Time and Tide* correspondents revealed how far she had moved from the image of God as a bearded patriarch – or mankind as sinful and frail. 'The insistence too that man is a poor sin-absorbed thing scandalises me. Surely man is the raw material of God?'

Esoteric 'Groups' made her shudder, devoted parish workers commanded her admiration. Her attitude to the Church of England was ambivalent – and made more so by her contact with the clergy to date. The then vicar of Tolleshunt D'Arcy had been both cavalier and unconcerned by the threatened closure of the Church school (of which Margery was now a Manager). Em's employer the Rev. Marcus Lawrence could seem 'an awful, narrow, over-educated type'. Over dinner in the difficult early months of their acquaintance he had asked her loudly whether she had 'Found Jesus' – and seemed disconcerted when she replied, 'Of course.' 'I must admit,' said Margery, 'that the only time my own natural, practical and unemotional faith wavers is when I am in Church or happen to hear some particularly idiotic religious broadcast.' She was however convinced that the traditional respect felt by ordinary Anglicans like herself for the episcopate, constituted a reserve of latent power. In a letter to Canon Roger Lloyd of Winchester, she stated her view of the potential for change that the crisis offered: 'The present time is bare, shivering and receptive and a strong line taken on essentials by the Church at the centre now might restore a unity and a subsequent authority that has been lost. That unity and authority have always been a need. Now it is a desperate one since the hour is even more dangerous spiritually than it is physically.'

Roger Lloyd had written several books on church matters and was a regular contributor to *Time and Tide*'s 'Notes on the Way' column. His question, addressed directly to Margery, 'Well, what do you want it [the Church] to do?' began a lengthy and amicable unpublished correspondence. He did his best to explain to her some of the internal problems of the Church (which appeared to centre on the age and ill-health of the then Archbishop of Canterbury, Cosmo Gordon Lang). He also worked energetically to carry out her reply to his question and initiate a period of specially focused prayer and teaching throughout his own diocese of Winchester. He had hopes of something similar from Southampton where the Bishop was known to be an appreciative reader of Margery's 'murders'.

There was excitement in August 1940 when William Temple, then Archbishop of York, took a hand in the debate. Roger Lloyd had told him of the discussion that had continued behind the columns of *Time and Tide* and 'I am sure you are right,' wrote Temple to Margery, 'when you say we have lost power because we so seldom talk with conviction and directness about God.' He then rather spoiled his argument by directing her to a recent contribution of his own in a Christian newsletter. In it he had advocated 'a gathering together of the great mass of Christian sentiment which undoubtedly exists and the direction of this to some definite goal'. To Margery, caught up by the extraordinary emotion of the Battle of Britain period, the goals proposed, federalism, abolition of the profit motive and worker participation on company boards, seemed at best irrelevant. She did not quarrel with his politics but with his priorities. 'I would not have you lead the people through socialism to God, but through God to socialism.'

She painted an emotional picture of her own disillusioned generation, picking themselves up from the 'shambles' of the Great War, reconstructing their lives through trial and error with no-one prepared to offer guidance, only to find themselves plunged back into chaos again. 'In this hour we need God.' It was a portrait on which she had started work as long ago as *Green Corn* and which had emerged from the camouflage of fiction in her letter to Meiggs. The discovery of Faith had been added to the canvas in *Traitor's Purse* and it would reach its most complete expression in *The Oaken Heart*, still a few months away. To William Temple she spoke of her own 'noticing' of God – and her consequent fears either 'of silly unnatural exultation (I am better, I am chosen) or of the more horrible sense of terror that one may somehow have got possessed by something which may turn out at any moment to be ordinary lunacy'. This was why she was looking to the Church. 'The Church holds one's hand. The Church gives one confidence to go on one's level way with the knowledge of God as the supreme asset and not as an over-balancing treasure.'

The Archbishop claimed to agree with every word. But, *how* to get the initial discovery of God as a vivid experience into people's hearts and minds? Margery replied at length and with sincerity. Then the correspondence lapsed. Disappointed, she pencilled a note onto her copy of her letter: 'No reply to this – not even an acknowledgement. They speak of him as a saint. It may be that the Blest can do without manners. Or that the posts are unreliable – ' Canon Lloyd was sure that there was 'a book in it' somewhere. He was deeply impressed by her analysis of her generation and offered to put her in touch with his publisher Robert Longman.

Other influences were pushing Margery towards a non-fiction project. From the Rockefeller Center, New York, Malcolm Johnson, now one of Doubleday's executive vice-presidents, wrote to Winifred Nerney in London, 'I have been brooding over Margery Allingham's various notes. I think she could do a most impressive non-fiction book about life in England and specifically in an English village during war-time. She speaks I think for the people who are England's backbone. She is a perfectly good reporter and a book written as her letters are written could hardly fail to find wide acceptance and to have values for England which I need not expand now.

'The difficulty is this: after a gap of several years we finally have a publishing schedule for her over here. I want her to continue to write mystery stories, if that is at all possible and to publish at least one and probably two a year. To ask her to interrupt her mystery writing for a book of non-fiction might be extremely unwise. On the other hand she may find it difficult to keep her mind on the arduous and complicated task of detective fiction writing, and if she does, this other book might give her an outlet for many things she would like to say, and might enable her to keep on writing steadily . . .

'I see a book with all the minutiae of village life as it is affected by the war, of what the ordinary person is doing and thinking about war and peace and the bombardment and the cost of food and the future of the children – a book full of the courage she expresses so well in her letters; the sort of book that would make the ordinary person here realise what war means.'

It was an astute letter. Margery had found herself 'ridiculous' as she plugged away at *Traitor's Purse* throughout the invasion scare and during her spells of duty at the Warden's Post. She stuffed it hastily into biscuit tins when there was an air-raid warning and 'tried not to see myself objectively for sanity's sake'. Three worlds jostled her consciousness: the international, as she read the newspapers and listened to the radio or Pip's military gossip; the domestic as she dealt with household, A.R.P. or First Aid business; and the fictional with Campion, Lugg and Amanda. Preserving a balance was hard. Her garden provided a refuge and spurts of defiant activity there may have been intended as unspoken reassurance that all would in the end be well. In the spring of 1940, when Pip was travelling to and from the barracks in Colchester, she asked him to design a rockery. Sam Taylor, the gardener, built it and Margery assisted in the planting of about sixty varieties. In the winter of 1941, when all the family were away, they put in one hundred apple trees.

Over the summer of 1940 and towards the autumn, aerial activity over the East Coast increased dramatically. The bomb map became pitted with black flags and Margery filled blank pages of her diary with four-leafed clovers. She had finished *Traitor's Purse* at the end of June and worked straight through the Battle of Britain summer to dispatch the first draft of *The Oaken Heart* to Paul Reynolds on November 20th. It reached America six weeks later. He passed it to Malcolm who was enthusiastic. Terms were agreed and Margery made herself a warm working corner in the breakfast room and started the book again. She had used two working titles; one, 'The Inner Island', touched lightly on those matters of psychological self-defence about which she had been writing to Meiggs, Roger Lloyd and William Temple. The other, 'Front-Line England', had the precise local detail Malcolm (and McFee) enjoyed. New material was coming in almost daily; from Londoners enduring the Blitz, from Joyce off to Singapore, Pip and Phil separately to the Middle East, news of the Tolleshunt D'Arcy Pig Club and the W.I. jam-making.

Margery's feelings about Tolleshunt D'Arcy and the house had changed completely since the time, three years ago, when she had wanted to sell it and get out 'of false position here'. After Munich, the Rev. Bobby Graves, formerly vicar for forty years, had written to her to express his pleasure at 'seeing you and Philip taking your proper place in village affairs'. Though in September 1939 Margery was still inclined to giggle at 'the remarkable collection of whiskery old gentlemen from all over the County who gathered in Pip's G.H.Q.' (and their accompanying 'troutage'), her First Aid and billeting duties changed her attitude decisively. She was bound to inspect her area and was frankly amazed by the conditions under which some country folk still lived – 'practically in *ditches*!' as she recalled years later. Her shyness and tendency to hang back from village life were jettisoned. 'The odd thing is the way it's improved the house. I used to hate the fact that it was so near the road. But now when I relieve Grog at the Post and sit down in the dining room with the window open, I know everyone who goes by and everyone knows me.'

It made *The Oaken Heart* both more absorbing and more difficult to write. 'Everybody in it is alive and living on my doorstep.' She had always been afraid of giving offence and this would be so easy when the new-found friends and neighbours saw their doings recorded in cold print – and for money. She chose deliberately to refer to everyone by their real names or nicknames and picked her words with the care of a referee. For the evacuees who had come and gone from the village and whom she therefore felt at liberty to portray more fully, she usually chose pseudonyms.

Because Margery could not risk attributing feelings such as bad temper, doubt or fear to others, she took almost all the emotional burden on herself. 'I wondered if we were all insane and so nearly squeaked aloud, as one does in nightmares sometimes, that I felt the blood rushing into my face with embarrassment.' 'I stuck my ground with the obstinacy of pure terror.' 'For myself I had never been more abjectly frightened in my life.' 'So I was hysterical, intermittently deaf and craven on that occasion, and also peculiarly angry.' The book recounts the slow process of 'hardening up'. 'Once you looked sideways, once you looked round, once you let your imagination out, you knew you might lose your head. Clearly the thing to do was to get yourself into a certain definite frame of mind and keep in it at all costs even if it made you slightly stupid. Everyone I met in the village seemed to be doing this instinctively but I . . . must always be watching and noting and putting things into communicable form.' *The Oaken Heart* became an important personal chronicle as well as a reflection of current history.

The overall theme of the book was a celebration of the character of 'the steadfast individual' – Margery's neighbours and their fellows up and down the country. The survival of civilisation now seemed to her to be dependent upon the personal integrity of ordinary folk. She herself was very frightened after Pip had been posted away in the summer of 1940 and during the 'noisy, bomb-filled winter' that followed. In the first year of war they had leased a small top-floor flat above the Doubleday office in Great Russell Street. The devastation Margery witnessed on her few visits there shocked her. The bombing of London was visible night after night from Tolleshunt D'Arcy as the German planes flew in over their heads. She was tempted to do as Nerney suggested, evacuate herself to some safer part of the country and carry on with the mystery story programme. Or perhaps set off and have 'an adventure', join up and know she was doing something directly useful like Cooee or Pip or Phil or Joyce, all of whom were in the Forces. By the spring of '41 even Grog was prepared to 'give himself up' to the recruiting officers. She wondered whether she would be called up, but knew this was unlikely. She was convinced that her duty was to remain at home, 'keep the roof tiles on' and ensure that the dislocation from which they had all suffered at the end of the First World War would not happen again. 'My new motto is "I Stay",' she announced on several different occasions. As her feeling for the village deepened, she added a second privately stated scheme – 'to earn all the money I can from America and spend it in the village'.

She remained fearful – and correspondingly filled with admiration for the people to whom dilemmas of staying or going never occurred. People like the Emeny family, Albert the handyman and Sam the gardener. Her admiration was not misty-eyed. She knew that they could be narrow-minded, suspicious, sharp-tongued and intolerant but that was all part and parcel of the great quality of rootedness. She remembered her grandfather saying of the Kaiser, 'He'll break his teeth on England.' A stubborn refusal to budge either from a place or from essential beliefs, seemed to Margery, in those unique days, to constitute the oaken heart of England 'which is old and hard and true still, in spite of surface rot'.

Throughout *The Oaken Heart* she attempts to 'clean old

words', words like 'good' and 'true', through the 'filter' of her own mind – a re-arming exercise analogous to the renewal of Christian understanding for which she had earlier hoped. 'Steadfastness' is the book's central quality and, to Margery, 'steadfastness' meant more than staying geographically put; it involved knowing who one was and staying within one's personal pattern, the very things she was struggling to do. Two people influenced her particularly through this period – and saw to it that she remained 'at her post' – Granny and Christina.

Christina Carter had been born in the village of Chappel, one of a large cottage family, and had had a happy country childhood. She and her brothers and sisters had been free to roam for miles across the fields, blackberrying, gathering wild flowers and herbs or playing, rather dangerously, along the railway line. Her father had died in the great 'flu epidemic of 1919 leaving her mother with a large family to provide for and little money. Christina went into service. She was the same age as Margery and had held several positions (including a spell with an English family in Washington) before she joined the household at Viaduct Farm. She enjoyed travelling and had only planned to work in Essex temporarily in order to spend some time nearer her mother. As she surveyed Margery's chaotic, even unhygienic household in the autumn of 1934, she remembers thinking, 'Oh my dear, you do need someone to look arter you!' She settled down and did so for the rest of Margery's life.

A stock figure in Margery's fiction, even before Christina's arrival, had been the devoted country woman who is the nurse, the housekeeper or the lady's maid. They were strong, taciturn figures equally able to deal with death, intruding detectives or the nerve-storms and waywardnesses of their lady charges. 'Chris' did not look like them at all. She was a plump, attractive country girl, ready to enjoy a joke, help with the parties and play with the succession of animals that passed through the house. Around 1940–41 she was busy making a pet out of a gander called Simpkin, one of two supposed to be a breeding pair who had been bought as an insurance against future food shortages. Simpkin, a notable character, was even allowed into Christina's kitchen – with a box tied underneath him to prevent him fouling the floor.

Even at Chappel it had not taken long for Margery to realise that her most junior member of staff was at least as strong-minded and dependable as the Alices and Dorotheas of her fiction. Chris knew what she was worth. She was frank about the wages she required and, if she felt she was being criticised unfairly, she had no hesitation in answering back. ('Her professional dignity is enormous.') This came as a great relief to Margery who was sometimes uncomfortable with the forcefulness of her own personality. Nothing she could do would 'rot up' Chris. If, for instance, she dared to suggest that the beds had been insufficiently aired, she risked having a pillow hurled across the room at her. Their relationship helps to make sense of some of Margery's more unexpected snatches of wisdom in *The Oaken Heart*: 'If the British people are prepared literally to die for freedom, then they may be expected to squabble and sulk for it also.' She could describe Chrissie as truculent, furious or flouncing without a shadow of anxiety that it would be taken in bad part. 'Oh yes, we had a lot of fights,' agrees Chris comfortably in her soft country voice.

A local Air Raid Warden coming on duty at the D'Arcy House 'Post' after Grog had left, remembers how cosy the kitchen seemed late at night with Chris and Margery sitting there chatting by the warm stove. When invasion was again discussed in the spring of 1941, Chris was confident that she could kill a parachutist or an enemy soldier 'if she had to'. They went shopping and to the cinema in Colchester together and when *The Oaken Heart* was finished, Margery and Chris went up to London for a few days. Chris helped Margery tidy up the flat for a small celebratory party and they went to lunch with Aunt Maud who was carrying on her magazines as normally as possible. She had moved into a hotel to be nearer the office and, when all the windows of her hotel room were blown out, she moved into the room next door and carried on as before.

Chris was, above all, invaluable in looking after Granny. Emily Jane had been living with Em and Marcus Lawrence on Foulness

Island when Marcus decided to move to a living further inland at Great Maplestead. The Vicarage there was huge and unfurnished. 'The work in the place and the size of it gave me a great respect for the old girl,' wrote Margery to Joyce about Em. 'She's got such a *nerve*!' Granny, however, was suffering an attack of bronchitis and came to D'Arcy House to be nursed by Margery. Once there she stayed until her death in 1952, her hundredth year.

She gave Margery someone for whom to keep the home going. Later on Margery often used to say that without Granny she would have left. She found her both comical and irritating. Her comments on the crisis provided much amusement: ' "Oh isn't it *wicked*!" she says, throwing down the paper. "Isn't it *naughty*! You'd think almost . . ." "What?" I say. "Well dear, I was going to say almost . . . you'd think *Gord* would do something." "Drop a brick on him?" "Or smite him," says Granny brightly. "All those poor nurses. Let me read you this bit . . ." '

She retained her desire to be helpful and a thriftiness from the days of her poverty. If Margery left any garment lying around the bathroom that Granny thought was getting a bit 'thin', she would whisk it away and patch it in the festive colours that she loved. 'I've got one nightshirt with a crescent on the stomach and a sort of swastika on the seat.' Granny liked re-cycling letters too and could not quite see why a communication from one dear relative to another should not simply have the name at the top altered and be sent on to give pleasure to a third. On her arrival, Margery made her promise that under no circumstances would she copy pieces from Margery's letters for general circulation round the various distant aunts and elderly cousins with whom she kept affectionately in touch.

During the nights of bombing and days of worry over those who were away, Margery's respect for the quality of Emily Jane's courage and faith increased. 'Her refuge is in manners and in God.' She could not share her Victorian conventions nor her social code but, 'better a shield covered with an anti-macassar than no shield at all.' Margery knew full well that the bombing they were suffering along the Essex Coast was as nothing to the pounding which Londoners had to endure night after night. She nevertheless had to struggle to control her fear when landmines came down and people in nearby Witham were reported to have been machine-gunned in the streets. The official censor cut five pages from *The Oaken Heart* which detailed their experiences with an unexploded mine and a variety of time-bombs. To Winifred Nerney, sticking to her own post at the Doubleday office, Margery wrote, 'Your news of London sounds very sad. I quake whenever I hear they've got through to you again. Do take care of yourself – I find it's the *continuous* bombing which gets one down. If we get a week off in between real excitement, almost everyone enjoys it but hefty crumps all round one every night are most demoralising. Granny even shows signs of boredom but not for long –' In one of the more distant 'crumps', audible from Tolleshunt D'Arcy, local people were shocked to hear that Em's fellow-executor and Mayor of Chelmsford, J. O. Thompson, and his family had been killed. All Dr Salter's diaries and the papers with which Em had helped him were lost.

The Oaken Heart was finished in May 1941. 'Am so tired I can't bear myself. I've written myself silly.' It is a book which today demands some effort of historical understanding and which, in its occasional lapses from clarity, may show the literary ill-effects of Pip's absence. He had been quick to complain that some early sections of *The Fashion in Shrouds* were 'incomprehensible'. Margery, about to start the second writing of *The Oaken Heart*, thought it 'queer stuff but very honnest'. It is a book written with minimal 'camouflage' and one which she remained proud to have completed. 'Previously I would have been afraid to say such things for fear of being misunderstood or of offending.' *The Oaken Heart* had helped her to make sense of a unique and testing time – and even to celebrate it. The published version ends,

'What a period! What an age to have been alive in!

'Oh, thank God I was born when I was.'

XV

'The World was Changing'

1941–1945

'The thing so few people remembered afterwards was the recklessness of that peculiar hour . . . The world was changing under his nose, between green shoot and stubble. The old order was going and the new one was rolling into place, gasping so painfully, retching and suffering so wretchedly in its agonising birthpangs that he might very well have been excused for mistaking them for death convulsions.'

Thus Margery's new novel, begun in the winter of 1941–2 when the theatre of war had become unequivocally world rather than European; when the momentary relief of good news from Pip in North Africa might be banished at any moment by realisation of the seriousness of the threat to Singapore where Joyce was stationed. Already the Battle of Britain summer, and the first heroisms of the Blitz, had receded from everyday consciousness. The sense of exaltation had been replaced by a grim determination to endure. What Margery termed the 'days of power' were slipping away.

The Oaken Heart, embodiment of those days, had been published in England in September 1941 and in America just a few weeks later. There, in the country for whom all the detail and the explanation had been intended, the book flopped. As soon as he had received the manuscript, Malcolm Johnson had written to thank Margery for 'the best expression that this war has seen of the spirit of a people – a record inspiring now and in a historical sense permanently valuable; in short, that rarity, an enduring book.' Paul Reynolds however wrote to her, 'I personally am very dubious now as to whether *The Oaken Heart* is going to have a large sale. It will be published in about four weeks now and the trade just isn't excited about it. The trade is sometimes wrong but not very often . . . I think it will be well reviewed and sell a few thousand copies.'

In Britain *The Oaken Heart* was not published by Heinemann but by Margery and Pip's friend from High Holborn days, Robert Lusty. At that time he had been with the somewhat amorphous mass of Hutchinson companies – one of which, Jarrolds, had published her first three Campions – but he was now managing the new, ambitious Michael Joseph Ltd. Margery was thrilled by this publisher's enthusiasm for her book. *The Oaken Heart* was being read in the office, Lusty told her, with an excitement only surpassed by the firm's first major success, Richard Llewellyn's *How Green Was My Valley* (published 1940). Margery's book never equalled that achievement but was nevertheless in its thirteenth thousand within two months – a respectable figure under wartime conditions, and a great improvement on her previous fiction sales. The first printing of *Shrouds* in 1938 had been 6,500 and of *Traitor's Purse*, earlier in 1941, 5,000.

The critics, too, were impressed. In advance of publication the *Time and Tide* diarist had written, 'In *The Oaken Heart* one hears the voice of a very old and very steady England,' and two weeks later the magazine's reviewer chimed in, '*The Oaken Heart* is something more than a true, touching and delightfully amusing study of England in wartime. It is England speaking . . .'

Pip wrote home later from the Middle East that 'elderly and unlikely persons came up with tears in their eyes' when they discovered that he was 'P.Y.C.' of *The Oaken Heart*, 'and assured me that it was the only classic they'd read since Scott.' For the first time in her career, Margery frankly enjoyed the publication of her book. It was not a matter of waiting for reviews and wondering about sales; readers felt that they had been caught up in the events of the book, and wrote or simply dropped in at D'Arcy House to say so. Margery described herself to Joyce (using one of her family nicknames) as 'Panda in Wonderland', never knowing what might arrive in the post or who might ring the front door bell. While the others were 'dancing round the world in this blessed circus', here was Margery's private adventure. Congratulations came from George Bernard Shaw and several years later (in 1948) an appreciative letter from someone even further back in Margery's past: Miss Holt, one of the assistant teachers who had attempted to champion her at Endsleigh House. 'It is the best book of the war years that I remember reading and what pleased me so much was that it was the kind of book I always hoped you would write. Unknown to you I have followed your career ever since you left school and it has always been a disappointment to me that the dark haired little girl with the straight fringe whose fingers were always inky and who wrote like a crab but whose ideas were always original should have gone in for writing thrillers . . . (P.S. Do you still spell language "langwidge"?)'

Among the most distinguished of *The Oaken Heart*'s admirers was Dr A. D. Lindsay, Master of Balliol, the college of which Russell Meiggs was now a fellow. In the way of eminent correspondents Lindsay sent both congratulations and a pamphlet of his own, *I Believe in Democracy*. On the last day of 1941, Margery replied, 'The immediate question you raise – how to keep this flash-in-the-pan of brotherhood is not an easy one is it? I have been thinking about it for a long time and, as I see it, what has happened is this, the danger has fused what is good (permanently alive) in each individual with the same thing in all his neighbours . . .' This new spirit of brotherhood was, in Margery's understanding, essentially Christian. It could she agreed, and indeed hoped, lead on to a form of socialism. She had raised no objections when *Time and Tide* dubbed her a Tory democrat (this was in opposition to J. B. Priestley, the 'socialist' tone of whose *Postscripts* had caused some offence) but in her letters to Lindsay she tried to make her position clearer. 'D'Arcy is Tory . . . and my job I felt was to put that down; it was D'Arcy's history not mine you see. I am if anything pure socialist, I suppose – Perhaps I ought to explain this. My father (who believed only in God and the Fabians) brought me up to be a novelist . . . I was discouraged from holding views. My only fixed stars lay in my religion, necessarily a very simple one (just the ten and one commandments) and all the rest was to be regarded as material to be observed, sorted and finally commented upon.'

Her opinion was as it had been when she replied to Archbishop

Temple in the summer of 1940 – that socialism was a word that had been desperately abused, and had led to untold disappointment, if not worse. She cited Russia and Germany. To Lindsay she spelled out what she had meant by 'leading people to socialism through Christianity'. She meant that the ideal 'love thy neighbour as thyself' had to be accepted first. For this it should be taught. 'Look, I think what I am saying is that it is not natural for most men to love their neighbours as themselves and that therefore they had better be taught how as well as why in a decent, simple, ordered fashion.'

She had lost confidence in the ability of the Church to act effectively. 'It looks as though Education will have to do it if it is to be done.' Her preparedness to try and legislate for good had grown firmer since the days of the evacuation. Then she had argued that 'no-one must ever be forced into doing good.' By 1942, she was prepared to be accused of indoctrination: 'It seems to me that the Germans are teaching some amazingly bad unconventional things and I don't see why we shouldn't teach some extraordinarily good ones.'

Once again Margery was in tune with her age. During 1942 there was a wave of social reforming energy. Discussions took place of the changes to be effected in the post-war world. It was the year of the Beveridge Report and the report from the Medical Planning Commission that laid the foundation for the 1944 National Health Service White Paper. Among the factors that influenced these attitudes was the shock many had felt, and Margery amongst them, during the evacuation as they discovered at first-hand the conditions under which their fellow-countrymen were normally obliged to live. Suffering the second of two world wars in a lifetime, Margery's contemporaries were determined to implement real change. 'This time we are doing the thing thoroughly and discovering the way to live pretty well from scratch . . . God is returning, like courage without fancy dress – if it can but survive its birthpangs this should be a very brave new world.'

One might expect that a novel written in this frame of mind would be something contemporary, even a little futuristic. In fact

Margery chose to write her only historical novel, *Dance of the Years*, as her contribution to human understanding at this time. As she explained to Dr Lindsay, she believed 'my value (if any) will always lie in this uncovering, pointing out, observing likenesses sort of way – the work, the constructing and altering is not for me – or at any rate not at this stage of my abnormally gradual development.'

She was ready now, she thought, to set aside the detective formula and 'attempt a real novel'. The expensive members of her household were away and she had slipped the leash of her regular publisher's schedule. This would be 'a great adventure'. 'I've got nearly a year to write whatever I like and I'm having a shot at something I want to say – It is a family history story with a plot, but its theme is an idea that has been growing in me for years. I cannot believe that the things people mean when they talk of "heredity", "environment" and "reincarnation" are not rather childish conceptions of a very big but also very obvious truth . . . and I thought that, if I could get away with it, it might be useful to put that point of view since from that angle things like the class question appear frankly silly.'

In her letters to these scholars and theologians, Margery developed a slightly disconcerting habit of characterising matters as 'obvious', 'simple', 'elementary' which, to this reader anyway, do not seem so at all. It may have been a form of defensiveness. She was always conscious, says Joyce, that she was 'uneducated'. Possibly she worried lest what was for her a new, exciting perception, might be, for them, bland, intellectual pap. Or it may have been that she was too much alone. Now that Pip was away, and Grog had joined the R.A.F., Margery was markedly less inhibited in her willingness to say what she had been thinking – she was not markedly clearer. Russell Meiggs had married late in 1941. She saw him only rarely after that date and the few letters that have survived stay on the surface of her life. At home she had lost her sounding-boards as well as her mockers. Charges of obscurity and over-didacticism can legitimately be levelled at some of her war-time writing. Nevertheless it was work of a philosophical and personal complexity that she might not otherwise have attempted and could not fail to enrich her post-war fiction. If Margery, like Dorothy Sayers, had to be judged on novels written before 1939, she would retain her place among 'Golden Age' crime-writers; she would not have staked such a convincing claim to full literary evaluation.

A clue to the 'very obvious truth' that links 'heredity' with 'environment' and 'reincarnation' comes when Margery tosses 'Christian philosophy' in brackets amongst them. 'Love thy neighbour *as thyself*' might, she thought, be a goal more capable of achievement if people were taught to attach more weight to their similarities than to their differences, and to see these differences as merely the accidents of their historical time and place – their contribution to an overall pattern. 'From one point of view,' she wrote, 'we are all one person really' – an interesting illumination of her literary as well as her philosophical aesthetics.

She did not believe in a personal soul: 'a peculiar unexplained spark individual to me, seems to my mind to be a sentimental idea'. Individuality lay in someone's 'pattern', their contribution of qualities: 'to put it baldly what I think is this; – I, Marge, am a composite thing. I am not a unit like, for instance, a pebble. I am a revolving muddle of a thing like a world and I am made up of millions of loosely related things not all of which are even sympathetic to one another.' Neither were these unique. She herself had ears, legs and a voice like Aunt Grace, her mind worked as her father's had, she was as likely to be impulsive as her mother and 'the peculiar, indefinable thing which is the kingpin of me' was something she could also discern in Granny. Such family likenesses, comparatively easy to spot, were manifestations of a larger truth. 'I think that out of other people could I be made up.' Because there were so many possible combinations of characteristics and because each individual combination was further modified by a person's position in space and time, exact replication, another identical Margery, was unlikely though not, by her theory, impossible.

These characteristics, mental and physical, were 'all mortal' but by that, she wrote, 'I mean capable not only of dying but of being reproduced.' She was interested in transferences of 'power' or 'force' between people and developed a theory that people could live on, in a limited sense, in others, by somehow 'bequeathing' certain of their qualities to their 'heirs'. She did not work out this theory fully for many years. Meanwhile, when Lilian Carter was suffering a terminal illness (she died in 1941), Margery wrote to Betty hoping that she would gain 'a sort of residue of strength' when her mother was finally released from pain. 'It's as if she's come to live in you for a bit.' She had felt this, she said, at the time of Herbert's death and it had been a tangible relief within her misery. Margery was 'so comforting and encouraging,' remembers Betty.

'I just work and listen to the wireless and read and read,' wrote Margery to Joyce. She was excited by what she read, by new ideas and intellectual pen-friendships. Writing to congratulate James Laver on his book *Nostradamus*, she suggested that 'time does not exist at all except as a measure of the growth and decay of each perishable thing'. Her reading had led her to consider all time as, in T. S. Eliot's phrase, 'eternally present'. Prophecy, then, she wrote to Laver, need arouse little surprise, the seer had caught a glimpse of events occurring simultaneously but outside the usual scope of his personal time – off the edge of the canvas as it were.

Paradoxically, together with the denial of conventional time, Margery possessed a sense of period that was as concrete as her sense of place. The historical novel, *Dance of the Years*, on which she worked during 1941–2, aimed to reflect as accurately as possible the slow alterations of certain attitudes through the Victorian age and on towards her own. It was also intended as a portrayal of a temporarily analogous experience – days of power passing away within the pattern of existence. In the same way that she had used her neighbours and herself to illustrate resolve growing towards the Battle of Britain days, she now used a version of her family's history to focus on the Victorians.

She begins *Dance of the Years* in the 'days of power' which she believed had existed while the country was under threat of Napoleonic invasion. Other writers had drawn this parallel as Britain looked anxiously across the water in the early 1940s and Margery relished analogies. To Lindsay, she quoted George

Borrow. 'I see from Borrow (Lavengro) that the same thing exactly happened in the early 19th century for about six months.' There is nothing quite so precise in *Lavengro*. The narrator tells of a time in his early boyhood spent near the French P.O.W. prison camp at Norman Cross. 'The dreadful struggle which long convulsed Europe and in which England bore so prominent a part was then at its hottest; we were at war and determination and enthusiasm shone in every face . . . Oh, those were the days of power, gallant days, bustling days.' It was in those days that he entered into his strange brotherhood with the Romany gypsies and earned his title 'lav-engro', romantically translated as 'word-master'.

This was a significant literary reference with which to embark. As well as the contemporary social motivation about which Margery wrote to Lindsay, *Dance of the Years* was intended as an exploration of components of herself through a history of her family. As she set out on it she wrote to Joyce telling her that this was to be The Novel, 'You know, the "Who-am-I?" one.' One of the stories that the Allinghams used to tell about themselves was that they were a 'second family'. Margery and Joyce played with the belief that their great- (or great-great-) grandfather had married twice and that his second wife, their ancestress, was a gypsy. Margery's American biographer, Richard Martin, commissioned genealogical research which discredits this theory and, at least towards the end of her life, Margery doesn't really seem to have believed it herself. Nevertheless, a gypsy ancestress offered her a convenient label for the streak of oddness she saw in her relatives. She had spoken of Phil's decision to join the fair people as something 'one of our family always has done'. She did not, thinks Joyce, mean this literally, but had in mind 'wild Uncle John's' exploits, Aunt Grace's disregard of convention and the slightly crude flamboyance of their mother.

Margery apparently suppressed all such characteristics in herself but she wondered whether her part of the family legacy was the gift of second sight. She had always attached great significance to her 'odd feelings' about things, her initial certainty, for instance, that she was 'destined' to live in D'Arcy

House. She consistently trusted her instincts above her intellect and took note of coincidences that others would have brushed aside. At this time particularly she noticed that premonitions about Pip's safety seemed often to have been justified. She might wake in the night gripped by fear for him, to discover later that he had indeed been in some danger on that date. This had happened on earlier occasions in their married life, once when he had been in a minor car accident returning from London with Phil, but he had not previously been away from her for any length of time.

The scene is set for *Dance of the Years* when the civilised, and desiccated, Squire Galantry takes advantage of the recklessness of his generation's 'days of power' to marry Shulamite Smith, the gypsy girl, and beget James, hero of the novel. 'This book is the story of James and the permutations of James.' Despite all the thought and hope Margery put into the novel – or, in part because of them – it was a failure. She was, perhaps, trying too hard. When, years later, she looked again at *The Fashion in Shrouds*, she found 'too many carefully hemmed turnings, not to mention feather-stitching all the way down the seams' and attributed this to 'over-anxiety'. This is far more obviously true of *Dance of the Years*. Though Margery's interpretation of the developing Victorian ethos is penetrating and interesting, her own voice is both too audible and too earnest. Not a facet of character, not a nuance of society escapes authorial analysis and in the process the life of the narrative is smothered, with never a murder to save it.

There was material enough for three books – something along the lines of Galsworthy's *Modern Comedy*, Arnold Bennett's Clayhanger trilogy or Kate O'Brien's Mellick novels. Volume one could have been the Victorians to the death of James (Margery's great-grandfather); volume two, late Victorians and Edwardians (grandparents and parents) and volume three a World War Two story of friendship and betrayal, love and work. Only the outline of the second and third parts was written. Little, Brown in America bought the book with enthusiasm on the strength of the first, early Victorian, section – and were so horrified by the way Margery rushed through the rest that they privately wished they were not obliged to publish. Michael Joseph published the novel in Britain, to polite reviews but disappointing sales.

Exact reasons for Margery's failure to carry out her intention are not documented. There are few letters or diary entries surviving from this period. Joyce believes that there was pressure from her publishers to deliver, and this may have come from Little, Brown. In November 1941 Margery received the first of a series of unexpectedly large income tax demands (£700) and may have hurried for the sake of some money. Equally, she may have lost confidence in the project herself. These were years when, in addition to her local wartime duties, she was always aware that her family were in peril. Occasionally she sought relief through verse. One notebook contains a poem, 'To my Husband'; unsophisticated lines, uncomplicated emotion.

'Today I set my teeth and hold my ground,
Tomorrow me, my heart, do not confound'

Her 1942 diary is threaded with lucky four-leaf clovers and little else – other than exclamations of relief when a cable or a letter from Pip arrived.

Pip had been posted to the Western Desert in 1941 and was now a captain. Initially he had little to do beyond censoring letters and coming to terms with the fleas and the flies. Then his unit moved on, its duty to supply the forward positions which were engaged in direct combat with Rommel's army. This was dirty and frequently dangerous work, culminating at the end of 1941 with the occupation of Tobruk. Through January and into February 1942 the situation was confused and uneasy. Pip was in and out of the line of fire as tank and artillery struggled to maintain constantly shifting and often untenable positions. Night-time bombing and aerial machine-gunning became commonplace. Half his platoon were lost on a single journey to Benghazi. Then in the summer came the long retreat from Tobruk. 'It was for us nightmare, often intensified by the futility of certain situations in which we found ourselves – times at which we just stood by uselessly and prayed we would get orders to move in time. A skin-of-the-teeth period.'

Pip missed Margery and hated the desert. He wrote to her frequently; easy, loving letters which described his daily doings as far as he could within the limitations of censorship. He was able to camouflage some criticisms of the headquarters staff and senior generals using their own Featherstone code. Lack of attention paid to the whole area of communications made him angry; the delays and unpredictabilities of the mail, the absence of channels for constructive comment by the ordinary soldier or junior officer and the insensitivity of sending men who had been two, three or four years in the desert, photographs of cheery American troops cuddling English girls at home.

'Dear Guffin,' he wrote in the spring of 1942, using one of his regular pet-names for her, 'Whatever adventures may hap (and pray God I don't have any more exciting ones) I can only regard all this as a stupid unnecessary interlude in our existence. Salutary perhaps, but on the whole a crushing bore and a cure for nothing except sophistication and preciosity. If I can't get a job soon that exercises my particular gifts I begin to think they'll atrophy and I shall become a normal case of the Desert Balmies.' 'And as for missing you,' he had written on an earlier occasion, 'my dear it occupies all my conscious thought all the time as a sort of orchestral background – will never let it happen again.'

After a period of reconnaissance duties, Pip was posted away from the battle lines, much to Margery's relief, and on to Baghdad as a Senior Army Press Officer – a matter of weeks before the battle of El Alamein. He left the desert gladly. 'I never want to see the mark of a tyre in the sand again, or to experience that continual cold gripe of terror that is so much like dyspepsia and which still haunts my dreams.' He too had turned to verse and a newspaper clipping survives from 1941, hailing the emergence of Pip Youngman Carter as 'a new war-poet'. This was his chance to tackle the problems about which he had groused. His duties in Baghdad brought out his real talents – the production of a daily paper *The Iraq Times*, as well as forces' newsheets, and broadcasting and public relations generally. He learned new, professional skills and Margery delighted herself with the belief that he was 'writing and drawing all day'. Certainly Pip enjoyed a burst of creativity at this time which suggests that he had found living at home with Margery artistically stultifying. He wrote several short stories and undertook a number of portraits including a commission to sketch the eight-year-old King Faisal II. Occasionally he was able to arrange meetings with Phil Allingham who was also posted to the Middle East. They recaptured their early camaraderie and exchanged bawdy details of their hospital experiences. Pip had gone down with an attack of pneumonia during 1943, Phil with a complex of maladies including acute sinusitis.

Pip also met Sean Fielding with whom he was to found *Soldier* (a monthly magazine for the forces which remains in production today). He worked in Cairo, Damascus and Teheran. The nature of his new job brought him in contact with a variety of people whom he found agreeable, interesting or useful and laid the foundations for his post-war career. He was himself a colourful presence. Jack Morpurgo, then a lieutenant in the Royal Artillery, paints a vivid picture of Pip's uninhibited social personality: 'I noticed that his capacity for gin was as enormous as his zest for work, that his enthusiasm for a tightly encased female bottom was as quick as his appreciation for a well-turned phrase . . . from that day too, I recall my sense of shame for the contrast between my sweat-laden, sand-encrusted officer's shop khaki drill and his immaculate, even resplendent dress, as fresh and well-cut as if every 24 hours there came to him on a magic carpet from Savile Row to Baghdad, a new uniform.'

Grog and Margery had protested when Pip put the final touch to his appearance and adopted a monocle in his D'Arcy H.Q. at the outbreak of war. Jack Morpurgo bears witness to what an effective adjunct to his personality this had become. When Morpurgo mentioned his plans for an anthology of Middle East Forces writing, 'Pip Youngman Carter . . . looked at me superciliously through his monocle, offered me the backing of *Soldier* magazine and took me to lunch at the Turf Club.' It could have been *The Tatler* already. Pip remained with *Soldier* magazine until the winter of 1945/6. Among his final assignments he travelled in attendance on the British Army of the Rhine viewing the devastation inflicted by Allied bombers on cities such as Hamburg. He was moved by the plight of the German people then. 'I never saw people so utterly bashed,' he wrote home to Margery.

His earlier removal from the Desert War to these more congenial occupations had lifted a burden of anxiety. In March 1943 Margery wrote to Dr Lindsay, 'I am glad your war news is good – so is mine thank God. There were one or two anxious moments naturally for my people were nearly all mixed up in the retreat but they all got away in the end and now PYC has been collected by the Public Relations people and is completely happy drawing all day . . . The others sound fairly happy. Grog is in Alexandria, Phil convalescing after what sounds like a slightly fractured spine, and my sister in Mombasa.'

She reported on her own war-jobs. There were seven of them, including 'emergency food officer' and 'minder of land girls'. 'While I cannot think that they are of much importance they are things that someone has to do.' Iron rations had been allocated to the village. These had to be stored and plans made for their swift distribution in a crisis. There was a village 'pig club' whose meetings Margery attended and on whose behalf she had sought advice from The Small Pig-Keepers Council near Henley-on-Thames. Visits to London were rare. She went to the theatre with Louisa, the zoo with Cressie and maintained her regular comfortable relationship with Nerney. These close friends came in their turn for quiet weekends at Tolleshunt D'Arcy. Small things were satisfying: eggs sent up regularly to the Doubleday office in Great Russell Street for distribution to friends and colleagues and the cartons returned by train the following week; a dress pattern successfully copied for Louisa; much bottling of plums from a good fruit harvest. Margery dispensed with a car and caught the bus or paid someone from the village to drive her when she wanted to go to the station or to Colchester. 'See all you can, feel all you can too,' she urged Joyce as she travelled to exotic postings. For herself, she scarcely left the parish.

The publication of *The Oaken Heart* had marked a moment when she felt accepted by the village and at home as she had never been before in a community. She was amused, she told Lindsay, by a tendency among her neighbours to adopt her as their mouthpiece, resident letter-writer and negotiator with Authority; and also rather pleased. 'It is impossible not to like them all very much and they are very easy to live with but I'm afraid I'm getting even more simple-minded than usual under their influence and it will be a good thing when the more sophisticated sides of the household return.'

She realised that *Dance of the Years* had not turned out as she had hoped but felt that she had benefited from a 'remedial year'. 'I am looking forward to my life of crime again and that had become rather stale. I was trying to put too much into the thrillers which was silly and unprofitable. Now I feel rather like an adventure or two with Mr Campion and Mr Lugg. The trouble I seem to have is that I must put down all I think to escape from it and a too constant devotion to one vein leaves me with a whole mass of fermenting ideas that have to be let out and aired. Not quite the right spirit in which to approach one's unfortunate readers perhaps but I don't see any other way out! I rather fancy I'm going to have a little trouble over this book . . .'

It appears that she did: *Coroner's Pidgin* was announced in a release written by herself and sent to *The Bookseller* by Louisa Callender in September 1943. It was not finished until the spring of 1945 – and then with a rush. Although the detective box was back in place, this book too said much about the period in which it was written: 'I don't like the way things are going just now . . . The "days of power" are over and now the great wind which blew everyone in one direction has died down, the view looks a trifle spiky to me.' There was a niggling persistent end-of-the-war feeling extraordinarily early in Britain – and a corresponding sense of frustration that the reality was so long in coming; the wait for the D-Day landings was wearisome; demobilisation schemes were discussed tantalisingly early then seemed slow and often haphazard in effect. The final terror of the V1 and V2 bombs strained tired nerves almost to breaking.

Coroner's Pidgin shares this pre-post-war uncertainty. Albert Campion cannot be certain whether or not he is home for good and his friend, Johnny Carados, attempting to commute between his London house and an R.A.F. base, is put at risk by the sheer incompatibility of the social structures and values in his two worlds. The Carados household invites comparison with the Sutanes – or with the Carters' 1930s *ménage*. But as Margery was to discover when her 'family' came home, such casual groupings could not be recreated in the post-war world. Mutual tolerance and communal responsibility – always qualities in short supply – have taken a knock from which they cannot recover. Taking thought for others is out of date and self-interest reigns paramount in *Coroner's Pidgin*. Even the grande dame is no longer a figure to be respected or obeyed. She is a spoiled, interfering nuisance. When the body of a murdered woman comes up the stairs in the very first sentence of the novel it is no longer the salutary shock that proves the basic health of a society. It is merely an inconvenience.

All this is fine and in keeping with the topical flavour and the title of the book – leave it for the coroner, it's his responsibility. Unfortunately something of the uneasiness of the period has crept out of the theme and into the timbers of the novel itself. Shuffling a surplus body from house to house or from bedroom to bathroom may offer a comment on the characters' attitudes but it may equally reveal callousness on the part of the author. Margery, always on the idealistic wing of her profession, does not usually allow a corpse to be so blatantly a prop.

World War II altered people's sensitivity to violence. In 1942 Hitler had unleashed the full force of his Final Solution; Pip, with deep repugnance, suppressed a report of the massacre of Polish officers by Stalin's Russia; and Margery reviewed Martha Gellhorn's searing *A Stricken Field* for *Time and Tide*. 'There will be people who will refuse to read this book and they will be human and natural but that does not alter the fact that they will be fools and cowards.' Canon Roger Lloyd worried with equal sincerity whether too much reading of the literature of atrocity might not gradually have a numbing effect on the reader's emotions and thus in some way extend the original evil.

Margery, only half-humorously, recommended readers of her review to 'say the sixty-fifth psalm over late at night' to gain some measure of relief from the graphic cruelties described in Martha Gellhorn's book such as 'flaying a sick man until his kidneys are laid bare before the eyes of his adoring sister'. Her return from contemporary horror to detective-story murder is unconvincing. Forty or so innocent train and van drivers are killed by Fifth Column sympathisers in *Coroner's Pidgin* with not one fortieth of the outrage that was generated by the suicide of a station porter's wife in *Dancers*. Motives too are ignoble. In *Traitor's Purse* the villain had a certain monomaniac stature. When only property, not lives or metaphysical concepts, is at stake, Oates' loathing of 'Double-crossing', of 'the Judases, the men who kiss and serve and sell; the lads who sit tight in one way of life and still serve the other . . .' has somehow lost its force. Who in this twilight world has the energy to care whether the Gryth Chalice has been tucked away for Goering? The novel, like its creator perhaps, is happiest with Lugg in the pig pen or Miss Pork down in the country.

Pip, 1942
by P. Youngman Carter

XVI

'Off the Chain'

1946–1950

The D'Arcy household did not reassemble after the war. Pip, who had been demobbed a Lieutenant Colonel, left *Soldier* magazine and took a job with *The Daily Express*. This involved his living in London during the week in their flat at 91, Great Russell Street. Cooee was married. Joyce stayed in the W.R.N.S. Phil married Francesca, an Italian girl whom he had met in London before the war. He settled down to build up a business supplying horoscope cards and other grafter's equipment. 'Madame Francesca' told fortunes for magazines. Only Grog made tentative moves to return to Essex but by then it was clear that their previous way of life was gone and he was gently discouraged. Margery, Chris and Granny continued their secluded domestic existence almost as if nothing had happened. Friends of Margery's own continued to visit her at D'Arcy and Pip usually, but not invariably, came home at weekends.

After the resolutions stated so often in Pip's letters of 1941 and 1942 that they would never again be parted and the few miles to neighbouring Maldon would be the furthest he would stir from the parish of Tolleshunt D'Arcy, Pip's post-war career decisions must surely have come as an unwelcome surprise. His letters of 1943 reveal how interesting he found the variety of media jobs into which he was pitch-forked, broadcasting, editing, writing, drawing, reporting. He relished the web of contacts which flourished within the press corps and, after the dirt and discomfort of the desert, made the most of hotel living and whatever entertainment was available. The commission to draw eight-year-old King Faisal II was exciting and the editorial sensation of having influence, heady. 'A sucker-up after people' Margery had damned him in 1925 but his sister Betty suggests more charitably that Pip returned from the war changed, as did so many others, and no longer wished to live as 'Mr Margery Allingham'. There are no diaries and only fragments of letters survive between 1943 and 1946.

The war had also to some extent weaned Margery from her emotional dependence on Pip. She had grown used to being 'off the chain' but she had not ceased to miss him. When she believed it safe to do so, she had looked forward to the return of his gay, sophisticated self and a renewal of their art-and-fiction partnership. There must have been a moment, probably early in 1946, when she realised that this was not going to happen. There is no record at all of whatever was said, thought or felt then. In February Margery sent a brief business note to their friend Arthur Underwood asking about separate tax assessment. In November she decided that she 'owed' Louisa Callender an explanation of her decision to postpone work on a promised Campion novel in favour of a magazine serial for sale in the United States. By the time this letter was written their new domestic arrangements appear to have been settled and the financial consequences of their situation are at the forefront of her mind. 'The alternative' (to earning money from a serial story) 'is to put Granny (and Grog?) in a home, sell the house and go and live at 91 with Pip. If I do that, I shall have to do the chores, won't be happy and won't write at all. Also he won't hear of the idea. If Pip lived *here* and went back to drawing and we spent his money on one home it might be different but I can hardly expect him to give up his career can I? We *could* part of course but we like each other.'

Pip's new way of life put even this 'liking' in some jeopardy. His job under Arthur Christiansen at *The Daily Express* was short-lived though the two men remained close friends. In the autumn of '46, 'that old social newshawk, Col. Carter', as Margery dubbed him, rejoined his *Soldier* associate, Sean Fielding, who had accepted the editorship of *The Tatler*. Sean was the author of a successful film, *Desert War*, and was poised to become an influential figure in post-war London café society.

The great houses and the aristocratic society hostesses whose milieux had provided glamorous 1930s settings for Margery's *Strand* stories and for several detective novels by her New Zealand-born contemporary Ngaio Marsh, had largely gone. In their place was a drabber, more ramshackle world in which new fortunes could be made and new reputations built up. The photographer, the couturier, the gossip-writer were key figures in the process. Alongside this tentative entrepreneurial excitement, there was war-weariness to combat, a sense of dejection at the battered state of London and at the prospect of reconstructing civilian lives after absences of five to seven years. Sean Fielding was at lunch with the photographer 'Baron' Nahum when 'The Thursday Club' was mooted 'to lighten the gloom that surrounded us all'. Baron's idea was that 'we should meet with friends once a week. No issues of importance would be allowed, no international questions would be solved – The club would be dedicated to Absolute Inconsequence. We would eat as well as we could, tell stories and swap reminiscences.'

Sean arranged the venue, Wheeler's Oyster Bar in Soho, and Pip was among the first men invited to join. Baron described these first members as an 'interesting cross-section of the post-war London Society that was just beginning to emerge; none of them were really nationally known figures, yet all possessed of the kind of Johnsonian vigour which is, in my opinion, the most interesting characteristic of present-day London.' The next batch of members were unarguably 'nationally known' – Peter Ustinov, James Robertson Justice, Gilbert Harding, David, Marquess of Milford Haven and Lieutenant Philip Mountbatten, R.N. A year later, in November 1947, Pip popped downstairs from the flat at No. 91 to show off his resplendent morning clothes to Winifred Nerney in the Doubleday office. He was on his way to the wedding of Prince Philip and Princess Elizabeth in Westminster Abbey.

There was only a marginal role for Margery in this. As other men returned to the countryside, Pip's enthusiasm for village cricket and summer parties was re-kindled and he occasionally invited London colleagues down with him. Margery rarely joined in the round of first nights, wine-tastings and private views that constituted much of his social life in London. She seems to have distrusted Sean Fielding, not for himself as much as for his influence on Pip, possibly holding him responsible for Pip's separation from her. Sean was brilliantly witty and stylish, a forceful personality. Margery found him alarming and 'a terrific snob'. Later she suspected that Pip had himself made the most of any 'rift' between Sean and her in order to preserve his freedom of manoeuvre.

The Tatler was then a weekly paper. Pip contributed portrait drawings – usually of actors or theatrical impresarios: Tom Walls, A. E. Matthews, Douglas Fairbanks and Ralph Richardson, sometimes with an accompanying character study. His versatility came into its own as he stepped into James Agate's place to cover films on the death of that distinguished critic; took on Anthony Cookman's theatre column or Sean Fielding's leaders when either went on holiday, and wrote occasional articles on wine or restaurants (often under the pseudonym Isaac Bickerstaff). Sean and Pip tried to retain a whiff of the eighteenth-century coffee-shop about their early articles for the magazine. Under their direction it moved perceptibly away from country sport to more extensive coverage of urban fashion. Pip's 'London Limelight' theatre column was a much praised feature during the 1950s. Immediately after the war, readers were more likely to holiday in Frinton-on-Sea than in Mustique but as the world returned to normal there were travel assignments too. Pip visited Paris, Madeira and Monte Carlo and went big-game hunting in Rhodesia. When Sean resigned from the magazine in 1954, Pip took over as its editor.

From 1953 he was also editor of *The Compleat Imbiber*, Gilbey's house magazine. It offered scope for fiction and illustrations as well as wine-trade articles and seems to have been a rather jollier venture than *The Tatler*. Work on *The Imbiber* could occasionally be done during weekends at D'Arcy House, with Grog and their friend Pippa involved. Margery provided a couple of stories and was talked into endorsing some advertisements for Martini. Pip, as George Gulley, wrote the leaders.

One of Pip's great qualities – one for which Margery missed

him especially – was his capacity to initiate projects and kindle enthusiasm in others. E. S. Turner, author of *Boys Will Be Boys*, a study of penny-dreadful adventure stories, published by Michael Joseph in 1948 (and the only critical study I have come across that mentions Herbert's contribution to the genre), paid special tribute in his preface to the encouragement given him by Pip. It was an invaluable asset to an editor. Jack Morpurgo remembers how he and other Old Blue friends might suddenly find themselves, notebooks in hand, at once 'face to face with a Society beauty and back to back with a Grand National winner'. At least two *Tatler* issues include a tiny sketch by Grog. Friends such as T. E. B. Clarke and Henry Rushbury had become fit subjects for features. There were photographs from Baron and from 'Franzi' Goodman who had undertaken some pensive studies of Margery at D'Arcy House; Robert Tredinnick (Record of the Week) and Anthony Cookman (theatre) were Essex neighbours and friends. Pip and Margery's summer parties had always offered an ideal opportunity for underwriting business with friendship. In the later forties and fifties the guest lists began to read like a media roll call.

This led to some awkwardness in 1949 when Baron decided to organise a cricket match – the Thursday Club against the locals – 'at Youngman Carter's country home'. Prince Philip and the Marquess of Milford Haven were in the team and although the occasion was private somebody told the *News of the World*. Their photographer snapped the Prince just as he was coming out to bat on the D'Arcy meadow and the picture, with Margery discernible in the background, was published next day. Margery, who with Chrissie and Joyce helping, had taken pains to do or say nothing that they would not normally do for any visiting cricket team, disliked this view of herself as a celebrity hostess. When, in the following year, the local tax inspector questioned her about her business entertaining figures and asked to see her visitors' book, she reacted with a degree of paranoia that derived directly from this embarrassment.

The cost of Pip's chosen way of life was considerable. Margery had fallen behind with payment of income tax during the war and Pip's new status as a salaried man was not the help that it might have been. He needed all of it – rather more than all of it it sometimes seemed – to finance his London living. There was little left for D'Arcy House, let alone arrears of tax. And all Margery's earnings were pushed into the surtax bracket. It was a situation about which several other successful married women novelists felt aggrieved in the later forties and fifties until the whole question of the taxation of artists was reconsidered.

Separate assessment, about which Margery had written to Arthur Underwood in February 1946, was not allowed. Margery then made what she afterwards realised was an error. She had written a serial story *Wanted: Someone Innocent* during 1945/6 which Paul Reynolds had sold advantageously to the *Saturday Evening Post*. Their wartime arrears were tackled but her annual income on which future tax assessments would be made was considerably boosted – and the serial money itself was immediately liable. Not quite seeing the consequences of her action, Margery set aside the novel she had promised Heinemann and wrote a second serial, *Last Act*, also for sale in America, mainly to pay off the tax on the first. She found she had thus set herself on a treadmill of accumulating demands which both terrified and exhausted her until Pip left *The Tatler* in 1957.

She was not in good health. The doctor who had helped her with her thyroid problems during the war had died. No specialist took his place. She had always been a heavy smoker and suffered increasingly from bronchitis, sinusitis and fluey illnesses. Food was scarce and dreary. 'The whole place,' she wrote to Nelson Doubleday in January of the bitter winter of 1946–47, 'is on a sort of half-baked reducing diet which keeps tempers scratchy but open revolt down as being too much effort.' She was lucky enough to receive regular food parcels from America – butter, sugar, flour, tea, tins of bacon, ham and beef. There are many letters which attest to the generosity with which she redistributed them among neighbours and friends. Paul Reynolds and his wife Ruth helped to keep Margery supplied with these and other 'luxuries' unobtainable in Britain. Nylons, pen refills and good quality typing paper were especially welcome.

It was difficult to summon the energy to fulfil her literary and financial obligations and she began to wonder whether she couldn't earn more from those novels she had written already. Almost all were out of print. Shortage of paper had affected many publishers' production during the war and it continued to be rationed and expensive. The metal type of books considered unlikely to warrant republication, *Cheapjack* for instance, had been melted down. At Heinemann Charles Evans had died and Dwye had returned from wartime service in the R.A.F. He could hold out little hope of reprints for any of the eight novels published by the firm before *Coroner's Pidgin*.

In Margery's opinion the 'news' in British publishing during the immediate post-war years was the dynamic expansion of Allen Lane's Penguin paperbacks, ten years old in July 1945. Penguin, who had been notably clever in manipulating the wartime paper situation to its own advantage, printed more copies and kept titles in print for longer than the traditional publishing houses. Margery by now was receiving regular letters from fans who wanted to read earlier episodes in what ordinary readers (but not the critics) were beginning to view as the Campion saga. She always replied to such letters, sent copies of unobtainable books if she possessed them herself and made friends. 'In England readers are quite amazingly faithful to an author,' she commented to Doubleday. If interest in an author was kept alive through a readily available backlist, then the new books from the hardback publisher would be more enthusiastically received.

Penguin could supply a readership numbered in tens, even hundreds of thousands rather than the 12–17,000 that was Margery's standard post-war sale in hardback. Her novella, *The Case of the Late Pig*, published in 1937 by Hodder and Stoughton, had been released to Penguin in 1940. It sold 75,000 copies then and 50,000 a year later. *Police at the Funeral, Death of a Ghost* and *Flowers for the Judge* had had similar wartime success. Allen Lane enjoyed Margery's books and they were on friendly terms. However, when the right to publish *Dancers in Mourning* in paperback was requested in 1946, attitudes at Heinemann had stiffened. In November Margery wrote to her agent, A. P. Watt, 'You say that if Miss Callender will not agree to waive her demand for 25% of the Penguin royalties, you will go and see her. If you do I hope you . . . will explain to her that in view of the present taxation on married people I am forced to do one of two things. One of them is to make extra money in the U.S. market to pay supertax due on my earnings. The other is to give up writing altogether and do my own housework and cooking as our government expects a married woman to do . . . I hope you will point out to Miss Callender that the cheap edition money on previous books which I should of course prefer to come from Heinemann themselves, *will have to come from somewhere* . . .'

Although she wrote simultaneously in more emollient terms to Louisa the surprising tone of this letter to 'Daddy' Watt may give some indication of the strain she was under. As well as her feelings of guilt and personal frustration over the Campion novel postponed in favour of the U.S. serial (it was *More Work for the Undertaker* and was not delivered until June 1948), one may suspect an alternative guilt that she was not behaving as a good wife should.

Rationally there could be no justification for this. Pip was consistently proud of Margery's achievements but he didn't want her with him in London and he wished D'Arcy House to be maintained in the style to which he had become accustomed. Margery felt excluded by Pip's new scheme of things. However she rationalised it, she could not escape some feeling of hurt. In moments of loneliness she may well have reflected how different their life might be if she, as well as he, was prepared to behave differently. She may even have experienced the first stirrings of suspicion that the womanly qualities which she was not offering Pip might be found by him elsewhere.

Early in 1949 Margery took an unexpected opportunity to demonstrate that she and Pip were still one team. Arrangements had been made by Paul Reynolds and her American publishers for her to visit New York in order to publicise her most recent novel (*More Work for the Undertaker,* completed at last) and to meet the magazine editors for whom she was writing the serials. The travel and currency restrictions in force necessitated formal invitations from Doubleday stating the business purposes of the trip. These had initially been completed for Margery alone. Pip liked such excitements too – as she had noticed when he dashed round London with Phil during the publication of *Cheapjack*. He wanted to accompany her.

Margery wrote to Paul Reynolds asking for new invitations to be issued. Whether to comply with the regulations, to bolster Pip's status or to strike a blow for their future, she laid great stress on their working partnership. He was virtually her co-author, she said, all their work was done together. Paul's amazement was undisguised; he confessed he had 'never really believed in Pip's existence even and now I find that he writes all your books with you'. Margery had been asked to write an article on detective fiction for *Town and Country*, an American magazine. She seized the opportunity to convince other sceptics of Pip's importance to her work. The editor was delighted – 'I believe I am being offered something of a scoop' – and stipulated that Margery should say as little as possible before publication.

Perhaps it was not too hard to comply. The only book of Margery's in which Pip could unequivocally be claimed as a 'co-author' had been *The Crime at Black Dudley*, written in the first months of their marriage. For the next three novels produced during their house swaps with Herbert and Em he had contributed to the plots and had been a valuable commentator. But from the time they moved to Viaduct Farm his involvement had dwindled steadily. After his brief resurgence of interest over *Traitor's Purse*, he had naturally been unable to take any part in *The Oaken Heart, Dance of the Years* or *Coroner's Pidgin*. Even after Margery's death when his decision to complete *Cargo of Eagles* pressed him to take what responsibility he could for previous books, Pip himself never claimed to have been more than a 'discusser'. And how many 1950s husbands talking over the progress of their work with their wives would ask that those wives be publicly recognised as equally responsible for it? Whether the *Town and Country* article reveals more about Margery's generosity or her insecurity is hard to determine. She was well aware that Pip was more firmly bound to her, financially, than she to him.

It is particularly hard to ascertain the nature of Pip's involvement in *More Work for the Undertaker*, the novel they were travelling to promote. Pip spoke of it as a book with which he had been particularly closely associated, and as 'probably her best'. There is some justification for the second claim and one can do no other than accept the first. Except to wonder when he found the time. Margery's letters to Louisa make it clear that the genesis of *Undertaker* took place during 1946 while Pip was establishing himself separately in Great Russell Street. Most of the writing was done when he was in his first year at *The Tatler* in 1947–8. No diaries have survived from this period but from 1950 when they can again be studied, it does not appear that Margery used to do a great deal of work at weekends when Pip was home. He was often tired and wanted to sleep late, read the papers and be provided with clean laundry for the coming week.

Other 'family' visitors like Joyce, Cressie or Aunt Maud were frequently present and Margery and Pip had picked up some of the threads of their pre-war social life such as visits to and from the Reids, the Maddens, and other local families. Margery had become friendly with Dr Francis Camps, the Home Office pathologist, who lived at nearby Purleigh. Jack Morpurgo was across the water at Bradwell which was also home of Tom Driberg the Labour M.P. for the area.

Pip loathed everything Driberg represented and would turn his back on him if they met in a public place. Margery was politely noncommittal. As she struggled to pay the taxes imposed by the Labour government, however, she grew more openly Conservative. She and Pip went to meetings at election time and entertained the prospective Conservative candidate, Aubrey Moody. Margery was pleased when she thought Moody had used some of her 'bits' in a speech. He, in common with the generality of their social visitors, found Pip and Margery hospitable and charming, a secure, successful couple in possession of a rather lovely house and garden.

They paid their visit to America in February 1949. Instead of crossing the Atlantic by boat, still the traditional route, they were slightly more adventurous and flew via Iceland. The trip appears to have made very little impression on Margery. She was glad to meet Paul Reynolds and his wife Ruth, made wary by the effusiveness of Isabelle Taylor who had succeeded Malcolm Johnson as her Doubleday editor. It was useful to meet the personnel of the New York office and the way was opened for many return visits by her American business contacts to D'Arcy House.

She saw Mac briefly and had a series of lunches with the influential editors of the fiction magazines, but perhaps only truly enjoyed the few days she and Pip spent with fellow Doubleday author Lavinia Davis and her husband Wendell at their country home in Connecticut. Barbara Noble, who was later to take over from Winifred Nerney as Doubleday's London representative, and who visited the Davises at Still Farm with her, remembers it as 'a lovely place and full of such well-mannered and charming children'. The Davises had six children all of whom became well-known to Margery through their mother's letters. The eldest, Ned, later spent several weeks convalescing at D'Arcy House after becoming seriously ill during an English Speaking Union exchange. Wendell and Pip liked one another and although this was the Carters' only visit to Connecticut, there was scarcely a year from that date when one or two – or six or seven – of the Davis family did not arrive in Essex.

Lavinia had been introduced to Margery by Winifred Nerney in 1948. She was a favourite too of William McFee who wrote to Margery after her death that 'the light has gone out of that house'. Margery's diary comment, 'a nice woman – very intelligent', seems less than fulsome yet holds a great relief. She could talk, or more usually write, to Lavinia about almost anything that concerned her in the certainty that she would be understood and that she risked nothing.

Margery's sister-in-law, Betty Carter, suggests it was not easy for Margery to make close feminine friendships because so many of the women she met were simply not on her intellectual level. Although Margery was generally more comfortable with women who complemented rather than competed with her, some of the 'other halves' who accompanied their husbands to D'Arcy House do not appear to have been stimulating company. A few women felt ignored by her and there is a suggestion that her uncontrollable fatness left her ill at ease with the beautiful ones. Though there are many patently sincere and affectionate letters from women paying tribute to Margery's warmth, kindness and generosity, the 'star' buried deep within her may sometimes have struggled to get out.

The independent women she met and liked – Mary Leonard, Louisa Callender, Theodora Bosanquet, 'Kay' Selby of Paramount Films and the ebullient Nancy Spain – were too often also influential business associates for someone as 'careful' as Margery not to hold back a little from full intimacy. When Nancy Spain descended on D'Arcy House or wrote exclamatory letters in red biro to 'my darling Maestro', Margery couldn't help wondering whether what Nancy really wanted was a book review for her magazine or the promise of a story for Joan Werner Laurie's *She*. Even dear Winifred represented her 'bosses'. During the war Margery had overcome her nervousness of Dorothy Sayers (who lived in nearby Witham) and decided that she was not 'headmistressy' but 'really quite a nice old duck when you get to know her'. The only close woman friend whose creative talents matched Margery's own had been Kate O'Brien, and about Kate there was an emotional intensity which could be unnerving.

Lavinia was neither a gifted novelist nor an obscurely troubled character. She was a prolific writer of books for children and teenagers, even of some detective/adventure tales, quite sufficiently a craftswoman to comment perceptively on Margery's work and to offer intelligent reassurance and support when it was most needed. Margery's letters to Lavinia cannot at this time be traced. Lavinia's to her are clearly one half of a wide-ranging exchange of domestic and working news, views on political and spiritual issues, jokes and concerned enquiries as to the other's well-being. The one topic which Margery seems to have avoided completely (judging only from Lavinia's replies) was her relationship with Pip. Their husbands were friends and Lavinia with her defined, slightly horsy, family background, personal uprightness and wifely devotion to her Wendell, was perhaps someone to whom it would have seemed disloyal to complain.

As well as being so truly 'nice', Lavinia also deserved Margery's compliment 'intelligent'. Of *More Work for the Undertaker* she wrote, 'the overall quality that comes up from this book as it does from so many of your others is style. I don't mean slickness or a highly developed expertise but the Real McCoy, the final art that hides all artifice – My dear, it must have been a fiendishly difficult book to write. Easy writing makes curst hard reading was one of the tags of wisdom taught us in school and the reverse is equally true . . .'

Other professionals were more confused in their response to the novel. *The Ladies' Home Journal* reported, 'Some readers were all for it thinking it had fine suspense and exceptionally polished writing. Others found it lacking in punch and too slow.' The editor of *Good Housekeeping* in America grumbled that the book was 'so very British that it will be outside the ken of any large American audience'. Yet it was the main choice for Doubleday's Detection Book Club and within the year Isabelle Taylor had printed 300,000 copies in her Pocket Books series. In Britain Heinemann underestimated the demand for the book in the difficult trading conditions of 1949. On its day of publication it was already reprinting.

Paul Reynolds expressed himself with ingenuous frankness as was his wont. 'I think *More Work for the Undertaker* will make a very good book. In fact I think it will make one of your best books and increase your reputation. I am going to offer it to the *Saturday Evening Post* but I can't pretend I think it's a serial in our sense. It is too quiet, too leisurely, too amusing in a nice sort of way, lacks the tension etc for a fast paced serial. However I am showing it to the Post and I do think it's a very good book.' He wrote to her after its publication encouraging her to try a serious novel next time – he thought she could probably write a satire. Actually he'd just been reading one.

Authorial responsibility for *More Work for the Undertaker* is unconventionally disclaimed. 'Every character in this book is the careful portrait of a living person, each one of whom has expressed himself delighted not only with the accuracy but with the charity of the delineation. Any resemblance to any unconsulted person is therefore entirely accidental.' Despite the reader who wrote worrying then that Margery 'must know some very odd people', no-one had, of course, been consulted. The Palinode family around whom *More Work for the Undertaker* is built are representative 'highbrows'. For Joyce they have always suggested the scholarly Luard family; this reader felt tantalised by her inability to make guesses at possible Victorian literary identities for 'Professor Palinode who wrote the essays' and his wife 'the celebrated Mrs Theophilia Palinode, poetess of the sixties' whose face 'had once smiled out at [Campion] from the frontispiece of a little red volume on his grandmother's chest of drawers'. Tantalised because, though identifications should not be attempted, yet the references sound so nearly plausible. The villain bears the name of a famous, indubitably 'literary' novelist. He manages Clough's bank and is assisted by 'old Congreve'. The fools (and they are dangerous fools) are those who think they can learn about life from books. They make matters easy for the villains who are out to make a quick speculative profit.

More Work for the Undertaker shows Margery's comic sense at its most expansive and most generous even at a time when her own life was not especially gay. Its literary comedy was written in the knowledge that her wartime attempt to achieve serious recognition for her work and ideas had failed. Margery no longer set out her beliefs for dons and archbishops and had become increasingly disenchanted with the groups she termed 'Bloomsbury'. After the war she resigned from *Time and Tide* to review books for the more popular (and better-paying) *Daily Graphic*. Her time in the country and her identification with the common man's causes left her as convinced as she'd been in her teens, that the 'academics', the 'honking highbrows' whose superciliousness reminded her of geese with their beaks in the air, had lost touch with the fundamentals of life. And yet although the Palinodes are satirised, they are left likeable.

Lawrence Palinode is neurotically revolted by his discovery that his seventeen-year-old niece has a boyfriend, ' "The itch is in you is it? Hot hands over the pavement in the yeasty dark and the shuffle of the curious rustling by. Do you know you make me retch? God! you disgust me! You disgust me! Do you hear?"

'The girl was shaken. She grew paler and smaller and her fastidious nose came down over her mouth. The resignation of long-misunderstood youth appeared in the droop of her body. She was silent for a long time.

' "Well?"

'She met his gaze suddenly and a faint irrepressible smile of sheer naughtiness ran across her lips.

' "It isn't like that at all," she said. "D'you know, I don't believe you know anything about it except what you've read." '

There may be a level of personal reference here (Lawrence believes, quite falsely, that Clytie's state of 'puberty' has bewitched her into writing obscene anonymous letters – Margery at the same age had shocked older gentlemen with the language of *Blackerchief Dick*), but any attempt to make scholarly points out of *More Work for the Undertaker* could quickly bring one within the scope of its satire. Earnest Miss Evadne notices a perfectly normal household practice and comments, 'I have always thought that Social Stratification would make a very jolly Second Subject if one wasn't so occupied already'. The novel's best readers were those who accepted its stylistic parameters, enjoyed it – and wrote to Margery thanking her for 'one of the nicest books I have ever read'. Correspondents like Dr (now Lord) Lindsay who worried because 'I don't think one should have to read a detective novel first for the third time so to speak' revealed an unconscious literary snobbery which put them among the Palinodes.

Some readers at the literal rather than literary end of the scale were made anxious by the novel for quite other reasons – where was Amanda? Why was Campion out detecting on his own? Was their marriage in trouble? Didn't he *love* her any more? – tell us, Miss Allingham, please!

Friends of Margery began to articulate similar questions – was Margery never in London? Was it right that she and Pip should spend so much time apart? Arthur Underwood, their conventionally-minded friend and solicitor, took it upon himself to write Margery a long letter advising her that when her grandmother died (Emily Jane's presence at D'Arcy House being one of Margery's reasons why she could not easily spend longer in town), she and Pip must take stock of their position. They should consider, he said, 'whether your grand establishment shall be in the country with a foot in London or your grand establishment as literary lights in London and a foot in the country in the form of a weekend cottage. I doubt whether either or both of you could be content with only one and in any case the one for one may not be the one for the other. I do not know quite why I am writing all this, but I personally think you are too much in the country . . .' Was the good Arthur trying to drop Margery a hint?

On a date early in 1951, the hint may have arrived in person. The year had started quietly enough. Pip was in London, Margery had spent a day in bed with 'flu. Some 'gigantum' lilies arrived for the garden and Margery's goddaughter Sally came to stay. After Sally had returned home, a man called Julian Clifford phoned. The reason for his call is not recorded. Margery jotted down a note, making an appointment, Julian Clifford, 4.30 p.m. On the following day she wrote to Arthur Underwood. Unfortunately her letter has not survived. On the next day, Wednesday January 10th, Margery records, 'Julian Clifford arrived –listened, sent home. Phoned Arthur. Phoned Pip in evening.' This biography assumes that these three actions had some connection with each other.

Margery's diary entry for Thursday is more colourful and much more confusing. The space is headed 'The Hour of the Angel'. 'Pip phoned lunchtime – went to Town. "Everywhere a friend" saw E. Seagrove, Louisa, Nerney, Vi. Went to French Club with Arthur and Betty and on to see Jour de Fete. Met Jean later. Most extraordinary day of my life – freedom. Something happened in my neck.'

'Most extraordinary day of my life'? Why? The people she met on this burst of sociability were all as it were 'regulars'. Edmond Segrave (Margery's spelling was as unreliable as ever) was editor of the trade magazine *The Bookseller* and a familiar figure in publishing circles. *The Bookseller* offices in Dyott Street were some fifty yards from Margery and Pip's flat at no. 91, Great

Russell Street. Nerney and Violet (Nerney's Doubleday assistant) were friends as well as business associates; Jean is most likely to have been Grog's sister 'Biddy', home briefly from South Africa.

On the day after the 'The Hour of the Angel' and 'The most extraordinary day of my life' Margery lunched with her friend Leslie Cresswell, phoned Arthur Underwood again and returned to D'Arcy taking Pip and a 'flu-striken Aunt Maud with her. The diary notes then begin to sound unequivocally as if duplicity of Pip's has been uncovered and a form of separation is being planned – 'Heard all about everything – am to have house' and 'heard more. Pip. penny drops perspective'. 'Beginning to understand, strange new clarity'. 'Pip home' she says – in direct reversal of her normal phraseology – when he returned to London after the weekend.

She saw her mother during the week. Em told her that her horoscope had read: 'Crisis in your family second week in January. You can do nothing so laugh it off.' Margery was more practical. Her first 'exhaltation' over, she settled down to 'planning cash' – and arranging for the transfer of D'Arcy House from Pip's name into her own.

XVII

'She Thinks I'm Dishonest'

1951–1955

No-one to whom I have spoken can remember who Julian Clifford was or what he came to tell Margery. Several people remember a story which Margery used to tell, and tell in at least three different versions, of an occasion when she rushed to London in reponse to a plea from a wronged husband and discovered Pip *in flagrante* in their flat. Richard Martin, who was the first to work through Margery's papers, claims to have seen a note in Margery's handwriting referring to this period. 'Husband having a liaison with another married woman.' It seems the most obvious explanation for a crisis which Margery described in her medical notes as an 'emotional moment' following a period of 'overwork and emotional difficulty'.

Whoever Julian Clifford was, however, he was not the husband of Pip's regular companion. Neither does Margery's diary mention any confrontation at the flat – merely that she found it 'as Coop left it'. It had been on loan to their friend Robert St John Cooper whose marriage was also in disarray. 'Whatever is happening at the flat?' her friend 'Biddy' (Jean) Gregory had written a few weeks earlier. 'Has Mr C. left Mrs C. or what?'

Margery's initial feeling of 'freedom', mentioned in her diary on the day of crisis, is not inconsistent with a revelation of unfaithfulness. Shortly after her trip to London she was able to talk to one of her closest 'domestic' women friends, Pippa St John Cooper. Pippa, noted Margery, 'has her own troubles' but was 'just feeling free at the moment'. Margery described such a reaction in the last of her magazine serials, *Safer Than Love* (written 1952–3 and the serial with which she felt most satisfied). A wife who has been silently enduring her husband's complete neglect and extraordinary lack of consideration stumbles upon proof of his infidelity. 'I ought to have been furious, sick, outraged. The conventional streak in me . . . was aware of all the right reactions, but I felt none of them. I felt freed.'

Whatever it was that Margery learned at this 'emotional moment', it caused her, in some sense, to give up on Pip. The tone in which she writes of 'The Hour of the Angel' is one of almost hysterical relief that her ignorance of Pip's activities is being swept away – however painfully. She need no longer be responsible for him. She could begin to sort out her own life. In *Safer Than Love* the heroine continues her explanation. 'I suppose it was the generations of proud, law-abiding religious women behind me whose legacies were deep within me forming my reactions despite any fancy thinking which I might be doing on my own account, who suddenly let up and washed their hands of [the husband]. I realised I could go. I was absolved . . . I could go free but I must not take revenge. I must not ruin him and above all I must not foul my own nest.' Granny, it may be remembered, now in her last years at D'Arcy House and telling stories of her youth to Margery and Christina, had finally, conscientiously, washed her hands of William Walter Hughes.

Whatever the details of the crisis, Margery used it as a spur to practical action. Hence the involvement not only of Arthur Underwood (who, as well as being a friend and a solicitor, had helped before the war with their tax-returns) but also, more puzzlingly, Sean Fielding at *The Tatler*. There was no row until three weeks after 'The Hour of the Angel'. By then financial arrangements were becoming contentious and Pip appears to have realised how seriously Margery was taking their situation. She was annoyed that he refused 'even to *think* about income tax' and that he had persuaded their accountant that it would be 'unfair' to ask him to contribute to the surtax. He was furious when he discovered that Margery had written to Sean inviting him down to Tolleshunt D'Arcy. Why she did so is not explained but probably it was for the straightforward reason that Sean was Pip's 'boss' and therefore the only other person likely to have any influence over him. The intensity and duration of Pip's anger convinced her that the 'famous rift' between herself and Sean had been manipulated wn ends, 'which are complete freedom of movement, for little Pippy'. She grew angry herself when she hat Pip 'must have read this diary the old bastard'. ly to her invitation revealed that 'Pip had told him I was mental etc.'

When Pip came down from London the following weekend he was still arguing. He revealed, thought Margery, 'the obstinacy of a moke and utter naivety'. 'Everyone writing kindly, seem to be preparing for death.' She then took to her bed with 'flu and Pip asked Dr Madden if her 'age had affected her head'.

The involvement of Sean in the quarrel confirms that the problem was not straightforwardly conjugal. Throughout 1950, Margery had grown increasingly desperate to resolve her income tax problems. She had learned, to her cost, that working harder and selling more increased the Revenue's demand the following year. 'All my life I have been one of those people who feel that when money is needed the thing to do is earn more. Now this is no longer the answer I don't quite see what to do.' For a while she had hoped that the high post-war levels of taxation would be short-lived. If she worked as hard as she could, sold as advantageously as she could, and paid over whatever she could afford to stave off the collectors, time would rectify the situation. Between 1946 and the end of 1950 she had written and sold three novellas, a scattering of reviews and short stories, a radio play (*Room to Let*), *More Work for the Undertaker* and was in the early stages of a major new 'Campion'. Her income had more than doubled and, like a relentless and unshakable shadow, so had her tax bills. By 1950 it was clear that there would be no early reduction in tax levels and Margery was well over £1,000 in arrears. When Paul cabled to say that the *Saturday Evening Post* had agreed to buy *Dark Invitation* (*The Patient at Peacocks Hall*) Margery was 'so relieved I was nearly sick'. Still she could not shift the burden. She became more and more tired – 'too tired to live' – and the official demands became increasingly peremptory. In December 1950 a collector arrived unannounced on her doorstep.

'We could part of course, but we like each other' – since she wrote that letter to Louisa Callender in 1946 Margery had been aware that divorce offered one way out of her predicament. In January 1951 with her belief in Pip's trustworthiness badly damaged, divorce could, for a moment, have appeared no more than a regularisation of their existing situation. Divorced, they would pay their taxes as single people. 'I am one,' she had explained to her accountant in the winter of 1950/1, 'I cannot afford to spend much time with Pip at all. We live entirely different lives.'

One may guess (but not assume) that Margery realised that the separate area of Pip's post-war life included other women, even before the occasion, whenever it was, that gave her irrefutable evidence. It was something she had long suspected. Nevertheless, although it had affected her private happiness and self-confidence during the 1930s, the continuance of their marriage had not been in question. After the war and as an older woman, it appears that Pip's infidelity was something to which she was usually capable of blinding herself. Observing the men of her generation to whom she was closest, she seems to have decided that it was in their nature to be promiscuous. What she called 'this balmy modern code' allowed, almost encouraged it. All a wife could ask was that extra-marital affairs were conducted 'off the premises'. Like many of her sex she set, superficially at least, a double standard. Men who were unfaithful might be condoned, the women they were unfaithful with, were 'tarts'. Or so she glossed over a similar situation when talking to her teenage goddaughter.

Supplying the money – or paying the tax – to support such liaisons was a different matter. To her accountant Margery might claim, 'Pip is the person who has the enormous expenses. His job which is to mix with people all the time costs an awful lot of money. I would not say that either of us were very extravagant personally but we have never hesitated to spend if the job in hand seemed to need it.' Privately however she was often shocked by Pip's personal extravagances. Whenever it was that she was forced to recognise the seriousness of Pip's affairs after the war, she is reliably said to have pointed out to his mistress that Pip was 'an expensive luxury'.

In the late 1940s both the income-tax officers and Margery's financial advisers were demanding that stricter accounts be kept and that business entertaining both at the flat and at D'Arcy House be more meticulously documented. Arthur Underwood suggested that Margery and Pip should run separate bank accounts. Margery undertook to arrange this – and was irritated when the bank would not deal with her without her husband. In a note to Pip on the subject, probably written in March 1950, Margery betrays an understandable insecurity. 'I would *like* to *own* something. This is just my private desire. You own the house. Let me own all it contains. I will get it done. You will make a declaration on a bit of paper prepared by a lawyer to prove that all the moveable content of the house is mine.' The events of January 1951 hastened her move towards assuring her own position. 'Heard all about everything. Am to have house.' On February 8th 1951, 'House became mine. Debt of £3,400 on it but glad to have it.'

'The Hour of the Angel' had brought a shock. Margery's 'body-mind' had registered its impact as definitely as her intellect had done. 'Something happened in my neck,' she wrote in her diary. She experienced a sensation of 'burst' and simultaneously 'great well-being coupled with fear'. Two days after her trip to London, she noticed that her neck was red and swollen, and asked Dr Madden to look at it. The swelling gradually receded and no lessons were learned and no connections made between the physical and emotional manifestations. Margery wrote afterwards to Lavinia Davis believing that her goitre had burst. Lavinia, who had recently had a lump removed from her own neck, urged Margery to consult a specialist. It was a pity she did not do so.

The *British Medical Journal* of 1949 had contained an article entitled 'Myxoedematous Madness'. Its author, Dr Richard Asher, coined the phrase in an attempt to draw the attention of his colleagues to the links between irregular thyroid activity, the condition from which Margery had now been suffering for twenty years, and disturbances in the mind. When mental symptoms were obvious, it was not always easy to diagnose the underlying physical condition. 'You get no history of myxoedema', Dr Asher wrote, 'if you are not thinking of myxoedema when you take that history.' In Margery's case, the opposite was true. Her myxoedema was recognised, if somewhat hazily, as connected with her weight gain. Its potential to exacerbate her natural volatility of temperament was not. Margery habitually chose to mix business with friendship. James Madden, for instance, asked to call and have a look at Margery's swollen neck and then stay on for supper or for a cocktail and a chat, was not well-placed to observe her in the detached fashion of a specialist.

As a friend, Dr Madden may have found the up-swing in Margery's mood perturbing. Pip certainly did so. His enquiry whether 'her age had affected her head' probably contained more fear for her equilibrium than he would have chosen to acknowledge. Margery had always experienced elation and despair in large measure. Her 'highs', however, usually manifested themselves in a surge of gaiety, forcefulness and energy which she poured into whatever was the work in progress; her 'lows' were so well concealed behind her facade of cheerfulness and competence, that it was not until Joyce, for instance, read Margery's diaries after her death, that she realised the extent of despondency that her elder sister had suffered.

Margery herself seemed reluctant to discover more about her health problems than was available at G.P. level. Her humour, her commonsense and her dogged determination to work almost always kept her inwardly steady through the ups and downs of her emotions. At this moment in 1951 and again four years later, she was not quite steady. On both occasions a moment of emotion came first then was further fuelled by the unacknowledged complexities of her metabolism.

The 'exhaltation', the 'miracle' of her first 'freedom' over, Margery felt convinced that the change in her relationship with Pip was permanent. By May her surge of assertion had subsided. She had been feeling ill for weeks and convinced herself that 'he'd be oke without me apart from material things'. Pip did not agree. It was her 47th birthday on May 20th. He gave her two 'very pretty' old paste brooches and Margery realised that he was trying hard to make matters right. She could not easily respond, 'feeling rather hopeless because I can't feel differently suddenly'.

Throughout the summer he remained attentive. He telephoned her regularly from London and kept her involved in his business happenings. She always enjoyed his metropolitan gossip. In the autumn and winter he promoted her work with enthusiasm and gained great marital credit for selling the British serial rights in her new novel for an unprecedented sum, 1500 guineas, to the popular magazine *John Bull*.

In the second week in January 1952 Margery came up to London. They went to the theatre, the Arts Club and the Café Royale together. On the 11th, the anniversary of 'The Hour of the Angel', she reported that they 'dressed up and went to the first night of *Much Ado*, John Gielgud – rapturous recep. Diana Wynyard – have seen better Beatrices but a lovely production. Went on to Ciro's. v. good.' Stripped of the glamour, this could have been an outing from the first days of their relationship in 1921. Margery concludes, 'A nice change from last year! Thank God all well.'

Between March and October of that traumatic year, 1951, Margery wrote the most part of the novel which is generally accepted as her finest achievement. *Tiger in the Smoke* is set in the same patched and peeling London 'manor' as *More Work for the Undertaker*. This was W.2, the area where she used to walk with her father looking from the outside at other people's houses, at high blank walls, dark streets and wondering what or whom they concealed. Reviewers made comparison with Dickens or the Stevenson of *The New Arabian Nights*. If Margery has a place in the honour roll of the English novel – as distinct from the detective story – it is through these post-war 'Bayswater' novels, *More Work for the Undertaker, Tiger in the Smoke* and her 1958 publication *Hide My Eyes*, that she earned it.

Tiger in the Smoke is Margery's morality drama. It offers expression to the idiosyncratically Christian view of existence by which she kept turmoil and despair at bay. She dedicated it with great seriousness to her goddaughter, Sally Reid. Sally, aged about sixteen and away at boarding school, was encouraged to consider the heroine, Meg Elginbrodde, 'my Meg'. Margery wrote regular letters to her reporting on Meg's predicaments and 'wondering' whatever she should do with her next.

Meg is not a lively heroine. Her importance to the tale is structural: her entire happiness must be seen to depend on being delivered from the evil of the Tiger. This answered a criticism Paul Reynolds had made of *More Work for the Undertaker*. To foster readers' involvement (and to make the tale more attractive to magazine-serial buyers) there should be, he felt, a character whose future was intimately bound up with the successful conclusion of the plot. This, as so often with Paul's suggestions, is interesting, well-meant and misses the point of whichever book is under discussion. After *More Work for the Undertaker* Paul had wondered whether Margery mightn't like to try a satire; after *Tiger*, he hoped she would feel able to settle to something serious! Margery teased Paul openly about his 'myopia' and his tendency not to like whatever she produced that was new. She also, unobtrusively, gave effect to several of his suggestions. Partly it was the 'editor's child' in her. More significantly it stemmed from her instinctive desire to redress one book's natural imbalance in the next. *More Work for the Undertaker* had made comedy of social change, *Tiger in the Smoke* considers individual moral choices in a markedly less genial world.

In terms of Margery's artistic development, the most significant progression revealed by *Tiger* lies in her portrayal of cruelty. It is hard to re-create gratuitous violence and the deliberate infliction of pain without melodrama. Margery's adolescent imagination had thrown up shards of such experience through the medium of 'the glass'. In her published work they had been smoothed away. Margery often described herself as a 'physical funk'. Despite her countrywoman persona, when the dog cut itself she ran to fetch Christina (or on one occasion the local policeman!). As a writer she did not make her characters suffer grossly. Primarily her novels were to entertain, not to harrow or to shock. 'It has always seemed to me,' she had written flippantly in *Time and Tide*, 'that, like amateur violin playing, shocking should be done in some good cause.' Yet her overriding aim was to achieve 'sincerity' – in the sense of wholeness as well as of truth-telling – and the experience of the Second World War demanded that the darker side of human nature be faced. Within

Tiger in the Smoke she confronts brutality through the minor creation of Tiddy Doll as well as of Jack Havoc himself.

To take a single example; a story Margery liked to tell to illustrate her early training from Reeves Shaw was the scandalised lecture he had given her when she allowed a character to use his feet in the course of a fight. " 'Fighting with feet is the beginning of sadism," he roared. "Do you know what sadism means?" I said, 'N-not entirely." And he said, "Sadism means IMPOTENCE and I won't have it in my paper. Tear that thing up, I don't want any part of it. Now go home and write something CLEAN!" ' *The Strand* and such attitudes had vanished early in the 1940s. When Tiddy in *Tiger* gives Duds 'something to go on with', he 'puts in the leather': that is, he kicks the head of the cringing, crying little man with his metal-tipped army boots. He kills him for fun, almost. Even when it may be against his own interests, Tiddy cannot resist the minor thrill of a sadist as he tears off an elastoplast gag to inflict maximum hurt. Jack Havoc does not even derive pleasure from his killing. For him human life has no value. He rips throats with a carelessness that is first terrifyingly, then somehow pitiably, insane.

The creation of Good in fiction is at least as great a challenge as the depiction of Evil. At first it seems unhelpful to discover that Margery claimed the character of the good Canon Avril in *Tiger* was 'a sort of portrait' of her father. A. M. Burrage, who had known Herbert in *London Journal* days, commented, 'I can see Mr Allingham in the Canon since you told me it was to some extent a portrait, but I am bound to admit that I should not have guessed if you had not told me . . . I daresay in his later years he grew like your Canon. I found him . . . cheery and broad-minded and more of a man of the world than the Canon. He was, I remember, a lover of the good old music halls. And I'll bet you first heard "More Work For The Undertaker" from him!'

Margery's portrait of Canon Avril is not obviously like Herbert, except insofar as she may have been imagining her father's development had he taken Holy Orders as William and Louise had once hoped. The significant likeness is found on the level of qualities rather than features. Burrage commented, 'the one thing

I remember most about him was that directly I stepped into his presence I knew that he was kind.' Kindness, tolerance and perceptiveness are the qualities common to Herbert and the Canon – the capacity to see other people as they really are and still to like them. Margery believed that this 'simple liking of mankind' had been her father's most distinctively Christian characteristic. Herbert did not achieve wholesale intimacy but the few friends he made had loved him – as his children had done. After his death, George Hearn wrote to Margery, 'You might say of him as was said of the strawberry, "Doubtless God might have made a better man, but doubtless he never did." '

Margery also mentioned the identification of her father with the Canon to Canon Luard, their landlord long ago at Layer Breton. It was unusual for her to point out a character's original so emphatically. Perhaps Herbert was often in her thoughts at this time because he had been 'One of the twin supports of my existence'. In her trouble with Pip, the second of these supports, she may have felt the loss of her father more than ever.

The ability to inspire lasting love ranked high in Margery's system of values. Towards the end of *The Oaken Heart* she had proffered some apology for her tendency to idealise the place. She continued, 'I love it as one does love one's home and if that has made me give it perhaps a very slightly prettier face than some would see at first glance . . . you must discount that much please, but not more I beg you, for remember only the really lovable is beloved for long.' This explains why it was important to the 'theology' of *Tiger* that the representative of Good should be based on the person who had inspired such enduring love in Margery. Good, like Canon Avril, is rooted in a family or a community. It is, as in *The Oaken Heart*, steadfast. Evil attacks from without. A note in Margery's 1951 diary reveals that Havoc gleaned several of his physical characteristics fortuitously from an unnamed commercial traveller who came to quote for the draught-proofing of D'Arcy House.

In her article for the U.S. magazine *Town and Country* in 1949, Margery had put forward her theory that the modern mystery story shared a function of the old Mystery play, 'to expound certain cheerful popular theories of Right and Wrong'. *Tiger* is her most successful expression of this aim. Readers responded in their various ways. Many found it pleasurably scary, one or two complained that they had guessed the identity of the murderer too early. The confrontation of Havoc and the Canon in the darkened church was generally admired. A scholarly reader from America wrote to enquire whether Margery had consciously intended the book to echo the epic struggle of Beowulf and Grendel. Others, more practically inclined, requested detailed instructions on how to make themselves a dressing gown like Avril's robe!

Tiger in the Smoke was the first of Margery's novels to be published by Harold Raymond at Chatto and Windus. Her incompatibility with Dwye Evans had finally decided her to leave Heinemann in 1950. However 'careful' both had tried to be in their dealings with one another, this parting seemed inevitable. Dwye was primarily a businessman with an overall grasp of the difficulties facing Heinemann in the post-war period: Margery was enmeshed in personal and money troubles. Her Campions were becoming more profound but taking considerably longer to write. Dwye considered that her sales did not warrant any increase in the amount of money advanced on each one; Margery believed that her books were written 'with the care and sincerity of novels' and that if Heinemann promoted them as such, her sales figures would rise accordingly.

The final split came after a meeting with Dwye in London during 1950. Whatever was actually said, Margery came away with the firm belief that what Dwye really wanted her to do was to write two books a year like Agatha Christie. If he had calculated to insult her he could hardly have done better. Margery was ready to be polite publicly about Christie's achievement, and to concede her mastery of the puzzle-plot. She had prepared appreciative obituaries for the files of *The Times* and *The Manchester Guardian*. 'She was the first of the procession of women writers who have specialised in this field,' wrote Margery in 1943, 'and it is generally accepted that she kept her place at the head of them. Her work had the blest quality of steady improvement, her

'My Garden My Love',
Margery outside the conversatory, c 1952 *(A. V. Swaebe)*

'The True Griffin', BBC programme on the formation of Army newspapers 1945 (including Pip on left, Sean Fielding and Richard Dimbley on either side of the microphone)

Members of the Thursday Club, c 1947 (including Robert St John Cooper, seated left, Pip, standing third from left; back row: Prince Philip, centre, Baron, second from right) *(Baron)*

Margery through friends' eyes (photograph taken by Baron in the bar at D'Arcy House)

Margery through Pip's eyes (photograph taken on holiday 1955)

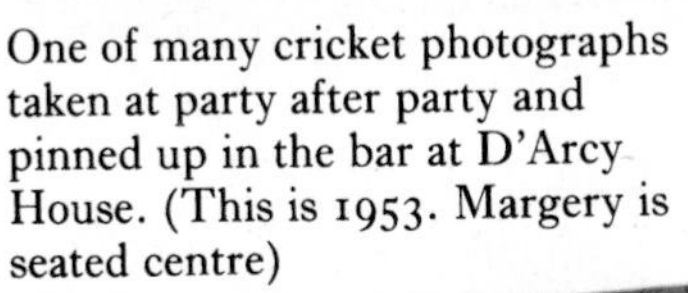

One of many cricket photographs taken at party after party and pinned up in the bar at D'Arcy House. (This is 1953. Margery is seated centre)

Christina and Brock

Granny *(Bertram Park)*

Pip and Margery in the garden at D'Arcy House immediately after the war. *(F. J. Goodman)*

Pip and Margery on the patio in the early 1960s *(Homes and Gardens)*

Isabelle Taylor

Mary and Ronnie Reid with Sally and her twin sisters

The Doubleday Christmas party, London 1956 (Barbara Noble at the end of table nearest camera. Clockwise from her left, Joan Kiddy, Louisa Callender, Vi Barton, Winifred Nerney, Edith Walsham, Margery, Kay Selby)

Top: Leslie Cresswell in the bar at D'Arcy House

Below left: William McFee, Nancy Spain and Joan Werner Laurie

Below right: Tom Carter

The 'Ladies of The Forge', Aunt Grace, Aunt Maud, Em

Pip in the studio

'A jolly old fruit', Margery, c 1964 *(Peter Hampshire)*

ingenuity was extraordinary and her invention unfailing.' But that her own publisher should prefer such fiction, however lucrative, to the novels she considered her 'children' was unforgivable. After other business partings she made strenuous efforts to salvage some appearance of amity with the former associate. But when her agent later suggested trying to smooth relationships with Heinemann, Margery replied that her rift with Dwye was 'deep basic stuff' and irreparable. She would not explain it further.

Word was soon out that she had no publisher. Margery's authorial reputation was high; few of her 1930s peers were thought to have adapted their style so well to the post-war world. Approaches came from her friend Robert Lusty at Michael Joseph, and, among others, from Agatha Christie's and Dorothy Sayers' publishers, William Collins and Victor Gollancz. All were asked to wait until *Tiger in the Smoke* was available to be read. Robert Lusty was charmingly persistent. Margery admired his skills as a publisher and was grateful for his championing of *The Oaken Heart*. Her fondness for that book had not lessened and had Lusty been in a position to offer an immediate reprint, she would probably have followed her inclination and offered *Tiger* to him. As it was, she determined to let her agents, A. P. Watt and Sons, make the selection. Money, it was assumed, would be forthcoming. Enthusiasm for Margery's work and willingness to present her as a novelist was to be the main criterion. Rumour had it that the by-now venerable firm of Watt did not work easily with the young, keen Michael Joseph Ltd. Additionally, 'Bill' Watt was a close friend of Harold Raymond at Chatto.

So, after an initial dinner 'to let the rabbit see the dog', as Margery put it, to Chatto she went. The initial contract was for one book only but although there was no dramatic expansion of her sales figures in their hardback edition, she settled and felt no inclination to change her British publisher again. She liked the way in which her books were presented, the regularity with which they were reprinted, and appreciated the taste and expertise of the editor, Ian Parsons, with whom she had most to do. Her reputation and her readership had anyway received a great boost in 1950 when Allen Lane at Penguin had at last negotiated successfully with Heinemann to publish an Allingham Million – ten of Margery's earlier titles simultaneously in runs of 100,000 copies each. This was a pointer to the esteem in which she was held 'among those wise men who like their nonsense to be distinguished', as the blurb of that edition had it. Her friend 'Biddy' Gregory wrote from Rhodesia, 'Some surprising *toffs* have the complete lot in the Penguin series. On reflection that sounds a bit rude but you know what I mean: bods whom you would think read nothing that is not tied up with Govt. red tape know them ALL!'

Her sixteen years with Chatto were not always smooth. Margery was too used to running her own affairs to be an invariably acquiescent author. Neither were any great friendships made. Ian Parsons and Pip met frequently in the Garrick Club but after one sudden and bruising spat with Ian's partner, Norah Smallwood, Margery resolved to keep her 'noisy personality' well out of affairs at Chatto. The quality that she was most glad to discover in her 'new bosses' was their willingness to leave her to work at her own pace. No letters survive from Chatto (among the many sent) which put any pressure on Margery to make haste. It is clear from her own correspondence that she did not feel that she had to be constantly promising, apologising or prevaricating to them. There were gaps of three and four years between each 'Campion', and as Margery's health and happiness declined these intervals were no longer packed with magazine serials and short stories.

For two years from the delivery of *Tiger* in November 1951 until November 1953, Margery had no novel 'on the stocks' at all. This was unprecedented. She was always prey to anxiety at the end of one book and the commencement of another. 'I have never sat down to begin a new book without feeling that I had mysteriously lost my gift and would never write again.' Yet there was usually something there, a bright idea, a technical challenge, the germ of a dissatisfaction with one book that was ready to lead her to the next. After *Tiger* there was nothing.

Pip had urged her to 'come to Town and write a play'. When he raised the idea even before she had completed *Tiger* her diary comment was succinct: ''ad to laff!' Letters from a 'fan' who became a regular correspondent, Canon Edwards of Norwich, suggest that she considered leaving the detective novel for overtly religious work – rather like Dorothy Sayers. Sayers last 'Wimsey' novel had been published in 1937. Since then she put her energies into popular theology through essays, addresses and religious plays. Canon Edwards warned Margery off this firmly. 'Miss Sayers is a very versatile person but in my view she was saying more in her detective stories and more influentially than she has ever managed to say elsewhere. What you convey with all the flippant nonsense and incredible situations is, without overtly saying so, a point of view of life.'

This barren period unsettled and worried Margery. All three Allingham children shared a need to work which, though it might be unconventionally expressed, was vital to their self-respect. Phil and Francesca had run a fortune-telling stall throughout the 1951 Festival of Britain celebrations in Battersea Park. Joyce had come out of the W.R.N.S. to help them. When Margery expressed some doubt over this decision, wondering whether Joyce would prefer to make her home at D'Arcy House, Phil was able to reassure her. 'You know how we all feel about earning our livings . . . to be ourselves, to feel well even, we've got to know we can pay our way and earn.' (In 1953 he wrote to Margery that he and Francesca, The Zodiac Circle, were 'turning out 200,000 readings a year if I include the gear we supply to the grafters. The other line – the Ancient and Modern nature preparations is also holding its own and looks as if it will eventually grow into something solid.')

Lavinia Davis understood Margery's anxiety over her temporary lack of inspiration. She had read a proof copy of *Tiger* and was generous with her praise. 'I think it is the best "thriller" I have ever read, bar none. I also think it is an astonishingly good novel and way above any I've read in a dog's age. And I think it is far and away the most truly reverent and moving tale I've read in I don't know when . . .

'I don't think we need cross our t's or even finish sentences to each other on the matter of the status of the writer when not writing. No one ever wants to write but we do want to in that we feel unbrushed, unwashed and horrid when we don't. The nub of the disorder is that serpent in the grass of noonday if one ever could again. But to think of you getting that way is absurd. Also, if I may sound off like a New England qahog (clam shell), the better and more profound the book, the longer the state of recovery and refilling of the wells afterwards.'

The Davises visited Tolleshunt D'Arcy later in the summer – scarcely a weekend passed without guests and Margery remained glad of American food parcels. Lavinia regularly sent a ham for the annual cricket weekend. Some of this entertaining was done 'for Pip'. Sean and Sheena Fielding, Frank and Gwen Shaw, David Milford Haven and several members of the Thursday Club came down. (Margery may have had some quiet fun at their expense with the 'Royal Augustes' of her 1954 novel, casting Baron, Vasco Lazzolo and the others as a group of high class clowns.) The garden was at its most glorious in July – deliberately planned thus, she suspected, for the Old Doc to scoop all the prizes at the local flower shows. She had dusted off his Victorian exhibition vases and did a little showing herself. Even before the war, she and Pip had revived the traditional garden parties, held on the first weekend of July and to which Em had taken her as a child. On the first weekend of July 1952, they entertained two hundred people.

A significant number of children had begun writing their own thank-you letters to 'Auntie Marge' by this time. Her most regular visitor and correspondent among her friends' children was Sally Reid, who wrote cheerfully to the 'famous fat authoress' about dogs and horses and school and her difficult relationships with her parents as she grew up. Another friend who wrote from boarding school was Andrew Hall. He sent Margery writing of his own to criticise and later had three detective novels published.

1953 opened with the shock of the East Coast floods but was otherwise a quieter year with a steady trickle of visitors but no grand scale entertaining. In July Margery performed the opening ceremony of the new Art School at Regent Street Polytechnic. A happy handful of old friends were there, including 'Chelly' (Josephina de Vasconcellos), now an eminent sculptress with commissioned work in galleries and cathedrals throughout the country. Margery's files are full of her polite refusals (often accompanied by a placatory donation) to perform ceremonies, give talks, award prizes – but the 'Polly' was an exception. After the reunion she attended a private view of Josephina's and her husband's work. Josephina remembers her 'flying in' looking lovely in a simple royal blue dress, full skirt and a big straw hat. Pip came in at the end of the day 'walking in curves'.

In this year, Margery wrote *Safer Than Love*, the most realistic of her 'woman's' serials. She called them her 'little bastards' and firmly resisted all attempts to publish them or have them reviewed alongside her Campion novels: 'I don't feel like giving them family status.' They were published in book form, two at a time, by Phyllis Alexander at World's Work (a division of Heinemann) in 1950 and 1954.

Beneath the veneer of good living, money matters remained troubling. By 1953 almost 2,000,000 copies of her books had been sold in Penguin. *Tiger in the Smoke* had earned high royalties from Chatto, had sold well as a serial and then had been a Reprint Society main choice. With all of her income taxed at 17s 6d in the £1, Margery had still not managed to improve her position. She felt bitter and rather frightened: 'a) go bankrupt b) leave Pip c) die' would be, she thought, her only options when she grew old or ill or her popularity declined. Nor was it an encouragement to work. Margery set herself to devising ingenious schemes which would enable her to produce another novel without seeing virtually all of the money earned going straight to the Revenue – and rendering her liable for another large demand in the next tax year. 'Anyone,' she wrote to *The Times*, 'who manages to pay out of the uncertain rewards for the sale of his brain children, taxes devised under a system designed to fit those earning a regular wage, is a bit of an artist.'

Eventually she drew up a Deed of Gift which transferred all the book rights in her next novel, *The Beckoning Lady*, to Joyce. She represented this to Joyce and others as enlightened self-interest.

ɔyce was helped to build up some security of her own, she would be better placed to assist in any family crisis: with Em, perhaps, now in her seventies and increasingly unsettled. Margery resented the time she had to spend juggling and justifying. 'Remember that I have only one head,' she told the local inspector. 'While I am explaining things to you I cannot be getting on with my work which is the only way in which I can make sure of paying you.' This same irritation finally helped her to break free of the barren creative patch about which she had worried to Lavinia.

For the plot of her next novel, she decided to kill off her tax adviser. Exasperated outbursts from denizens of *The Beckoning Lady*, an artist's estate, explain why he dies unmourned. 'That man was one long prying nose,' says Emma Bernadine to Campion. 'Hasn't it occurred to you that we're all taking your inquisition remarkably calmly? Don't you think it peculiar that we're all getting on with our work and letting you poke about as if you're nothing out of the ordinary? Well let me tell you that you're not. We're used to this sort of thing. We have it every day. We're not surprised to open our kitchen doors and find that someone has undone the stove to find how much fuel we're buying. We're not astounded to be asked who we've telephoned and why, or where that half bottle of gin that was on the sideboard last week has got to, or if the new piece of soap in the cloak room is really necessary. That's the kind of insane life we've been leading and the reason is that Minnie let the little brute into the house and then daren't get rid of him.'

Minnie is one of Margery's most easily identified self-portraits. Was she named for the other little girl from Emily Jane's childhood stories? The donkey cart from Layer Breton days is there and *The Beckoning Lady* is thick with other personal references. 'Granny' had died in 1952, just missing Margery and Pip's silver wedding anniversary and her own hundredth birthday. More importantly the 'old cad, Tonker Cassands' in the novel is a partial version of Pip, recognised by himself as such. 'Tonker' endorses Emma Bernadine's account of Minnie's beleaguered existence. 'She's given herself over to them. She's let them into her life so her existence is lunatic farce.'

Margery had not physically let either her accountant, Aubrey Christlieb, or the Witham tax inspectors into her house – but her family could well feel that they had forced their way into her mind. She had been disproportionately upset by a letter received in October 1950: 'Approximately how often did your client entertain visitors in the year under review who may be regarded as professional connections and contacts, and on how many occasions did such visits involve sleeping at D'Arcy House? Also how many bedrooms were used? If your client keeps a visitor's book no doubt this information can be readily compiled.' The unannounced arrival of the collector in December of that year had encouraged her to feel that the Inland Revenue were very close and that they might watch her every move. Unused to expense account discipline she found the detail of her accountant's well-intentioned questions thoroughly intrusive and resented the humbug she found herself obliged to use in her replies.

She used the novel to give vent to her feelings. Behind the portrait of the murdered man, be he accountant or revenue official, are 'hundreds and hundreds of screwed up buff forms'. Minnie's problems are Margery's. She too has tried to step up production. 'That appears to be fatal,' explains Tonker. 'Once you do that the problem behaves like wages chasing prices, round and round and up and up until the bell rings and we all fall down . . . Minnie having had the wind-up and made a superhuman effort has now reached the stage where she can't humanly hope to earn more in a single year than she does now and as time goes by she is pretty certain to earn less. They [revenue officials] see this, I suppose, and . . . they've pointed out to her that if she was single she could call a halt to the dash up the spout . . . she's not got it wrong. She trotted up to London and got Counsel's opinion.' *The Beckoning Lady* claims that it is he who is completely outraged by this suggestion.

As much as a divorce from Pip a divorce from D'Arcy House might, as Arthur Underwood had cautiously suggested in his letter about their 'grand establishment', have solved Margery's problems. So for Minnie in *The Beckoning Lady*. The 'little estate' that gives its name to the novel is in part a loving portrait of

Pope's Hall where Aunt Grace was losing her long battle for financial survival. In the oddly titled *Beckoning Lady* Margery hints at witchery, at a bond stronger than reason yoking house and owner. So many of the daily irritants that Margery endured were caused by her struggle to keep D'Arcy House by putting as much as possible of its cost 'on expenses'. She could bring out any amount of cerebral justification for this: she needed the house to borrow money on because she was paid so irregularly; she needed it because it was actually quite small though it looked so grand; she needed it because it was quite grand and so encouraged visiting American publishers to take her and her work more seriously and pay her better for it. The truth was that D'Arcy House and its surroundings were essential to her – and to her work – in more profound ways than she could easily explain to Arthur Underwood, Aubrey Christlieb or the Inland Revenue. Sally Reid says 'she was never the same anywhere else. Away from that house, she was diminished.' If, in the difficult fifties, Margery had been forced to jettison either her home or her husband to survive, her choice would have been hard to predict. Convincing herself that she might lose either gave a frenetic quality to her grapplings with her financial affairs.

Margery wrote *The Beckoning Lady* to please her fans as well as to exorcise herself from the 'tax-botherers'. Since *More Work for the Undertaker* and her readership boom from 1950, she had been inundated with requests for more Campion, more Amanda, more Lugg, more Luke. Puzzle-plot aficionados begged for a tale where they had to guess the villain. Margery herself longed to recapture the happy days – as they now seemed to her – when she could write *Sweet Danger* and *Death of a Ghost* in almost a single year and still have the energy to keep up the weekly film story. She felt middle-aged and jaded. What would become of her if she had really lost her appetite for work? She whipped herself into action, flinging a character or a situation from almost every book she had written into the autobiographical concoction and striving to make all gel into the rich atmosphere of a D'Arcy summer party – the one moment of the year when she could be sure that she and Pip were working as partners.

The novel was written very fast (between January and April 1954) and with a consciousness of self-indulgence. 'I am so happy doing it that I don't care if no-one else likes it,' she wrote defensively to Isabelle Taylor. A massive injection of penicillin for sinusitis had put her in an 'exalted' mood. There is a flurry and breathlessness about its literary style and it hovers disconcertingly on the borderline between autobiography and art. Some critics have praised its 'cumulative power', others its 'supercharging' of reality. For some readers, Joyce for instance, and those who attended the midsummer parties, it is an especially dear and characteristic achievement. Other admirers have felt puzzled and excluded by it.

For the biographer this novel is fascinating but as a quarry rather than a story – 'a purely personal picture of my own mind' perhaps, like the wild doodle Minnie the artist-heroine must not allow herself to look at too often. There is a truth-telling about the marriage of Minnie and Tonker, Margery and Pip, that makes disturbing reading. However hard the author tries to present this fictional marriage as sound and satisfying in its unconventional way, neither it, nor by implication her own, can quite shake off Tonker's bitter summary of a situation where 'I think she's mad and she thinks I'm dishonest.'

Margery, 1953
by Thurston

XVIII

'I Think She's Mad'

1955–1958

In April 1955, when Chatto brought out *The Beckoning Lady*, Margery was in a nursing home undergoing electro-convulsive therapy.

She had found herself, towards the end of 1954, putting 'a mental d.v.' by all arrangements because of the precariousness of her health. Her diary says nothing about the nature of her ailments. Presumably they were, as was now usual for her in the winter months, bronchitis, sinusitis and bouts of 'flu'. Like her father before her she was a heavy smoker and at the end of 1953, had had a spot on her lung. Perhaps too she was suffering the slowness, tiredness and depression of her low periods. *The Beckoning Lady* had been completed with a fine flourish of energy in April '54. Grog had come down for a long weekend, as he had done for *Tiger in the Smoke*, and the whole book was re-dictated to and typed by him. Gloria Greci, who had been helping Margery with her typing since 1950 and was by 1954 Margery's regular secretary, did not realise the traditional importance of this procedure to Margery and remembers feeling rather hurt. Pip was fully involved. He still designed the jackets for the English editions of Margery's 'Campions'. A dead white female mask, slipping by on a virid river, adorned *The Beckoning Lady*.

The second half of 1954 had been obscurely difficult. There was entertaining to be done through the summer – including Pip's 'bi-annual celebrity party' as Margery now referred to the Thursday Club visitation. In October, Pip took over the editorship of *The Tatler* after Sean Fielding resigned. Aunt Maud, as dedicated as ever to *The Picture Show*, but feeling the wear and tear of her seventy years, looked to Margery for weekend cossetting. Em's time with Marcus Lawrence had ended. She needed financing, accommodating in pensions and apologising for. 'My mother is not really safe with people,' explained Margery to the solicitor whom she employed to pay Em's bills for her. Dealings with the Inland Revenue degenerated further and sections of Margery's diary become no more than aide-memoires of business guests entertained and bottles of champagne consumed. Managing this swallowed the dregs of her energy. She had promised her American editor, Isabelle, that she was working on a new 'Tiger-type' tale but made little progress.

Phil, Francesca, Em, Maud and Joyce joined Margery and Pip for Christmas and the Madden family came over on the day itself. In the New Year, Deirdre Reid, the eldest daughter of their close friends, Ronnie and Mary – and 'a dear girl' in her own right – had a splendid London wedding to Neil, Lord Primrose, only son of the Earl of Rosebery. Margery enjoyed several days of festivity but returned home ill. A 'massive' dose of penicillin injections similar to that which had set her on such a high for *The Beckoning Lady* was tried but her sense of exhaustion persisted. Her thyroxine prescription was sharply increased and she went on a fashionable weight-reducing diet which required her to eat almost nothing but bananas.

She continued to feel ill. In mid-April 1955, Russell and Paula Meiggs came to stay with their two daughters, Sylvia and Rosalind. Though Pip had paid occasional visits to the Meiggs in Oxford, Margery had not seen Russell for many years, probably not since before his marriage in 1941. She had agreed to stand godmother to his elder daughter Sylvia but it was not a close relationship. Paula and Margery had never met. Paula remembers her nervousness at meeting Margery and was glad to find her willing to talk about her work and to show her guests the tiny writing room. Getting up late after a D'Arcy breakfast in bed, the Meiggs found Margery and Pip already out on the lawn with a bottle of champagne. The children were dispatched to a nearby point-to-point meeting, a novelty which amazed them as much as the house-party lifestyle.

The visit, not wholly satisfactory and never repeated, had given Margery an extraordinary sensation of pleasure. Joyce dropped in after the weekend. She had been visiting friends locally and had experienced some trouble with her car. Margery led her into the garden and announced dramatically, 'The *Meiggs* have been here! Can't you *feel* it?' Joyce noticed that her sister was a trifle 'high' emotionally but thought little of it. 'People often were in our family.' Her own mind was on her car, about which Margery gave her sound, if somewhat extreme, advice.

Two days later Margery suffered a second 'burst' in her neck. There was blood in her throat. This must have been caused by a cyst on her goitre haemorrhaging. Although she tried to keep up appearances and work normally when Gloria came in the mornings, as the week wore on she became convinced that she was going to die. Pip did not return that weekend. Margery describes herself as 'overwraught' and by the following Monday as 'out of hand – faster and faster, wilder and wilder'. Her neck was large and red.

An Australian journalist, Jean Hind, who had not met Margery before, had an appointment to interview her on that day. On arrival she was greeted by 'a comfortable looking servant' and handed a note which read 'Dear Miss Reporter – I am so sorry I cannot greet you and give you my life story but there is a story here if you will look for it I think. Be very honest or the consequences will be disastrous. God bless you, my dear, Margery Allingham.' Jean Hind waited, reading the book titles on Margery's shelves. Encouraging messages continued to arrive but some hours later the author had still not emerged. She was about to abandon the interview when unexpectedly the door opened and 'Miss Allingham stood there in a long green housecoat, her short grey hair in wild curls all over her head.' She dashed away at once calling for 'champers'.

It was a sad and distracted meeting. Asked about her husband, Margery replied, 'We've been married for twenty-seven years and I'm very fond of him . . . I'm always delighted to see him when he comes.' And asked why she chose to write detective stories, 'Because I felt I knew nothing of love, my dear.' She seemed confused about time and the journalist concluded politely that she had encountered an example of 'the great tradition of English eccentrics who placidly indulge their quirks of personality and are only too happy for everyone else to do the same'.

It was not so straightforward. Margery might be exuberant, she might be depressed but she was invariably well-groomed and courteous. Neither was she a habitual drinker. The ubiquitous bottles of 'champers' waved around through this period are all too obviously a prop, a clutching for the party spirit. By Tuesday Margery was writing farewell notes and making unhappy, incoherent telephone calls to friends and neighbours. Orlando Greci helping in the garden at D'Arcy House returned home to tell his wife Gloria that Margery was walking there barefooted, talking to herself. Doctors were called – Jimmy Madden and Ronnie Reid. Christina was glad of Dr Madden's help in tracking down Pip in London. Pip contacted Joyce. The men conferred. Pip and Ronnie remembered how Em had reacted after the death of Dr Salter. She too had been 'over-excited' and unmanageable. In 1932 this had been ascribed to shock – plus the female mysteries of the 'change of life'. Jimmy Madden had seen her when she again seemed close to breakdown in 1937.

Like mother, like daughter? In their crisis of 1951, Pip had asked Jimmy whether Margery's 'age was affecting her head'. Margery had laughed to herself then and on other occasions about their tendency, as she saw it, to ascribe everything to 'a woman's age'. Later in 1951 she had wondered whether she was approaching the menopause and had started recording her menstrual cycle in her diary. Any anxiety appears to have been groundless. Her periods continued to occur regularly late into the decade and she records none of the other symptoms, hot flushes or sweating, usually associated with this phase. In 1955, however, Pip and Dr Madden were convinced that she was suffering just as Em had before her and needed treatment urgently. 'Boys decide "change of life mental trouble" I open champagne and take inhalants by nostril.' (Margery is known later to have been afraid of suffocation and to have used inhalants to combat feelings of breathlessness; she might have been doing something similar now.) She was hurried away in an ambulance, accompanied by Christina – but not, it seems, by detailed medical notes. On the journey Margery invited all the ambulance crew to a party. She arrived in a Chiswick nursing home 'fighting but very happy'.

The day after her arrival at the nursing home, Margery was given the first of a series of four sessions of electro-convulsive therapy. There were three on consecutive days (unusually closely spaced) and one after a two-day gap. She was severely disorientated and, with everything else, 'forgot' her own knowledge of her health. It was two weeks before her normal memory returned.

E.C.T. was a treatment widely used to combat depression during the 1950s, including 'involutional' depression, the condition frequently diagnosed among women in their menopausal years. It could be frightening for patients if not handled sympathetically and today, though it is highly effective in certain cases, it is used more sparingly. One of the main contra-indications for its use is that the patient's normal job demands a high level of concentration. Ronnie Reid disagreed with this proposed treatment. He thought it a blunt instrument to wield in Margery's case but as a surgeon his opinion carried little weight.

Margery found it terrifying. She was not confident or sophisticated about mental illness or institutions. Her *Answers* serials of the '30s had gained their most harrowing melodramatic effects from the appalled helplessness of her heroines faced with pseudo-medical assaults on their minds. There is every reason to believe that Margery would have felt similar emotions. Even in normal times she had needed reassurance that her recurrent attacks of sinusitis could not damage her brain. As a writer, she both developed and guarded her mind. She had not been in hospital or a nursing home before. The women close to her – Joyce, Christina and Gloria – were sure that E.C.T. given with such haste, if it should have been given at all, was a cruel mistake. 'She was crying out for help,' says Christina, 'and that's what they did to her.' When Margery emerged from the nursing home, she put up an unconvincing show of cheerfulness, but had 'lost' one week from her memory permanently and believed that she would never write again.

She was calmed certainly. After four E.C.T. sessions results were pronounced 'most gratifying' and the treatment discontinued. It took two weeks for the disruption of her normal memory to subside. During this time, while she was slowly 'piecing together some sort of emotional history', a new doctor noticed the condition of her neck. Gradually Margery remembered her thyroid condition and the specialist advice she had received during the war. To help herself explain matters clearly she made chronological notes of her various problems from teenage years. At last her troubles with her 'temperament', her thyroid, her periods of overwork and emotional stress, her sinusitis and her 'fears' were all gathered together.

Medical attention switched back from her mental to her physical health. From Margery's very few explanations to her closest friends, it is not quite clear whether the doctors blamed the penicillin dose in January or the alteration in her thyroxine prescription for her loss of control. Intangibles, such as Margery's personality type and the effects of stress on her metabolism, appear to have been left out of the equation again. When she was referred to an eminent physician, Dr Raymond Greene (brother of Graham and Hugh), it was first for a new thyroxine prescription and then for a thorough physical check-up. Dr Greene is said to have been unsympathetic to psychiatric medicine and here again an opportunity may have been lost. Though Margery's physical condition was certainly overdue for expert attention, her unexpressed and unrecognised fears and phobias were inwardly growing to such an extent that they militated against the effectiveness of even physical treatment. This unhappy experience of E.C.T. left her less inclined than ever to discuss her depression or specific neuroses. She was afraid that if she did, the treatment might be given to her again.

Most acquaintances heard nothing of Margery's illness or assumed that she had suffered yet another bout of sinusitis. Some weeks after she came out of the nursing home, she vanished quietly. First to Thorpe Bay with Joyce where she was persuaded to write a single short story (*A Word in Season*) for *The Tatler* Christmas number, purely to reassure herself that she could continue her career; and then to Cornwall. August and the first two weeks of September were spent at Tolleshunt D'Arcy.

Entertaining was subdued; first Nerney came to stay, bringing with her the American detective novelist Dorothy Gardiner, and then, for a few days, Mac and his second wife Beatrice. In mid-September Pip took her on his kind of holiday – Monte Carlo and Paris.

The photographs that Pip took of Margery on this trip are charming. Her hair by now was grey, and somewhat scanty, but her dresses and accoutrements are beautifully chosen to convey the smartness appropriate to his or her professional status, combined with a consciously feminine appeal. She looks prettily plump (which meant, says Christina, heavily corseted) and poses with a parasol, wearing short white gloves or with her ever-present cigarette encased in an elegant ebony holder. On their way home from Monte Carlo they stopped to visit a colleague of Pip's. This was Meg Catusse, a former dancer, friend of Colette, once mistress of Willy. She had been writing a *Tatler* column 'Priscilla in Paris' since 1909 and was determined to see out her fifty years on the paper. She and Margery had become most affectionate correspondents but had not previously met. The Carters arrived at the Gare du Nord. Meg wrote rapturously of her delight when she first saw Margery 'come sailing down that platform like a lovely ship'.

Meg was not a person with whom to be shy. During their stay Margery described the 'extraordinary experience' of her illness – and afterwards wrote to apologise if she had, as Pip had suggested, bored Meg. Quite the contrary, Meg replied, she had longed to ask for more detail but refrained as 'I was overcome with the feeling that your blessed old Tonker hates to have it spoken about.' She was entirely right, and subsequently chose to exercise diplomacy in her concern for Margery's health. 'I am timing this to reach you at a time when Pip is in Town and not likely to make any enquiries about it. I can understand his somewhat ostrich-like attitude re illness, bless him. Men are all like that and in his case it is so obvious that his inmost self begins and ends with you that he must find it somewhat disruptive when you are ill.'

Meg's generous attitude was to a great extent also Margery's. Joyce, who came, at Pip's request, to live permanently at D'Arcy

House after Margery's breakdown, looks back with amazement at the trouble they all took, led by Margery, to save him from being discommoded by her illnesses. This was Margery's choice. In 1955 she insisted that she had returned from their autumn holiday feeling fitter that she had 'for years'. It was obvious to Meg in Paris and to Joyce in Essex that she remained draggingly tired.

In November she went to see Dr Greene in Harley Street and in the following January spent a week under his supervision in the (private) St David's Wing of the Royal Northern Hospital. In the course of a series of tests Dr Greene discovered a lump in Margery's breast. He wished to make a small exploratory operation. The words 'cancer' and 'biopsy' were not used, as far as Joyce remembers, but Dr Greene made it clear that the condition could be serious. Margery allowed herself to believe that the lump was yet another manifestation of her sinusitis, a glandular clogging. She said she wished to take a second opinion from an ear, nose and throat specialist. During 1956 she spent time and money with physiotherapists endeavouring to clear the 'toxic matter' from her glandular and vascular system but she refused any operation. Dr Greene warned her that if the lump was what he feared, she would come to him in ten years' time and he would be unable to help her.

Margery claimed not to 'agree' with operations unless they were directly to save life. Joyce found her whole attitude so puzzling that she could not argue against the decision to ignore Dr Raymond Greene's advice. She did not wish to 'trespass' on Margery's privacy and, with a lifetime's habit, she accepted that her older sister would do as she thought best. She wondered whether Margery was afraid of the general anaesthetic – her weight and bronchial problems could have made this dangerous. A great-aunt of theirs had died unexpectedly under anaesthetic for a minor operation and so had a friend of Margery's in the 1930s. Margery was afraid of suffocation. She was also afraid of knives and blood and usually referred to operations as going 'under the knife'. When Phil was in the Middle East he had been so ineptly operated on for sinusitis that doctors in England assumed he was suffering from head wounds. Choosing surgery meant choosing a risk not just for herself but for those who depended on her. There is no indication that she discussed the matter seriously with Pip; on all the evidence she is unlikely to have done so. She did talk about it – Joyce remembers Margery telling them what Dr Greene had said and what she had decided – but not as if she expected any advice or action from anyone other than herself. There was no proper discussion.

Doctors might say that a refusal to accept treatment implies a desire to pretend that nothing is really wrong and that this in its turn reveals that all is not well psychologically. The hormone, thyroxine, in which Margery was deficient, is such an important catalyst within the body that a lack of it, over a long period of time, can cause more than just weight-gain, slowness, sensitivity to cold, nasal congestion, dry skin and hair loss – all symptoms suffered to various degrees by Margery. It may also, insidiously, allow a fear to become a phobia; a neurosis, a psychosis. When a psychiatrist finally saw Margery, at the end of her life, problems of this nature were threatening to engulf her.

Margery was no mean psychologist herself. It would be over-simple to suggest that she had to keep writing murder stories to hold at bay her fear of violence, but there might be an element of truth in it. As she had said to Dr Lindsay, 'I seem to have to put down everything I think to get rid of it.' But, as she would also have agreed, observing a situation and taking action to rectify it are two distinct processes. In 1956, Margery set Dr Greene's specific warning aside, gave up smoking and settled back to work. Originally, in the autumn of 1954, her projected novel had been entitled *Tether's End* (the title under which it was eventually sold in the U.S.). Now it had a new name, perhaps a new theme, *Hide My Eyes*.

Margery's starting point for *Tether's End/Hide My Eyes* was a comment upon the ending of *Tiger in the Smoke*. The tone of the second novel has changed. Whereas *Tiger* can be read as a Morality Drama, a battleground for cosmic forces, *Hide My Eyes* is a black comedy in which there is no place for beauty. Its characteristic locale is a dump or a deserted bar or a museum of oddities. Despite Tiddy Doll and his street-band of degenerates,

Tiger in the Smoke is finally optimistic. Its good character, Canon Avril, embodiment of Christian Charity or, in Margery's later phrase, 'disinterested love', has wisdom and a certain stature as he confronts Jack Havoc in the darkened church. If Avril is not quite a prudent citizen when it comes to assisting the police, nevertheless his detection is clear-eyed and he comes close to saving a soul. Polly Tassie, vehicle of love in the second novel, is a fool and worse, for she deliberately shuts her eyes to the clues scattered in her path and does all within her power not to recognise the monster of callous selfishness and duplicity that her love has created.

Both Canon Avril and Polly Tassie are fortunate to remain alive at the ends of their respective novels but whereas it is obviously valuable that Canon Avril should survive, Polly Tassie's resuscitation is a mixed blessing. The villain of *Hide My Eyes* is the nearest Margery came to a portrait of an actual criminal. Her friendship with the pathologist Francis Camps left her no illusions about the grisly realities of forensic evidence. In 1953 Camps published an account of his investigation into the Christie case – and Pip was commissioned to produce a drawing of the murderer. 'Two days association with it [the portrait]', wrote Pip afterwards, 'made me almost physically sick.' Christie's crimes prompted comparison with another multiple murderer, John George Haigh, who disposed of the bodies of his victims in an acid bath. Reviewers of *Hide My Eyes* were quick to notice that Margery's murderer was using that identical method. She was determined that the villain of this novel should be the most evil person she could conceive. Nevertheless, at the end of the novel, the reader knows, as does the murderer, that Polly will once again forgive him. More than that, she will expend any money she has left to buy the ablest lawyers for his defence – just as, so long ago, Emily Jane Hughes had sold the last of her jewels to help her worthless husband. To reasonable people this is almost incomprehensible. As Margery's Sergeant Picot concludes, ' "Then she's a fool . . . because that chap really is the cold-blooded monster that the papers are going to call him. D'you honestly think she'll stick by him when it all comes out?"

'Luke sighed and went back to his report. His vivid face was furrowed with weariness.

' "I know it," he said. "She'll forgive him without question whatever he's done to her and however high we hang him. And he knows it. It's no use you blaming her. She can't help herself. She's only a vehicle. That's Disinterested Love, chum, a force like nuclear energy, it's absolute." '

Disinterested Love was the one great quality that Margery had believed she and Granny shared. More than the 'Christian liking of mankind', which had been exemplified by Herbert and by Canon Avril, this love goes further in its unstinting acceptance and unquestioning forgiveness. It has a dynamic quality – and in *Hide My Eyes* it has begotten evil. The anguish in the book is the anguish of a parent who has seen a child go wrong and can trace it directly to loving indulgence or the realisation of a spouse who has trusted unwisely and discovered the harm caused to others through this abrogation of responsibility. Many of Polly Tassie's personal quirks hint that she is a bitterly comic portrait of Margery herself.

Polly Tassie is ridiculous, just as Margery feared that she herself was. They share a desire for cosiness in their surroundings and their relationships which is laughable. Margery's perceptions worked characteristically on several parallel levels. Polly would make a snug little home out of Euston Station if she had to. Margery was ignoring the realities of her life to make comfy little stories out of betrayal and mass-murder. The desire that all should be cosy is not only laughable, it is dangerous. In the mid-years of the '50s and 1956 in particular, Margery was draught-proofing, insulating and heating D'Arcy House. Polly Tassie's veritable passion for draught-exclusion facilitates her near-death from asphyxiation. A sudden gust of fresh air sends her entire museum up in flames. A sudden gust of insight in her relationship with Gerry makes it inevitable that he should try to murder her. As he prepares to kill her, Gerry gives her chloral, reassuring her the while,

' "Darling, it's all right, it's all right. Don't be frightened. It's only a little. Only enough to put you out."

'He was agonised, weeping even, suffocated by the relentless compulsion. Polly looked so very earnestly and stupidy at his face so close to her own.

' "I . . . am the last thing you love," she said thickly, struggling with the drug as its waves broke over her. "If . . . you . . . kill me, Gerry, you will lose contact with . . . your kind. There'll be nothing . . . to keep you alive. You'll wither like a leaf off a tree." '

The character of Gerry has charm, impudence, a sense of style – all the qualities claimed for Tonker in *The Beckoning Lady*, never there so convincingly demonstrated. He takes opportunism, 'the Science of Luck', further even than Jack Havoc in *Tiger in the Smoke*. Havoc is a man with a dream, lured by the spurious glitter of 'treasure'. Gerry has no vision. He is the arch-manipulator, endlessly rearranging other people's plans, possessions, bodies to suit his own convenience. His habitual establishing of alibis becomes a joke: he needs alibis to alibi his alibis. He name-drops with panache and is nonchalantly impressive as Major Chad-Horder, hinting at a world of exciting goings-on, glamorous company and grand schemes. Margery could not make a murderer from the bare bones, as it were, of Camps' scientific investigations. She needed to convey feelings and motives. The most intense anger as well as the most enduring love that Margery had felt for anybody had been felt for Pip. In their row of 1951, the moment her fury was aroused was the moment when she discovered the extent to which he had 'misrepresented' her and Sean to one another and 'manufactured' the rift between them 'to suit little Pippy's own ends'. 'YOU WILL COME TO A BAD END my little diary reader.' There are aspects of Gerry's character and actions which suggest the cruellest caricature of aspects of Pip that Margery had ever written.

Years later, when Pip and Margery were dead, and Joyce was living on alone in D'Arcy House with Christina, she was asked to write a preface to Pip's fragmentary autobiography *All I Did Was This*. In an unpublished draft she expressed, movingly, why she had loved and missed her brother-in-law 'for all his faults'. He was 'lavishly gifted and appallingly selfish,' she wrote. 'He revelled in his prejudices and intolerance, grasped all the best things in life with the minimum of effort for himself or concern for others . . . And if he happened to look over what I am writing now, I rather think he might say "Well, ye-ess!" Then glance sideways at me and flash that naughty grin.' In the bar of D'Arcy House Pip hung a cartoon of himself as 'Uncle Pip' trussing up and gagging some hapless little boy in order to filch the child's train set. He and Margery shared an ability to look objectively at versions of themselves and laugh. There is no evidence that he admitted to recognising anything of himself in Gerry as he agreed he had in Tonker. Neither is there any evidence that he would have been wounded or made angry if he had.

Some readers may find it illuminating to see versions of Margery and Pip behind the masks of Polly and Gerry. Others may fairly consider that such emphasis on personality obscures what the novel is attempting to convey, not only about the quality of love, but also the relentlessness of the existentialist 'logic' that drives Gerry on. He comes to the end his doctrine demands when he betrays himself by leaving indisputable proof of his presence, deeds and motives in his victim's wallet in a café. He has been so nearly successful in constructing his own life and identity without reference to beliefs, systems or personalities outside his own, that he has cast himself as his own destroyer. If one succeeds completely in caring about nothing except oneself, thought Margery, one will eventually grow careless even of that.

Gloria Greci, Margery's secretary from 1950 onwards, believes that the writing of *Hide My Eyes* was Margery's greatest achievement. So much self-doubt and downright fear had to be overcome. The ordeal (as it had been for her) of the E.C.T. left her in need of constant reassurance. Yes, it was good. Yes, it made sense. No, Margery had not lost her gift. Every page was typed and re-typed, yet from the first Gloria sensed how well the story was moving. She had worked with Margery on *The Beckoning Lady* though hardly at all on *Tiger in the Smoke*. She had made many copies of Margery's serials and short stories. Sometimes she typed from Margery's rough manuscript and as they grew more used to one another, Margery dictated directly to Gloria at the typewriter. Despite the author's uncertainty, this book seemed to Gloria to be far more assured than anything she had been asked to do before – 'slicker' even.

Endeavouring to compare like with like, objectively, there are fewer characters, less description, less meditation in *Hide My Eyes* than in *Tiger*. The elaborately constructed opening scene has a bizarre quality that marks it out even among Margery's characteristically challenging first chapters. Whodunnit purists cite this as Margery's single lapse into 'cheating'. Accepted as an icon of the novel's message, however, it stays readily in mind. Two old people sit in a lighted bus in the pouring rain. They witness a murder but do nothing. That's because they are not human. What then are living people who deliberately choose to act thus?

Ronnie Reid was depressed by his belief that the E.C.T. had done lasting damage. He detected a subtle change in Margery's personality, some clouding of the intellect perhaps. He found it hard to define. His daughter Sally thought that she didn't understand Aunty Marge's books so well after *Tiger in the Smoke* – and some reviewers would have agreed with her. The novels that came after Margery's treatment – *Hide My Eyes* (which was published in 1958), *The China Governess* (1963), *The Mind Readers* (1965) and *Cargo of Eagles* (left incomplete at her death) – failed to please critics as dependably as had her earlier titles. *The Beckoning Lady* had also been accorded a mixed reception. Margery ascribed this, publicly at least, to the natural progression of a career. She was now an established figure in the world of crime-writers, voted one of the world's top ten living practitioners by the Mystery Writers of America and thus a target for younger writers and critics wishing to mark out their own stylistic territories. 'I am at that stage of authorship,' she said, 'when it is fair game to wallop Auntie.' Privately she was depressed to find *Hide My Eyes* still reviewed as a Whodunnit.

The four, or more fairly the three, post-1955 novels are too varied for it to be easy to point to any single new flaw or feature. Sally said perceptively that they didn't seem to her to 'fit together' so well. First readings of these novels may induce an uncomfortable feeling of confusion which a second reading dispels. There is an increase in visible contrivance. Possibly Margery is taking less care to disguise her invention, possibly her inspiration is more cerebral, less instinctive. There is, until *Cargo of Eagles*, a significant absence of Lugg, or of similar comic characters who used, as Margery claimed, 'to write themselves'. Whatever the change in Margery's writing, if there is felt to be such a change, it would be rash to ascribe this to E.C.T., and not to natural intellectual development – or ageing.

For Sally the change in Margery herself was more grievous than any change in her writing. When she was twenty in about September 1955 she became engaged and took her fiancé to meet Margery at D'Arcy House. 'She seemed strange, distant and agitated. He, quite clearly, was not the sort of person she hoped I would marry and she believed that I was marrying for the wrong reasons. In the past (with her old kindness and wisdom) she would have written at length to me or asked me to come and stay for a couple of days and talked with me. On this occasion, she just waited till he was out of the room for a few moments and then raved at me – called me a "bloody little fool". I think she was very fond of me and desperately wanted to prevent me from making what she thought would be an unhappy marriage . . . For my part I was very hurt and very angry. This led to a rift between us that lasted several years, by which time I had moved to another part of the country and had four young children to look after. Perhaps it was significant that she sent me two magnums of champagne on the birth of my only daughter!'

Not many weeks after the completion of *Hide My Eyes* in 1957, Margery and Pip's married life took an unexpected turn. Pip resigned his editorship of *The Tatler*. Gloria remembers being called in to D'Arcy House one Saturday afternoon in late September to type Pip's letter of protest and resignation. There was a thunderous atmosphere, raised, wrathful voices in the next room, expressing outrage at the way Pip had been treated. Her fingers slipped, her spelling went haywire.

No-one can remember now quite what the problem was. The magazine's staff were apparently happy. Colleagues wrote to Pip thanking him for his championship of their interests and for the harmonious working atmosphere that he had created as editor. His disagreement appears to have been with the paper's proprietors, Illustrated Newspapers. Margery was not sorry that Pip had left *The Tatler*. She coupled it with 'the War' as one of the two major hiatuses in their life together. Writing to Isabelle Taylor at Doubleday, she spoke of her relief that 'twelve years of sitting out a Hunt Ball' had ended. Friends wrote kindly, some appreciating the effort he had made to 'bring intelligence' to the paper, others hoping he would soon find 'an editor's chair that fits him better'. Meg Catusse, shrewdly, sympathised with the strain Margery would experience living with 'Pip with a sore head' until his next career was underway.

Meanwhile other problems had become acute. In November 1957, an officer of the Inland Revenue Enquiries Branch notified the Carters that 'information in the hands of the Inland Revenue suggested that their accounts and taxation returns might not always have been correct.' He 'had no authority' to tell them what this information might be. It was in fact a simple book-keeping error made by the Revenue themselves but since that could not be disclosed, it was not discovered for another two years. In 1958 the lengthy process of an Official Enquiry was launched.

Margery was certain that they must put their financial affairs on a more business-like and comprehensible basis. With Pip a free agent there was nothing to prevent them taking a course of action she had discussed with Arthur Underwood in 1950 and forming themselves into a company. In August 1958, P. & M. Youngman Carter Ltd undertook 'the manufacturing and marketing of literary and pictorial ideas and properties invented or drawn or written by one or other of us'. D'Arcy House and all available rights in Margery's earlier novels were 'sold' to the company. Margery and Pip owned shares and were paid a salary. Joyce was company secretary.

'The old art-and-fiction factory' was formally back in business.

Pip
by Emmett
(The drawing he hung in the bar)

XIX

The Art-and-Fiction Factory

1958–1962

Pip's 'return' and the formation of their Company precipitated a series of changes. Finding herself under Inland Revenue investigation, but with no knowledge, at first, of the discrepancies that had prompted such investigation, was nerve-racking. Margery's ready imagination only fuelled her worry. *Hide My Eyes* was an immediate financial success as it was her first book to be selected by the Reader's Digest organisation. This brought a lump sum payment as well as publication and translation across the world. When Paul Reynolds suggested negotiating a new contract with Doubleday in order to save tax by spreading payment for her novels over more than one financial year, Margery replied in terms that show her galloping anxiety:

'I do not think you have any idea of the attitude (both official and public) over here towards any suggestion of attempted tax evasion. If you will think of your own country's attitude towards communist subversive activities of some years ago, you will get a faint picture of the present British attitude towards any hint that one is even thinking about ways to avoid paying out in full on any unexpected gain . . . Now Paul, do not misunderstand me but your letters to me, full of kind and bright ideas for saving tax are more than dangerous to me. If I was suspect (and the very fact this deal is a big one and I gave my last book away legally makes me so) my mail could be examined. So do not think out ways for me to avoid tax and above all do not put your ideas in writing.'

In the first shock of the enquiry she had wondered whether Aubrey Christlieb could have been either inefficient or dishonest. Neither, she discovered; it had merely been a case of poor communication and unnecessary acrimony. 'It emerges,' she wrote later, 'that our accountant suffered from arrogance, not dishonesty. He was absolutely sure of his facts and so, instead of explaining them, told the not unreasonably inquisitive inspectors to go to blazes – with just the results you'd expect!' Margery's own tendency to over-react had not helped. When she complained to Christlieb about the Witham Inspector's mention of her 'visitor's book', he wrote angry letters to the Chief Inspector in London, 'Do you suggest that my client runs her authoress profession as if it were a boarding house?' Her need to set D'Arcy House expenses against the cripplingly high rate of tax had led to some even more ludicrous expedients than those guyed in *The Beckoning Lady*. For a while between 1957 and 1958 Margery and Joyce did not feel able to sleep in the house at all – unless 'business guests' were present. At the end of every working day they conscientiously crossed the Square to Norry Emeny's former blacksmith's forge which Margery had bought for Joyce after his death. They wondered as they did so whether anyone stood in the shadows observing them.

From 1957 Margery felt the disgrace of being under investigation so acutely – as the letter to Paul Reynolds indicates – that she found it almost impossible to admit. When, in due course, the officers explained that the area they were investigating was her American earnings, and asked her to arrange for confirmation of all figures to be sent from her publishers and the editors of the magazines to whom she had sold serials and short stories, she demurred. Notwithstanding her actual innocence, she believed her reputation would be hopelessly tarnished if she had to explain why she needed the figures. All the years she had spent building up her transatlantic pen-friendships would go for nothing – or so she feared.

Finally she was obliged to supply the information: it was nothing more than a book-keeping error. Gross amounts paid from Doubleday had been entered by the Inspectors as part of Margery's earnings; the same amounts paid by Paul Reynolds, less his commission, had been entered again. The total therefore was far greater than the amount correctly declared by Margery. There was a stormy meeting in 1961 with the officers involved. Pip, who normally sat through such affairs in silence, suddenly, unexpectedly, spoke out. In his best Colonel Carter manner, he berated those present for their incivility to his wife. He demanded, and received, an unqualified, written apology. It was a moment for which Margery remained deeply and (thought Gloria) rather pathetically grateful.

After two and a half years of the enquiry, the semi-permanent condition of financial anxiety and official intrusiveness was ended. With the formation of the company and a new accountant came a change of tax district. No longer need Margery worry that watchers from Witham might be counting the number of visitors to her house and dividing them by the bedrooms available – or whatever phantasms had assailed her in the vulnerable 1950s. The problem of D'Arcy House's new status as company property was neatly solved by Margery renting herself sleeping accommodation there – on bed and breakfast terms!

The existence of the Company and the day to day administration by Joyce at D'Arcy House lifted Margery's burden of responsibility. Winifred Nerney had retired as Doubleday's London representative in 1954 and Margery had missed her soothing, cushioning influence. Now, when negotiations became difficult, she could take refuge behind 'my bosses'. 'I'll set the family on it' became a favourite phrase when tedious detail needed checking. ('Family' included both Joyce and Gloria.) Much of the anxiety of financial planning – could she 'afford' to sell another serial, complete another novel in any particular tax year – was removed by the business framework. All monies went to the Company, meticulous accounts were kept and all expenditure on business entertaining and on the two offices at D'Arcy House and the basement of no. 91, Great Russell Street, met from Company resources.

A change of British agent strengthened Margery's position further. It was not easy to leave the firm of A. P. Watt and Sons. They had represented her in Great Britain since the day when she had stood before the desk of 'Hansard' Watt and heard that Sir Ernest Hodder-Williams would be prepared to publish *Blackerchief Dick* on condition she deleted that offensive 'blasting, wilting swine'. But by 1958 Margery, now so business-like herself, considered that the heyday of the firm was over and its efficiency questionable. Letters went unanswered and there was a 'scary moment' when 'Daddy Watt seems to have forgotten all the dealings we have had with Penguins'. The new contract made with Chatto was discovered to be flawed and she wrote anxiously to her friend Edward Terrell Q.C. for confirmation that a proportion at least of the large *Reader's Digest* payment would actually come to her – that contingency had not been covered.

She decided that she must seek a change 'if I am not to fade out into a dusty heap of old papers'. Melancholy letters reached her from older authors, friends of her father: A. M. Burrage, Dick Starr, even Mac, who had found no enthusiasm left in the publishing world for themselves or their work. (Margery was an early advocate of the public lending right, a small fee paid to authors or illustrators each time their book is borrowed from a public library, and an aid to authors' security in old age. 'I think we should demand a penny a read and stick to it,' she wrote in 1961.) She had been worrying about the decline of her own capacity for work ever since the beginning of the 1950s. Her anxiety that her past novels be kept in print was, in part, another manifestation of this insecurity.

Relations with Heinemann improved markedly in the 1960s when Charles Pick became managing director and instituted a uniform library edition of the earlier Allingham novels in his care. Three omnibus editions published by Chatto in 1963, 1965 and 1967 were prompted by a suggestion from Margery that younger readers might be introduced to her work in this way. Three novels in each; an original introduction by the author and a new short story 'in the toe of the stocking', neatly gift-wrapped in a jacket from Pip. What attractive Christmas presents they would make, thought 'Auntie Marge' whose list of honorary nieces, nephews and godchildren lengthened every year.

At the same time as she set herself to consolidate her family readership, Margery tried to ensure that her work didn't date. As a critic she had shown an acute ear for period in a novel's content and attitudes; in her own work, atomic clouds had mushroomed up from young Rupert Campion's drawings as early as *More Work for the Undertaker* (published 1948/9). In the later novels come urban redevelopment and high-rise flats, advanced scientific research and cold war spying, mods, rockers and purple hearts often in slightly odd conjunction with the ripe romantic language and 1920s slang which remained her natural mode of expression.

Outside the text, almost all her business changes in this later period were prompted by her desire to be treated as an author with a future. To the end of her life she fought to have her new books 'published', not simply 'brought out'. When she had left Heinemann in 1950 she had made a principled decision not to trade solely on her reputation when finding a new publisher. Interested parties had had first to read, and like, *Tiger in the Smoke*. She was to do the same in 1963 when moving from Doubleday to Morrow in America for the publication of *The Mind Readers*. Such decisions were also shrewd. She understood the hesitations a firm might feel in taking over an author in mid-career. Were they being asked to pay too high a price for work on the verge of decline?

Her new agent, Graham Watson at Curtis Brown, found that working with Margery was a challenge he enjoyed. She was not quite the easy author she had liked to describe herself as in the thirties. She could, says Graham, be thoroughly 'devious' – if, he insists, that word is used without pejorative associations. Curtis Brown was a leading agency. He became its managing director in 1965 and had every reason to consider himself pretty good at his job. Margery, he says, kept his adrenalin flowing. She had always been business-like about her own affairs and the 'ink in her blood', her Allingham upbringing, ensured her wider interest in trade matters. Graham came to admire her foresight and her ability to spot trends in publishing – even from the Essex marshes. Public lending right (finally established in 1982) might be one example, the increased popularity of spoken word recordings was another. In the early 1960s Margery was predicting a boom in such alternative editions and insisting that authors' rights must be contractually safeguarded. Unabridged recordings of her major novels were finally made in the later '80s.

The establishment of a formal business partnership with Pip meant much to Margery. It seemed to promise a re-creation of the early days of their marriage to which she had so often looked back nostalgically. She tried to change her way of life in order to spend more time with him in London. They had earlier rented extra space from Doubleday (principal leaseholders at 91, Great Russell Street) and set up an office – and a bar – as an extension to the flat. Margery's new Penguin 'blurb' stated firmly 'Miss Allingham, who is married to P. Youngman Carter, divides her time between a house in Essex and a flat in Bloomsbury once the studio of Victorian illustrator and novelist George du Maurier.'

P. and M. Youngman Carter spent many weekdays in 1958–9 in the flat entertaining agents, publishers and journalists with all the optimism of a pair of entrepreneurs. The 'London Limelight' column that Pip had written for *The Tatler* was continued in *The Evening News*, portrait commissions were discussed and an exhibition of his work at the Moulin d'Or restaurant arranged. The film rights for *Hide My Eyes* were also the subject of eager, though ultimately fruitless negotiations. One company signed up the singer Cliff Richard to take part. The *New Musical Express* reassured its readers that although 'it is a murder thriller, Cliff will sing at least three songs'. The film of *Tiger in the Smoke*, made by Rank in 1956, had merely cut out the character of Albert Campion!

In the years after he had left *The Tatler*, Pip was able to make more use of his range of talents, writing and selling articles and short stories as well as reviving some of those he had written during the war. He produced some limited edition prints and wrote witty captions for a satire on traffic wardens, *Parker's Lot*. He both wrote and illustrated a travel book, *On to Andorra*, and produced three books on wine all of which were published by Hamish Hamilton, their neighbours in no. 90 Great Russell Street. The production director (ex-Christ's Hospital student and friend since 1934), Max Martyn, remembers how solicitous Margery was for their success. She was still, he sensed, anxious lest it was her accomplishment that had blighted Pip's creative career.

The most speculative of the projects undertaken jointly by Pip and Margery in the later fifties, the one that was always about to make their fortune but never did, was a new gaming machine called first Zoe, then Orion. They had visited the casino in Monte Carlo on their recuperative holiday in 1955 and had amused themselves on their journey home by devising their own novelty item. This was their spiel. 'This remarkable new device, which is a thing of great beauty in its own right, combines three elements: the appeal of fantastic odds, the chic and familiarity of roulette with the lure of astrology which has more followers now through the popular press than ever before.' They made a provisional application to the patent office as soon as they returned home and produced complete specifications in 1957 (with help from Cressie, the technical draughtsman). By 1959 they had negotiated U.S.A. representation and produced a working model. Optimistically they continued renewing the patent until the end of their lives. Though a few publicity paragraphs were generated nothing more came of the idea.

It has been suggested that Margery's decision to 'divide her time' between D'Arcy House and no. 91 was a direct strategy to prevent Pip spending his weekdays with anyone else. It was, however, the working rather than the sexual relationship which she sought to recapture. She did not like his continuing infidelity but succeeded in keeping it a side issue in their marriage. Friends who knew Pip in London knew about his 'London wife'; those who heard Margery at D'Arcy House mention 'Pip's Mistress' with jokey casualness, comfortably assumed that there was no such person.

In June 1959 she wrote to Isabelle Taylor with undisguised satisfaction, 'Pip and I are both working on the synopsis of the new book, and we haven't done that for years.' A formal synopsis was something she had not produced for years either – since she had been writing *Answers* serials for Messrs Tiltman and Yates in fact – and then it had been a thoroughly uncongenial exercise. In yet earlier days when she and Pip had worked together on *Mystery Mile* and its companions, a page of notes planning a chapter might be generated from their talks, but no formal scheme embracing the whole development of a book. Brief and occasional chapter jottings for other novels are scattered at random through her notebooks. More diligence was evident in planning the novel that became *The China Governess* but possibly less conviction.

Margery embarked on an unusual amount of research for the novel, in this case extending her knowledge of Staffordshire pottery. She regularly did a certain amount of what might be called 'professional' reading. As well as the novels of her fellow crime-writers, which she read somewhat sparingly, her bookshelves contain memoirs of retired policemen, accounts of actual crimes and reports by forensic scientists. Their neighbour, Francis Camps, helped confirm detail. In 1946 he had proposed Margery for membership of the Medico-Legal Society and she read its and similar journals. Only rarely did she need to carry out specific research. Pip's former school friend, Littley Wright, an army engineer, had checked the functioning of the bicycle grenade in *Dancers*; for *The Patient at Peacocks Hall*, Dr Jimmy Madden had advised on a G.P.'s altered role after the inauguration of the National Health Service; Phil had been asked to comment on the street-band scenes in *Tiger*. Generally speaking Margery had been writing from well within her own or her family's experience. She had needed to think about, not read about it.

The imagined pottery group depicting the governess and her charges provides no more than a starting point for the novel. In an interview given in 1963 Margery spoke of it as a 'decoration'. Pip thought it might be a useful marketing aid and endeavoured to have an actual model produced to accompany the book. That Margery should feel the need to construct what is essentially a gimmick could indicate a faltering of confidence in her inspiration. There are other indications that she was ill at ease with the nature of her craft. *Time and Tide* was attempting its own rejuvenation in 1958. Viscountess Rhondda had retired and the new editor, Anthony Lejeune, wrote to former contributors asking for copy. Margery called her piece, 'What to do with an Ageing Detective'. It began, 'I came out of my interview with Mr Albert Campion feeling rather sad. He had been so nice. As we parted he took my hand.

' "My dear girl", he said, looking at me with that kindly wryness that no longer wrung my heart. "How *can* I?"

' "Can you what?" I was abrupt with him.

' "Well . . ." He was still modest, still shy, still a trifle vague, not to say incoherent for a modern world. "Hop about. Pull guns and shoot lines. Pretend I like the Police . . . I mean everybody knows how old I am. *You* saw to that, fixing it at the same age as the century so we shouldn't get muddled. I'm not complaining, dearest. I only point out that by the time the next tale comes out I'll be . . ." He blushed faintly, "Well, sixtyish."

' "Yes," I murmured colouring faintly myself. "Yes, I see. Don't you like the police any more?"

' "Not awfully." The pale eyes betrayed a blue severity I had not noticed long ago. "They're all right. Good chaps doing their job I suppose but it's a tatty old job, Sweetie. Don't you think so?"

' "No," I said hastily kissing him firmly and pushing him back inside his front door in Bottle Street. "No, I don't. If I did we'd neither of us be here. Bless you, see you soon. You get set in your armchair." '

In the article Margery hints that she is considering a new detective, someone younger than Campion and equally gentlemanly but someone who has to work for his living and is thus more involved in the altered society she observed around her. In the later 1940s Margery had created a policeman detective, Divisional Detective Inspector Charles Luke, to move her work on from Campion's upper-class amateurishness. Luke was a Londoner, his personality more colourful, his attitudes fiercer and more robust than those of her Superintendents before him. He became a major character within her fiction, never quite a hero. Margery kept her youthful vision of the detective as a romantic adventurer, 'the rescuer, the dragon slayer, the wanderer in search of other people's troubles'. Like his predecessors within the Force, Luke was ill at ease off his own mental patch, his humanity bounded by his profession. Luke was an objectively conceived character; Campion was different. 'As the only life I had to give anybody was my own,' Margery explained, 'we grew very close as the years went by.'

By the turn of the decade, Margery had become somewhat disillusioned with the role of the police in society and impatient with their centrality in detective fiction. 'It's a very sour world where the romantic heroes masquerade as police in uniform.' From 1958 Margery showed a new willingness to talk directly about her craft, not merely through asides as she had done in her reviews. She felt ready to pass on her 'trade secrets' and possibly by so doing to help her own work through a period of transition. 'I am by nature an intuitive writer whose intellect trots along behind, tidying, censuring and saying "Oh My!" It has taken me a very long time to comprehend this and to allow for it,' she wrote in 1965.

The debate surrounding the partial abolition of capital punishment (by the Homicide Act of 1957) demanded that detective novelists reassess their craft. The appalling consequences of mistaken deduction in a society where murder is swiftly punishable by death had given edge to the genre since H. C. Bailey's *Trent's Last Case* (published in 1912). Writers had abandoned the essentially Edwardian world of jewel-thieves, coiners and sinister international conspirators, the world in which Margery had started her career, in order to focus with virtual unanimity on the crime of murder. 'It must be murder,' she had explained to their friend Paul Holt for *The Daily Herald*, 'because that is the only crime you get hanged for. Increase the number of crimes for which there is capital punishment and we'd all move away from murder tomorrow.'

In fact readers of 'Golden Age' detective stories are as little encouraged to consider the fate of the villain after his unmasking as readers of romantic novels are conventionally expected to think about life after the Happy End. Dorothy Sayers' Lord Peter Wimsey attended one condemned man to the morning of his execution, and that was the last book she wrote in the genre. *Tiger in the Smoke* (1952) was the first of Margery's novels explicitly to consider the conviction and hanging of the murderer – and only Luke is keen to dispatch his prey. Avril could not accept the responsibility of pronouncing sentence and Campion 'was no great man for blood sports'. Neither was Margery. However, the fact that Havoc was never captured nor his body found caused unease to some readers and to Margery's publishers. She later admitted she had deliberately let him slip through Luke's fingers. In *Hide My Eyes*, she said, she had attempted to compensate and to imagine a villain for whom the death penalty would be appropriate. 'Contrary to my usual reaction,' says Campion of Gerry Hawker, 'I rather hope this chap will hang.'

By 1958 there were not more but fewer crimes punishable by death and Margery's attitude to the fictional device of murder had become very much more sophisticated than the explanation she had offered Paul Holt. In a talk entitled 'Crime for our Delight', she spoke of the old 'puzzle-novel' growing on into the 'novel of suspense'. It was the 'death of an aspect' which had interested her. 'The killing we harp on is not just an ordinary killing [it is] the new and main literary idea of this century. We seem to be catching up with the Greeks at last. Enormous amount of our stories have this second meaning or main meaning: the way one keeps on murdering one aspect of a person to give birth to another. We kill one relationship and another takes its place. We lose one of ourselves and find another.' This she claimed was true 'of all stories, love, adventure, travel but now we are starting to see it like this and do it deliberately'. In the future 'I see more and more serious writers taking up this two-dimensional kind of story as they begin to see not only the elementary problem but the curious symbolical way in which it can be used.' The old 'chess-problem type of story', she added dismissively, would be 'better served by the cross-word puzzle'.

Pip, however, was a dedicated cross-word puzzler. The plot of *The China Governess* is elaborate and there are moments when it gives the impression of having been imposed on the themes of the novel rather than having sprung from them. Margery promoted her new book as being the third of the 'group' which included her greatest successes, *Tiger in the Smoke* and *Hide My Eyes*. Perhaps, as had earlier been the case with *Look to the Lady*, this turned out to be 'the third of a series that usually convinced me that it was time to push on and try something elsewhere'. In *The China Governess* Margery is writing in a style with which she appears bored and about characters and places who are no longer of prime interest to her.

The twin poles of the novel are the Keep at Angevin, a name reminiscent of her pre-war 'Suffolk' novels, supremely gracious but striking as chill as a mausoleum, and the termite horrors of the Turk Street Mile, 'wiped out utterly and for ever in a single night by four landmines and a sprinkling of incendiaries'. Hope for the future centres on a concrete monster: 'The design was some way after Corbusier but the block was built up on plinths and represented an Atlantic liner swimming diagonally across the site.' The first of many high-rise blocks of council flats had been built in London by 1959 and *The China Governess*'s characters divide into those appalled and those excited by this vision.

The author is (with reservations) in the second group. Her portrayal of the barren Kinnits, civilised, economically comfortable and conservative, the characters most like her surface self, is bitterly comic and angry. A glance back to the Palinodes of *More Work for the Undertaker* helps define Margery's change in tone. The Kinnits, chilly connoisseurs and owners of The Keep, help run The Little Society for the Preservation of the London Skyline. They use the remnants of their class power to oppose the plans of the crusading Counciller Cornish who dreams of 'social rebirth' in the sincere belief that 'decent conditions make a decent community'. Their old retainer, Nanny Broom, constructing her life on a shoddy romance of little princes and princesses and the importance of 'nice manners', is presented with an extraordinary disgust.

Satirising this world, the world she had worked to afford, Margery's aim is sure. In her most distinctive new character, the socialist urban planner, Councillor Cornish, she fails to achieve consistently a distinctive new voice. There are good moments – for instance the brief scene when Cornish confronts his unknown son and berates him with the special venom that Margery believed was reserved for family quarrels, but too often, unfortunately, Cornish speaks in Allingham cliché, 'a pleasant, matter-of-fact voice with a hint of pure steel in it'. Several of Margery's characters had used that one.

Unevenness of this kind, even self-pastiche, mars *The China Governess*. This may be attributed to the transitional nature of the book. The focus of Margery's interest in her last novels is moving unobtrusively away from questions of Good and Evil, away from houses and families, towards a new look at a changing society, and 'the communal mind at work'. Her failure to achieve a consistent tone may equally have been caused by sheer tiredness and ill-health. Gloria Greci remembers the novel being written, revised and re-written over and over again. Commenced in 1958, it was not published until 1963.

All too soon it had become obvious that Margery's well-being could not stand up to so much business entertaining and the demands of London life. The other visitors to and residents of 91, Great Russell Street remember her as indefatigably ebullient and hospitable. 'Wherever Margery was there was always a bottle of champagne to be found.' Barbara Noble however, who had taken over from Winifred Nerney as Doubleday's London representative and who was therefore also Pip's and Margery's immediate landlord, grew aware that behind the laughing lady who passed by her office laden with jokes and hat-boxes, there was a tired, unhappy woman. Her own relationship with Margery was far from easy; there were frequent bickerings about repairs to the building, and Barbara was too often made aware that, in Margery's eyes, she could never take the place of Nerney. She nevertheless gives Margery generous credit for the 'gallantry' with which she kept up appearances.

At D'Arcy Christina disapproved thoroughly of the London visits and so was 'cross'. Joyce felt Margery's exhaustion when she returned home from the flat and Gloria remembers how many of the days Margery planned to give to *The China Governess* were spent in bed. Attacks of 'flu, sinusitis and bronchitis laid her low for weeks at a time. Margery, as usual, claimed that there was nothing to worry about. 'All goes fairly well with us. I am still wandering around London with Pip but I shall be glad when he gets a quieter job again and I get back to my homework. The break is doing me good though.' Eventually she accepted that she could not keep up with Pip in London. The firms of Chatto, Heinemann, Penguin, A.P. Watt, Curtis Brown and Paul Reynolds Associates, were requested not to address their letters to the Youngman Carter office at Great Russell Street but direct again to D'Arcy House.

There were compensations. The existence of the Company meant that the maintenance of D'Arcy House need no longer be the piecemeal affair satirised in *The Beckoning Lady*. Despite the facility of the bar at no. 91, major business entertaining took place in Essex. Not only visiting publishers, agents and journalists but their sons, daughters and friends arrived expectantly from all parts of the world. American guests were the most frequent and their standards of domestic comfort were high. Even after her retirement from Doubleday Winifred Nerney thought it her duty to write to Margery hoping she would soon be able to install an 'en suite' bathroom in the main bedroom 'at least'.

In a moment of exasperation Margery decided that her house reminded her 'of nothing so much as a potting shed'. Local workmen joked about the narrow track left up the middle of the stairs by the piles of magazines and paper heaped at the side of every tread. It is a house rich in crannies and alcoves and cupboards at the base of sloping ceilings. When Margery and Pip arrived in 1935 many of these were still filled with the Doctor's bric-a-brac. Now they were full again with sketches and stories and old business letters, Margery's fabrics, Herbert's sagas and Pip's and Joyce's souvenirs. Nevertheless the house could look impressive when the occasion demanded. Out came the old silver and napery, and in came extra help to polish the fine furniture Margery had collected over the years. A 'fan' of her books who visited the house in 1965 wrote, 'I knew you would have all this of course – it just brought to life one of your many descriptive pieces of opening the door of a lovely old house to be greeted by the smell of well-polished oak.' There was usually some new planting or project underway in the garden, and in 1959 Pip and Margery put a huge Flemish sideboard into Dr Salter's former stables converting them into a spacious studio for him with a cosy writing room tucked under the roof for her – plus a darkroom for Joyce who was a keen amateur photographer and an office for Gloria. *Homes and Gardens* magazine 'did' the house in 1960. Margery wrote to Paul, 'The young firm of P. & M.

youngman Carter Ltd is pursuing a gay (and somewhat Ritzy) progress . . . and Christina is once again telling me how they do things in "good" houses. One of the picture magazines are featuring us next month . . . I saw the pictures on the wide lens and hardly recognised the old place we looked so clean, tidy and big!'

Though the Thursday Club cricket matches had come to an end, the tradition of big summer parties continued. Business and personal friends were entertained together, so often they were one and the same. The raffish crowd who had used to descend on Viaduct Farm had grown eminent and remained congenial. A letter from 'Rush' of the old days, by 1960 Sir Henry Rushbury KCVO, Keeper of the Royal Academy, written after a visit to D'Arcy House said, 'Years rolled back and I saw you in your bar, surrounded by the jibes and jokes and household fun, and you, my dear Marge, standing there with the real magic of friendship making all about you happy.'

Jack Morpurgo thought that Margery in 'her' bar deliberately acted up to a Toulouse-Lautrec/Folies Bergères image. Dorothy Watson speaks of her 'arranging her bosom' over its flat surface. Oriel Malet recalls her infectious laughter; Sally Reid, her uninhibited conversation, punctuated by invisible exclamation marks and 'ducky's' and 'bless you's'. Margery's talent for Essex dialect speech was such that another friend arranged for her to be officially recorded. From earlier times, Sally and her sister Deirdre also remember how Margery helped them to feel included in a conversation when they were children, sometimes simply by putting her hand on their shoulders and drawing them close to her while other adults were talking over their heads.

Even when the visitors were gone and Pip busy with his London activities, D'Arcy House was a more populated place after 1958. It became, unexpectedly, a family home again. As a younger woman, Joyce had been reluctant to make a home with Margery. She had felt the force of her elder sister's personality so acutely that she had wondered whether she could ever sustain her own selfhood in constant proximity. When Margery had suffered her breakdown in 1955 Joyce came without hesitation – and wondered afterwards why she had ever thought there would be a problem. Joyce was glad to be reunited with Brock, her collie dog who had lived at D'Arcy House since the war. He had been Choc in *The Beckoning Lady*. A second Brock and then his 'wife', Belle, joined the household at the turn of the decade and contributed their own strand of family affairs.

It took Margery a little time to discover just how competent her younger sister was. Initially she had planned to have Phil, the successful, if unorthodox, businessman, as chairman of P. & M. Youngman Carter Ltd. Then there was talk of bringing Grog in as secretary but soon it became clear that no token men were required. By the time Margery came to make her will, she knew that all she needed to do was to pass complete control of all matters, financial and sentimental, to Joyce.

The final interdependence of the sisters came to maturity under challenging conditions. With rather the same sense of shock that billeting officers had experienced when required to accommodate the pathetic groups of evacuee mothers and children in 1939, so, early in 1958, Margery and Joyce had realised that it was their inescapable duty to take on geriatric care of the surviving older members of their family – Em, Maud and dear Aunt Grace.

XX

How to Become a Jolly Old Fruit

1959–1966

The advent of the old ladies, just as life at D'Arcy House had settled into its new routine, was an alarming prospect. 'Whose survival was at stake?' Margery wondered. 'Whose life? Yours or ours?' In *The Relay*, an account of this experience, she set out the situation as it first appeared to herself and Joyce in 1958: 'They were all very strong, powerful, self-opinionated, egotistical women who did not want any help from any body. None had quite enough money. We loved, respected and were very grateful to them all' but 'I remember thinking when I was little more than a girl that I would give my parents anything except my life. Old people sometimes take lives without noticing it. It is up to everybody to protect his own.'

Maud, widowed in 1946, had continued to devote herself to *Picture Show*. Joyce remembers her working long hours, being parsimonious to her staff and hard on herself, all for the greater good of Fleetway Publications. For Margery, Maud was the ultimate 'fan'. She and her paper had succeeded because Maud understood instinctively what other fans would want to know about films and those who starred in them. There was no distance between Maud and her readers. Regular weekends at Tolleshunt D'Arcy House throughout the 1950s had helped keep her at work. Margery would tint her hair, smarten up her clothes or put her to bed and nurse her. In 1958, Maud suffered a stroke after a showing of Cecil B. de Mille's epic *Ten Commandments* and could continue no longer. She was left bitter, bad-tempered and, because she had only paid herself a minimum salary, short of money.

Em had been on Margery's conscience ever since she had left Marcus Lawrence. In *The Relay* Margery described her mother flitting restlessly from one pension to another leaving a train of minor quarrels and financial difficulties in her wake – 'a heart-breaking and unhappy figure'. Margery covenanted her an allowance and employed a tactful solicitor to administer it. The question of Em coming to live in D'Arcy House lurked unresolved in the background. Unlike 'Granny', whose unfailing good manners carried her through the difficulties of dependency – 'I don't know who you are,' she had said to Margery and Joyce as they turned her during her final illness, 'but I'm sure I'm very much obliged to you' – Em had never made it easy for Margery to welcome her into her home. On any visit, especially if other guests were within earshot, she was almost bound to pause in the hall and sigh, 'Ah well, I expect you've put me in the garret again.' She was only too clever at uncovering the lowest motives to any act of kindness. Cooee, recipient of much generosity from Margery, remembers being taken aside by Em who explained, 'Margery doesn't do it because she likes you, you know. She just likes to see herself being generous.' Pip had remained adamant that Em could not live with them. At a time when their marriage, their money and her health were all under pressure, it is not surprising that Margery had shied away from her mother's company. Into *The Relay*, which was written after Em's death, Margery slips a covert admission that it was aspects of their likeness that had frightened her. She did not think that she could continue to control her own fluctuating moods when Em was there letting rip with hers.

After Maud's stroke, some decision had to be taken. Maud was in her mid-seventies, Em approaching her eighties and both needed care. Too many state-run geriatric institutions looked like the workhouses in which they had often been sited. Private retirement homes were expensive, depressing and, thought Margery, 'unnatural'. 'The general artificial segregation of the old', she wrote later, 'is as dangerously unnatural as general artificial insemination and, in a way, rather like it. Integral pieces of human experience are by-passed and lost by both.' D'Arcy House with its steep stairs and multiplicity of steps, thresholds and rooms on different levels was not especially suitable for two infirm old ladies. Her own reluctance aside, Margery believed it would be unfair to Pip to compel him to accept such a concentration of her family under one roof.

Joyce's cottage, the Forge, on the opposite side of the Square supplied the perfect solution. Margery and Joyce prepared as if for a 'typhoon'. Stripped to its essentials the Forge provided on a single level one large room with two beds (a pair of four-posters with curtains round each for warmth and privacy), smaller rooms for washing and cooking, some storage space and separate accommodation for a resident carer. Maud was a big woman and unsteady on her feet. Em's bones had become fragile. Support rails were set into the floor and the furniture checked for solidity. Once the old ladies had moved in, Joyce kept meticulous accounts so that their money could be seen to be used directly for their own maintenance, and so the three children could contribute as they thought best.

It was typical of Margery that she should always be seeking further levels of significance in the events of her daily life. Faced with the particular needs of Em, Maud and then Grace, she thought about the wider problems of caring for the elderly in contemporary society – as she had with the evacuees. She tried, at the same time, to include an acceptance of ageing and death in her understanding of life's metaphysical pattern. During 1958, she had attempted to console the young novelist, Oriel Malet, on the death of her 'Marraine' (the actress, Yvonne Arnaud) by sharing, as she had done earlier with Betty Carter, the thoughts that had comforted her after the loss of her father. Margery described to Oriel her understanding of inheritances – some little while after the actual bereavement, she said, the survivor may find that they have gained something new; some fragment of the dead one's personality or belief reappears in the living. Margery's trust in a kind of immortality was not based on belief in a personal soul but on this idea that salient characteristics may be reincarnated in those who are ready to inherit them. Margery was aware of family characteristics as tangible, discrete things. Death allowed the re-absorption of a person's characteristics 'back into the family where all that is going to remain of him here must be preserved'.

From presenting life as a dance, Margery came to think of the period of old age as the intricate takeover in a vital family, and human, relay. In her relay image she saw the elderly person finding his or her moment to move to one side of the track and the two generations travelling some distance together while the 'batons' of inheritance were handed across. These batons were various; not material possessions but, as she had described to Oriel, definite if intangible things which the younger generation had not had before the dying person passed them over. The initial act of handing over and accepting responsibility – Em and Maud's decisions to give up managing their own lives, Margery and Joyce's new readiness to manage for them – was the important first baton in a series of hand-overs. It was their compulsion, she thought, to find the proper recipient, the person who would keep and treasure pieces of knowledge, fragments of their personality or experience that often made old people garrulous, repetitive and somehow urgent.

Existence, thought Margery, was a process of making oneself, of 'doing one's honnest best' (one of her favourite phrases) to respond intelligently and constructively to each of life's challenges, seeking to discover, and to carry out, whatever it was for which one was meant. By the time of old age, that process was almost complete and the old people could show themselves as they essentially were: they could reveal the 'hard bright core' of themselves. This, in turn, could help the younger people, the 'heirs', to gain greater understanding of their selves and proceed more purposefully within their own pattern.

Expressed thus, the process sounds elevating. More often it was gruelling. Margery and Joyce made a conscious decision 'that no attempt to steer our old ladies must be made by us that was not absolutely vital to their physical well being.' In Margery's words the aim of the Forge 'dower house' system was to be 'the converse of the nursery, not a repetition of it'. She continued, 'In practice this resolved itself into an honest attempt, within the limits of sanity, to give them everything they wanted, the moment they wanted it. They had all lived for over seventy years trying to get just this.' When Em demanded steak for lunch every day, Margery did not hesitate. Steak it was every day until Em herself became weary of it. Although a 'carer' was employed, the two old ladies were constantly 'playing the goat'. Joyce hurried to and fro across the Square to sort out endless minor upsets and to ensure that their companion's conditions of service did not become intolerable. If they were unwell she too slept at the Forge. Margery was the person of last resort.

Joyce remembers a sense of gaiety surrounding the project. The Ladies of the Forge, as Margery took to describing them, were 'naughty', even 'obstreporous'. They were also uninhibited and so 'alive'. Maud would think of some way to stir up a fuss and Em would put it into action. They bickered in old age just as they always had. Former colleagues of Maud's who came visiting were rather shocked to find Miss Hughes so bad-tempered 'for she really is in clover. Everything there is so beautifully bright and fresh. What more could one want?' Em's tongue had lost little of its facility. *The Relay* is scattered with sarcastic little gibes which sound as if they have been noted verbatim. There were squabbles, sulks and 'set-outs'; there were also moments of great merriment.

Em died first in June 1960, peacefully and completely in control of herself. 'I think I'll go now, darling,' she said to Margery when she had finally been moved to hospital in pain from a broken bone. After fifty-six difficult years, mother and daughter parted on good terms.

Aunt Grace arrived in her stead. She had passed on Pope's Hall to a nephew and had tried to return to live in London. She had become confused and could be headstrong. Margery wrote to Isabelle Taylor, 'At eighty nine [she] just won't have it that anyone has died and we are always being called upon to prepare for visits from either of her husbands (deceased), her Papa (Granny's elder brother) or the full cast of *Floradora* with whom she appeared nightly in 1889.' When Grace sat by the Forge window watching the Queen's Head pub across the square, happy in the conviction that it was a theatre putting on regular evening performances, all was well. When she climbed out of the windows and employed her charm and plausibility to beg passing motorists for a lift to town, she could precipitate a crisis.

Grace died at Christmas 1960 and Aunt Maud in the autumn of

1961. The support rails were unscrewed from the concrete floor and the 'dower house' returned to its condition of an ordinary small dwelling. By 1964, Margery was looking speculatively at her own house and wondering 'how I can re-jig this old heap for my own and Tonker's final phase – the very idea gives him apoplexy'. She wrote *The Relay* in the summer of that year between 'virtual' completion and final revision of *The Mind Readers*. Part metaphysical explanation, part autobiography and practical handbook, *The Relay* is characteristic of her non-fiction approach to life. Pip disliked it. Old age was another subject on the list of those he 'refused even to think about' and *The Relay* was never published. Reconsidering the book, Margery agreed that though it had some 'good stuff' in it, it was 'served up in untidy heaps'. Nevertheless, writing it 'seems to have taken a weight off my own mind'.

Margery did not properly reach old age herself. She was 60 in 1964, the last year for which her diary is complete. It shows her in an almost constant state of tiredness and vague, unidentified ill-health. Two days of visitors or an early morning spent arranging flower show exhibits and she was in bed exhausted for another day. Joyce remembers seeing her rub some soreness in her breast when she thought she was unobserved. She may already have given up her visits to a Colchester doctor for thyroid treatment. 'The doctors have decided that I am born fat and fitter fat so they leave me alone as hopeless,' she wrote in July 1965. Photographs taken around this time show her very bulky indeed. Intellectually she felt full of ideas. During 1964, she wrote *The Relay* – 40,000 words, cut 29,000 from *The Fashion in Shrouds* and produced a preface for the omnibus *Mr Campion's Lady*. She gave some help to Pip with *Drinking Bordeaux* and with the captions for *Parker's Lot*. Margery's main effort, however, went into the completion and final revision of her new Campion novel, *The Mind Readers*.

This novel was in stark contrast to its predecessor, *The China Governess*, almost an implicit criticism of it. She had laboured to make that novel '100% comprehensible at least'; in *The Mind Readers* she did not. 'One takes a great risk by being intelligible I always feel,' she wrote defiantly. Pip disagreed with her but Phil thought it 'one of your very best'. *The Mind Readers* was modern, experimental and written 'to please myself'. 'The subject of the book fascinated me,' she wrote. And again, 'I can't bear to leave it.' It was, though she could not know it, to be the last novel she would complete. It took as its subject the phenomenon that had sparked her first, extrasensory perception.

Margery had once explained that thought, to her, had a circular quality; if she followed a 'think' right through, neither giving up nor being diverted, she would inevitably find herself returning to her starting point – '*but from the other side*'. 'Receiving' the plot of *Blackerchief Dick*, long ago in 1921, had been a formative experience. It had seemed to show her that there were worlds and personalities existing alongside, or within, her surface life and that she had the power to reach them by the 'chemical flash' of perception. It had sent her out on her career as a novelist. Over the years her awareness of parallel existences had influenced her attitudes to place and time, to inspiration and to the potential of her own mind. In 1963–4 she approached a similar happening again, from the other side, from the point of view of the observer not the medium. The detection in *The Mind Readers* had abandoned convention and aims to uncover not, 'Who did it?' but 'What is going on?' How are the schoolboys at the centre of the story performing their feats of clairvoyance? Margery considered that she was investigating a 'technical mystery', some aspect, not of an individual personality, but of 'the common mind'. If telepathy could become as commonplace as wireless or telephones, what were the implications? Who would control its use? 'What to do with an ageing detective' is no longer an issue in *The Mind Readers*. Campion, Amanda, Canon Avril and Luke are relegated effectively to spectators and commentators as two small boys, Sam and Edward, take the real action into their own hands.

Technologically, Margery believed that the time was right for this novel. She felt as convinced as she had with *Traitor's Purse* that her 'unconscious mind had sniffed the air' and that her plot expressed something that was topical. Research for *The Mind Readers* had the need-to-know urgency that had been absent from *The China Governess*. Gloria remembers how keenly Margery collected newspaper articles on 'bugging' and thought-control, how real the issue of Government surveillance of individuals seemed to her. Entering other people's minds, tampering with their thoughts – 'bloody dangerous, ducky' she warned Gloria earnestly. She dedicated the novel 'to my technical advisers in gratitude for their astonishing new world and in the hopes that I get this book out before they do'. *The Mind Readers* complete, she was unsurprised to read a report in *The Times* that the Navy were considering experiments with simple telepathy to improve communication to the new generation of nuclear submarines. Just as she had suggested in Chapter Two.

Ideologically, *The Mind Readers* was written for the cold war world. Margery had left behind the great symbolic clash of Good and Evil. The world she feared in the 1960s was the world of men who would sell their country for 'just a little bit more money'. In part *The Mind Readers* may be seen as Margery's idiosyncratic (even eccentric) response to the same set of circumstances that produced John le Carré's *The Spy Who Came in From the Cold* (published 1963). She was immediately impressed by le Carré's work and was sure that this was the direction in which the adventure novel (and the romantic hero) should go. In 1965, before the publication of *The Looking Glass War*, Margery took part in a trans-national 'conversation' with le Carré for the American magazine, *The Ladies' Home Journal*. Le Carré was interviewed in Switzerland, Margery in Essex and the copy cabled to America. After filing his first draft, the reporter received a telegram from New York, '*ALLINGHAM MARVELLOUS BUT GREATLY REPEAT GREATLY UNDERPLAYS HERSELF. SHE GREAT WRITER WHEN CORNWALL STILL WASHING ELEPHANTS*.'

In the 1990s the scientific and even the political aspects of *The Mind Readers* look dated. If the book was entirely the tract for its times that Margery claimed, this would lessen its stature. But was it really intended thus straightforwardly? Margery's nomenclature – her 'iggy-tubes', her 'nipponanium', the grubby sticking plaster wrapped round the bland, sinister capsules – has a flippancy out of place in the world of Smiley or even Bond. The inventions at the centre of the tale are only amplifiers. Schoolboys have salvaged them from transistor radios. Margery had been nineteen in 1924 when she had first listened to Aunt Maud's wireless; 'a wonderful thing it is'. The action of her 'iggy-tube' is the crackle of a sudden intuition. Sam, the most skilled of the boys at receiving and interpreting individual flashes of emotion, is a 'sympathetic' child. He understands 'what people feel' and can attain surprising insights even after discarding the device. Sam is interested in horoscopes and is writing a book of poems. Unlike his friend Edward, a future scientist, Sam resembles the young Margery, his 'iggy-tube' her writer's questing antennae.

'All sincere authors,' wrote Margery in 1965, 'must be psychoanalysing themselves all the time.' In this period she was ready to take her craft apart and examine both the techniques and the instincts that made her the writer she was. Under its camouflage of cold war attitudes and advanced technology, *The Mind Readers* would seem to play a major part in the exploration. It was certainly a novel in which she had invested a great deal of personal preoccupation and hope for the future. It was to be the first of a new type, the A.A.A. – Allingham Adult Adventures in which 'the killing is almost always incidental and the mystery concerns an idea'. This was her chance to 'bust out of the AWFUL Gollancz/Symons/MWA stale blood and fumbling sex blanket bath and have FUN again'.

In the spring of 1964, she finally braced herself to tell Doubleday, her American publishers, that notwithstanding they had published every book of hers since *Blackerchief Dick* (except *Dance of the Years*), she had decided to offer *The Mind Readers* elsewhere. She penned a sheaf of letters to John, Isabelle, Ken, Lee, Paul, Winifred and Barbara. 'Made careful job and explained that I needed change – no blame anywhere.' Doubleday's current vice-president, Milton Runyon, and his wife, Laura, both of them valued friends, were actually staying at D'Arcy House when Margery wrote her letters. Milton understood her wish to seek the stimulus of a new publisher and could guess at the dissatisfactions she had left unstated.

There were some specific business reasons for the change:

frustration with Doubleday's attitude to the paperback rights of her novels, and a feeling, shared by Paul Reynolds, that they were having to haggle over every contract. But principally, the reasons were personal. For some time Margery had feared that Doubleday thought of her as an 'old' author; that they were no longer interested in promoting her books and that, despite oft-expressed friendship, they would jettison her without compunction as soon as she slipped from form. Ken McCormick, then a senior editor in the New York office, says that this was not so. He 'adored' Margery for herself and confirms that she was highly regarded by the company. 'We had a lot of mystery writers at Doubleday, but Margery was a mystery *novelist*.' Unfortunately, Margery was not convinced. Winifred Nerney's retirement had left her acutely aware, over-sensitive indeed, to anything insincere in the protestations that flowed from her Crime Club editor, Isabelle Taylor. 'I notice,' she commented to Paul Reynolds, 'that when my books are selling well I am "my dearest Margery" and when they are not, I get a note from a secretary.'

From her many letters to Margery, Isabelle Taylor comes over as a highly intelligent, forceful, charming and somewhat egotistical lady. Many of 'her' authors were devoted to her. 'I have for her a very great admiration and much gratitude for a very unusual author–editor relationship, a sympathy and a friendliness far beyond the line of duty and I'm sure you must feel the same way,' a fellow author, Dorothy Tillett (alias John Stephen Strange), had written to Margery in 1952. From Margery's side of the Atlantic, the Doubleday style of publishing with Isabelle as its most immediate exemplar, used the pretence of affection as a business counter. 'It's a barmy game they play,' she grumbled to Paul Reynolds. At the same time she played along energetically, writing newsy letters, choosing tasteful gifts and issuing invitations to D'Arcy House. Among the welter of endearments, Isabelle may never have had a chance to realise that Margery was secretly both frightened of her, and increasingly angry with herself for being so.

Part of Margery's attitude to her publishing 'bosses', the part she had inherited from Herbert, was mingled subservience and resentment. It was too well hidden by her powerful charm and friendliness. While she craved reassurance and shrank from confrontation ('the instinct to keep the editress happy is in my blood'), she was inwardly very sure of her own work – a difficult combination for her publishers to manage. Margery could project a tremendous presence which blinded even those closest to her to the extent of her insecurities. By 1963 she was writing to Paul about Isabelle, 'I feel I have now reached the stage where I don't feel I have a publisher anymore so much as a capricious headmistress who is quite likely to want to humiliate me or beat me down or not sell my work simply to get it into my head that I am not very important.' Recalling Isabelle's attitude to *The Beckoning Lady*, the last book before *The Mind Readers* that Margery had written 'purely to please myself', she could not bear to offer her this new, experimental and personally significant work.

As at the break with Heinemann in 1950, Margery gave her agent a free hand to take her and her new book wherever he would. Paul chose Larry Hughes at Wm. Morrow. Margery was delighted. 'I like the way they keep me in the picture without fussing. I also feel safe with them and not that everything I write may be held as evidence against me at some future date.' Larry Hughes expressed himself pleased with his purchase. 'It [*The Mind Readers*] has a freshness about it which I liked and it also has a good mixture of suspense and movement.'

Sales were good but reviews, as was now usual, were mixed. Margery was untroubled. She had said what she had set out to say and promised her Chatto editor, Ian Parsons, that her next story would be 'a straightforward whodunnit with a corpse in Chapter One'.

She did not now conceal her longing to be 'discovered'. This was something apart from reviews or sales for any single book. She wanted reassurance that her life's work had been worthwhile. She was pleased when *Tiger in the Smoke* and *Hide my Eyes* were taken onto school exam syllabuses and thrilled when Mlle Suzanne Dutruch from the Sorbonne came to visit her in the course of research for her doctoral thesis *Les Techniques et les*

Thèmes du Roman Policier Anglais (*Auteurs Féminins*). '*Nice* girl. Good day.' Her moment of greatest satisfaction came in September 1965 when Charles Champlin in the *Los Angeles Times* suggested that the entire corpus of Margery's Campion novels should be considered together as making one 'super-novel'. Thank you, said Margery. 'I think that this is the very nicest thing that can happen to an author. One plods along sending one's work out into the blue and getting a fair share of award, but without ever knowing if anyone sees the main "grand programme" until suddenly after years and years one gets a truely splendid appreciation which shows that every point has been taken and the whole exercise really has come off after all.'

Margery liked the 1960s – never mind the manners, habits and hairdos of the younger generation, they reminded her of her own Gang in the twenties. The 'dreary days of dun-coloured spectacles' were coming to an end. Modern youngsters were tougher, she thought, but attractive. 'Look at all those little girls screaming at the Beatles like a dawn chorus,' she wrote. 'Awful of course, but so healthy.' In 1965 she wrote an article for the Society of Women Writers comparing fashions and attitudes of the two decades. 'The Programme Is Continuous' she called it. She hoped to capture the spirit of the times in her new adventures in the same way that those first 'plumpuddings' written with Pip and Grog from 1927 had expressed the zest and mocking humour of the 1920s.

But the Bright Young People were ageing fast. From looking eminent in the fifties, by the mid-sixties some were beginning to look old. They were no longer keen to join the cricket team, preferring to sit in a deck chair on a long hot summer's afternoon and watch the Tolleshunt D'Arcy gymkhana. Of Margery's friends, Meg had died in 1960 and Lavinia Davis, suddenly, in 1961. 'I was horrified and broken-hearted,' she wrote at the time. 'She leaves a gap in life.' Two years later she wrote to Lavinia's husband Wendell worried that she might have appeared cold when he had first broken the news. She had been stunned, she said, unable to express her feelings. She told Wendell that she continued to keep Lavinia's letters in her desk, and re-read them frequently. 'I miss her very much.' In April 1964 she was shocked when Nancy Spain was killed in a light aircraft with another friend, Joan Werner Laurie. There was worse to come. When, in May, the unfortunate Barbara had to telephone and inform Margery that her beloved Nerney had died, Margery broke down utterly.

Margery rarely visited London in the last years of her life. Mobility was becoming a problem. When she did make an unusual effort and attended a signing session at a Penguin bookshop in Southampton, she wheezed and hobbled and returned home exhausted, though claiming to have enjoyed it enormously and found it all most interesting. Pip spent most weekdays at the flat. Sometimes he came home tired and snappy, sometimes keen to enlist Margery in his various projects. On their wedding anniversary they drove to Ely for the day and then back via Long Melford. The poet Edmund Blunden, a Christ's Hospital pupil rather older than Pip, was spending his last years propped against the bar of the local pub. *Cargo of Eagles*, the book Margery started in 1965 and Pip completed after her death, takes something from Blunden for its faded Georgian, H. O. Wishart.

Cressie came to live in Tolleshunt D'Arcy. There was a disused pub in the village which Margery helped him convert into a cottage. He was old now and irritable and prone to quarrel with the neighbours. Joyce was busy with local affairs and with her dogs. They provided the bright spots in many of Margery's letters. Brock won a working trials championship in 1964 and in 1965 he and Belle produced a litter of puppies.

Margery thought of the Old Doctor. It was one hundred years since he first sat down to dinner in the dining room at D'Arcy House and she no longer felt threatened by his presence. Instead she felt a kinship with him, especially when she considered their garden, its capricious loveliness and its endless demands for new plants, time and toil. She wrote two articles describing it and considered a short biography of Salter. It is some testimony to Pip's determination to complete Margery's unfinished business that he made moves to start on the research for such a book after her death.

The Relay had expressed Margery's fascination with old age but her business changes showed that she feared it. She agreed that she had dreaded the approach of her sixtieth birthday and claimed that her change of U.S. publisher had made her feel 'happier and younger'. Whatever could be salvaged by determination and what Barbara had called her 'gallantry' would be attempted. 'Life proceeds along a plan,' she told one interviewer, 'until you either rot and drop off the tree or become a faded old pressed flower – and believe me there are a lot of pressed flowers around growing brown at the edges. If you're lucky you turn into a jolly old fruit.'

In January 1966 she wrote facetiously to Sir Allen Lane about death. 'Since our generation seems to have laughed off almost all the other hazards in the calendar, I was hoping we'd meet this one with the same aplomb, and so indeed it seems to promise. The question of taste keeps cropping up. One hovers between titles like "Old Age and How to Get Rid of It" and "A Funny Thing Happened on the Way to the Cemetary" or, more simply, "Euthanasia, Here I come!" '

Facing death squarely just a month after this letter was written, took all the courage and humour Margery had ever possessed, and remained obstinately tragic for those around her.

Sail Lofts, Tollesbury
by P. Youngman Carter, 1963
– the setting for *Cargo of Eagles*

XXI

Queen Beetle

1966

In February of 1966 Margery went down with what was described as a 'rheumatic virus infection'. Her blood pressure was high and she was exhausted. A Colchester doctor observed a mastitis in her left breast and called Ronnie Reid in urgently. On February 14th Ronnie examined Margery. He found the lump on her breast so palpable that he could not believe it had been missed during her regular examinations. He wanted to perform a biopsy and insisted Margery should attend hospital immediately for an irradiation dose. Margery became frightened. A cancer seemed to her to be an evil thing. The notion that she could be harbouring one within her body seemed horrible. After her first dose of treatment with the cobalt ray, Margery stayed in bed, trying to hide from the medical truth. It was obvious to the household that she was very ill and a local nurse who had attended her during her bouts of bronchitis was called in to look after her.

Beneath the blankets, as it were, and in her own mind Margery realised that she was going to die. On February 17th she asked for Gloria and dictated a remarkable description of her state of mind as she faced up to the final 'adventure'.

She presented herself as 'Queen Beetle', a 'large, white slug-like' creature preparing for some unknown metamorphosis. Around her is the 'swarm', directed by their 'first head worker', Joyce. They feed and look after her. She is 'pushed around' but in a 'cared for way'. Sometimes the Queen Beetle accepts this, understanding that she is surrounded by affection and must be kept 'flat on her back' and calm as she waits for the change that will bring 'rejuvenation'. At other times she finds their behaviour irritating and attempts to assert herself. She demands that the open window be shut or that she be given her own hot water bottle. There are 'strong differences of opinion' with the first head worker, then moments of pain and real fear when she realises that this is death she is facing. She struggles with paranoia: 'Is the window going to open and someone or something come in? Will the bottom drop out of the bed? What is going to happen to me?' She knows that she must face 'the black pit when you are absolutely alone'.

In the background is her husband hopelessly attempting to stop the process. He 'goes to her and the group, community, swarm and says "stop her doing this. I don't want her to be dead. Leave her alone." And swarm say "Let her keep on with it" and she says "Yes, will be up, will be up." He keeps wailing "Why are they mucking about?" ' The Queen Beetle thinks about her friends, 'men and women – more men than women but all thought of with equality of feeling'. She endeavours to occupy her mind with light literature and puzzles and ordinary everyday things 'because when you have the adventure you will be out of key with fright'. In moments of resignation, lying flat on her back, she hopes that if she can only accept that she is going to die, then perhaps it will not hurt and there will be somewhere to go to.

The *Queen Beetle* account is amusing in places, profoundly sad in others. It is complicated by Margery's endeavours to describe the physical changes in her body, 'warm and sweating, no widdles, very convenient'. She feels that she is stretching, that her body is coming to pieces, her joints dislocating. 'Now felt back pelvis slide out – neck slipped out – back flat against mattress – felt shaky.' In parts of her account she tries to set out what she is experiencing in almost textbook fashion, as if she is trying, for the last time, to offer what is happening to her as a guide to others – a ludicrous, moving, brave attempt. Finally she broke off her dictation to Gloria and asked for a cup of tea.

Taking down such a description had not been easy. Though she had been able to move her head and even to give a pale impression of her usual vivacity, Margery was clearly very weak. Her speech was occasionally indistinct and Gloria had to strain her concentration to catch all that she said. She did not doubt that Margery was perfectly lucid after her own fashion. Her mode of speech was obscure, certainly, but Gloria felt sure that whatever Margery was trying so hard to express was worth struggling to transcribe as accurately as possible. She felt anxiety about the competence of her shorthand coupled with intense curiosity to learn what Margery was going to say. The nurse, she recalled afterwards, glanced across at her, conspiratorially, as if she understood that Margery was delirious or insane and that Gloria was merely humouring her.

It is obvious from the *Queen Beetle* account that Margery's moods were very volatile. She was seriously ill. Perhaps when the writing was over, she could no longer keep at bay the fear which she had described so long ago to Russell Meiggs, the 'stages ranging from acute nervous pain to downright hallucination and then to a dreadful apathy and a lot of dreadful fear which is like nothing I ever read of'? However hard she struggled to fit death into her pattern and to convince herself that there was something afterwards, she could not be sure.

That evening Dr Madden called in Dr Russell Barton, a psychiatrist and physician superintendent in charge of Severalls, the Colchester hospital that specialised in treating mental illness. Dr Barton reported that Margery was 'agitated, over-active, garrulous, at times jocular, at times depressed'. She was preoccupied with 'bizarre' ideas about the fluid levels in her body and with 'rituals' intended to right them. He made a note that Margery was '*Terrified* of ECT'. He promised her that, under his care, even if it were considered desirable, E.C.T. would not be given without her express consent. The matter with Margery, thought Dr Barton, was that she knew there was something badly wrong with her and could not bring herself to admit it. He prescribed sedatives and anti-depressants.

Dr Barton had only been allowed to feel the lump in Margery's breast through her clothing. He described it as 'large, hard and unmistakeably malignant'. During the night Margery grew worse. She could not sleep, became more agitated and was still refusing treatment. The dread word cancer was in everybody's mind and Joyce felt determined that whatever could be done, must be done. She could not understand how they had allowed Dr

Raymond Greene's warning, given ten years previously, to remain unheeded for so long. She could not cope with Margery at home and requested she be admitted to Severalls.

Pip stepped back. As *Queen Beetle* recognises, he loved Margery and could not face the situation – 'I don't want her to be dead.' She, when she could, wasted her energy trying to reassure him, 'Yes, will be up, will be up.' Margery refused to go to hospital.

Dr Barton decided to take full responsibility and admit Margery compulsorily. He hoped that this would minimise the risk of family bitterness and recrimination later. Joyce did not think that it mattered what admission procedure was used as long as Margery's illness could be treated. She knew how forceful her sister could be and believed that only some legal sanction would enable a hospital to keep her.

So Margery was taken to Severalls Hospital and placed in Dr Barton's care. Severalls in the 1960s was perceived by the local public as the 'loony-bin'. Its name, among the general uninformed, carried vague connotations of shame and fear, very different from the straightforward emotions aroused by the Essex County Hospital where Ronnie Reid presided. Her first reaction was anger. She felt that she had been dragged forcibly from her bed and carried to the hospital without any authority. When Dr Barton saw her on the first day, he thought she seemed 'amiable' but there is no doubt that she felt trapped and very frightened. She wrote to him twice, urgently, begging to be allowed to go home. Losing control of her life thus suddenly was in itself traumatic. She would have been more at ease if she could have been a private patient, as she had been at Chiswick and at Dr Greene's St David's Wing, but Dr Barton did not take private patients. Illogically Margery also began to worry about the financial state of the D'Arcy household if she were not there getting on with her work.

Dr Barton refused to sanction a return home. After consultation with Joyce, he thought it best to face Margery with the situation as directly as possible. 'At the moment,' he wrote in reply, 'you are compulsorily detained here under section 25 of the

Mental Health Act 1959. Your relatives are not able to discharge without my consent for twenty-eight days from the date of your admission.' He did what he could to soften the blow. He hoped Margery 'would be able to accept' her temporary stay in Severalls. He attempted to allay her anxiety about being away from her work and confirmed that she could be allowed to play her radio in her room – as long as it did not disturb other patients. 'Sorry not to be able to do as you ask,' his letter ended, 'I hope your stay won't be long.'

On the reverse of Dr Barton's letter is a desperate appeal in Margery's handwriting:

> Oh Tonker save
>   poor Marge –
> Get Edward and if necessary
> Camps on to this and try try try again.
> I am ill, not at all
> balmy –
>   all my love
>   Marge

Evidently Dr Barton's efforts to be reassuring as well as firm, to dispense small privileges as well as to forbid, had done nothing to reconcile Margery to her legalised loss of freedom – and to the terror of being considered 'balmy'. Edward, mentioned in the note, was Edward Terrell, the Q.C. from whom she had sought opinions so often; Camps, was Sir Francis, whom she had requested most recently to read *The Mind Readers* before its publication. She sent other similarly urgent pleas to Pip but he had gone to London. He visited the hospital at weekends, reluctantly, unhappily. Their friend, Max Martyn, remembers the 'heartbreaking' phone call Pip made later to tell him that Margery was dying, 'this from one of the stiffest upper lips I have ever known'. Margery asked Joyce to tell Cressie she was ill. He chose not to visit. Only Joyce and Christina went in day after day. Chrissie gave Margery the baths she enjoyed when she had been ill at D'Arcy House. Joyce did her best to liaise between Margery and her doctors and to reassure her that practical matters at home were being attended to.

Slowly Dr Barton and his colleague Dr Ristich helped Margery regain her equilibrium. They checked her responses, her levels of cerebral activity and prescribed appropriate medication. Margery's room was in a villa set in a garden within the hospital grounds and Dr Barton took to dropping in at the end of his day's work for snatches of conversation which Margery called 'complines'. He tried to explain that she had no need to be frightened of his 'nuthouse'. He pointed out that Severalls now treated many other patients besides those who were mentally ill, that less than five percent were compulsorily detained or certified and only two of his thirty wards and villas were locked. Although he understood that she felt imprisoned she was not.

By the end of February Margery had improved. She was friendly with the nurses and accepted both her treatment and the need to remain in hospital. The nurses mentioned her talkativeness, her 'flight of ideas' and her 'infectious jollity'. Dr Barton recollects that Margery spoke occasionally of painful matters and her private griefs 'but seemed to regard this as a sign of weakness, maybe disloyalty, and could quickly dismiss the conversation with a bon mot or subtle crack'. He developed a great respect and liking for Margery in the course of these chats. 'Her mind saw associations which delighted her listeners and diffracted topics into their constituent parts with humour and insight.' Her perception of people's motivations, their meannesses and kindnesses, were, thought Dr Barton, 'quite remarkable'. In his word, Margery's imagination was 'untrammelled'. He found her uninhibited, entertaining, clever. He also diagnosed her as suffering from manic-depressive illness (bipolar depression) – pinning down the condition which Margery had observed for so long in herself and perhaps in her mother too. It is a condition in which, as Dr Barton explains it, periods of 'hypervigilance and abounding energy seem to open doors in the mind' but alternate, painfully, with phases when 'a true perspective of the human condition is etched with despair and hopelessness'. Dr Barton uses the phrase 'the genes of genius'. Margery, he remembers, laughed and spoke of her 'cuckoo times'.

Her physical condition received its due attention. A biopsy was delayed but she was given high doses of irradiation (appropriate to the advanced state of the growth) from a cobalt bomb which she nicknamed 'fiery Fred'. As she commented later to her American friends Milton and Laura Runyon, 'the cure (which appears to involve a sort of hygienic flame thrower) is unamusing. Still I progress and everyone says how lucky I am to be big and strong – I'm glad to hear it.' She became a non-certified patient on March 15th and left Severalls on March 18th and returned home to Tolleshunt D'Arcy. She kept no diary in 1966 and there is nothing more after *Queen Beetle* to tell of her state of mind. Gloria remembers that her most characteristic expression through her last months was 'guarded'. She would pause before she spoke when responding to an enquiry as to her well-being, perhaps to spare a companion's feelings, perhaps to ensure that she said nothing more that might strike her hearers as 'bizarre'. Joyce found herself treating Margery as a valetudinarian, taking her for gentle drives around the leafy, spring-time lanes to help her relax. Margery joked that she felt as if she was in her pram again. 'I loved being in my pram.'

The Queen Beetle had been interrupted in her dying, not deflected from it. Though she assured various acquaintances that the lump in her breast had been neither painful nor malignant, she was more honest to others. To Graham Watson she reported, 'I am waiting for the ray to die down . . . my chest looks like something on the Sainsbury's bacon counter . . . However the bosom is remarkably free of submerged cardboard boxes now and I think they have conquered the trouble but I am keeping my fingers crossed. As far as depression is concerned I alternate between feeling one hundred per cent for ten minutes then having an hour's complete exhaustion.' To Grog's sister Biddy in Rhodesia she said she was 'limp, crawling about and feeling like hell'.

After she returned home, Margery made a last revision of her brief will, confirming her complete trust in Joyce as her essential, non-material heir. 'Joyce is going to *be* me.' It was an important concept to her. She may at this time have destroyed the many letters Cressie had written to her, especially during the troubled years of the 1950s. She asked Joyce to burn all Pip's 'courting' letters which until then had been carefully kept in a large Meissen dish. She attended St Mary's Hospital, Colchester, for further irradiation treatment and was visited at home by Dr Barton. When she became too weak to manage the stairs, a bedroom was made for her in the old wash-house a few steps across the yard from the kitchen door. This was Margery's choice, avowedly to avoid disturbing Pip's arrangements in the breakfast room, partly perhaps as her makeshift version of the transitional 'dower house' that she had described in *The Relay*, a place in which she could see the life of the main house continuing yet be a little detached from it; a place from which to hand over responsibility.

In June of that year Joyce reported that Margery was suffering attacks of panic. She was particularly fearful that she would die of bronchitis. Because of this, she liked to be kept propped up on pillows in a semi-sitting position. She, and Joyce with her, worried about yet more fluid collecting in her congested lungs and yet in the *Queen Beetle* she insisted that she be kept 'flat on her back' for the moment of change. One of the nurses in Severalls remembers how frequently Margery resorted to the inhalant that helped her breathing. Her fear of suffocation was deeply ingrained. 'A terrifying preoccupation,' comments Dr Barton, 'with a very real and rational basis in view of the recurrent bronchitis and bronch-spasm she had experienced.'

Despite these attacks of panic, the subsequent exhaustion and the partial paralysis of one side of her mouth which could have been caused by exhaustion and mental trouble, by cerebral bleeding or a secondary tumour, she managed with Pip to entertain the Runyons in early June. Pip said later that her good spirits then gave him his last ray of hope that all might yet be well. Almost before their thank-you letters had time to reach her, she relapsed. She had suffered a left-sided stroke and was re-admitted to Severalls for diagnostic X-rays. Afterwards it was discovered that the cancer had metastasised to her heart and brain. Ronnie Reid wrote to Joyce, 'From the day I saw Margery a few months ago I saw what an awful thing had happened to her. We did our best to mitigate the thing's effect without hurting her and we failed completely.'

Margery's last words to Pip, before she was taken from D'Arcy House for the last time, were cheery: 'Forty years, forty years, not so bad eh?' And to Christina, 'I can't do any more for him. It's up to you now.' Joyce remembers herself calling out suddenly to the ambulance men, begging them to be very careful with her sister, 'She's so old you see, she's so old.'

Joyce visited Margery once more in Severalls and read her the Runyons' letter. Margery said she would like to talk to a priest and Joyce promised to arrange this. The next day when she came with Christina, Margery was being wheeled out of her room for X-ray. Joyce and Christina went out into the garden to wait for Margery's return. Not many moments later, Dr Barton came to find them and told them she had died. She had not been distressed and she had not suffocated. Her heart had given out.

Margery's death was announced on television and radio and in newspapers across the world. Obituaries were printed and public tributes paid. More comforting than these were the heartfelt letters of sympathy that began to arrive at D'Arcy House. Almost unanimously the writers mourned Margery for her kindness, her wit, her generosity, her vitality. Those who had known her well felt that something 'splendid' had gone out of their lives. Those who knew Tolleshunt D'Arcy considered that it would seem an ordinary place without her. Many people wrote who had known neither Margery nor the village. They had read and re-read her books, followed her characters, laughed at her jokes. They had escaped into what a fellow novelist called 'her own lovely world of imagination and humour'. Those people too said that they felt they had lost a friend.

Margery's funeral was held at Tolleshunt D'Arcy and she was buried in the churchyard there. The service was taken by Canon George Armstrong, the priest to whom she had wanted to speak in her last days. He asked those present to remember Margery's 'essential humanity'. The church was full. It was the first week of July – a good time of the year for flowers.

*

A fete had been planned later that summer to be held in the D'Arcy House garden. It was a village affair, in aid of the Church School, the school that had been reprieved from closure almost thirty years before. Pip and Joyce decided that the fete should go ahead and be the best they had ever held, one final big occasion to commemorate all the parties Margery had given. There were sideshows and baby shows, and opportunities for Tollesbury and Tolleshunt D'Arcy to renew their traditional rivalry. Some last remaindered copies of *The Oaken Heart* were put on sale.

A local woman whose husband had been a warden during the war but who had known Margery only slightly, vividly remembers Pip at the fete, sitting among a selection of his etchings, looking abstracted and utterly forlorn. This was an image that remained with several of his friends. Occasionally theirs had seemed an 'extraordinary' marriage, especially to those who knew Pip in London, but in Pip's diminishment after Margery's death the extent of his dependence and devotion became obvious. As he said more than once to his friend Jack Morpurgo: 'You know, Jack, now Marge's gone, I'm only half a chap.'

Pip suffered feelings of guilt as well as grief. Not long after her death he poured his emotion into a memoir of Margery which was published to introduce the third of her omnibus collections, *Mr Campion's Clowns*. A few months later he set to work, as Margery had asked, to complete *Cargo of Eagles*, the novel she had left unfinished. Joyce managed the business, Christina kept house and Gloria came in as secretary. A collection of Margery's short stories followed, then two detective novels, *Mr Campion's Farthing* and *Mr Campion's Falcon*, written by Pip alone. The first was based on a plot that he and Margery had discussed, the second was entirely his. Albert Campion renews his membership of an exclusive London club, acquires a Jaguar and a more discerning palate. He retains some personal idiosyncrasies and a few characteristic turns of phrase. These are as empty and as sad as favourite old clothes from a dead woman's wardrobe. They may still have plenty of wear in them – but never look quite right on anybody else.

Pip's Campions were published by Heinemann and Morrow to kind reviews. He commenced a third novel but died in 1969. Joyce and Christina lived on in D'Arcy House until 1984 when they moved into a bungalow built onto the end of Dr Salter's former stables, Margery and Pip's last studio. Though the art-and-fiction factory had finally ceased production, Margery's fear that she would 'fade out into a dusty heap of old papers' has so far proved unfounded.

St Nicholas' Church, Tolleshunt D'Arcy
by P. Youngman Carter

Afterword:
'What Will Survive of Us'

Margery died in 1966; Pip in 1969. Margery's brother Phil became ill and ended his life in the same year. He and his wife Francesca (who died in 1980) had no children. Neither did Pip's sister, Betty Carter, who died in the 1990s. Nor Joyce Allingham who died in 2001. Genetically, this would seem to be end of story.

In the late spring of 1952, a half century earlier, a young man named Dick Laurie was visiting his older sister Joan in the house she shared with her lesbian partner, Nancy. Joan had previously been married and had a son, Nick, who was about six years old. Nancy, however, was a famously 'trouser-wearing' character. She was Nancy Spain, *Daily Express* journalist, writer and broadcaster; Margery and Pip's friend. Nancy was a personality who managed, rather brilliantly, to persuade the media world to accept her unconventional style without having to spell out her sexuality at a time when homosexuality was still a criminal offence and lesbianism officially unrecognised. Dick was under no illusions as to the nature of Nancy's relationship with his sister and regarded Nancy with great affection. She was fun to be with, clever, kind, and someone who he knew he could turn to if he ever had a problem. She had even offered practical help if Dick wanted to be alone with a girlfriend: they could use her and Joan's house – and she wouldn't tell Joan if Dick didn't want her to.

'The only thing I won't do is go to bed with you myself,' she said.

Dick remembers being privately horrified by this suggestion – he was in his late teens, Nancy was in her mid thirties and anyway, she was a chum.

On this particular visit he tried to go through the kitchen doorway at the same time as Nancy. And they stuck.

'You might as well know: I'm pregnant,' she explained matter-of-factly.[i]

Once Dick had recovered from his immediate surprise he wanted to know who the child's father was. But Nancy wasn't telling. It could be her boss, Lord Beaverbrook; it could be Stirling Moss; it could be … anybody. She wasn't telling many people about the pregnancy either. When the time came to give birth, in August, she went into a private nursing home and then passed the baby off as Joan's. The lies told on the birth certificate shake one's faith in the registration system. The mother was, allegedly, one 'Anne Brooker Seyler, formerly Brooker' (Nancy's second name) and the father, Joan's former husband, Paul Seyler, who at that time had been missing, presumed dead, for two years.

The baby was Thomas Bartholomew Laurie Seyler and his actual father was Pip Youngman Carter. There's no evidence that Pip knew that Nancy had had a child or that the child was his. Nick Laurie, looking back as an adult to the arrival of his 'baby brother', finds it almost inconceivable that there wasn't any gossip about Nancy's altered shape that summer. Rose Collis, Nancy's biographer, quotes Dick Laurie's explanation: 'You have to remember that those people who knew her would have imagined it so unlikely that she could ever have been pregnant that even if she looked like she was, they would have discounted it. "Nancy going to bed with a man and getting pregnant? No, no, no – it must be too many lunches at the Ivy …"'[ii]

Had there been chatter, it could have travelled as far as Pip. Not that he was an intimate member of Joan and Nancy's circle – his name was nowhere on the speculative fathers' list – but Pip was then deputy-editing the *Tatler,* still spending every week in London, and gossip was part of his stock in trade. Something that he regularly shared with Margery on his phone calls home.

If Tom, born on the 27th of August 1952, was a full-term baby, he would have been conceived sometime in the later part of November 1951 – at the end of the year that had started so catastrophically for Margery and brought her close to divorce. She had seen over the summer that Pip was trying to make amends but she probably guessed that this did not include monogamy. A note in her diary for September mentions that he was sleeping ('by amicable arrangement') in another room 'because I snore.'[iii] During October Margery was battling with sinusitis and finishing *Tiger in the Smoke.* In early November her American agent Paul Reynolds sent her his 'typical letter … very disappointed tale not like the last one – doesn't see where he can sell it etc.' At that point Pip was 'rather cross' with her and returned to his idea that she should write a play. 'Rather dubious,' notes Margery, 'as first job is to make some real cash.' In the middle of November, however, Pip sold *Tiger's* serial rights for £1500, a justification, if one was needed, of the time he spent networking in town. Although there are many blanks in the diary over the next few weeks, the general tone is businesslike and cheerful until Pip returns to Essex in time for a celebratory family Christmas with the Reids and the Maddens. After Christmas Margery spent several days with him in London. 'A nice change from last year!' she notes. 'Thank God all well.'[iv] A month after Tom was born in August 1952, Margery and Pip made it to their silver wedding anniversary.[v]

Nancy Spain's career proceeded energetically. She made her first broadcast for BBC *Woman's Hour* when Tom was a fortnight old and continued travelling and writing for *Good Housekeeping* and the *Daily Express* with no discernible intermission. Her eagerness for life and adventure, for experimentation and even risk, were qualities that many found attractive – Pip and Margery included. She told Dick Laurie that she had refused an abortion because she wanted to see what having a baby was like. Going to bed with Pip might also been in the nature of an experiment – for both of them, perhaps?

There was a business element to the friendship between Nancy and Joan, Pip and Margery, as well as genuine liking. Nancy and Joan needed material to fill Nancy's columns and Joan's magazines; Margery knew that the right publicity was good for sales and Pip at the *Tatler* was unblushingly convinced of the importance of puffing one's friends.[vi] Nothing in Margery's diaries or in the pattern of their meetings suggests that Tom's existence made any difference to the established pattern of social meetings and literary back-scratching. In October 1955 Nancy produced a special edition of *Woman's Hour* which included Tom, Nick, Dick, Pip and Margery in the one programme (though not as a single item).

This was all very cosy for the adults; occasionally less than ideal for the children. Dick Laurie speaks of the two boys being 'shunted off' as Joan worked the hours expected of a magazine editor in non family-friendly Fleet Street. Nancy did write from home sometimes but both her job and her inclination required her to go out socialising and she was also a frequent traveller. Rose Collis reports that after her death other 'love-nests' were found across the country.[vii] When she was around she was the warmer and more loveable partner, making up stories with the boys and sometimes finding ways to involve them in her assignments. Tom recalls the last summer they had together in 1963 when they went to Bournemouth for Nancy to interview the Beatles and 'John Lennon read my comic'.[viii] Other holidays, however, were spent at school in North Wales or being minded.

Aspects of Tom's childhood recall Margery's portrait of the young teenage boy Sinclair in *The Fashion in Shrouds*. Sinclair's particular difficulty was that his celebrity mother's constantly changing lovers meant that he had constantly to be remaking his own life and fending off the comments of his school fellows. 'I don't want to be bogus and pretend. I only want to be something definite ... It's my *life*, you see.'[ix] Tom's problems of identity were still more acute. He was deliberately misled about his mother and denied all knowledge of a father. Nancy's assumption had been that she and Joan would be sufficient parents for both children. They amalgamated their names on his birth certificate and made wills in which they left everything to each other.

These private acts of trust were hopelessly inadequate to secure Tom's future when both women were killed simultaneously in a plane crash in the spring of 1964. The boys were away at their separate boarding schools and it was only after her death that Tom learned that Nancy, not Joan, had been his birth mother. At the funerals Nick was told that Tom was not in truth his brother. Neither was Dick Laurie Tom's uncle, though he became Tom's trustee. When the interchangeable wills were examined the fact that Tom was Nancy's child, and Nancy, as the older, was technically deemed to have died first, meant that Tom inherited nothing.[xi]

Amid such wholesale loss Tom gained an aunt, Nancy's sister, a socially conventional former fashion designer. She acted as one of his trustees, helped rectify the financial situation and made some attempts at kindness but they did not form a lasting relationship. In the end Tom was fostered by his prep-school headmaster and wife. No father came forward to claim him and there appears to have been little concerted effort to discover who this person was. Margery noted her shock at the deaths in her diary: Pip was among the four hundred people who attended Nancy's memorial service.

Once Tom reached university he decided that he wanted to know his father's identity. None of his trustees could help. Eventually he asked the man who had been Nancy's doctor. The doctor couldn't remember Pip's name but told Tom that it was whoever had been married to Margery Allingham. Tom went away and consulted an old copy of *Who's Who*. He rang the doctor back. Was it Pip Youngman Carter? Yes, that was the name. But by this time both Pip and Margery were dead. Tom changed his surname from Seyler to Carter but made no new family contacts until a distant cousin researching the family from Canada wrote to him in 2007. Meanwhile he suffered the first of a series of serious nervous breakdowns and lives a life disabled by mental illness.

Tom Carter is an unusual person, much loved by his brother Nick and uncle Dick. His resemblance to drawings and photographs of his father is quite startling and when I met him I felt I had understood for the first time how charming Pip might have been. Tom also has a good brain and strong opinions. In the past he has been known to drink too much and shout to put his point across but since 1997 he has been safely on the wagon. He's a regular reader of *Private Eye* and doesn't hesitate to write in and set the editor straight if he feels that the magazine has missed a trick. Ian Hislop says: 'A note from Tom Carter, often but not always about the Balkans, is likely to be forceful, detailed and, most irritatingly for editors, right.' Tom's sharing of *Private Eye* with a pen friend from Romania recently led to a collaborative translation into English of six children's fairy tales. The first concerned a confused prince, brought up alone in his palace with every luxury and no knowledge of the world at all. He sets out on a quest to find someone even lonelier than he is and finds himself, as in so many good fairy tales, in a dark black forest.

But this is the end of Margery's biography, not Tom's. And it has to end with questions. The obvious question – how would Margery have felt had she known about Tom? – was an unwelcome addition to her sister's emotional inheritance. Joyce learned that Tom was Pip and Nancy's child from an article in the *Daily Telegraph* one Saturday morning in 1997, in advance of the publication of Rose Collis's biography. She was shocked and deeply saddened on Margery's behalf. She knew that Pip's disinclination for fatherhood had been the major reason for her sister's childlessness, though she accepted that there were others, 'Kid v car, really.'[x] The childless Joyce loved children too. This seemed a final betrayal. Some of us wondered whether Joyce might want to reach out to Tom in some way but Jack Morpurgo, publisher of Pip's fragmentary autobiography *All I Did Was This* (a title that goes on getting worse), convinced Joyce that the information should be ignored.

An alternative question is how far Margery herself, by her very existence and measure of celebrity, was responsible for the misinformation that clouded Tom's childhood. She would have been appalled by the lies on the birth certificate, the false assertion of motherhood, the total denial of the father. Margery was deeply interested in genetics, in inheritance and in people knowing who they were. 'It's my *life*!' as her teenage character, Sinclair, said. I think she would have considered such irresponsibility to be criminal. The awful irony is that had she not been who she was, none of these lies would have been necessary. 'Whoever was Margery Allingham's husband, was your father,' the doctor told Tom. If Margery had divorced Pip in the early spring of 1951, Tom might still have been conceived – the extent of Pip and Nancy's mutual attraction remains their secret – but the corollary, Nancy's fear of hurting Margery with the truth, would have been effectively diminished. If indeed this was (as Nancy's friend Sheila Van Damm claimed) the central reason for Nancy's silence on the matter of paternity.[xi]

There are other possible reasons: that Nancy wanted to be a father, not a mother, or that the social stigma of child-bearing outside marriage was still too great even for such a redoubtable individualist to face. Those are not Margery's responsibilities, except insofar as she hid her eyes and went along with the 'balmy modern code' that condoned male promiscuity then called their lovers 'tarts' and unplanned children 'bastards'.[xii] Someone should have told Pip to go get himself a vasectomy.

But then there would have been no Tom at all. And that, despite the pain of his illness and the frustration of his latent talents, would be a loss.

On the day that I met Tom Carter I had attended a memorial

service for one partner in an incomparably literary, high-achieving, childless couple. There was a moment when the bereaved husband read Philip Larkin's 'An Arundel Tomb', a poem that expresses the incomprehension later generations feel as we contemplate monuments to past lives.

'Time has transfigured them into/ Untruth.'

It should be every biographer's screen saver. Yet through the misunderstandings and myopia comes a final, famous, almost-reassurance that 'Our almost-instinct (is) almost true: / What will survive of us is love'.

The mums and dads in this situation may have messed up, to bowdlerise Larkin's even better-known line, but Nancy loved Tom and Nick and the non-genetically-related brothers have remained truly brotherly. Margery continued loving Pip and, as she said of her village, 'if this has made me give it perhaps a very slightly prettier face than some would see at first glance (although I would not admit this), you must discount that much please, but not more I beg you, for remember, only the really lovable is beloved for long.'

i Conversation with Dick Laurie 5.12.2008. Conversations with Nick and Dick Laurie, Ann Capon and Rose Collis are central to this chapter.
ii Rose Collis *A Trouser-wearing Character: the Life and Times of Nancy Spain* Cassell (1997)
iii MA diary 21.9.1951
iv MA diary 11.1.1952
v MA diary 29.9.1952. (This was also the day of Granny's funeral.)
vi *All I Did Was This* Sexton Press (1982)
vii Collis p.276
viii Interview with Tom Carter 10.12.2008 Tom's comic was the *Topper.*
ix This situation was later rectified by Tom's trustees
x *The Fashion in Shrouds* (1938 edition, some of this is cut in the 1965 revision) p.148 & p.150
xi above p.175
xii Collis p.130 Hmm ... Margery was pretty shrewd about Pip and I can't help noticing that the description of Edna, Gerry Hawker's mistress in *Hide My Eyes* (p.68), would fit Nancy nicely.
xiii above p.279 & cf p.291 where Margery calls her non-Campions her 'little bastards'
xiv *The Oaken Heart* p.275

Pip and Margery at the time of their wedding by A.J. Gregory

Notes and Sources

Abbreviations

A.C. Aubrey Christlieb / A.D.L. Alexander Dunlop Lindsay / A.J.G. Alan Joe Gregory / A.M.B. Alfred McClelland Burrage / B.C. Betty Carter / Christlieb C.C. Christina Carter / C.H. Christ's Hospital / E.J.A. Emily Jane Allingham / G.G. Gloria Greci / G.W. Graham Watson / H.J.A. Herbert John Allingham / I.T. Isabelle Taylor / J.A. Joyce Allingham / J.deV. Josephina de Vasconcellos / J.T. Julia Thorogood / L.C. Louisa Callender / L.D. Lavinia Davis / M.A. Margery Allingham / M.B. Mary Brown / M.J. Malcolm Johnson / M.L. Mary Leonard /N.D. Nelson Doubleday / P.R.R. Paul Revere Reynolds / P.W.A. Philip William Allingham / P.Y.C. Philip Youngman Carter / R.B. Russell Barton / R.M. Russell Meiggs / W.M. William McFee / W.N. Winifred Nerney / W.P.W. W.P. Watt / W.T. William Temple

Introduction

p xvii 'Golden Age': idea from John Strachey, *Saturday Review*, Jan 1939.
Source of drawing room story, Sally Everitt (Reid).
Margery was surprised to receive £4 14s 4d from Japan in 1951 – and spent it all on a four-poster bed. She built up considerably more in the Iron Curtain countries but couldn't spend it as the money was not allowed out.
Fan letter to Mr Campion in Margery's files at Tolleshunt D'Arcy.
Detective novels as 'folk literature': theory from *Mystery Writer in the Box* article reprinted as preface to *The Mysterious Mr Campion* omnibus volume (Chatto, 1963). Theory also put forward by D.L. Sayers.

p xviii See Bibliography. I have especially in mind: *Mr Campion's Career* by B.A. Pike (Bowling Green State

University Popular Press, 1987), the biography *Ink in Her Blood* by Richard Martin (U.M.I. Research Press, 1989), *Deadlier Than the Male* by Jessica Mann (David and Charles, 1986), also books and articles by Mary Craig and Patricia Cadogan, Julian Symons, Eric Routley, Colin Watson, Susan Asbee, Suzanne Dutruch.

'an instinctive writer': from M.A. preface to *Mysterious Mr Campion*.

'as I have to': from letter to Paul Reynolds 23.6.64. The whole passage reads: 'I think I want to be a novelist but mainly I suppose I just write as I have to. Sometimes the books work out more seriously than others. It depends on how serious life has been in the gestation period, which is reasonable after all.'

'The whole of life': interview with Arthur Pottersman, *Daily Sketch*, 1962.

p xix 'In the course': *The Oaken Heart*, p249.

'Mr Campion': preface to *Mysterious Mr Campion*.

p xx 'I envy you': M.A. letter to J.A., 1941/2.

Mother-in-law 'old Mrs Carter' – on p1 of *Police at the Funeral*, Joe Gregory in *Mystery Mile*, M.A. and P.Y.C. in *The Beckoning Lady*. Uncle Ted's comment was made in a letter (4.3.36) after reading *Flowers for the Judge*, Gloria Greci's hands given to Miss Pinkerton in *The Beckoning Lady*.

'I should be': M.A. to Isabelle Taylor 12.3.63.

p xxi Margery's diary is reasonably complete for 1921–4, 1934, 1937–8, 1951, 1964; partial for 1925, 1931, 1935–6, 1940–1, 1950, 1952–3, 1955; fragmentary for 1927, 1942, 1956; non-existent before 1921 and for 1926, 1928–1930, 1932–3, 1939, 1943–1949, 1958–9, 1961–3, 1966. Letters received were kept fairly systematically from Gloria Greci's arrival in 1950.

'Nobody blamed': from preface to *Mysterious Mr Campion*.

p xxii 'My bet is': ibid.

Chapter I

p 1 Conversations with Joyce are central to this chapter.

'men were beasts': letter from William McFee to Herbert John Allingham 14.11.32.

William McFee (1881–1966): ship's engineer and prolific novelist, emigrated to America.

p 2 Margery on her parents: e.g. letter to P.R.R. 24.9.65: 'My parents were unusually advanced newspaper folk in their own day.'

Annie Besant (1847–1933): advocated birth-control in a widely circulated pamphlet published with Charles Bradlaugh in 1876. From 1889 A.B. was a leading exponent of the theosophy of Madame Blavatsky. Em possessed A.B.'s *Autobiography* and a biography, gifts from Herbert.

ABC café: cf. *In the First Watch*, William McFee (Faber, 1947); also H.J.A. diary 1909.

'Guard her well': H.J.A. diary 1920.

p 3 Joyce's family notes were intended for use as an introduction to Margery's autobiographical book, *The Oaken Heart*, but were never published.

e.g. M.A. makes virtually no mention of Em in *The Oaken Heart* (1941) which was written in Em's lifetime; the tone of references in *The Relay* (written 1964, unpublished) is guarded, as is the preface to *The Mysterious Mr Campion*.

p 4 'poorest': *Dance of the Years* (Michael Joseph, 1943), p207.

Police at the Funeral (Heinemann, 1931).

The Oaken Heart (Michael Joseph, 1941); edition used: Sarsen 1987; ref. to great-grandfather, p259.

p 5 Many of Emily Jane Hughes' (Granny's) anecdotes were told to Christina Carter.

Margery on Granny: *The Relay*.

p 6 'the kind which gave': *Dance of the Years*, p209.

p 7 Ref. to Granny's novel from unpublished autobiographical notes collected by Joyce from M.A.'s drafts.

p 8 'the prospect': *The Oaken Heart*, p213.

Alfred McClelland Burrage, b. 1889, prolific author, best known for his account of service in the First World War using pseudonym, ex-Private X. Quote comes from letter to M.A., 1953.

The manufacturers of Beecham's Pills were among the 'J.G. Francis' accounts. Joyce remembers her grandfather privately cursing the inefficacy of the product!

p 9 Herbert claimed to have based his first school stories on his experiences at Ardingly. Similar claims were commonly made by writers in that genre.

'My thoughts wandered': H.J.A. diary 1886.

'bearded patriarch': P.Y.C. in *All I Did Was This*, Youngman Carter (Sexton Press, 1982), p31.

The History of Old Boys' Books, 'Ralph Rollington' (publ. 1913).

Account of publication: H.J.A. diary 1886.

p 10 'James "remembered" ': *Dance of the Years*, p207.
'the right and reasonable': W.M. to H.J.A. 18.6.18.
The Edwardians, J.B. Priestley (Heinemann, 1970).

p 11 'that gentle, austere man': *All I Did Was This*, p32; cf. P.Y.C.'s description of H.J.A. in his preface to *Mr Campion's Clowns* (Chatto, 1967).
'sultanic': *The Oaken Heart*, p355.

p 12 'children were lost': *All I Did Was This*, p31.
'All my dull days': H.J.A. to W.M. 19.8.20.
H.J.A. diary 1923.
W.M. to H.J.A. Jan 1916. In 1920, however, he wrote, 'I really am surprised that a sensible woman like Mrs Allingham can't see the bunkum of Christian Science.'

p 13 'that terrible old building': W.M. to M.A. 5.6.48.
'just below me': from 'London, My Market Town', M.A. notes for talk, 1963.

p 14 *London Journal* history: Pierce Egan etc. from *The English Common Reader*, R.D. Altick (Chicago, 1957).
'ghastly Victorian weekly': A.M.B. letter to M.A. 1953.

p 15 'In these days': H.J.A. *New London Journal* editorial, 1906.

p 16 'Looks as though': H.J.A. diary 1909.

Chapter II

p 18 Information from parish roll in Essex Record Office and H.J.A. correspondence.

p 19 'little Margy': *New London Journal*, July 1906.
H.J.A. diary Jan–April 1909. Despite headaches he wrote 36,678 words in January, 22,990 in February and 35,000 in March.

p 20 'parrots and monkeys': *History of Old Boys' Books*.
'Nelly Vaughan' contract in family papers.
Details of purchase of Pope's Hall etc.: Richard Starr letter to M.A. 1958.
Christina Carter's memory of childhood in Chappel.

p 21 *In the First Watch*, McFee, p302.

p 22 'the hard, paraffin-lit': *Oaken Heart*, p213.
When I Was Young (unpublished typescript poems).

p 23 'I would not go': M.A. notebook, c 1923?
'I spent': *Oaken Heart*, p115.

p 24 Surveyor's report: in H.J.A. papers.

p 25 Letter from Florence Pudney, 5.10.64.
Letter from Miss Fegan, 29.9.64.
M.A. draft letter to Kate O'Brien c 1933.

p 26 'We were': M.A. preface to *Mysterious Mr Campion* (Chatto, 1963).
The Love Story, in *Girl's Cinema* 25.3.22.
'snobbish': M.A. diary 23.6.23.

p 27 Sybil Fletcher letter c 1963.
'a man who was': *Dance of the Years*, p208.
'Father, mother, aunts and uncles': this and subsequent quotes from draft autobiographical material collected by Joyce from Margery's papers.

p 28 'I'm Sarah Sutane': *Dancers in Mourning* (Heinemann, 1937), p50.

p 29 'I was allotted': this and next two quotations from draft autobiographical material, as above.

p 30 'I have been trained': *Oaken Heart*, p245.

Chapter III

p 31 'where a man': *Dancers in Mourning*, p119.
'preoccupied': M.A. draft autobiographical material.

p 32 'My mother': draft version of material published in preface to *Mysterious Mr Campion*.
'We are in need of a good holding story of the *East Lynne* type,' wrote an editor to Herbert in 1918.

p 33 e.g. In June 1904 four instalments (20,000 words) of a serial were returned at once without payment as the third was thought to be 'suggestive'. There was no opportunity for Herbert to appeal. A scene of drunkenness was 'unpardonable' in 1908 whereas 'gambling may be introduced occasionally but it must be very nicely done and the habit condemned.'
M.A. interview with Phyllis Meras, 'Miss Allingham Loves to Write', *Providence Sunday Journal*, 1963.
H.J.A. letter to Anne St John Cooper 1934.

p 34 *The Study Fire* (unpublished poem).
'were lined with': M.A. draft material.

p 35 Development of school stories to adventure detection: cf. *Boys Will Be Boys*, E.S. Turner (Michael Joseph, 1948).

p 36 'We were all smart men': *Pearson's Weekly*, Jan 1901.
'Bloods': these were melodramatic adventure stories written for the penny magazines.
'charming fairy tales': H.J.A. correspondence.
The Darings of the Red Rose: see Ch. X.
'apparently aged seven': this is the age at which Margery is

said to have produced the *Wag-Tale*. The relatively competent handwriting and the style of material suggest that she was somewhat older, perhaps nine, when she returned to school after her convalescence. McFee is quite likely to have visited then as well.

p 37 'Editress of The Wagtail': letter W.M. to M.A. 1922.

p 38 In 1922 McFee wrote an article describing the labours of the Burlingtons (the Allinghams), a family of hacks. Herbert enjoyed it but reminded him that 'the joy of craftsmanship comes to the maker of doll's houses as well as the builder of cathedrals'.

'Many an hour': *In the First Watch*, William McFee, p303.

Mac reminded Herbert in 1923 that he still possessed Margery's first letter to him written 'in letters an inch high'. It was found among his books in the 1960 s.

Aliens was republished in a second, longer edition in 1918, still with its dedication.

p 39 'suffragette': W.M. letter Nov 1913.

'murder mystery stories': W.M. letter to H.J.A. 27.7.29.

M.A. draft for *Mysterious Mr Campion*.

p 40 'not a hack': H.J.A. correspondence.

'run loose': *Dancers in Mourning*, p51.

p 41 Letter from Miss Fegan, 1964.

'my education': M.A. to Wesley Hartley 1959.

Source of cheating story P.Y.C.

p 42 All 'the Misses Dobson' quotations from draft autobiographical material.

p 43 'I enjoyed myself': M.A. to H.J.A. winter 1918.

p 44 The publisher was Joan Kahn from Harper and Row.

'our little fiction factory': H.J.A. to Anne St John Cooper 1934.

Dr Salter's Diary, ed. J.O. Thompson (Bodley Head, 1933): 'Five or six submarines' 14.11.1914.

Dr Salter – For his achievements see also essay by J. Wentworth Day, 'The Astounding Dr Salter', in 'Rum Owd Boys' (*East Anglian Magazine*, 1974).

p 45 'That half contemptuous': *Dancers in Mourning*, p110.

p 46 *Dr Salter's Diary* 28.2.16.

Pamela Horn article in *Essex Countryside Magazine*.

'The Old Doctor': this and subsequent quotes from *Oaken Heart*, p246.

Chapter IV

p 49 Chapter heading from *Oaken Heart*, p28.
'War simply meant': ibid., p25.

p 50 'My father hated': ibid., p207.
'strain': ibid., p24.
H.J.A. correspondence 1915.

p 51 'exasperating': *Oaken Heart*, p299.
'whose idols': *Dance of the Years*, p209.

p 52 'a Master of Men': Emily Jane Allingham MS 1932.
'dull but pleasant dream': M.A. draft material.
'roused his gardener': Dr Bouverie in Margery's *Dancers in Mourning* does just this and Dr Salter's former gardener Herbert Bullard confirms that this was his common practice.
'her husband': E.J.A. MS, 1932.

p 53 'Pigeons': *Oaken Heart*, p28.
'Everybody at all the farms': ibid., p97.

p 54 'We were not alone': ibid., p28.
The Romance of the Amalgamated Press, George Dilnot (1925).
'It was in 1916': *The Record*, Fleetway House magazine 1961.
Women's Magazines 1693–1968, Cynthia L. White (Michael Joseph, 1970).

p 55 'she was a tartar': ibid.
'Aunt Maud': *The Relay.*
H.J.A. diary 1918.
Margery's first published story, *The Rescue of the Rain Clouds* (*Mother & Home* 14.4.17), was a version of 'The Change', a fairy story in *The Wag-Tale*. A third version has survived making it likely that this was the story M.A. was thinking of when she said she had written 'the same fairy-story five hundred and forty five times'.

p 56 'Sarum did not merely': contribution made by Margery to Perse 75th anniversary history, 1956.

p 57 'I'll be very scared': M.A. letter to H.J.A. 1918.
'A brilliant teacher': from *The Perse School for Girls 1881–1981*, M.A. Scott (Cambridge, 1981).
'above clothes': M.A. draft version of contribution, ibid. Her comments on her teachers' dress were cut by the then headmistress lest they cause hurt.
Green Corn: unpublished novel written 1923–4.

p 58 'sea-cook': an expression used frequently by M.A. It comes from the original title of *Treasure Island*.

'I never, never': W.M. to H.J.A 1929.
'Their method': M.A. draft letter to Russell Meiggs c 1938. A letter from Miss Rose Luard to J.A. after M.A.'s death shows that she had been aware of M.A.'s feelings at school.

p 59 'almost physical': M.A. letter to Wesley Hartley 1959.
'the old boy': M.A. diary 1921.
'a nervy, big-boned, exciteable child': M.A. draft for 'I Seem to Have Won a Medal' (*Homes & Gardens*, June 1963).
a contemporary: Mrs Saunders.

p 60 Miss Georgina Luard letter to H.J.A. 1920.
a fellow-pupil: Alice Narborough in touch with Margery around 1956.
The Persean, Dec 1922, mentioned *Soldier of Fortune* in connection with the public production in London of *Dido and Aeneas*.
'for her type': *Green Corn*.
So Said the Blackbird: *The Persean*, early 1920.

p 62 'little stone bridge': *Green Corn*.
'Board of Trade': *In the First Watch*, William McFee.
'Margery needs': this and following quote from Miss Georgina Luard's letter 1920.

p 63 'I left school': this and following quotation from draft material from 'I Seem to Have Won a Medal'.
'stammering and snobbery': P.Y.C., *All I Did Was This*, p32.
'in a year or two': H.J.A. to Edith Heald 1919.
'Margery wants': H.J.A. diary 1920.
'chaffs her mother': H.J.A. letter to W.M.
'sweedles': *Green Corn*.

p 64 H.J.A. diary and correspondence.
'industrious apprentice': M.A. dedication to *Death of a Ghost* (1934).

p 65 'take up the whole': *Green Corn*.
Charlotte Corday etc.: roles played or recited by M.A.

Chapter V

p 66 First section of this chapter based on M.A. draft for article 'I Seem to Have Won a Medal', conversations with Josephina de Vasconcellos and material in the Polytechnic archive.

p 67 H.J.A. diary 1921.

p 68 Foyle's lunch 1938.
'It's not what I can't say': from 'I Seem to Have Won a Medal'.

p 69 'Betty recited': M.A. diary 24.10.21.
Conversation with Betty Carter.
'a peasant girl': this was probably M.A.'s poem 'Jerry Abbershaw', the tale of a highwayman's execution. It was one of her most popular.
The Witch: Tib Merryweather, the witch, has been ducked and curses her enemies and the entire village. The poem ends: 'The fire shall dance motley, the wind shall howl loud / And Sennifer's daughter shall sew on her shroud.'

p 70 **George Bernard Shaw** (1856–1950): influential dramatist essayist, critic, central figure in Fabian Society 1884–1911. H.J.A. and W.M. constantly refer to and argue about his characters and ideas in their letters. M.A. went to many of his plays. At this time she had most recently seen *John Bull's Other Island* and read *Love Among the Artists*.
'B. Shaw sent back my play': M.A. diary 26.3.21.
Without Being Naturally Qualified (unpublished play).
Congratulations on *Oaken Heart*: P.Y.C. preface to *Mr Campion's Clowns*.

p 71 'I am too young': M.A. diary 7.3.21.
H.J.A. letter to W.M. 1920.
Romeo and Juliet seen 7.2.21, *Romeo Domino* written 28.2.21. *The Tempest* seen twice in that month, poem on Caliban written 27.2.21.
Description of M.A.'s clothes from J.de V.
'a short, simple undergarment': Polytechnic prospectus.

p 72 'squiffy' etc.: all this gleaned from M.A. diary 1921.
'uncanny': M.A. letter to P.R.R. 1965.

p 73 'authentic evidence': *Without Being Naturally Qualified*.
'she would have nothing more': H.J.A. unpublished account of events on Mersea Island, summer 1921.
'Our world': *Toasted Cheese and Cinders*, Sybil Brand (Book Guild, 1986).

p 74 'bleak wasteland': John Fowles, introduction to *Mehalah* (Boydell & Brewer).
'Sunset over Mersea' and 'Moonlight': unpublished poems.

p 75 'smuggling': unpublished draft of preface to *Mysterious Mr Campion*

pp 75–7 Herbert's account was written as a possible introduction to *Blackerchief Dick* but set aside in favour of McFee's preface. He made use of it in correspondence with other interested persons mainly 1922–1923.

p 77 'my daughter is': H.J.A. letter March 1922.

'politely ironical': phrase occurs in the transcripts made during each session. H.J.A. describes the levity with which they started playing the game.
Blackerchief Dick (Hodder, 1923); edition used – Kaye & Ward, 1974.
The Mind Readers (Chatto, 1965).

p 78 Stories which seemed to M.A. to be true elsewhere included the novels *Traitor's Purse* and *The Mind Readers*.
Strong Poison, Dorothy L. Sayers (Gollancz, 1939).
H.J.A. correspondence.

p 79 Stevenson on language: essay on the composition of *Treasure Island* and The Art of Writing.
'ripping' etc.: M.A. diary.
H.A. is said: conversations with Joyce.

p 80 *The Mind Readers* e.g. chapters 6 and 10.

p 81 'It was an astounding': M.A. draft letter to Russell Meiggs c 1938.
Hearn was younger than Herbert, not then married and was certainly fond of Margery. When she had what otherwise seems to have been her first love affair (with Angela Doubleday in 1922), she writes in her diary, 'I'm for it *again*' (my emphasis). This may of course be simple over-dramatisation by M.A. or refer to some earlier schoolgirl crush).
'We drank': from transcripts of seances.

p 82 'Oh Hal': *Blackerchief Dick*, p37.
'the jewel': ibid., pp294ff.

p 83 bookseller gossip: source, Tony Doncaster, Colchester bookseller.
Editorial attitudes: while magazine editors exercised close control over the style, content and development of their material, the editors of books were less closely involved. In matters of clarity and grammar they relied on the printer's reader. Explanation from Sir Robert Lusty: no 'desk-editors' then.

Chapter VI

p 85 'it sold': quoted from M.A. draft material. Actual sales figures were 752 copies home, 800 colonies.
'Sewed, wrote, read': M.A. diary 25.9.21.
'chord': from M.A. draft material.

p 86 'Dear, oh me': M.A. diary 4.10.21.
'she with her head full': M.A. diary 7.10.21.

Reactions to *Dido*: M.A. diary 5 & 6.10.21.
'If I cry': M.A. diary 9.7.21.
'Mother worried': M.A. diary 9.10.21.

p 87 'we're not just kids': *Green Corn*.
Dido and Aeneas was performed on June 1st 1922 at the King George's Hall W.C.1 and on the 29th at the Cripplegate theatre E.C.2 (possibly again in Dec 1922).
Margery tried to be business-like from the start. As soon as she began paid work for Aunt Maud, she started to keep accounts in the back of her diary. She didn't keep them up invariably but they record the titles of many of her film stories.

p 88 'Devised on ingenious': Dilnot, *Romance of Amalgamated Press*.
Later, when Margery was more expert and living out of London, Maud's office might only send the notes.
'an outstanding': Polytechnic magazine.
Water in a Sieve published by French's acting editions 1925.

p 89 'Pip came': M.A. diary 13.10.21.
'The true connection': *All I Did Was This*, p34.
'You and I': H.J.A. to Lilian Carter April 1927.
'could know him': this and following quotations from *All I Did Was This*, p8.

p 90 'big, bouncing schoolgirl': P.Y.C. preface to *Mr Campion's Clowns* (Chatto, 1967).

p 91 '1911!': *Fanny's First Play* was written by George Bernard Shaw in that year.
'Charles': M.A. diary 12.5.22.

p 92 'I love her': M.A. diary 20.5.22 (cf. note to p81 above).
'Got up late': M.A. diary 21.5.22.
'clever young . . . dramatist': *Daily Sketch* 1923. Margery's first interview was with *The Daily Chronicle* who considered hers 'an astonishing performance'.
M.A. to W.M. 10.6.23.

p 93 'Charles came': M.A. notebook 5.7.23.
'a bit of a mollycoddle': M.A. diary 16.7.23.
'Saw Charles': M.A. diary 23.5.24.
'Oh lord': M.A. diary 24.3.25.
The Sexton's Wife in *The Allingham Minibus* (Chatto, 1972).

p 94 *Hill of His Ancestors* – unpublished story.

p 95 Ferdal of the Dark Hills etc.: seance notes.

p 96 'girls who haven't': *Green Corn*.
Theatre: *All I Did Was This*, p35, and Margery's diary.

'Granny thinks': M.A. diary 6.5.23.
Comments from M.A. notebook 10.5.23, 19.6.23, 20.6.23, 25.6.23, 30.6.23.

p 97 M.A. diary entries concerning Pip's proposal 12–14 August 1923.
'secret engagement': P.Y.C. preface to *Mysterious Mr Campion*.

p 98 'I am not fair' and subsequent quotes: M.A. diary Jan–Feb 1924.

Chapter VII

p 100 'an extraordinary indifference': M.A. to Charles Evans 1937.
All review comments from H.J.A. collection.

p 101 'They made a great fuss': M.A. diary 30.12.21.

p 102 Edith Shackleton Heald, journalist, Layer Breton visitor, reviewed in *Time and Tide* during 1930s, in touch with M.A. in 1950s.
'I so frightened': M.A. diary 12.2.21.

p 103 'I do not think': P.Y.C. preface to *Mysterious Mr Campion*.
'cuckoo in the nest': M.A. notebook 25.6.23.

p 104 'This was discouraged': M.A. draft material.
'hills and sheep': M.A. letter to W.M. Dec 1923.
'was bitten': preface to *Mysterious Mr Campion*.
'synopsis': M.A. diary 28.9.23.

p 105 'Phil': M.A. diary 2.3.24.
M.A. diary entries for 1924 and 1925 only half complete.

p 106 'I had the family figure': preface to *Mysterious Mr Campion*.
'His face': this and subsequent quotes from *Green Corn*.

p 107 'I don't know': M.A. diary 10.3.24.
'Hear they've': M.A. diary 26.1.25.
'trial and error': *Oaken Heart*, p26.

p 108 'the fragments': *Green Corn*.
'Read G.C.': M.A. diary 8.3.24.
H.J.A. correspondence, July 1924.
Letter George Hearn to M.A. 21.10.24.

p 109 'My poor father': M.A. draft preface to *Mysterious Mr Campion*.
'Find I am': M.A. diary 4.8.24.
The Barbarian publ. in *Allingham Minibus* (Chatto, 1973).

p 110 'I wish': E.J.A. to W.M.
'she embraced': P.Y.C., *All I Did Was This*.
Letter to J.A.

p 111 H.J.A. to W.M. 19.8.20.
H.J.A. diary 1923.

M.A., 'My Garden, My Love' (*Homes & Gardens*, 1965).
'a wonderful': M.A. diary March 1931.
'Things not joyous': M.A. diary 1924.

p 112 'Miss 1925' was in the first issue of *Joy* (Feb 1925).

p 113 'Dead Sea fruit': preface to *Mysterious Mr Campion*.
Show at the Poly: several of Margery's ballads were included in Miss Bagley's Poetry Revues with Margery as the tale-teller during 1925 and 1926.
'potential saint': M.A. diary 20.3.25.
the GN: this was a small, cheap, sporty two-seater, the 1920s equivalent (roughly) of an MG Midget into and onto which Mary Brown (Cooee) remembers cramming numbers of people – and being stopped by the Mersea Island policeman.

p 114 'So, Marge has': W.M. to H.J.A.
'I believe': M.A. diary 8.7.25.
'I would chuck up': M.A. diary 30.8.25.
'No phone': M.A. diary 21.8.25.
Recollections of Mary Brown (Mary Orr).

p 115 'In some ways': *Oaken Heart*, p354; Pip's recollections of General Strike in *All I Did Was This*, p43.

Chapter VIII

p 118 'future husbeing': M.A. to W.M. July 1927.
'no money': H.J.A. to W.M.
H.J.A. to Lilian Carter.
'At the time': M.A. draft for *Mystery and Myself*.

p 119 'Madam Virginie': *On to Andorra*, P.Y.C. (Hamish Hamilton, 1964).

p 120 'sex was of minor': preface to *Mysterious Mr Campion*.
'talking grandly': *All I Did Was This*, p38.
'hitting each other': M.A. diary Mar 1931.
'Virginie': *Oaken Heart*, p283.

p 121 *The Lieabout* in *The Allingham Casebook* (Chatto, 1969).
Bound to be Read, Robert Lusty (Cape, 1975). Lusty locates the flat in Raquet Court but is referring to Middle Row Place. The area was heavily bombed during W.W.II.
'fat and furry': M.A. to W.M. 1928.
'happy': H.J.A. diary Dec 1927.
The Hovel was in Neal Street and is described by P.Y.C. in *All I Did Was This*, p45.
'like a power-drill': M.A. article 'London, My Market Town', 1963.
'the surprising intimacy': *The Lieabout*.

p 122 Christina Carter, member of household from 1934.
e.g. Stukely Wivenhoe in *Sweet Danger*, Towser in *Fashion in Shrouds*.
'I think I must be': M.A. to W.M. July 1927.

p 123 'the strain': M.A. to W.M. 1928.
The Gang: from Christ's Hospital came Littley and Bunny Wright, Elton Box (a song-writer) and Sydney Carter (a poet and writer of hymns). Arthur Underwood, a lawyer, was also a friend from this time, though not from C.H. Pip remained friendly with Hamilton Fyfe and Roger Pippett from *The Daily Herald*. The publisher Robert Hale was a friend from this time.
Robert Lusty, 1909–1991, publisher, Hutchinson and Michael Joseph, Chairman National Book League, Governor B.B.C.
Henry Rushbury, b. 1889, drawings, watercolours, prints, Keeper of the Royal Academy from 1949. His wife, Birdie, was a close friend.
Edmund Blunden, b. 1896, educ. C.H. Many published works esp. *Undertones of War* (1928).
cf. *The Company We Kept*, Barbara Muir autobiography. Barbara's father Sidney Gowing wrote serials as John Goodwin. Material in this chapter comes from conversations and letters.
Robert St John Cooper was for many years editor of *The Daily Express* home page.
T.E.B. Clarke autobiography *Jeremy's England* publ. 1934. Recollections from Bill Gee.

p 124 'barmy nights': this was from an advertising slogan, 'Make Friday night Amami night, then Saturday night's a barmy night'.
'Today the young woman': H.J.A. letter to W.M. Nov 1927.
'a party for a dozen friends': P.Y.C. preface to *Mysterious Mr Campion*.
Sexton Blake: *The Men Behind Boys' Fiction,* Lofts and Adley (Howard Baker, 1970). Margery was consulted during the preparation of this work. While she was helpful regarding her father and 'Ralph Rollington', her own entry shows a certain reticence.

p 125 'an epic serial': P.Y.C. preface to *Mysterious Mr Campion*.
The Darings of the Red Rose, in *Weekly Welcome*, 1930.
The Bookseller, Jan 1927.
Q.D. Leavis, *Fiction and the Reading Public* (Bodley Head, 1931).

White Cottage Mystery (Jarrolds, 1928). New edition prepared for Chatto and Windus by Joyce Allingham, 1974. Penguin edition, 1978.

p 126 'a surprise every tenth': from preface to *Mysterious Mr Campion*.

'Pip is starting': H.J.A. diary Dec 1927.

'Hitherto': M.A. draft autobiographical material.

p 127 ' "Yes," she said': *White Cottage Mystery*, p24.

The Crime at Black Dudley (Jarrolds, 1929). Edition used Penguin 1950. Campion appearance p11, exit p168.

p 128 'Mornington Dodd': More was made of this alias in the earliest editions of *Black Dudley*. Abbershaw has seen his face in Scotland Yard's files and describes a 'neat little confidence trick' which 'Dodd' pulled off at a house party. Prenderby 'goggled' at Dodd/Campion. 'Do you mean to say you're a *crook*?'

Anecdote from *Important to Me*, Pamela Hansford Johnson (Macmillan, 1974). Jack Morpurgo thinks Edmund Campion the Christ's Hospital martyr was in M.A.'s mind, H.R.F. Keating mentions the flower similarity to Baroness Orczy's Scarlet Pimpernel, Agatha Christie thought the likeness to Dorothy L. Sayers' Wimsey was so marked at this time that 'Margery Allingham' might have been a pen name for D.L.S.

'As the only life': preface to *Mysterious Mr Campion*.

p 129 'There are only': H.J.A. to W.M. 1929.

'In the centre': *Black Dudley*, p5.

p 130 From London to saltings via Chelmsford – Witham – Kelvedon – Birch.

Mystery Mile (Jarrolds, 1930). Penguin edition (1950) used, not the Penguin revised edition (1968).

p 131 'I shan't be afeard': *Mystery Mile*, p77.

p 132 Letter and page of working notes sent by A.J.G. to J.A.

Pip's work exhibited R.A. on at least three occasions between 1927 and 1931.

'And any word': M.A. draft autobiographical material.

p 133 'The sun': *Mystery Mile*, p92.

'the putting away': ibid., p209.

'mixed ping-pong': ibid., p213.

'a hillock': Lugg's first appearance, ibid., p122. Magersfontein was a Boer War incident where barbed wire was first put to military use. In *Green Corn* Margery had a comic porter named Sebastopol Toms.

p 134 His sense of humour: M.A. preface to *Mysterious Mr Campion*.

'writing himself': In her introduction to the Penguin 1950 series, M.A. wrote, 'He is the only character whom I never consider. He appears when he thinks he will and talks without effort . . . Sometimes he has to be censored.' Reviewers who disliked Lugg included Nicholas Blake (*Spectator*), Raymond Postgate (*Time and Tide*), Val Gielgud (B.B.C.).
'You may Kiss': *Mystery Mile*, p254.

Chapter IX

p 136 *Look to the Lady* (Jarrolds, 1931). Edition used Penguin 1950.
'Right hand writing is the story one tells spontaneously at the party. Left hand writing is the one one is made to tell by somebody else'. Preface to *Mr Campion's Lady*.
'One to break' and 'Plumpudding': preface to *Mysterious Mr Campion*.

p 137 Corresp. W.M. and H.J.A.
'I had tried': *Cheapjack* (Heinemann, 1934). Edition used publ. by Geo. Mann (1973).

p 138 'The village of Sanctuary': *Look to the Lady*, p51.

p 139 'women-with-a-'; ibid., p47.

p 140 W.M. to H.J.A. 30.7.30.
'Hurrah': M.A. diary 28.2.31.

p 141 'a deliberate attempt': M.A. to Malcolm Johnson.
'touching beards': M.A. to Mary Leonard.
Police at the Funeral (Heinemann, 1931). Edition used Penguin 1939.
Deerstalker: ibid., p13.

p 142 *Thor Bridge* first publ. in the *Strand* magazine in the early 1920s, republished in *The Case Book of Sherlock Holmes* (1927).
'a chastening ride': preface to *Mysterious Mr Campion*.
'seven paternal uncles': Herbert's view of his brothers, conveyed to Margery, may well have been over-anxious. Tod, at least, managed his affairs sufficiently well to be able to send his son, Michael, to Ardingly and to retire early to play golf to a professional standard. His brother Claude arrived regularly for Sunday lunch. The only other member of the family whom Michael Allingham, as a child in the 1940s, remembers seeing on a regular basis was Margery's brother Phil. He helped Phil graft in Shepherd Market and named his own son after him.

p 144 'no vent': *Police at the Funeral*, p43.
Twin solutions: *Death of a Ghost* is the prime example.

p 145 'very, very trying': this and subsequent quotations from M.A. diary Jan–Mar 1931.

p 146 Heinemann and Charles Evans: information mainly from the company history, *A Century of Publishing 1890–1990*, by John St John (Heinemann, 1990).
Without My Cloak, **Kate O'Brien**'s first novel, was publ. by Heinemann (1931).
John Dickson Carr (1906–1977) wrote 27 of his Carter Dickson novels for Heinemann between 1934 and 1956.
Philip MacDonald (1900–1981) was averaging five crime novels a year between 1930 and 1933. They were published by Collins and Doubleday.
Agatha Christie's, **Dorothy Sayers'** and **Ngaio Marsh's** first detective novels were published in 1920, 1923 and 1934 respectively.
Sir Philip Gibbs was an editor and prolific novelist, **Mary Griggs** wrote her first novel in 1931.

p 147 'If a girl': M.A. letter to W.M.
'Marge still a bit': H.J.A. diary Oct, Dec 1931.

p 148 'billowing': *The Company We Kept*, Barbara Muir.
'blest': preface to *Mysterious Mr Campion*.
'a scene in the studio': *The Pioneers*, 1937 (publ. in *The Allingham Casebook*).
'a complete ape': draft letter to R.M. c 1938.

p 150 'Her personality': E.J.A. letter to W.M. c 1923.
'so very fearful': E.J.A. to W.M.
Dr Russell Barton met M.A. in his capacity as Physician Superintendent of Severall's Hospital, Colchester. He was later consultant psychiatrist to the World Health Organisation and now lives and works in New York.

Chapter X

p 152 P.Y.C. letter Christmas/New Year 1931/2.

p 153 'where every tenth' and subsequent quotations: M.A. to W.M. 31.2.32.
'very promising': H.J.A. diary.

p 154 Dedication to *Death of a Ghost* (Heinemann, 1934). Edition used publ. Penguin 1942.
'The sales figures': M.A. to M.L. 1.4.32.
Heinemann printed 2,000 copies of the first edition of *Police*

at the Funeral, sold at 7s 6d; 2,000 one year later, sold at 3s 6d; first printings of next three novels, *Sweet Danger*, *Death of a Ghost* and *Flowers for the Judge*, in the 7s 6d edition were all 3,000.

p 155 Wages: Em was offering £52 p.a. for a maid of all work; presumably Margery paid something equivalent.

p 156 Timetable: M.A. notebook.

Description of *Answers* editors: preface to *Mr Campion's Lady* and letter to M.L.

Books by Maxwell March: *Other Man's Danger* (serialised as *Man of Dangerous Secrets*) (Collins, 1933), *Rogue's Holiday* (Collins, 1935), *The Shadow in the House* (serialised as *The Devil and her Son*) (Collins, 1936).

p 157 Dr Salter last will and testament.

H.J.A. diary.

p 158 The hospital report mentioned Em's confusion, depression/excitability, tendency to delusions of a religious nature. Her 'gonads' were said to be 'in Menopausal change'. The report also mentioned an enlargement of Em's thyroid gland and a tendency to gain weight and suggested she should take thyroid extract. It was, apparently, a remedy popular around this time though the specific connections with mental illness were not fully explored until the late 1940s. Joyce does not remember hearing that this treatment had been suggested for their mother.

Sweet Danger (*Kingdom of Death*/*The Fear Sign*) (Heinemann, 1933).

Introduction to *Sweet Danger* in *Mr Campion's Lady* (1965)

p 159 'alarums': review comment.

'People like': short story *Nurse Marjorie* (undated, publishing details not known).

'an escape': M.A. interview 1962 with Arthur Pottersman. See above, Introduction p xviii.

p 160 'Mr Campion's yard-stick': preface to *Mr Campion's Lady*.

'And I shall shout': *Beckoning Lady*, p178.

p 161 'Aw Gawd, Pa!': *All I Did Was This*.

'Cocky beat me up': M.A. diary 15.9.35.

'If you have to': M.A. to G.G.

'Only wanted to send': M.A. to M.L. 1.4.32.

p 162 'Margery Allingham thinks': M.A. to M.J. 1935.

M.A. diary 20.1.34.

p 163 'Do not want': M.A. diary 1.3.34.

Descriptions of early parties from Joyce, Mary Brown

(Cooee) and Noel Gee. Grog sometimes drew a party in progress. One such picture of a party at Chappel still exists.

p 164 'half a dead thing': M.A. diary 21.5.34.

p 165 Phil was not a regular 'knocker-worker' (door-to-door salesman). *Cheapjack* tells how he and a friend cashed in selling 'No Hawkers' signs in an area that had been over-worked door-to-door.

Autobiography of a Super-Tramp was first published in 1908 with an enthusiastic preface from G.B. Shaw.

p 166 'not quite nice': M.A. diary 17.5.34.

'having sex': *Cheapjack* draft.

'Phoned Phil': M.A. diary 18.1.34.

p 167 'temporary depression' M.A. to M.L.

p 169 'Eve': M.A. diary 1.7.34.

'had a scean': M.A. diary 11.10.34.

'horridest': M.A. diary 31.12.34.

'Cocky has no time': M.A. diary 13.11.34.

p 170 'commercialism': *Death of a Ghost*, p40.

'In private life': press release prepared by M.A.

Chapter XI

p 172 'Fell for it': M.A. diary 5.9.34.

Dr Salter Will.

p 173 'bad improvements': *Oaken Heart*.

Descriptions of Tolleshunt D'Arcy and Dr Salter from conversations with Herbert Bullard and Mr and Mrs Beckwith.

p 174 E.J.A. record of her feelings 1932.

'Decided': M.A. diary 9.9.34.

p 175 'I suppose': M.A. diary 20.11.34.

'Have uncomfortable feeling': M.A. diary 5.5.34.

'Joint project': M.A. diary 24.1.34.

p 176 Sarah Sutane: cf. p28 above.

p 177 **Louisa Callender**: described in Heinemann company history as 'very large with chestnut hair and a memory like a filing cabinet'. She was Charles Evans' secretary and became a director of the firm in 1943.

'pregnant': M.A. to L.C. 27.10.37.

Written 'for lonely exiles': preface to *Mr Campion's Lady*.

Margery's first published review was written for Roger Pippett at the *Daily Herald*. The book was *The Private Life of Sherlock Holmes*. She earned 3 guineas and was 'very impressed'.

p 178 *Flowers for the Judge* (Heinemann, 1935).
Margery's copy of *Jeremy's England* is inscribed by the author to 'The Staff and Clientele of the Viaduct Arms Hotel'.

p 179 M.A. letter c 1936.
H.J.A. account of travels with Phil.
'Suppose': M.A. diary 18.1.34.

p 180 'was always an event': *Oaken Heart*, p105.
'unbearable young puppy': M.A. diary 12.4.21.
'went over': M.A. diary 4.12.34.

p 181 Small boy: information from Piers Barker.
Conversation with Hon. Mrs Richardson (Valentine Crittall).
'hell of a set-out': M.A. diary 17.6.38.

p 182 Sir Claude de Crespigny and Dr Salter regularly organised boxing matches in D'Arcy, possibly bare-knuckle.
Dancers in Mourning e.g. tea-party in ch. 3.
Edward Terrell, O.B.E., Q.C., b. 1902, Recorder of Newbury, legal author, inventor, sailor.

p 183 **Sir Valentine Crittall** (1884–1961): local industrialist and philanthropist, represented Maldon for Labour 1923–4. From 1942 to 1955 Tom Driberg held the seat first as an Independent and then for the Labour Party.

p 184 Anonymous letter crisis: M.A. diary and notes. Mary Brown (Cooee) remembers this episode. She comments that in her view Margery had no idea of the amount of rumour-mongering in the local community about the nature of the 'goings-on' in D'Arcy House in this pre-war period.

pp 184–7 All quotations from M.A. diary are from January 1936.

p 186 *Beauty King* publ. in *The Return of Mr Campion* (Hodder, 1990).
I have assumed that the 'new Campion story' was *Dancers in Mourning*. The novella *Case of the Late Pig*, publ. Hodder 'new-at-ninepence', was also written during 1936/7 and includes Albert Campion.
The first print run of *Dancers in Mourning* was 5,000.

p 187 'Who was the little god': *Dancers in Mourning*, p345.

p 188 Campion and Bouverie: ibid., ch. 4.
'rural factory': an art-and-fiction 'factory' was how Margery liked to describe her home. The local council had ordered that the shop next door to D'Arcy House be demolished and rebuilt because it stuck out too far into the road.

p 189 'Oh dear': M.A. diary 17.1.36.

Chapter XII

p 191 Quotes from M.A. diary Jan 1937.
'an emotional finish': M.A. diary 24.1.37.

p 192 Sutane, 'the worker': *Dancers in Mourning*, p345.
'try a novel': quoted M.A. letter to W.M.
'Of course': M.A. letter to M.L.
'Bloody good story' and other quotes from M.A. diary Jan–Feb 1937.

p 193 Winifred Nerney is described as 'the perfect secretary' in *Arnold Bennett*, Margaret Drabble (Weidenfeld and Nicolson, 1974).
Margery wrote *Sweet and Low*, *'Tis Not Hereafter*, *The Black Tent*, *Miss Amber Wore Pearls*, *The Correspondents*, *The Mistress in the House* and *The Pioneers*.
Mr Campion, Criminologist (Doubleday, 1937) contains *The Case of the Late Pig* and six stories.
'I'm praying': M.A. diary 28.4.37.

p 194 '1837': E.J.A. letter to W.M. 11.5.37.

p 195 'dictated story': M.A. diary 19.5.37.
'heap of up-ended egg-boxes': *Oaken Heart*, p134.

p 196 All M.A. diary entries from August 1937. S. Paws was Shaky Paws, a nickname for *Strand* editor Reeves Shaw.
'conceived a nausea': M.A. letter to M.L.

p 197 *The Fashion in Shrouds* (Heinemann, 1938); revised version included in *Mr Campion's Lady*, omnibus collection; edition used Dent (1986).
'Having great difficulty': M.A. diary 12.11.37.
'Getting interested': M.A. diary 7.2.38.

pp 197–8 *Between the Wars*, James Laver (Vista Books, 1961).

p 198 'never go pretending': *Oaken Heart*, p115.
Sleuths' Corner: see article 'Practising to Deceive', *Time and Tide* 5.11.38.
Frank Swinnerton, b. 1884, novelist and critic, particularly admired Margery's character Amanda. Introduced M.A. to H.C. Bailey, Freeman Wills Crofts, E.C. Bentley.
A.A. Milne, b. 1882, creator of Winnie-the-Pooh etc. Margery thought of him in connection with *Punch*. Wrote 'Notes on the Way' articles for *Time and Tide*, also wrote detective stories.
Francis Gerard, prolific writer of thrillers, later emigrated to South Africa.
Jan Struther (Joyce Anstruther), b. 1901, had just started writing her 'Mrs Miniver' articles for *The Times*.

p 199 **Lady Rhondda**, Margaret Haig Thomas, b. 1883, businesswoman, founder and editor of *Time and Tide*.

Theodora Bosanquet, b. 1880, had been secretary to Henry James, had written several books, edited journal of Society for Psychical Research, and was Lady Rhondda's companion.

'lent Miss Bosanquet': M.A. diary 9.4.38.

Extracts from M.A. reviews for *Time and Tide*: 'earnest, cultured works' 12.2.38, 'a fine straightforward style' 2.4.38, 'to have read it is' 21.5.38, 'slovenly' construction and 'written to entertain or educate' 2.7.38.

p 200 'On to Ronnie's': M.A. diary 3.3.38.

'No blame': M.A. diary 11.3.38.

'Grand meeting': M.A. diary 22.4.38.

p 201 'They lead very dull': M.A. letter to Russell Meiggs 1937.

'To the police': *Fashion in Shrouds*, p188.

cf. *White Cottage Mystery*, p43: 'The whole of our civilisation is one network of little intrigues . . . a crime calls the attention of the community to one point.'

'prop': M.A. letter to W.M.; 'box': preface to *Mysterious Mr Campion*.

p 202 'worked like a fiend' etc.: M.A. diary Mar–Apr 1938.

'I have written': M.A. diary 7.2.38.

'running on the wrong force': M.A. medical notes.

'Their several responsibilities': *Fashion in Shrouds*, p228.

p 203 'bland': *The Lady Investigates*, Patricia Craig and Mary Cadogan (Gollancz, 1981), p207.

'It's not what I can't say': M.A. 'I Seem to Have Won a Medal'.

'Does she always': *Fashion in Shrouds*, p138.

'one of those people': *The Relay*.

p 204 'a wife, not a mistress' and subsequent quotes: *Fashion in Shrouds*, p287.

'pretty elementary': *Time and Tide* review 21.11.42.

'exactly what one needs': *Fashion in Shrouds*, p288.

'far from the norm': *Dance of the Years*, p17.

p 205 'put M. off': various M.A. diary notes Mar–Apr 1938.

Russell Meiggs, 1902–1989, educ. C.H., fellow of Keble Coll. then Balliol Coll., Oxford. Ancient historian, author *Roman Ostia* etc., 'a great Oxford figure' said *Independent* obituary.

There are other letters from M.A. to R.M. c Dec 1936 onwards which are not now available. I am grateful to Dr Richard Martin for extracts quoted in *Ink in Her Blood*.

'a personality': *Traitor's Purse* (Heinemann, 1941). Edition used, Penguin 1950, p27.

p 206 'promising people': M.A. letter to R.M. Oct 1938, quoted *Ink in Her Blood*, p94

'infatuation': M.A. to R.M. 12.8.38 and ibid.

The Mistress in the House, publ. in *Mr Campion and Others* (Heinemann, 1939).

'difficult, emotional': M.A. diary March 1937.

'sex-to-do': e.g. in le Carré interview 1965.

'worked together': *The Pioneers* publ. in *The Allingham Minibus*.

p 207 'Box and Joan': M.A. diary 24.2.37.

'I am nervy': *Fashion in Shrouds*, p67.

'Cocky has': M.A. diary 1934, quoted p169 above.

'decent, sensative': M.A. draft letter to R.M., Dec–Jan 1937/8.

p 208 'The thing people': M.A. letter to Dr A.D. Lindsay, undated, c 1942.

'Was just a tiny bit': M.A. diary 16.4.38.

M.A. letters to Joyce, written winter 1941 – spring 1942.

p 209 'I don't think': this and following quotes from M.A. draft letters to R.M., winter 1937/8.

Her reading: Don Marquis, *Chapters for the Orthodox*, a book not unlike C.S. Lewis' *Screwtape Letters*. G.K. Chesterton was a major influence on M.A.

p 210 'had the horrors': M.A. diary 12.1.36.

'One day': M.A. draft letter to R.M., as above.

'Man is the': M.A. letter to Theodora Bosanquet 1940.

'the terrifying web': *Time and Tide* 5.3.38.

'I now know': M.A. to W.N., Nov 1938.

Russell Meiggs married Pauline (Paula) Gregg, author and social historian, Dec. 1941.

p 211 'for Meiggs': source Paula Meiggs.

'Torquemada' (Powys Mathers) in *Observer* 1938.

'The August party': *Oaken Heart*, pp33 and 40.

Chapter XIII

p 212 Much of the material for this chapter comes from *The Oaken Heart*. In it the names of villages are disguised (Tolleshunt D'Arcy becomes Auburn as in Goldsmith's *Deserted Village*). This was retained by M.A. in the 1959 reissue of the book as she thought that the experience of her village had a representative quality.

'Phosgene': *Oaken Heart*, p44. These sheets of instructions are still among Margery's papers, together with other material dealing with A.R.P. matters or evacuee reception.
'Collect seven hundred': ibid., p46.
'The notion': ibid., p55.
p 213 'You cannot attempt': ibid., p50.
'You will wake': W.M. letter to M.A. 10.10.38.
'Don't judge England': M.A. letter publ. *New York Sun* 10.11.38.
'An outrage': W.P. Watt to M.A. 26.11.38.
p 214 'My editor': W.M. to M.A. 4.10.39.
'that extraordinary': M.J. to M.A. 17.2.39.
'hundreds and hundreds': *Oaken Heart*, p25.
'almost mitigated': ibid., p66.
'I felt': ibid., p118.
Time and Tide on evacuation shortcomings Oct 1938.
W.V.S. letters to M.A. Dec 1938 – Jan 1939.
'Strangers at the Gate': article Feb 1939.
p 215 'the mind wandered': H.M. Tomlinson in *Time and Tide*. Cf. J.B. Priestley, 'Notes on the Way' article 5.11.38 on difficulties for the creative writer. Also Lettice Cooper, 'How Can I Write a Novel in the World Today?' Jan 1939.
p 216 'hopeless grief': M.A. review 4.2.39.
'She writes': M.A. letter to W.N.
Letters from Paul Revere Reynolds, Jan 1940.
p 217 'A few months ago': M.A. review, *Time and Tide*, 21.10.39.
'shadows in the mind': *Oaken Heart*, p88; phrase also used *Time and Tide*.
p 218 'virgin and sinister': *Oaken Heart*, p132.
'medical stuff': ibid., p106.
p 219 'Among the number': Report to Medical Officer, Dr Bullough.
'came up': *Oaken Heart*, p125.
Low Company, Mark Benney (Peter Davies, 1936). Cf. comments in *The Thirties*, Malcolm Muggeridge (Hamish Hamilton, 1940). 'Mark Benney' was in fact a pseudonym for Henry Ernest Degras. It was the name by which Margery usually referred to him.
M.A. review of *The Scapegoat Dances*, *Time and Tide*, 21.5.38.
p 220 'The inhumanity': *Oaken Heart*, p160.
p 221 'an Authorised Matron' and 'It's taken me some time': both from M.A. draft letter to R.M.

In her medical notes Margery names this doctor as a Dr Torrens.
'To blunder into': *Oaken Heart*, draft and p276.
p 222 'feel we're a three-legged': M.A. diary 6.3.40.
Source: conversation with Mary Brown (Cooee).
p 223 'Without you': poem in M.A. notebook, no date.
'Love is not a cement': frequently used phrase, e.g. *Fashion in Shrouds*.
'contented weldings': preface to *Mr Campion's Lady*.
'You proved': *The Pioneers*.
'because he was': *Dance of the Years*, p30.
'no sudden changes': ibid., p348.
p 224 'off the chain': *Fashion in Shrouds*, 24.4.40.
'Finally we agreed': *Oaken Heart*, p244.
'A mad day': M.A. diary 7.4.40
p 225 'One result': *Time and Tide* 25.5.40.
'To see them': *Oaken Heart*, p271.
'Trying to work': M.A. diary 25.5.40. *Oaken Heart*, p269.
p 226 'an odd life': ibid., p277.

Chapter XIV

p 228 'The thriller': *Time and Tide* 6.4.40.
H.J.A. diary 9.1.18.
Himmler: article in *Sunday Despatch* 16.10.55.
p 229 'blows on the head': M.A. draft letter to R.M. 1937/8.
'It had been something': *Traitor's Purse*, p116.
'The capitulation': *Oaken Heart*, p289.
p 230 'elderly in soul': ibid., p111.
'the most uncomplicated': ibid., p276.
M.A. letter to *Time and Tide* 13.7.40 'The Church: a bridge or a barrier?'
p 231 Replies quoted from Edwyn Bevan and Evelyn Underhill.
'I am in conscience': M.A. letter to *Time and Tide* 22.7.40.
'academic': Theodora Bosanquet to M.A. 20.7.40.
'as well as a fundamental niceness': M.A. to Roger Lloyd 24.7.40.
'awful, narrow, over-educated type': M.A. diary 20.5.37.
p 232 'Found Jesus': M.A. draft letter to Freeman Wills Crofts.
Canon Roger Bradshaigh Lloyd, Residentiary Canon and Diocesan Missioner of Winchester, religious author and frequent contributor to *Time and Tide* 'Notes on the Way' column.
William Temple (1881–1944) was Archbishop of York from 1929 and of Canterbury from 1942.

'I am sure you are right': Wm. Temple letter to M.A. 7.8.40; article in Christian newsletter.
p 233 'I would not have you': M.A. to W.T. 12.8.40.
'No reply': pencilled on draft of M.A. letter to W.T. 27.8.40.
'a book': R.L. letter to M.A. 31.8.40.
p 234 'I have': M.J. to W.N. 11.9.40.
'ridiculous': *Oaken Heart*, p264.
p 235 Rockery: M.A. diary 13.3.40; apple trees: M.A. diary 3.1.42.
'seeing you': Rev. Graves to M.A. 28.9.38.
'old gentlemen' and 'troutage': M.A. draft letter to R.M.
p 236 'ditches': source, Tony Doncaster, Colchester bookseller.
'The odd thing is': M.A. letter to R.M.
'Everybody in it': M.A. letter to Dr A.D. Lindsay Jan 1942.
Real names: cf. Vera Brittain, *England's Hour* (1941), which uses assumed names to recount the same happenings that are retold without disguise in *Testament of Experience* (1957).
'I wondered': this and the following quotes from *Oaken Heart*, pp73, 161, 227, 300.
'Once you looked sideways': ibid., p245.
p 237 W.N. suggested Margery move away when Tolleshunt D'Arcy became a Defence Area, spring 1940.
'give himself up': M.A. diary 23.5.41.
'keep the roof tiles on': J.A. letter to M.A.
'I stay' and 'earn all the money': M.A. letter to R.M.
'He'll break his teeth': *Oaken Heart*, p369.
'which is old': ibid., prefatory letter.
'clean old words': M.A. letter to W.T. 12.8.40.
p 238 Source: conversations with Christina and Joyce. Also Christina's Age Concern essay, 1990, Essex Record Office.
p 239 'professional dignity': *Oaken Heart*, p289.
'If the British': ibid., p76.
Local Air Raid Warden, Mr Beckwith.
'if she had to': M.A. diary 3.5.41.
p 240 'She's got such a nerve': M.A. to J.A. 18.10.41.
'Isn't it wicked?' *Oaken Heart*, p360.
'nightshirt': M.A. to J.A. 7.2.42.
Re-cycling letters: *The Relay*; also M.A. to J.A.
'Her refuge': *Oaken Heart*, p315.
p 241 Landmines: M.A. diary 3.1.41 and in *Oaken Heart*, draft version.
Machine-gunned: M.A. diary 6.1.41.
'Your news': M.A. to W.N.

'Am so tired': M.A. diary 18.5.41.
'queer stuff': M.A. diary 11.1.41.
'Previously': *Oaken Heart*, p221.
'What a period': ibid., p372.

Chapter XV

p 242 'The thing': *Dance of Years*, p7.
'days of power': ibid., p9, and letter to A.D. Lindsay 1942.
'the best expression': M.J. letter to M.A. 1941.
'I personally': P.R.R. to M.A. 3.9.41.

p 243 6,500 copies: *Fashion in Shrouds* (at 8/6) was the highest first printing of M.A.'s pre-war novels. According to Howard Haycraft the average sale of a detective novel before 1940 was 1,500–2,000. Agatha Christie was regularly selling 10,000 copies. Dorothy L. Sayers claimed 6,000–10,000.
'In *The Oaken Heart*': *Time and Tide* diary Aug 1941.
'*The Oaken Heart* is something more': *Time and Tide* review 13.9.41.
'elderly and unlikely': *All I Did Was This*, p82.
'Panda': M.A. to J.A. 7.2.42.

p 244 'It is the best book': Christine Holt to M.A. 25.1.48.
'The immediate question' and following quotes: M.A. to A.D.L. 31.12.41.
Alexander Dunlop Lindsay, b. 1879, Master of Balliol College Oxford since 1924, moral philosopher, writings on democracy and Christianity. Sent M.A. his most recent pamphlet 'I Believe in Democracy'.

p 245 'This time': M.A. diary 25.5.41.

p 246 'my value': M.A. letter to A.D.L. Jan 1942.
'a great adventure': M.A. to A.D.L. Jan 1942.

p 247 'From one point of view' and following quotes: M.A. draft letter to R.M. 1937/8.

p 248 'It's as if': M.A. to Betty Carter 1941.
'I just work': M.A. to J.A. 7.2.42.
'Time does not': M.A. to James Laver 1942.
'If all time is eternally present: opening to 'Burnt Norton', first in T.S. Eliot's *Four Quartets*, which were written between 1935 and 1942.

p 249 'I see from Borrow': M.A. to A.D.L. Jan 1942. *Lavengro*, George Borrow (John Murray, 1851), ch. 2.
'You know': M.A. to J.A.
'one of our family': *Oaken Heart*, p106.

p 250 Pip's safety: M.A. diary 20.10.40 and 25.1.34.

'This book': *Dance of the Years*.
'carefully hemmed': introduction to revised version of *Fashion in Shrouds* (1965).
Galsworthy comparison made by Louisa Callender. He was a Heinemann author.
Little, Brown admission of reluctance from letter in Chatto archive.

pp 251ff P.Y.C. experiences from *All I Did Was This* and letters to M.A.

p 252 'Dear Guffin': P.Y.C. to M.A. Feb 1942.
'My dear': P.Y.C. to M.A. Sept 1941.
Pip war-poet: clipping 31.10.41.

p 253 'I noticed': *Master of None*, Jack Morpurgo (Carcanet, 1990), p69.
'Pip Youngman Carter': ibid., p143.

p 254 'I never saw': P.Y.C. to M.A. Nov 1945.
'I am glad': M.A. to A.D.L. 2.3.43.
Pig club: M.A. diary 6.7.42.
'See all you can': M.A. to J.A., winter 1941/2.

p 255 'It is impossible' and 'I am looking forward': M.A. to A.D.L. 2.3.43.
Coroner's Pidgin (Heinemann, 1945); edition used Penguin.
'I don't like the way': M.A. to A.D.L. 2.3.43.

p 256 'There will be': review of *A Stricken Field*, *Time and Tide*.
'Notes on the Way', R.L., *Time and Tide* 8.8.42.

p 257 'Judases': *Coroner's Pidgin*, pp159–60.
'Double-crossing' was a term with more visual impact then than now. The double cross was the swastika, contrasted with the Christian cross. Cf. *Time and Tide*, Dec 1942.

Chapter XVI

p 260 'The alternative': M.A. to L.C. Nov 1946.

p 261 'we should meet': *Baron* by Baron (Muller). Cf. also *Portrait of a Decade: London Life 1945–55*, Douglas Sutherland (Harrap, 1988). Cf. Ngaio Marsh, *Death in a White Tie* (1938).

p 262 'a terrific snob': M.A. diary 29.4.51.

p 263 'face to face': J.E. Morpurgo, postscript to *All I Did Was This*.
'at Youngman Carter's': *Baron*.
News of the World 27.6.49.
Pip's salary (between £1,500 and £2,500) was taxed at normal

levels. Surtax started around £2,000, therefore almost all of Margery's income was liable for an additional higher-level tax. At its highest point this meant that she paid 17s 6d (87.5p) out of every £1 earned.

p 264 'The whole place': M.A. letter to Nelson Doubleday Jan 1947.

Typing paper: authors' manuscripts sent over from Britain to America at this time were regularly retyped on arrival as the paper quality was so poor.

p 265 'Penguins continue to be the outstanding venture over here': M.A. letter to N.D. Jan 1947.

On Penguin and paper rationing see J.E. Morpurgo, biography of Allen Lane (Hutchinson, 1979).

'In England': M.A. to N.D. Jan 1947.

For more information on Heinemann's attitude to paperbacks see *A Century of Publishing*, John St John.

Penguin copies printed during W.W.II: *Police at the Funeral* 75,000 in 1939, 80,000 in 1940; *Death of a Ghost* 70,000 in 1942, 60,000 in 1944; *Flowers for the Judge* 60,000 in 1944, 60,000 in 1945 (figures from Chatto archive).

'You say that if': M.A. to A.P. Watt Nov 1946. She appears to use the terms 'surtax' and 'supertax' interchangeably. The taxation system was a problem to other married women writers: see Jane Aiken Hodge's biography of Georgette Heyer. Margery kept a copy of a letter from Barbara Cartland on the subject of tax written to *The Daily Telegraph* 16.5.53.

p 266 *The Patient at Peacocks Hall* written during 1950 makes reference to the change in the hero which may be autobiographical observation.

p 267 'never really believed': P.R.R. letter to M.A. 31.1.49; M.A. letter to American Embassy claimed P.Y.C. as 'my partner and co-author of works of fiction under the pen-name *Margery Allingham*'. Letter from Helen Grey of *Town and Country* 11.2.49.

'discusser': P.Y.C. to Chatto sales conference on publication of omnibus *Mr Campion's Clowns*.

M.A. article 'Mystery and Myself' published *Town and Country* August 1949. 'Our stories were published under my maiden name because of my earlier work . . . It amused us to observe that if I had taken his name he had also taken mine.'

p 268 M.A. attitude to Tom Driberg: see his autobiography *Ruling Passions* (Cape, 1977).

p 269 'a lovely place': Barbara Noble, letter to J.T.

'the light': W.M. to M.A. 24.9.61.
'a nice woman': M.A. diary 19.1.50.
p 270 'really quite': M.A. letter to J.A. 1941/2.
p 271 'the overall quality': Lavinia Davis to M.A. 1.2.49.
'Some readers': *Ladies' Home Journal* 9.12.48.
'so very British': *Good Housekeeping* Dec 1948.
'I think': P.R.R. letter to M.A. 29.6.48.
More Work for the Undertaker (Heinemann, 1949). Edition used, Penguin 1952.
'every character': M.A. preface to *More Work for Undertaker*.
p 272 'must know': fan letter, M.A. papers.
'Professor Palinode': *More Work for Undertaker*, p16.
'the celebrated Mrs': ibid., p68.
p 273 'honking highbrows': in the *Oaken Heart* M.A. speaks of her geese 'honking like highbrows at a private view'. In *More Work for Undertaker* Lawrence Palinode has a 'honking' voice and 'goose-tones'.
The *Daily Graphic* paid 20 guineas per 600 words each week Mar–Oct 1947.
'The itch': *More Work for Undertaker*, p195.
The household practice is tradespeople visiting downstairs, professions coming up; see *More Work for Undertaker*, p59.
'I don't think': A.D.L. to M.A. 13.7.50.
p 274 'whether your grand establishment': Arthur Underwood letter to M.A. 21.6.50.
'Julian Clifford arrived': M.A. diary 10.1.51.
'Hour of the Angel': M.A. diary 11.1.51.
p 275 'Heard all about everything': M.A. diary 12.1.51; 'heard more' 13.1.51; 'Beginning to understand' 15.1.51.
'Crisis in your family': M.A. diary 17.1.51.

Chapter XVII

p 276 'Husband having': quoted *Ink in Her Blood*, p168.
'emotional': M.A. medical notes from 1955.
Flat 'as Coop left it': M.A. diary 12.1.51.
'Whatever is happening': Biddy Gregory to M.A. 28.11.50.
'has her own troubles': M.A. diary 28.1.51.
Safer than Love published in book form (with *The Patient at Peacocks Hall*) under the title *No Love Lost* (World's Work, 1954). Edition used, Penguin 1959.
p 277 'I ought to have been': ibid., p138.
'Hour of the Angel': contemplating the end of the world in an

atomic explosion, Granny had remarked with placid certainty, 'We shall see the minor angels first.'

'Pip refuses': M.A. diary 28.1.51.

'unfair': M.A. diary 31.1.51.

'famous rift' and following quotes: M.A. diary 4.2.51.

p 278 'the obstinacy' and following quotes: M.A. diary 9.2.51.

'All my life': M.A. to Aubrey Christlieb.

M.A. income 1946/47 £1,719, £658 (U.S.), owed approx £750 tax. Income 1951/2 £3,406, £1,685 (U.S.). At the end of 1950 her accountant had estimated that 'at least' £1,400 tax would be due, 'probably much more'.

'so relieved': M.A. diary 22.2.50.

'too tired'; M.A. diary 16.2.50.

p 279 'I am one': M.A. to Aubrey Christlieb Dec 1950.

'this balmy modern code': in a *Time and Tide* review 21.11.42 M.A. spoke of 'the rules of the time which demand complete emotional freedom for the individual unhampered by any purely moral rules' – these 'spartan if barmy modern and intelligent rules'.

'Pip is the person': M.A. to A.C.

'an expensive luxury': source B.C.

p 280 'I would like to own': notebook, no date, relevant diary entry 2.3.50.

'House became mine': M.A. diary 8.2.51.

'Something happened': M.A. diary 11.1.51.

'burst' and 'great well-being': M.A. medical notes.

'Myxoedematous madness' reprinted in *Richard Asher Talking Sense*. Another article I found helpful was 'The Neurologic Manifestations of Myxedema' by Vernon Sanders in the *New England Journal of Medicine*, March 1962.

p 281 'my age': M.A. diary 15.2.51. Later in the year she found she needed to take a regular sedative to enable her to sleep. This suggests she was suffering from depressive illness. Later still in the year her sleeping improved but she mentioned that she and Pip were sleeping apart ('by amicable arrangement') 'because I snore'. This is a symptom typical of myxoedemics.

'he'd be oke': M.A. diary 19.5.51.

'feeling rather hopeless': M.A. diary 20.5.51.

p 282 'dressed up': M.A. diary 11.1.52.

The Tiger in the Smoke (Chatto & Windus, 1952) (dedicated to Sally Reid). Edition used, Penguin 1957. The *Spectator* reviewer made the comparison to Dickens: 'Like him . . . she has an infinite capacity for conveying the essence of varied eccentricity in supporting characters and is absorbed by the macabre possibilities of London.' The comparison with Stevenson was made most tellingly in the *Times* obituary 1.7.66 re *Tiger in Smoke* and *Hide My Eyes*: 'she shares his feeling for London as a place of dark magic and mysterious doors.'

p 283 Paul Reynolds' suggestions made in letters 3.1.49, 22.3.49, and 16.11.51.
'physical funk': *Oaken Heart*, p220.
'It has always seemed': *Time and Tide* 23.4.38.

p 284 'fighting with': M.A. preface to *Mr Campion's Lady*.
'something to go on with': *Tiger in Smoke*, p85.
'a sort of portrait': Canon Luard to M.A. 28.6.52.
'I can see': A.M.B. to M.A. 2.7.53.

p 285 'liking of mankind': *Oaken Heart*, p207.
'You might say': George Hearn to M.A. 10.4.34.
'One of the': M.A. diary Jan 1936.
'I love it': *Oaken Heart*, p371.
Havoc: 'Hermaseal man came – very exasperated at delay but it now occurs to me that he'd do for Havoc – may be sent by Gawd!' M.A. diary 21.6.51.

pp 285–6 'to expound certain popular theories': the *Town and Country* article formed the basis for 'Mystery Writer in the Box' which was in turn used as the preface to *Mysterious Mr Campion*.

p 286 All 'fan' letters cited are among M.A.'s correspondence.
'with the care': from letter drafted by M.A. to assist A.P. Watt in explaining where the incompatibility had lain and what Margery was hoping to find in a new publisher.
'She was the first': from M.A. *Manchester Guardian* obit. of Agatha Christie written in 1943 and revised in 1955. In 1950 she wrote an appreciation of A.C., 'Half-way House', which was published in the *New York Times*.

p 287 'deep basic stuff': letter to Graham Watson 1963.
Adapting style: achievement mentioned by several commentators including writer of M.A.'s obituary for *The Times*.
Publishers' letters are among Margery's papers. There are also relevant letters in the Heinemann archives. I am grateful to Dwye Evans for communicating his pragmatic view of the disagreement.
'to let the rabbit': M.A. to W.P.W. 25.11.51.
Sales figures: the first printing of *More Work for Undertaker* had been 12,500. It was reprinted before publication and very soon afterwards was selling 16,542 (1949). *Oaken Heart* had reached 17,000 copies and the first printing of *Tiger in Smoke* was 17,500.

p 288 'some surprising Toffs': Biddy Gregory letter to M.A. 22.11.51.
Letters in Chatto archive and among Margery's papers.
'noisy personality': M.A. to G.W. June 1962.
'on the stocks': phrase from preface to *Mysterious Mr Campion*.
'I have never': M.A. draft letter probably to R.M.
'come to Town': M.A. diary 21.9.51.
p 289 'Miss Sayers is': Canon Edwards to M.A.
'You know': P.W.A. letter to M.A. 1951.
'turning out': P.W.A. to M.A. 25.3.53.
'I think': L.D. to M.A. 8.6.52.
p 291 'I don't feel': M.A. to Harold Raymond 9.3.54.
Reprint Society choice meant a special edition of 200,000 copies.
'Anyone': M.A. letter to *The Times* Jan 1955.
p 292 'Remember that I have': M.A. draft letter c 1954.
The Beckoning Lady (Chatto & Windus, 1955). Edition used, Penguin 1960.
'That man': *Beckoning Lady*, p138.
'She's given': ibid., p114.
p 294 'she was never the same': Sally Everitt (Reid) to J.T.
p 295 'I am so happy': M.A. letter to I.T. 9.2.54.
'cumulative power': Susan Asbee, *The Feminist Companion to Literature in English*; Elizabeth Bowen (*Tatler*): 'Imagination with knowledge of the extraordinary'; H.R.F. Keating: 'supercharging of reality' *D.N.B.* entry. Eric Routley, who doubted whether the detective story 'ever reached a point of maturity higher than that to which M.A. bought it in *Tiger in Smoke*', found *The Beckoning Lady* unreadable. He felt as if all the characters were 'talking with their backs to him' and 'wanted to put his fingers in his ears' (*The Puritan Pleasures of the Detective Story*, Gollancz, 1972).
'a purely personal': *Beckoning Lady*, p112.
'I think she's mad': ibid., p113.

Chapter XVIII

p 298 'My mother': M.A. letter to J. Hines, solicitor, 1951.
'massive': from M.A.'s own medical notes.
Account of the Meiggs' visit: conversation and letter from Paula, Sylvia, Rosalind Meiggs. Conversation with J.A.
p 299 'overwraught': M.A. description in own medical notes.
'Dear Miss Reporter': article by Jean Hind in *The Age*, Melbourne 25.5.55.

p 300 'boys decide': M.A. notes.

p 301 E.C.T.: in his autobiography, *Ways of Escape*, Graham Greene mentions that, at this time, he was refused such treatment. I am indebted to *A Short Practice of Clinical Psychiatry* by Dr Russell Barton for a practical understanding of what is involved in giving this treatment.

'most gratifying': M.A. notes.

p 302 *A Word in Season* was altered slightly and reprinted in the omnibus *Mr Campion's Lady*.

p 303 I am indebted to Oriel Malet for information about Meg Catusse.

'come sailing down': Meg Catusse to M.A. Oct 1955.

'I am timing this': Meg Catusse to M.A. Jan 1956.

p 304 **Dr Raymond Greene**, b. 1901, was Hon. Consultant Physician to the Royal Northern Hospital, Vice-President of the Royal Society of Medicine and a specialist in endocrinology. (He was also a mountaineer and the eldest of the three Greene brothers.)

Some of Margery's letters at this time suggest that she was thought to be suffering from hypoglycaemia, a condition produced by a disturbance of the endocrine glands. She is also known to have suffered, probably from an earlier date, from hypertension (high blood pressure).

p 305 *Hide My Eyes* (Chatto & Windus, 1958) (dedicated to Maud Hughes). Edition used, Penguin 1960.

p 306 *Medical and Scientific Investigations in the Christie Case* by Francis E. Camps (Medical Publications, 1953).

'Two days association': Pip's comment quoted by Robert Jackson in his selection of Camps' case histories (Hart Davis MacGibbon, 1975). Pip made the same comment in various articles.

'Then she's a fool': *Hide My Eyes*, p223.

p 307 'Darling': ibid., p200.

p 308 'to suit little Pippy': M.A. diary 4.2.51.

'for all his': J.A. unpublished draft.

p 310 'slicker': conversation with G.G.

'I am at that': M.A. letter to G.W. 11.4.63.

p 311 'to write themselves': cf. note to p134.

p 312 'twelve years': M.A. to I.T. Nov 1957.

'Pip with a sore head': Meg Catusse to M.A. Mar 1958.

Chapter XIX

p 314 'I do not think': M.A. to P.R.R. 17.5.58.

'It emerges': M.A. letter to I.T. 1960.

p 315 'Do you suggest': A.C. Oct 1950.

pp 315–16 Material in these pages comes from M.A.'s correspondence and conversations with J.A. and G.G.

p 317 'Daddy Watt seems': M.A. letter in Heinemann archive.
'if I am not': M.A. letter 1958.
'I think we should': M.A. to Gilbert White 9.1.61.

p 318 *Book Society*, Graham Watson's autobiography, was published by André Deutsch in 1980.
The National Library for the Blind regularly requested permission to make braille editions of her books. On 1.10.1952 the secretary wrote, 'We already possess 11 of your books comprising 46 volumes. They weigh over 2cwt and to read them in braille involves a finger journey of over 35 miles. I thought you might be interested in these slightly odd statistics.'

p 319 'it is a murder': *New Musical Express* 28.10.60. Margery said that the film of *Tiger* was so bad that 'even I laughed in all the wrong places'.
Pip started writing his autobiography in 1959 (eventually published as *All I Did Was This*). Margery nicknamed it 'How I Became a Snob' and wrote its opening paragraphs.

p 320 'divide her time': *Ink in Her Blood* takes this view.
'both working': M.A. to I.T. 1959.

p 321 'Miss Allingham Loves to Write' by Phyllis Meras, 1963.
'What to do with an Ageing Detective', *Time and Tide* 6.12.58, reprinted in *The Return of Mr Campion* (Hodder, 1989).

p 322 'the rescuer': M.A. preface to *Mysterious Mr Campion*.
'As the only life': ibid.

p 323 'It's a very sour world': M.A. preface to *Mr Campion's Lady*.
'I am by nature': ibid.
'It must be murder': M.A. quoted by Paul Holt 9.7.49.
Lord Peter attended a hanging in *Busman's Honeymoon* (1937).
'no great man': *Tiger in Smoke* p173. With the pervasive metaphor of blood sports in this novel it is interesting to note that Pip had been big-game hunting in Rhodesia in autumn 1950 while Margery was thinking out *Tiger*.
Canon Avril on hanging: ibid., p181

p 324 In a draft article, 'My Characters', Margery claimed that she had let Havoc escape out of pity. 'I knew him so well I got sorry for him.' This is an over-simplification. In the metaphysics enunciated by Avril in the darkened church, Havoc's journey is ever down towards nothingness. The ending is perfect. Harold Raymond at Chatto queried it as soon as the manuscript was read there and Margery insisted it must stand. *Hide My Eyes* was to be 'the other side of the coin'.

'Contrary to my usual': *Hide My Eyes*, p209.

'Crime for our Delight': notes for talk 1958.

'the third': M.A. preface to *Mysterious Mr Campion*.

The China Governess (Chatto & Windus, 1963).

p 325 'wiped out utterly': ibid., p7.

'The design': ibid., p9. Cf. *The New Look*, Harry Hopkins (Secker & Warburg, 1963), chs 34–5.

'decent conditions': *China Governess*, p14.

Berating son: ibid., ch 7.

'a pleasant matter-of-fact': ibid., p13.

p 326 'the communal mind': M.A. to Oliver Ellis 1965. Professor Oliver Ellis had been an occasional correspondent of Margery's since 1940 and paid her the compliment of placing her in 'the great succession of Anglo-Irish writers of beautiful English' 14.10.65.

'All goes fairly well': M.A. to P.R.R. 29.1.59.

p 327 'a potting shed': M.A. to Milton and Laura Runyon 1965.

'I knew': 'fan' letter in M.A. correspondence 16.8.65.

'the young firm': M.A. to P.R.R. 29.8.60.

p 328 'Years rolled back': Henry Rushbury to M.A. 1960.

Descriptions of 1950s parties at D'Arcy House may be found in Jack Morpurgo's introduction to *The Return of Mr Campion* and in Oriel Malet's forthcoming book on Daphne du Maurier. Guy Wilson, son of Molly Wilson who helped Margery type *More Work for Undertaker*, and Julie Ramos, daughter of Henry and Birdie Rushbury, remember how exciting the parties were for them as children.

Chapter XX

pp 330–4 'Whose survival': this and subsequent quotes come from M.A.'s unpublished typescript *The Relay*. Details confirmed by J.A.

p 330 Maud as the 'fan': M.A. letter to Sir James Waterlow 1961.

p 331 'the garret': source J.A.; 'Margery doesn't': source M.B.

'A family of daughters can be driven almost insane by a condition of thyroid gland in their mother since every unreasonable symptom of hers appears to be a blown-up version of one of their own known and controlled temperamental weaknesses.' M.A. *The Relay*.

p 334 'for she really is in clover': letter 27.6.60.

'I think I'll': source J.A. Different version in *Ink in Her Blood*.

'At eighty nine': M.A. letter to I.T. 29.8.60.

p 335 'how I can re-jig': M.A. letter to G.W. 8.12.64.

'good stuff': M.A. letter to G.W. 1.6.65.

'The doctors have decided': M.A. to Allen Lane 29.7.65.

'100% comprehensible': M.A. to I.T. Dec 1961.

'One takes a great risk': M.A. to P.R.R. 16.6.65.

p 336 'one of your': P.W.A. letter to M.A. 1965.

'subject fascinated': M.A. to James Keddie ('Cheetah' of the American Society The Speckled Band, and a regular correspondent) 8.3.65.

'I can't bear': 1964.

The Mind Readers (Chatto & Windus, 1965).

p 337 Article in *The Times* 5.9.64.

'just a little': *Mind Readers*, p203.

M.A. letter to P.R.R. 27.1.65 said le Carré was 'like Graham Greene but not so miserable . . . he'll be one of the big sellers'.

p 338 Explanations for E.S.P. cf. Ch. V above.

'All sincere': M.A. 1965.

'A.A.A.': she had forgotten that she had already used those initials to comment on *Traitor's Purse*.

'bust out of the': 1964.

'Made careful job': M.A. diary 24.2.64. The people involved were John Sergeant, Isabelle Taylor, Ken McCormick, Lee Barker, Paul Reynolds, Winifred Nerney and Barbara Noble.

p 339 'We had': Ken McCormick to author.

'I notice': M.A. letter to P.R.R. 29.1.59.

'I have for her': Dorothy Tillett letter to M.A. Nov 1952.

'It's a barmy game': M.A. to P.R.R.

p 340 'the instinct': M.A. to P.R.R. 1965.

'I feel I have now reached': M.A. to P.R.R. 26.11.63.

'I like the way': M.A. to P.R.R. 13.7.65.

'It has a freshness': Larry Hughes to M.A. 1.12.64.

'a straightforward': Ian Parsons to M.A. 18.1.65.

p 341 '*Nice* girl': M.A. diary 20.8.64.

'I think that': M.A. to Charles Champlin 10.9.65.

'Look at all those': M.A. 1965.
'I was horrified': M.A. to I.T. 29.8.61.
p 342 'I miss her': M.A. to Wendell Davis 1.8.64.
Articles 'My Garden, My Love', *Homes and Gardens*, 1965; 'Just a Few More Roses', *Woman's Realm*, 1967.
p 343 'happier and younger': 1964.
'Life proceeds': Sylvia Duncan article, *Modern Woman*, 1960.
'Since our generation': M.A. to Allen Lane 3.1.66.

Chapter XXI

p 345 Most of the information in this chapter comes from conversations with Joyce Allingham, Gloria Greci and Dr Russell Barton; also from Margery's papers.
Queen Beetle: unpublished typescript prepared by G.G. from dictation by M.A.
p 347 'stages ranging from': from draft letter to R.M. quoted p209 above.
p 348 'you are compulsorily': letter from R.B. to M.A. 24.2.66.
pp 349–50 Source of quotations: Dr Barton and Margery's medical notes.
p 351 'the cure': M.A. to M. & L. Runyon 6.6.66.
'I am waiting': M.A. to G.W. 5.6.66.
'limp, crawling': M.A. to Jean Gregory 6.66.
'Joyce is': M.A., *Queen Beetle*..
p 352 'From the day': Ronnie Reid letter to J.A. 4.7.66.
'her own lovely': Oriel Malet to P.Y.C. 9.8.66.
p 353 'essential humanity': from Canon Armstrong's funeral address.
p 354 Impression of P.Y.C. from Mrs Beckwith.
'You know, Jack': Jack Morpurgo to author.
p 355 'fade out': cf. note top p317.

The Published Works of Margery Allingham

(First British Editions)

(This does not include any of M.A.'s work published in *Girl's Cinema*, *The Picture Show*, *Joy* or the D.C. Thomson magazines. Neither does it include any of her published juvenile or anonymous work.)

Novels and Novellas

Blackerchief Dick: A Tale of Mersea Island (Hodder and Stoughton, 1923)
The White Cottage Mystery (Jarrolds, 1928). New edition prepared by Joyce Allingham (Chatto & Windus, 1975)
The Crime at Black Dudley (Jarrolds, 1929)
Mystery Mile (Jarrolds, 1930)
Look to the Lady (Jarrolds, 1931)
Police at the Funeral (Wm. Heinemann, 1931)
Sweet Danger (Wm. Heinemann, 1933)
Other Man's Danger (as Maxwell March) (Wm. Collins, 1933)
Death of a Ghost (Wm. Heinemann, 1934)
Rogue's Holiday (as Maxwell March) (Wm. Collins, 1935)
Flowers for the Judge (Wm. Heinemann, 1936)
The Shadow in the House (as Maxwell March) (Wm. Collins, 1936)
The Case of the Late Pig (Hodder & Stoughton, 1937)
Dancers in Mourning (Wm. Heinemann, 1937)
The Fashion in Shrouds (Wm. Heinemann, 1938)
Black Plumes (Wm. Heinemann, 1940)
Traitor's Purse (Wm. Heinemann, 1941)
Dance of the Years (Michael Joseph, 1943)
Coroner's Pidgin (Wm. Heinemann, 1945)
More Work for the Undertaker (Wm. Heinemann, 1948)
Take Two at Bedtime (World's Work, 1950) – contains two novellas, *Wanted: Someone Innocent* and *Last Act*

The Tiger in the Smoke (Chatto & Windus, 1952)
No Love Lost (World's Work, 1954) – contains two novellas, *The Patient at Peacocks Hall* and *Safer Than Love*
The Beckoning Lady (Chatto & Windus, 1955)
Hide My Eyes (Chatto & Windus, 1958)
The China Governess (Chatto & Windus, 1963)
The Mind Readers (Chatto & Windus, 1965)
Cargo of Eagles (completed by P.Y.C.) (Chatto & Windus, 1968)

Omnibus Editions

The Mysterious Mr Campion (Chatto & Windus, 1963) – contains Author's Preface, *The Case of the Late Pig*, *Dancers in Mourning*. *The Tiger in the Smoke* and a short story, *On Christmas Day in the Morning*
Mr Campion's Lady (Chatto & Windus, 1965) – contains Author's Preface, *Sweet Danger*, abridged edition of *The Fashion in Shrouds*, *Traitor's Purse* and a short story, *A Word in Season*
Mr Campion's Clowns (Chatto & Windus, 1967) – contains Memoir by P.Y.C., *Mystery Mile*, *Coroner's Pidgin* and *More Work for the Undertaker*

Short Story Collections

Mr Campion and Others (Wm. Heinemann, 1939) – contains *The Case of the Widow*, *The Case of the Name on the Wrapper*, *The Case of the Hat Trick*, *The Case of the Question Mark*, *The Case of the Old Man in the Window*, *The Case of the White Elephant*, *The Case of the Frenchman's Gloves*, *The Case of the Longer View*, *The Meaning of the Act*, *The Perfect Butler*, *It Didn't Work Out*, *The Mistress in the House*, *Publicity* and *They Never Get Caught*. There is some variation of titles with the Penguin edition publ. 1950 which also contains *The Definite Article* and *The Danger Point*, *A Matter of Form*, *The Meaning of the Act* and *Safe As Houses* and omits the final five titles of the Heinemann edition (as above). *It Didn't Work Out* had been M.A.'s contribution to a series with other members of the Detection Club, *Six Against the Yard* (publ. 1936)
The Allingham Casebook (Chatto & Windus, 1969) – contains *Tall Story*, *Three is a Lucky Number*, *The Villa Marie Celeste*, *The Psychologist*, *Little Miss Know-All*, *One Morning They'll Hang Him*, *The Lieabout*, *Face Value*, *Evidence in Camera*, *Joke Over*, *The Lying-in-State*, *The Pro and the Con*, *Is There a Doctor in the House?*, *The Borderline Case*, *They Never Get Caught*, *The Mind's*

Eye Mystery, *Mum Knows Best* and *The Snapdragon and the C.I.D.*

The Allingham Minibus (Chatto & Windus, 1972) – contains *He Was Asking After You*, *Publicity*, *The Perfect Butler*, *The Barbarian*, *Mr Campion's Lucky Day*, *'Tis Not Hereafter*, *The Correspondents*, *He Preferred Them Sad*, *The Unseen Door*, *Bird Thou Never Wert*, *The Same to Us*, *She Heard it on the Radio*, *The Man With the Sack*, *The Secret*, *A Quarter of a Million*, *The Pioneers*, *The Sexton's Wife* and *The Wink*

The Return of Mr Campion (Hodder & Stoughton, 1989) – contains Introduction and Notes by J.E. Morpurgo, *The Case is Altered*, *My Friend Mr Campion*, *The Dog Day*, *The Wind Glass*, *The Beauty King*, *The Black Tent*, *Sweet and Low*, *Once in a Lifetime*, *The Kernel of Truth*, *Happy Christmas*, *The Wisdom of Esdras*, *The Curious Affair in Nut Row* and *What to Do With an Ageing Detective*

Uncollected Stories

A Proper Mystery (publ. in *Lights of Essex*, 1942, a pamphlet in aid of Welfare for the Forces, and republished in *Essex Countryside Magazine* Oct. 1986)

The Day of the Demon (publ. in *Essex Countryside Magazine* Nov. 1986)

Jubilee For Two (publ. in *Answers*, 11.5.35)

Sleuth's Corner (story for National Book Fair Competition, 1938)

Other Books

Water in a Sieve (French's Acting Editions, 1925)

The Oaken Heart (Michael Joseph, 1941)

Book Reviews and other articles

Published in *The Daily Herald*, *Town and Country* (U.S. magazine), *The New York Times*, *Time and Tide*, *The Daily Graphic*, *The Tatler*, Simpkin Marshall's house magazine (edit. Nancy Spain), *Homes and Gardens*, *Town and Country Review* (a British magazine briefly edited by P.Y.C.) and others.

Unpublished Work

Early Poems, Short Stories, Dramatic Monologues and Plays including *Without Being Naturally Qualified* (1920–1), *Dido and Aeneas* (1921) and *The Hill of His Ancestors* (1923)

Green Corn (novel, 1923–4)
The Lover (incomplete novel, 1925)
The Relay (on the care of the old, 1964)

Typescripts of broadcast plays and talks
Meet Albert Campion (talk for B.B.C.) 17.6.35
Room To Let (B.B.C. radio play) 11.11.47. (May also have been filmed.)
Man at the Window (B.B.C. radio play) 21.10.43
My Characters (notes for 'Woman's Hour' talk, 1958)
London, My Market Town (talk) B.B.C. 'World Of Books' 6.4.63
She was interviewed on the radio by Nancy Spain for 'Woman's Hour' 13.1.55, by John Sherwood for the European division in 1958, for 'Meet the Author' 25.7.62, and 'Writers Talking' (Oct 1965). She appeared on B.B.C. TV's 'Panorama' programme, 22.12.58, in Associated Rediffusion's 'Late Extra' on 7.10.59 and plans were made for an appearance on Anglia Television 19.11.65. Her Essex dialect was recorded by Basil Slaughter for the W.E.A., 9.8.60

Other typescripts and notes for talks or articles
'Toast to literature' (Foyle's, 1938)
'The English Countryman' (Oxford, 1942)
'Crime For Our Delight' (Harrods, 1958)
'The Thriller' (possibly prepared for Suzanne Dutruch)
'On the Writing of Dialogue in Detective Fiction' (possibly as above)
'The Book as a Possession'

Barry Pike, a founder of the Margery Allingham Society, has performed invaluable service to all collectors of detective fiction with his meticulous work in describing and dating various editions of her detective novels and in listing her short stories with their variant titles.
Tony Medawar, also of the Margery Allingham Society, is preparing the complete bibliography

Books by Pip Youngman Carter
On to Andorra (Hamish Hamilton, 1963)
Drinking Bordeaux (Hamish Hamilton, 1966)
Drinking Burgundy (Hamish Hamilton, 1966)
Drinking Champagne and Brandy (Hamish Hamilton, 1968)
Mr Campion's Farthing (Heinemann, 1969)
Mr Campion's Falcon (Heinemann, 1970)
All I Did Was This (Sexton Press, 1982)

Preface to *Mr Campion's Clowns* (Chatto, 1967)
Short stories and articles in a variety of magazines from 1942 onwards. These include the forces magazines *Gen* and *Soldier*, as well as *The Tatler*, *The Compleat Imbiber*, *Argosy* and *John O'London's*.

by Phil Allingham
Cheapjack (Heinemann, 1934)

Book Plate
Designed by P. Youngman Carter

Index

The Last Word

'What people should really ask is: "How many of the detective stories you read do you remember?" Not very many and there Margery Allingham stands out like a shining light. Everything she writes has a definite shape. And she has another quality not usually associated with crime stories. Elegance.

If I say I don't know at all what she was like, that is the truth, and it makes her interesting to me, because one so often thinks one knows more or less just what someone one has met is like. She did not seem reserved, but I think she may have been. She talked and smiled – she was nice.

But there was a great deal more to her writing than that. I know little about her except that she lived mostly in the country in East Anglia. Her whole intriguing personality seems gathered together there. How sad it is that there are no more of her stories to which we can look forward. Not only to enjoy on publication but to read often and often again, enjoying them anew each time.'

Agatha Christie

Woodcut
by PipYoungman Carter for Margery's play
Dido and Aeneas, 1922